# CHASING ZEBRAS

# CHASING ZEBRAS

## THE UNOFFICIAL GUIDE TO HOUSE, M.D.

### BARBARA BARNETT

ECW Press

Published by ECW Press
2120 Queen Street East, Suite 200, Toronto, Ontario, Canada M4E 1E2
416-694-3348 / info@ecwpress.com

LIBRARY AND ARCHIVES CANADA CATALOGUING IN PUBLICATION

Barnett, Barbara Shyette
Chasing zebras : the unofficial guide to House M.D. / Barbara Shyette
Barnett.

ISBN 978-1-55022-955-4

1. House, M.D. (Television program).  I. Title.

PN1992.77.H63B37 2010          791.45'72          C2010-901371-9

Developing editor: Sarah Dunn
Cover and text design: Tania Craan
Typesetting: Mary Bowness
Cover photo: © Armando Gallo / Retna Ltd.
Interior photo credits: pages 61, 103, 115, 125, 135, 141, 149, 153, 157: Armando Gallo / Retna Ltd.; 222: Greg Gayne/NBCU Photo Bank via AP Images; 258, 308: Adam Taylor/NBCU Photo Bank via AP Images; 356: Darren Michaels/NBCU Photo Bank via AP Images; 382: Michael Yarish/NBCU Photo Bank via AP Images.
Printing: Solisco Tri-Graphic    1    2    3    4    5

PRINTED AND BOUND IN CANADA

ECW PRESS
ecwpress.com

*To my soul mate, Phillip, with love and gratitude*

# Table of Contents

Preface 11

Introduction: Elementary, My Dear Wilson 13

    The *House* Online Fan Community 16

    Finding a Holmes in (the) House: An Interview with a *House*-Loving Holmesian 17

Differential Diagnosis: A Character Study Wrapped in a Mystery Wrapped in a Medical Procedural 21

    Department of Diagnostic Medicine? 21

    Chasing Zebras 22

    Case in Point: A Closer Look at "Sports Medicine" 26

    Formulas Are Made to Be Broken 30

    Drama vs. Medical Accuracy: A Balancing Act 31

    Diagnostic Medicine: Life Imitating Art 33

Words on the Page: Crafting *House, M.D.* 35

    When It Doesn't "Fit" 36

    Plucking Threads 37

    A Script Is Born 38

    A Flair for Their Characters 40

From Bach to Eddie Van Halen: The Music of *House, M.D.* 47

    An Emotional Language 47

    Musical Diagnosis 49

    The *House* Soundtrack 50

    Sometimes You Might Get What You Need 51

House's Haunts 53

    House's House 53

    House at Work 55

    The "Ball of Unknown Origin" 56

    House's Inner Sanctum 57

    The Mutual Admiration of Stephen Colbert and Dr. Gregory House 58

    Around the Corner to Wilson's Place 58

    The Dean's Domain 59

God, Religion, and Hypocrisy 61

Mad, Bad, and Dangerous to Know: Dr. Gregory House 63

    A Literary Hero on Prime-Time TV 64

    House's Genius 65

    Is It Luck — Or Is It Memorex? 67

    In the Orbit of House's Energy Field 68

    House's Troubled Past and Painful Present 70

    The Disillusioned Idealist 72

    The Buraku of Princeton-Plainsboro Teaching Hospital 74

    Survival 101: Change and Adaptability 75

    Rebel with a Cause: The Maverick of Princeton-Plainsboro 77

    The Fine Line Between Right and Wrong 78

    A Sacred Calling: House's Passion for Medicine 80

    When House's Objectivity Fails Him 81

    Feeling Too Little — Or Too Much? 83

    Mad and Bad . . . 85

    . . . And Dangerous: House's Self-Destructiveness 87

    House the Linguist 88

    . . . Yet Vulnerable 89

Broken: House, Pain, and Drugs 91

Doing the Right Thing: House and Ethics 99

    House's Influence 101

    The Case of Ezra Powell 102

Boy Wonder Oncologist: Dr. James ("Jimmy") Wilson 105

    Wilson's Defining Moment 106

    Symbiosis or Codependence? 108

    Amber and House 110

    Wilson in Love 111

    The Impact of Amber's Death: A Closer Look at "Dying Changes Everything" 112

    It's Not *All* About the Neediness 114

Smart, Funny, and Full of Sass: Dr. Lisa Cuddy 117

    Managing Dr. House 119

    Enter Rachel 123

An Overcapacity for Caring: Dr. Allison Cameron 127

    Cameron's First Husband 129

    Cameron's "Insane Moral Compass" 130

House and Cameron 133

Cameron and Chase 135

His Father Made a Phone Call: Dr. Robert Chase 137

The Transformation and Redemption of Robert Chase 138

Family Matters 140

Chase and Cameron 140

Like House, But Nicer: Dr. Eric Foreman 143

Looking Out for Number 1 144

A Welcome Thorn in House's Side 146

Ready for Prime Time? 147

House's Fellows: Imprinting on the Daddy Doc 149

The Love Doctor 149

The Enigmatic, Unlucky 13: Dr. Remy Hadley 151

"Some People Take Pills; I Cheat": Dr. Christopher Taub 155

The Tragedy of Lawrence Kutner: Dr. Lawrence Kutner 159


Guide to the Guide 163

Cast of Characters 165

Season 1: Patients Make Us Miserable 169

An Odd Sort of Humility: A Closer Look at "DNR" 182

Struggling to Do the "Right Thing": A Closer Look at "Role Model" 194

Before the Leg 201

Season 2: Settling into the Story 205

House and Medical Mistakes 217

House's Windmill — Death: A Closer Look at "All In" 233

Ketamine: A Closer Look at "No Reason" 243

Season 3: Finding Meaning 245

Setting Up the Downfall: A Closer Look at "Meaning" 247

The Happiness Scale: A Closer Look at "Lines in the Sand" 254

Season 4: A Shake-up at Princeton-Plainsboro Teaching Hospital 287

Learning to Be a Doctor from a Doctor Like House 298

Diagnostics Team 2.0 304

Truth Begins in Lies: A Closer Look at "It's a Wonderful Lie" 307

People Don't Change: A Closer Look at "Don't Ever Change" 311

A Truth Just Beyond His Grasp: A Closer Look at "House's Head" 317

To the Limit: A Closer Look at "Wilson's Heart" 320

Season 5: Upheaval and the Ultimate Escape 323

        Coincidence vs. Divine Intervention: A Closer Look at "Unfaithful" 345

        On the Edge of Reality: A Closer Look at "Under My Skin" 358

        It's a Nice Story: A Closer Look at "Both Sides Now" 362

        From the Writer's Mouth . . . 364

        Kutner's Death and House's Crash 365

Season 6: People Don't Change . . . Or Do They? 367

        A New Journey Begins: A Closer Look at "Broken" 370

        Diagnosing Dr. House: A Conversation with a Clinical Psychologist 374

        On the Couch with Dr. House: A Closer Look at "Baggage" 411

        Redemption: A Closer Look at "Help Me" 416


Appendix A: And When It's Very, Very Good: Awards for House, M.D. 421

Appendix B: "Time Is Not a Fixed Construct": Continuity and the Series

        Timeline 423


Acknowledgments 428

# Preface

It is an axiom of medicine: "when you hear hoofbeats, you think horses, not zebras." Dr. Gregory House and his elite team of diagnostic fellows chase medicine's "zebras" — the anomalies, the odd presentations, the diseases so rare that most doctors would not have encountered them in a normal medical practice.

*House, M.D.* is, itself, a zebra in a herd of horses. It is a rare find of a show blessed with consistently sharp, intelligent writing: densely packed and multifaceted. It features one of the most complex characters ever to have been written for the small screen, Dr. Gregory House, brought to life through Hugh Laurie's brilliant and nuanced performance.

I grew up on TV. By age nine, I was hooked on *The Man From U.N.C.L.E.* and by 11, I was addicted to *Star Trek* classic. Nowadays, I have little time for series television. But when I get hooked on a television show, I really get hooked, and so it is with *House, M.D.*

Whenever the media say that women are attracted to House because he's a "bad boy," I tend to cringe first and then shake my head in disagreement. I don't like "bad boys" — real or fictional. I like my heroes, well . . . heroic. Heroic, but tragically flawed: equal parts Mr. Knightley and Edward Rochester; Mr. Spock and Rick Blaine.

House has a "public persona" and also one he keeps tightly under wraps, reluctant to reveal — to anyone. Publicly, he's a brilliant diagnostician, intuitive, deductive, and eerily smart. He's also a risk taker and more than a tad reckless. In many ways he's an adolescent boy constantly hatching his next manipulation or elaborate game. He's crude and rude. House's closest associates tell us that House cares only about the puzzle. No messiah complex for him; he has a Rubik's complex instead. But how does this image reconcile with the times we've seen him gazing yearningly from behind the glass into patient rooms, watching them with their families? How often do we observe the arrogant and egotistical Gregory House late at night, alone in his office or apartment, desperately searching for answers inside himself long after everyone else has gone home? Like the show that bears his name, House is as complex and rare as the medical cases he takes on: a zebra amongst the horses.

This book is a highly subjective look at a great television series through one fan's perspective. Another writer might focus on the medicine, the humor, or the mysteries. But I view *House, M.D.* fundamentally as a detailed character study: House's journey, his struggles, and the people in his orbit. This is the lens through which I enjoy *House* — and through which I understand it.

There are chapters here on the writing, the structure, and the elements that make *House, M.D.* such a fascinating series. There are chapters on each of the characters and some of the show's oft-visited themes viewed through "closer looks" at key episodes. I've also included an extensive six-season episode guide. Although there are episode guides all over the Internet offering episode recaps and credits (and even in-depth analyses, including my feature at *Blogcritics*), this guide is slightly different. It's a road map through the series, showing you the highlights from six seasons: memorable scenes, House's patented eureka moments, clinic patients, relationship highlights, music, and more — all from a fan's perspective.

> *Spoiler Warning: These narrative chapters contain many spoilers, giving away major character and plot points from episodes throughout the first six seasons of* **House**. *If you are new to the series and do not want to be "spoiled" about episodes you haven't yet seen, I'd suggest moving first to the book's six-season episode guide!*

Scattered throughout the book, I've shared quotes from the numerous exclusive interviews I've been privileged to conduct for *Blogcritics* through the years with *House* producers, writers, crew, and actors, including: Katie Jacobs, Jennifer Morrison, Lisa Edelstein, Garrett Lerner, Russel Friend, Doris Egan, Eli Attie, David Foster, and production designer Jeremy Cassells.

Enjoy!

Barbara Barnett
May 2010

# Introduction

## Elementary, My Dear Wilson

Dr. Gregory House is an unrepentant jerk. He's rude, brusque, and harsh — suffering no fools and taking no prisoners. He's not conventionally pretty; he's not young. In addition, he's crippled, limping along with a cane. Yet, he's the central character on the hit television series, *House, M.D.* (just *House*, for short). It's a completely unlikely proposition. How do you sell the network on a series created around such an irredeemable bastard? Who would even want to watch it? Millions do.

*House* is one of the highest-rated television series on American television. More than that, it's a hit around the world — from the United Kingdom, France, Spain, Eastern Europe to the Middle East, and in lands as far flung as Australia and Hong Kong. In Canada, *House* has even outranked *American Idol*! Eurodata TV Worldwide, which tracks and ranks television across the globe, reported in June 2009 that *House* was the most-watched television show worldwide, with nearly 82 million viewers tuning in from 66 countries.

Why would more than 80 million viewers tune in week after week to see Dr. Gregory House verbally spar with his patients, staff, and colleagues at Princeton-Plainsboro Teaching Hospital? There has to be something more to it (and to him) than just a brilliant jerk packing a stethoscope and a toxic tongue.

Is it the bizarre medical cases? That's probably one reason, and the starting point for most episodes. Inspired by physician Lisa Sanders' *New York Times* feature "Diagnosis," the *House* writing team, with creator David Shore at the helm, conjure the most unusual of cases, fitting for an elite Department of Diagnostic Medicine.

Perhaps the series owes its success to the snappy dialogue: the quick wit and rapid-fire pace of the writing. The show's scripts are certainly dense and swiftly paced: a stark counterpoint to the physically disabled and slow-of-foot Gregory House. And the humor, with its one-liner "House-isms" and snarky banter, supplies balance to the intensity of the weekly medical and character stories.

Or do people simply live vicariously through House's unfiltered voice? He is certainly capable of saying things the likes of which we normal, well-adjusted worker bees can only dream. Some may be intrigued by House's uniquely personal code of ethics. Or perhaps House's personal struggles resonate with us.

Much credit in making *House* compelling television goes to the nuanced and genuine performance of Hugh Laurie, who stars as the genius diagnostician with serious personality issues. Through his expressive eyes and masterful acting, Laurie's flawless interpretation of House's frustrations, fears, hopes, and hurts guides us through House's morass of bullshit and elaborate game playing and deep into his heart and soul.

> "Hugh has contributed not only in front of the camera — and has contributed in a way nobody else could — he is such a partner. Contributing in so many ways from the very beginning, which is why the show is so successful."
>
> **— Showrunner/executive producer/director Katie Jacobs, January 2009 interview**

It's ironic that executive producer Bryan Singer, the director of the *House* pilot, had difficulty casting the role of the quintessentially American Gregory House with an American actor. It was not until Laurie, legendary British comedian (and novelist, musician, and actor), sent in an audition tape, complete with perfect American accent, that Singer found an "American" actor capable of handling the complex role. But perhaps that's because Dr. Gregory House has more in common with a particular English literary hero than he has with any American television character.

Take a classic British literary hero, bring him into 21st century American medicine with a vengeance, and create a modern television phenomenon. The parallels to House's literary grandfather — Sir Arthur Conan Doyle's 19th century detective Sherlock Holmes — are many and intentional. House . . . Holmes; Wilson . . . Watson. Holmes fiddled with his fiddle; House plays piano and guitar. Both House and Holmes reside at 221B. Holmes solved cases with associative leaps — a combination of genius and deductive reasoning, superheroic observational skills and deep intuition about the human psyche. So does House.

Like his Victorian ancestor, House applies logic, reasoning, an encyclopedic knowledge (of everything), plus his intuition to solve medical mysteries and save lives. Holmes uses cocaine to forestall boredom; House uses Vicodin for more than just the pain in his leg.

Unlike the British Sherlock Holmes, House is very much American. Yet, the Eton- and Cambridge-educated Laurie — a quintessentially British actor —

completely captures the character. It's no accident that Holmes fans have often suggested Laurie as the heir apparent to the role of Holmes.

But Sherlock Holmes isn't House's only literary or pop culture ancestor. House's heritage includes a long history of literary and cinematic heroes and antiheroes. Part Byron, part Sherlock, a bit of Quincy, M.E., perhaps a hint of Dr. Kildare's mentor Gillespie, some of the *The Dark Knight*'s Batman, and a generous dollop of truth-seeking antihero Fox Mulder (*The X-Files*), House joins the ranks of classic dark angels and iconoclasts.

Conceived by David Shore (*Hack*, *Family Law*, and *Law & Order*), a Canadian former corporate attorney, *House* was intended to fit into a network need for a new "procedural" series. Shore's partner in this venture, writer Paul Attanasio (*Quiz Show*, *The Sum of All Fears*, *The Good German*) "came up with this medical idea that was like a cop procedural. The suspects were the germs," Shore noted in an interview with Dylan Callaghan for the Writers Guild of America. Or, as Shore put it in an interview for the *House* season one DVD set, they were "trying to do a cop kind of show in a medical setting . . . a group of doctors trying to diagnose the undiagnosable." But astutely, Shore recognized that a "procedural" was simply not enough.

"I quickly began to realize that we needed that character element. I mean, germs don't have motives," he said in the Callaghan interview. Shore told John Doyle of Canada's *Globe and Mail*, *House* is "not about the medical stories as much as it is about that character who's so clever, philosophical, and ethical." Around that character, Shore and company — Attanasio, executive producer Katie Jacobs, and Bryan Singer — constructed a well-realized universe where this tough, clever, strangely ethical, abrasive, and wounded Dr. Gregory House could play.

*House* debuted November 16, 2004, with an audience of slightly more than 7 million, and ranked 62nd in the ABC Medianet Weekly Television Rankings. Critics generally liked the show, but most wondered how long a show about bizarre illnesses — and featuring such a cranky, even misanthropic, doctor — could really last on network television.

The series viewership dropped below 7 million by its second week and stayed there until January, when an a little show called *American Idol* premiered its fourth season in January 2005. The coveted post-*Idol* spot on Fox's schedule was a welcome elixir to the fledgling series. Curious *American Idol* viewers stayed tuned to watch the new series and got hooked. Following *Idol*, *House* nearly doubled its viewership to more than 12 million viewers, and soared from 53rd to 25th in the national rankings.

Produced by NBC Universal, *House* was nearly rejected by Fox, which had purchased the rights to the show nearly a year before it went on the air. Fox's viewership is typically young, and the network "powers that be" were concerned about airing a series about a craggy middle-aged misanthrope, according to Shore.

Although the show *seemed* to have hit its peak in United States in season three, especially with its coveted post–*American Idol* slot, the show has maintained a viewership well above 12 million for Fox Network's first-run broadcast, with many more tuning in for the rebroadcast on the Universal-owned USA Network the following week. Although the numbers dipped somewhat when *House* moved to Monday nights at 8 p.m. after losing the *American Idol* lead-in entirely, they have remained consistently strong. Even in its sixth season, the series has the ability to draw 14 million ("Remorse," 6.12) to 16 million viewers ("Broken," 6.01, 6.02), even without the lead-in.

No one knows how much longer *House* will remain on the air. Entering its seventh season as this book goes to press, the series seems to still be going strong. There appear to be no end to bizarre medical cases, and the tireless Hugh Laurie continues to pour his soul into every performance, even directing an episode during season six ("Lockdown," 6.17). But every series ends eventually, and whether it's Laurie's desire to return to the U.K. or to go on to other things (or if the series simply runs out of steam, which would be a terrible shame), it will end someday.

Will House go riding off into the sunset on his motorcycle with Dean of Medicine Lisa Cuddy sitting behind him? Perhaps ex-girlfriend Stacy, former fellow Dr. Allison Cameron — or maybe even best friend James Wilson? Or will the series end on a more somber note? No one knows, but until that time, we'll sit mesmerized by one of television's most compelling characters, hoping the journey never ends.

### The *House* Online Fan Community

The Internet is host to dozens (if not hundreds) of places where you can explore your *House* passion. Medicine your thing? PoliteDissent.com takes apart the medicine of each episode, grading it for accuracy as well as story quality. Interested in one or another of the relationships on the show? Explore the numerous Live Journal communities that specialize in everything from "Hameron" (House/Cameron) and "Huddy" (House/Cuddy) to "Hilson" (House/Wilson) and any other pairing your imagination can conjure. Fox.com hosts the official *House, M.D.* site with an active discussion forum, videos, links, and a *House* wiki. And of course for in-depth discussion of everything *House*, you must visit *Blogcritics* magazine's *House* feature "Welcome to the End of the Thought Process: An Introspective Look at *House, M.D.*"

There are a multitude of other blogs and comprehensive websites provide the discerning *House* fan with endless hours of entertainment and much opportunity to talk, read, debate, and argue with fellow fans about everything from House's latest scheme to Cuddy's latest hairstyle. For those so inclined there are places where you can find "spoilers" to divulge what's coming up on the series, and fan fiction sites where you read some excellent (and even novel-length) stories about the show's characters with content ratings from "G" to "Adults Only."

The online community is incredibly diverse, with pre-teens to grandparents participating in the discussion. The community is admittedly skewed female, but you'll find fans from all over the globe with whom to share your interest in the series. It's easy to locate the perfect group for your specific interest in the show: just Google, click, and shop around.

## Finding a Holmes in (the) House
### An Interview with a *House*-Loving Holmesian

As you might imagine, a television series (however loosely) based on the Sherlock Holmes stories might incorporate a nod or two (or 10) to the famed literary series. For example, observant viewers might have noticed *The Complete Sherlock Holmes* on House's living room end table during seasons four and five.

The show creators have scattered numerous subtle — and not so subtle — Holmesian references throughout the series fabric since episode one. However, the most interesting connection between the two characters originates in the creation of Sherlock Holmes himself.

Holmes' creator, Sir Arthur Conan Doyle, a physician as well as a writer, trained at the University of Edinburgh under Dr. Joseph Bell (a physician to Queen Victoria). Bell would often amaze and amuse his friends at parties by diagnosing a roomful of people on the spot, using only his keen observational skills. Conan Doyle, of course, later went on to write the Sherlock Holmes stories and novels, loosely basing his creation on his amazingly observant mentor.

Dr. House has also occasionally demonstrated the same flair, for example, diagnosing a clinic waiting room full of patients in the series' third episode

"Occam's Razor" (1.03). Unlike Bell, though, House doesn't do it so much to amuse as to dispose of his patients ASAP. But the literary lineage is clear: Bell to Conan Doyle to Holmes to House.

David Shore has often remarked that the names House and Wilson are a play on Holmes and Watson, and as we learn in season two ("Hunting," 2.07), like the fictional detective, House lives at "221B." We've not yet learned whether he actually resides on Baker Street, which would extend the parallel.

The patient in the "Pilot" episode is Rebecca Adler, clearly a reference to "the woman that got away" in the Holmes canon, Irene Adler. Besides the name, there is little to connect Rebecca and Irene. But Holmes' Irene comes up again in "Joy to the World" (5.11) when House's best friend Dr. James Wilson confabulates a tale about how House acquired a copy of Joseph Bell's 19th century medical book *On Surgery*. Describing House's obsession with "Irene Adler," a patient treated years earlier — someone he couldn't diagnose, Wilson calls her "the one that got away." (Of course, that wasn't at all the case; Wilson had actually given House the book. He is simply screwing with one of House's fellows.)

Arachne Jericho, a Holmes blogger (Holmesian Derivations) and occasional contributor to the science fiction Internet site Tor.com is also a *House* fan. Jericho sees numerous connections between the genius detective and his medical descendant. Like Holmes, Jericho says, House is a bit messy with books piled all over the place, papers stuck in odd places, etc. And whereas Holmes keeps tobacco in a Persian slipper, we learn at the end of season five that House has been known to keep a secret stash of Vicodin in his sneaker ("Under My Skin," 5.23).

Watson would continually be irritated with Holmes' sloppiness (Watson is Holmes' roommate). And, says Jericho, "When Wilson ended up staying with House — well, we know how that ended up. You don't want to be the roommate of House or Holmes!" Circa season six, House seems at least marginally more inclined to neatness, perhaps because he's living under Wilson's roof this time.

In the Holmes canon, notes Jericho, Scotland Yard detective Inspector G. Lestrade is often portrayed as Sherlock's "semi-nemesis." He's a policeman who plays it by the book, and "the book" doesn't work any better in Holmes' universe than it does in House's. Who is House's Lestrade? Jericho argues that the conventionally thinking doctors who dwell in House's universe collectively represent him. "We can see it any time House is up against a doctor who works more traditionally than he does, whether it's a regular like Cuddy, one of House's team, or some poor guest star."

Holmes fans think of Professor James Moriarty as his archenemy. A criminal mastermind, Holmes dubbed him the "Napoleon of Crime." So who is House's

Moriarty? So far, the only "Moriarty" has emerged from House's own psyche. In season two finale "No Reason" (2.24), House, who has been shot by a former patient, hallucinates about him while unconscious. The man is House's intellectual equal, challenging, and taunting him about everything from his sanity to his misery and self-destructiveness.

Although he is never actually called "Moriarty" during the episode, the shooting script refers to him that way in a clear shout-out to Holmes. So, is House his own Moriarty? House is often his own worst enemy, sabotaging his life and relationships — as his therapist in "Broken" (6.01, 6.02) suggests — almost as if that is the goal. He is also, in many ways, much harder on himself than anyone knows, so why not?

At least nominally, Wilson is intended as House's Watson. But Robert Sean Leonard, who plays House's best friend, Dr. James Wilson, disagrees. He has said that House's team of fellows are the Watson of this Sherlock Holmes retelling.

Arachne Jericho observes that Wilson is certainly not as much of a hero-worshipper of House as Watson appears to be in the Holmes stories. On the other hand, both Wilson and Watson seem to "need to be needed," and have chosen especially needy friends in House and Holmes, respectively.

A new film adaptation of *Sherlock Holmes* was released in 2009. Not exactly Conan Doyle's Sherlock, the movie, starring Robert Downey Jr. as Holmes and Jude Law as Watson, gave a shout out to *House, M.D.* bringing the relationship between Holmes and House full circle.

In the movie, Watson is ready to quit his relationship with Holmes, tired of whole game. But Holmes manages to suck Watson completely into a new case. And pulling a quotation right out of the *House* episode "Birthmarks" (5.04), he harangues Watson to "Admit it! Admit it! Admit it!" — admit that he really doesn't want to quit the game — or Holmes. Coincidence? I think not!

# Differential Diagnosis

## A Character Study Wrapped in a Mystery

## Wrapped in a Medical Procedural

Rebecca Adler engages with her kindergarten students about how they spent their weekend. Suddenly she starts to babble incoherently, much to the amusement of the five-year-olds in her class. But as she tries to scrawl the words "Get help" on the blackboard, they quickly realize something's not right with Miss Rebecca. A normal life disrupted abruptly: something *House* fans will soon recognize as the episode "teaser." It sets the stage for the medical mystery to be solved in the hour to come. Rebecca's symptoms point to something wrong with her brain. But what?

By the end of the episode, we'll know: it's a dying tapeworm in the brain. The medical gymnastics to get from "incoherent babble" to the final diagnosis frame the pilot episode of *House*.

After the "teaser" segment, the camera focuses on two men walking in what appears to be a hospital foyer. At first, only their legs are visible; one man wears a white doctor coat and the other leans heavily on a wood cane, walking with pronounced limp.

We are about to meet Dr. Gregory House, legendary, "world-famous" doctor. He's a specialist in infectious diseases and nephrology (kidney diseases) — and head of the Diagnostics Department at the fictional Princeton-Plainsboro Teaching Hospital. And big hint: the famous doctor is *not* the one wearing the white lab coat. The one in the coat is House's best friend, head of oncology, Dr. James Wilson, who wants him to take the case of our young kindergarten teacher from the teaser. He tells House that his cousin "Rachel" (note, not "Rebecca") has seen several doctors, but is still sick.

### Department of Diagnostic Medicine?

Outside House's universe, in the *real* world, there is no such medical sub-specialty as "diagnostic medicine," although this may be changing. In 2009, the National Institutes of Health established the Center for Rare and Undiagnosed Diseases to evaluate patients for diseases "resistant to diagnosis," which is essentially what House does on a smaller scale.

Most doctors are diagnosticians in one way or another, and they perform "differential diagnoses" all the time. You don't feel well; something hurts. And it prompts you to see your family physician. After you describe your symptoms, the doctor takes a medical history, does a few tests, and, based on all that, delivers a diagnosis — hopefully.

But what if the symptoms, the history, and the tests don't add up? Or what if the doctor thinks he has the answer, you do what he tells you to do, but you're still sick — and getting worse by the hour? *And* what if you have consulted doctor after doctor and still come no closer to finding out what's wrong?

The Princeton-Plainsboro Diagnostics Department is one of a kind, created especially for Dr. Gregory House, who happens to have a genius for diagnosis. He is a sort of medical court of last resort. People seek him out when no one else can help.

### Chasing Zebras

Standard medical practice warns that when you "hear hoofbeats, think horses, not zebras." Don't get exotic; consider the easiest explanation first. And usually, that works. But House and his elite group of medical fellows — board-certified physicians acquiring advanced training from a brilliant practitioner — are equipped to hunt down the medical zebras, the cases other doctors miss. In "Pilot," House explains that if Rebecca's illness "is a horse," her family doctor would have figured it out, and the case "never gets near this office."

As they consider the case, House's fellows process new information through their own specialties: Eric Foreman is a neurologist; Allison Cameron is an immunologist; Robert Chase is an intensivist (critical care specialist). House's dual specialties of infectious diseases and nephrology (diseases of the kidneys) round out the constellation of expertise. His holistic way of looking at symptoms, coupled with vast medical knowledge, helps him finesse the team's educated guesses into probable new diagnoses.

As the medical story unfolds in "Pilot," we begin to learn more about House and the rest of his team. This debut episode begins to sketch out the key roles and relationships of the series. House is the sardonic, embittered antihero, misanthropic and disillusioned. His philosophy of life is "Everybody lies." Wilson, his best friend, is the classic straight man or sidekick. House's team is young, pretty, smart. (Hey, this *is* a Fox show, right?) We meet Dr. Lisa Cuddy, the chief hospital administrator, and dean of medicine at Princeton-Plainsboro. She is also House's boss and main adversary. But we quickly observe that their banter sparkles with the hint of something more than mere antagonism between boss and difficult employee.

For the first time, we see what will become familiar components of House's unique modus operandi. He holds court either in front of the whiteboard in his office or rapidly walking the hospital's corridors, guiding the team in a way that would make Socrates proud. On the surface, House's dismissive process with his fellows in these differential diagnosis sessions seems brutal. As House himself describes the process: "I thought I'd get your theories, *mock* them, then embrace my own" ("Merry Little Christmas," 3.09). But that's not really what House does. Instead, he acts like a giant filter for his team's theories, educated guesses, even wrong diagnoses, which through this process become the seeds of something potentially lifesaving.

House assigns his staff to run tests (often rerunning tests already done by other doctors, who, of course, cannot be trusted because "they're idiots"). They often take a patient history, even breaking into a home or workplace to identify possible toxins or environmental factors (as well as family secrets) that might affect the diagnosis. In "Pilot," Foreman breaks into Rebecca Adler's home, and there he finds a key piece of medical evidence, which indirectly leads to the final diagnosis. Throughout, the team constantly evaluates new information and re-evaluates what they've already done, often revisiting discarded theories as some new bit of relevant information comes to light. If they're right, another piece of the medical puzzle is in place; if they're not, they've still learned something they hadn't known before about the culprit.

House leaves no stone unturned or oblique angle unexplored. Not even House's own ideas are sacrosanct. He is willing to be wrong — and wrong again — until the answer is found and the patient is diagnosed, treated, and fixed. It doesn't matter to House whether it's his idea or someone else's — as long as it's right.

As the team hones in on the most likely diagnosis, House often uses imaginative metaphors to explain what's going on in the patient's body. Antibodies may become blitzing linebackers; a blood clot is represented as a terrorist sleeper cell (with a tumor being represented by Osama bin Laden). The metaphors not only enlighten the fellows, but help make the complex medical issues and physiology more understandable to the viewers.

And then it comes: eureka! Something triggers a faraway look in House's eye. If *House* were an animated series, a lightbulb would appear over House's head. He has his answer, and most of the time, it is in time to save the patient, who by now is likely hovering at death's door.

Sometimes the answer strikes him when he's alone. At a dead end, House becomes withdrawn and introspective. He knows he and his team are missing something, but doesn't know what. He stares at the whiteboard; maybe he plays with one of the toys on his desk, always deep in thought, and deep inside himself. This is as much a part of his process as tinkering with test tubes and MRIS.

But House usually needs a muse to spark that final flash of brilliance. Often Wilson or Cuddy serve that purpose; perhaps a clinic patient says something that makes the final puzzle piece click into place. On rare occasions, the doctor who refuses to see patients pays a rare visit to sit at his or her bedside. But this is the moment of his medical magic; it's where objective science and logic give way to intuition and inspiration.

In "Pilot," House pays Rebecca one of these rare visits towards the end of the episode, and it's the first time she has met the elusive Dr. House, although she has been inquiring about him since being admitted. They already have come up with the correct diagnosis, but having undergone so many tests, Rebecca is ready to die, refusing to be guinea pig to even one more of House's experiments. To her, it's over, and unless they can prove the diagnosis to her, the next procedure is just one too many.

As he will do in several episodes over the years, House shares an important (and personal) piece of himself — as if it is only that keeping the patient from giving up entirely. In "Pilot," Rebecca insists on knowing why she should keep fighting to survive — not give up when she sees that *he* so obviously has. "What makes you think I'm so much better than you are?" she persists.

Ultimately, House comes away from this encounter willing to let Rebecca die, honoring her request to simply be left alone because they have no proof. "No more tests," he explains to his staff. But when Chase suggests a simple procedure to confirm House's diagnosis, something clicks and House realizes they can, indeed, obtain the proof Rebecca demands — and cure her.

This pilot episode only begins to render the remarkably textured (but even after six seasons, essentially unknowable) central character. A recluse, particularly during the first five seasons, House avoids patients at all costs. He doesn't return phone calls, answer his mail, or honor requests for speaking engagements. He is brusque and blunt with no readily apparent bedside manner. He tells it like it is, usually not the way you would want to hear it. But when you're dying, House might inquire, would you want a nice doctor who held your hand while you died, or a not-so-nice doctor who got you well?

Gregory House is a man uncomfortable in his own skin. He hides from patients; he hides from everyone. Is it laziness? Is House a slacker? Or is there something else? We soon realize House's attitudes have as much to do with his self-image as a general contempt for society. "See that?" House observes to Wilson as they walk the hospital foyer in "Pilot," "They all assume I'm a patient because of this cane."

Wilson's solution is simple. All House needs to do is "put on a white coat like the rest of us." House counters, "People don't want a sick doctor." And therein lies House's dilemma. That one sentence defines, within the first 10 minutes of the series, an essential key to his character, helping us understand and sympathize with him, even as his other actions might repel us.

House's wounded spirit doesn't prevent him from making outrageous remarks and snarky snipes, "House-isms." Snappy, often insightful one-liners populate his speech: "Everybody lies" and "Treating illness is why we became doctors. Treating patients is actually what makes most doctors miserable."

In juxtaposition to the intensity of each week's diagnosis, House "does time" in the hospital's free clinic, treating patients who could be as easily treated as by a "monkey with a bottle of Motrin." These "clinic beats" provide a break in the tension, sometimes a bit of comic relief during the main action of the episode.

House hates working in the clinic, finding it boring and beneath his skills. By treating Rebecca, he has come out of hiding to take on a patient as a favor to Wilson, exposing himself to the prospect of making up six years of neglected clinic duty. Too bad for House, but those "clinic beats" are much beloved by series fans and sorely missed when they went largely AWOL by season four.

### Is Formula a Bad Thing?

The series signature formula makes it in some ways predictable, and indeed, television critics and some fans have nailed the show as a bit *too* predictable. In fact, at one point in season two, House self-referentially remarks to Wilson, "People will think I'm formulaic" ("Hunting," 2.07), certainly a nod to the show's critics at the time.

Yes, *House* is often formulaic. It *has* a formula, and nearly every episode revolves around that formula — even the occasional "special" episodes (with some notable exceptions, including the two-hour season six premiere, "Broken").

Perhaps in the beginning, when David Shore first struck pen to paper (or keystroke to pixel), the series *was* intended as a straight-on medical mystery — a "procedural" drama similar to the wildly popular *CSI* — except that instead of criminal perpetrators, *House* battles rare diseases and death. If you were tuning in only for the show's main plot, just stopping by for the differential and to see House work his medical magic, your criticism would be valid. But you also would not be doing justice to the series, which is not really a medical procedural — except at its topmost layer. The heart of the series is everything that happens beneath the skeleton of the case's predictability. It's between the lines and under the surface, deep within the relationship exchanges, ethical dilemmas, social commentary, and most crucially, the detailed character study of the show's complex central character.

On *House*, the formula isn't a negative; it is the pivot point for House's story and the story of his universe. It is the constant in nearly every episode, the framework upon which everything else is layered to create a complex, elegant, and nuanced story.

### Case in Point: A Closer Look at "Sports Medicine"

So how does it all fall together, this mix of medical mystery procedural and detailed character study? An episode in the middle of first season, "Sports Medicine" (1.12), is a good place to search for the answer. Like all *House* episodes, "Sports Medicine" revolves around a patient with a mysterious set of symptoms. The main medical plot drives the action, and feeds several subplots and character reveals, creating a rich and intricate story.

Directed by film director Keith Gordon, "Sports Medicine" introduces us to Hank Wiggen, a star baseball pitcher. (According to the plot, he struck out the great Sammy Sosa!) Wiggen is getting back to his career after being suspended from professional baseball for drug use. In the teaser, he is filming an antidrug public service announcement directed, in a self-referential cameo, by series executive producer and director Bryan Singer. While softly lobbing a baseball, Wiggen inexplicably breaks his arm.

Wiggen's history and easily broken bones suggest steroid abuse to House. Testing, talking, and brainstorming, he and the team refine the diagnosis to Addison's disease plus steroid abuse. But then Wiggen's liver fails, putting his life in immediate danger. It's not until the hyper-observant House — in a classic series epiphany moment — discerns a subtle symptom in Wiggen's wife, Lola, that House uncovers an important lie, and puts it all together.

Wiggen has cadmium poisoning from smoking contaminated marijuana. Despite his episode-long protestations to the contrary, he is not at all "drug-free."

Test, guess, treat, guess some more, more treatment, "aha!" moment, and, voila! Another life saved by Dr. Gregory House. It's the classic *House* formula: part science, part intuition and observational skill, part unearthing secrets and lies. House's genius puts together seemingly disparate bits of information to figure it all out. But the mystery of Hank Wiggen's broken arm is but one thread of this multifaceted episode.

At the end of "Sports Medicine," House attends a monster truck rally, something we've learned is a particular passion of his. The planning of this outing, winding through the episode, at first appears to be there simply as comic relief. Admittedly, it's pretty amusing to watch House obsess over monster trucks, score $1,000 tickets, and act like a 10-year-old who's gotten a Wii for his birthday. But this subplot provides the vehicle (so to speak) to delve into several crucial character threads explored later in the first season — and on into the next.

House loves monster trucks. He loves to watch these gigantic vehicles crush smaller vehicles into flattened metal pancakes. It's such a "regular guy" thing, that it's hard to imagine the dour and miserable House getting excited about it. However, the gleam in his eye when he asks Wilson to share this treasured event — complete with "owners' passes" at a $1,000 apiece — is a classic moment in the series.

Wilson begs off, explaining that he has a speaking engagement. The disclosure drives an important secondary plot woven into the episode's main fabric. As House tries to find an alternate companion for the event, it seems everyone on the staff will be attending Wilson's lecture. But House learns by chance that the lecture has, in fact, been canceled — and that his best friend Wilson has lied. The news hurts House, and he wonders why Wilson would be avoiding monster trucks for a speaking engagement that doesn't exist. The answer, uncovered by the episode's end, springboards into one of the series' most important story lines.

Wilson has lied to conceal a dinner date with a mutual friend named Stacy. But believing the meeting would upset House, Wilson lies to protect his feelings. Although feelings are not something one would readily ascribe to House at this point in the series, it's clear that Wilson's concerns are justified, although House tries to conceal it all behind a veil of sarcasm.

Brushing it off, House assures Wilson that he can have dinner with whomever he chooses. "You two are friends, you *should* see her," he encourages less than convincingly. "Say 'hi' for me." However, House's tone of voice suggests much more to the story than a dinner date with a mutual acquaintance. We may not know it yet, but this pivotal scene sets the stage for a big reveal to come about House's disability — and his longtime relationship with Wilson's dinner date.

But, for now, this is a small plot thread; we're not sure how, or even if, it's relevant to the show's overall narrative. But this is how *House* works: a tiny reveal, an offhand remark, and a fragile thread that takes on significance only at some later date.

Through this plot we begin to get a sense of House's wariness with women —

at least those he cares about. Until this episode, we only see him as a leering, loudmouthed sexist (particularly towards Cuddy — and to a lesser degree, Cameron). But, like so much about him, the crudeness is but a smoke screen. When House is inspired to ask Cameron to the big event, which he acknowledges is a "date except for the date part" — he is reticent and unexpectedly shy.

But House is also quite capable of playfulness, and the monster truck rally gives us an opportunity perceive House's "inner child." He seems uncharacteristically relaxed acquainting Cameron with the wonders of "Grave Digger." He's actually having fun! The "date, except for the 'date' part" seems an awful lot like a date. (It evidently fools Cameron as well, because in episodes aired soon after, she begins to wonder about House's feelings towards her.)

As Cameron and House walk the grounds of the monster truck rally, we see — in a very subtle use of props — House uses an ornate, silver-tipped cane. It's something we learn that he saves for special occasions (we won't see it again until late season two at a formal affair). It's one of those incredibly subtle cues and clues into House's inner life — a minor detail that the creative team does so well. To House, this outing is a special occasion, one befitting this fancy walking stick. Whether that's due to the monster trucks or to being on a non-date with Cameron, we're not entirely sure.

At the end of the evening, House playfully steals Cameron's cotton candy and they actually talk, free of the guardedness surrounding most of his conversations. It's a great moment between the two of them. Then, when Cameron asks House if he's ever been married, the moment ties back into House's earlier conversation with Wilson about Stacy. When he reflectively reveals to Cameron that he "lived with someone for awhile," we are left contemplating whether the "someone" might be Stacy, Wilson's dinner date.

*Dr. Gregory House — Rock Star*

In another subplot, Foreman hooks up with a new pharmaceutical company sales rep. As the rep continues to hang around, it becomes increasingly clear she is not only pursuing Foreman. House believes the beautiful young rep is actually trying to get closer to him through Foreman and the other fellows. As House explains it, it's like groupies, who get closer to rock stars by hanging out with the roadies.

The rep is trying to get House to attend a medical conference in Bermuda. But why go to so much trouble just to interest a reclusive, misanthropic doctor? Who would care whether House attends or not?

It's another tiny detail, almost a throwaway line, the rep asks Foreman in an intimate moment whether they might convince House to attend. The point is made: House seems to be an influential enough doctor to warrant the rep's attention. The series, of course, has already alluded to House's importance by this time. But it's different hearing about Princeton-Plainsboro's "Picasso" ("Socratic Method," 1.06) from Wilson — or Cuddy or the fellows — than from an outsider to House's insular little universe.

### Patients' Rights and Other Ethical Dilemmas

Enmeshed within all the other plots and subplots is the story of Lola Wiggen's pregnancy. When Wiggen's liver begins to fail, his wife offers a piece of hers for transplant if it's a match. Testing reveals that Lola is pregnant, and although her liver is a match for Wiggen, her pregnancy makes her ineligible for the procedure. Lola wants to abort the fetus. And as with so many *House* episodes, we are presented with an ethical dilemma.

When Wiggen learns that Lola insists on an abortion to save his life, he attempts suicide, using his manager's heart medicine, which, until House figures it out, sends the team off on a tangent, pursuing new, unexplained symptoms. Lola is still insistent, but House reminds her that Hank is free to choose, even though he might die.

Despite Lola's — and the team's — protests, House protects Wiggen's right to make this decision. A patient's right to choose death over life after they have all the relevant information is an often-revisited theme on *House*, first raised in the pilot episode. He may browbeat his patients into procedures and treatments while he's seeking the diagnosis, but once all the information is in, House generally accepts the patient's decision, sometimes in direct opposition to his staff, Wilson, and Cuddy. And, as we'll learn by the first season's end, this approach is something that ties directly back into House's own history.

"Sports Medicine" touches on another key *House* trope. House knows that disclosing his tainted marijuana diagnosis will probably end Wiggen's baseball career, given the athlete's history with drugs. So, in his final medical report, House omits this detail, mentioning Hank's Addison's disease. Omitting this key medical fact is likely against the rules, but is it the "right" thing to do in this case? Explaining the omission to Cuddy, House reflects that no one should be destroyed because of one mistake. It's an interesting comment on fairness, and House's worldview.

Woven into the episode's fabric between the several plot threads, the Princeton-Plainsboro clinic provides comic relief as House diagnoses an entire waiting room full of people in about 70 seconds. House and Wilson's glee over having a famous ballplayer as a patient adds another element of "guy stuff" playfulness. Of course, no first season episode of *House* is complete without at least one *Fantastic Voyage*–like journey into the patient's body, courtesy of the program's special effects.

All of this fits into a densely packed 43-minute episode, a very typical season one offering. A well done, but standard "formulaic" episode, it attempts nothing extraordinary or out-of-the-box. Yet it nicely showcases the deeply layered richness of every episode and reveals what makes the series great.

### Formulas Are Made to Be Broken

What good is a formula if you can't mess with it once in awhile? Every season has played around with the *House* formula: season one's "Three Stories" (1.21), season two's "The Mistake" (2.08) and "No Reason" (2.24) are tinker-with-the-formula episodes. They are all framed by medical mysteries of one sort or another, so none of them dispense with the formula completely. "Three Stories" diagnoses three leg problems, "The Mistake," a liver ailment, and "No Reason," the surreal predicament of a man with a swollen tongue.

By season three, the producers felt they could tinker even more, breaking the formula entirely in "One Day, One Room" (3.12), which focuses on House's encounter with a young rape victim, Eve. The season four episodes "House's Head" and "Wilson's Heart" (4.15, 4.16) use non-linear storytelling to break through House's trauma-induced amnesia with very little differential diagnosis involved, except as it involved unlocking House's memory.

David Shore and company really shook things up at the beginning of the strike-shortened season four, feeling the need to refresh the series while it was still hot. Partly due to bad timing, the attempted metamorphosis was not quite as successful as hoped. A Chicago political axiom teaches, "If it ain't broke, don't fix it," but clearly Shore had never studied Chicago politics.

After all three members of House's original team leave under different conditions at the end of season three, House needs to hire a new staff. So, season four begins with House conducting an overlong and highly unrealistic *Survivor*-esque competition to find his new team. The length of this story arc seemed exaggerated after the Writers Guild of America (WGA) went on strike in November 2007, which pressed "pause" mid season for most of network television. The hiring story arc would have been only a fraction of the ordered 24-episode season, but with the season shortened by a third, it dominated the season, creating a top-heavy, unbalanced feel, completely redeemed only by the two-part finale "House's Head"/"Wilson's Heart" (4.15, 4.16).

Ultimately, House hires three new fellows and the original three eventually return to the hospital. But the producers seemed to have a difficult time successfully incorporating the now much-larger cast in the already complex 43- to

44-minute episodes. Chase and Cameron in particular got short shrift, just as they were striking out on their own in new specialties, and had very little screen time. And at the beginning of season five, even House's screen time was sacrificed. Some chagrined fans began to compare his screen time to that of new fellow "13," upset that her time on-screen seemed to eclipse even that of the central character. But by the end of season five, the producers seemed to find the correct balance between the fellows, Wilson, Cuddy, and our hero House.

Season five also explored some novel storytelling techniques. "Last Resort" (5.09), plays out against a hostage situation. Although there is a diagnosis, it's done under a highly pressurized situation unlike any we've seen before in the series. "Locked In" (5.19) tells the story from the patient's point of view while he lies immobile, unable to speak. And the final several episodes of the season play with House's (and our) sense of reality within his universe.

The season six premiere spans a three-month period, completely outside House's world, as he is treated at Mayfield Psychiatric Hospital. None of the other series regulars appear in the episode, except for a brief telephone call from Wilson. But back at Princeton-Plainsboro, there is another (albeit less dramatic) shake-up. And when the dust settles by mid season, House's team is a mix of old and new: Foreman, Chase, "13," and Taub.

The late season six episode "Lockdown" (6.17), scuttles the diagnostic process entirely. Framed around the search for a missing baby, the episode focuses on the dynamics between most of the series regular characters. Season six concluded with two outside-the-formula episodes. "Baggage" (6.21) is framed by House's psychotherapy session with his psychiatrist Dr. Darryl Nolan, and the season finale, "Help Me" (6.22), is mainly set outside the hospital at the site of a crane disaster. Both have medical mysteries, but are far less about the medical case and much more about House's emotional state as season six comes to an end.

### Drama vs. Medical Accuracy: A Balancing Act

Like any television drama, watching *House* requires a healthy suspension of disbelief, especially if you happen to be a medical professional or knowledgeable about the way hospitals operate. In the *House* universe, doctors perform most of the tests — from simple blood tests to elaborate brain procedures. In the real world, nurses, technicians, and other medical professionals would undoubtedly do the procedures performed by Gregory House's staff.

There is a reason behind this bit of dramatic license, however. Although *House* is a show about diagnostic medicine, which involves a lot of testing and interpreting of results, it also focuses on the personalities and personal lives of

House and his staff. How much fun would it be to watch our central characters simply sitting around reading reports and hanging around the whiteboard? If all the cool stuff was done by peripheral characters, however realistic that might be, there would be much less opportunity for the main cast to interact with the weekly patients, witness their inevitable crises, and be part of the episode's drama.

Diagnostic medicine is even a fictional medical discipline. But as unrealistic and overly dramatized as the medicine may seem, some of the unlikeliest medical moments on *House* are based on real cases. Many of the conditions House treats are so rare, few doctors would ever encounter them, which is kind of the show's point.

In "The Itch" (5.07), the patient, who has an intestinal gas issue, catches fire — internally — as the team tries to cauterize his intestine after a procedure. It's easy to believe that the stunt was simply for dramatic (or creepily comic) effect. But it wasn't. The incident is actually based on something that happened with a real patient, according to Dr. Lisa Sanders, whose *New York Times* feature "Diagnosis" provided part of David Shore's inspiration for the series.

Sanders serves as one of several *House, M.D.* medical consultants, along with Dr. David Foster, who also serves as a *House* writer/producer. Bobbin Bergstrom, a real nurse who also plays one on the show, is often on set to make sure the actors actually look like they're doing proper medical procedures. And, in season six, as the show began to seriously address House's emotional issues, the producers hired a new medical consultant — a psychiatrist — to bring realism to the handling of this important story line.

While the broader medical picture is in the capable hands of the show's consultants, the details of how the medicine is practiced often takes a backseat to the story's dramatic needs. The show's medical inaccuracies are legendary, documented on the Internet and in books like *The Medical Science of House, M.D.* (Andrew Holtz, 2006). On a weekly basis, the blog Polite Dissent picks apart the medicine of the series procedure by procedure, grading each episode for its medical accuracy, the elegance of the diagnosis, and the creativity of the solution.

Everything on *House* — all the tests, and the length of time to get results — is compressed to fit into a week or less. Genetic testing isn't actually as instantaneous as is often portrayed on the show. The fellows all seem to have expertise in multiple disciplines: the neurologist does what a cardiologist might, and the immunologist shows her expertise in endocrinology. Then there are the times when House goes from to A to B to X with his diagnostic puzzle, when in reality, A to B really leads to Z. And sometimes a more straightforward procedure is sacrificed for something riskier — and more dramatic.

The diagnosis of Mark Warner's acute intermittent porphyria (AIP) in "Honeymoon" (1.22) would not have required House to wait until an actual attack to test for the disease as suggested by the episode. As dramatically crucial as the attack scene is (with its opportunity for House and his ex-lover Stacy to argue about her role in his disability), the doctors could have tested Mark's urine at any time. The levels of the chemical marker for the disease are always present in an AIP patient, say Internet medical experts.

However, the series' exploration of rare diseases, medical ethics, and the nature of right and wrong often make *House* "must-see" TV for medical students around the world. The series has also served a higher purpose in bringing much-needed attention to some diseases, including lupus, which pops up frequently among the usual suspects considered during each week's diagnostic chase.

The Lupus Foundation publicly thanked the series and its creators on its website for bringing new awareness to this disease, which is difficult to diagnose since its symptoms mimic many other conditions. The show has also raised awareness of Spinal Muscular Atrophy (SMA), the number one genetic killer of children under two, according to the Families of SMA website. In "Merry Little Christmas" (3.09), House has a conversation with a little girl afflicted with the disease, leading him to the diagnosis of his patient. The following season, "97 Seconds" (4.03), features an adult SMA patient as the week's main case. Garrett Lerner, whose son has SMA, and Russel Friend wrote the episode.

Huntington's chorea, which afflicts *House* fellow Remy Hadley ("13") and other diseases have gained public awareness as well. And in season six, as Gregory House begins to finally address some of his psychological issues, the series partnered with the National Alliance on Mental Illness to support its work.

---

### Diagnostic Medicine: Life Imitating Art

There is an old South Asian legend about a group of blind men who encounter an elephant. The men are tasked with describing the large animal. Because each has touched a different part of the elephant — the tusk, a leg, the ear, and the tail — each of their descriptions greatly differ. Each man has only experienced a small part of the whole and is unable to understand the larger picture.

A similar phenomenon can occur when a specialist doctor examines a patient's symptoms. As oncologist Wilson observes in "Dying Changes Everything" (5.01), "I'm an oncologist; I see cancer." Cameron would look at the same results through her perspective as an immunologist, and Foreman through his specialty of neurology.

It's a narrow lens, but that's the nature of specialization. House is different. When he diagnoses a patient, he relies not only on his dual specialties of nephrology and infectious diseases, and the specialties of his staff and colleagues, he mines his vast knowledge of everything from history to chemistry, language to music, math to psychology. He endeavors to see the entire picture.

Unfortunately, as Dean of Medicine Lisa Cuddy points out in the season six episode "Epic Fail" (6.03), departments like House's don't exist in "real life." The one at Princeton-Plainsboro Teaching Hospital was established specifically to make use of House's unique gifts and skill set. Outside of House's fictional world, his patients would remain undiagnosed for years, shuttled from specialist to specialist, never obtaining an answer to the question "what's wrong with me?" But what if a doctor (or a team of doctors) like House existed outside of the fictional Princeton-Plainsboro Teaching Hospital?

In February 2009, the U.S. National Institutes of Health (NIH) established the Center for Rare and Undiagnosed Diseases to research just the sorts of rare presentations and often-genetic diseases House's department tackles. Only the NIH has taken House's game and gone pro.

According to Dr. John Gallin, director of the NIH Clinical Center, they are "taking a formal multi-disciplinary approach so that every patient is going to really be looked at from the perspective of 25 senior attending physician-scientists here who will consider the nature of the illness from a multi-system perspective of every problem." Sound familiar? The program, designed to admit about 100 patients each year, will give hope to many people who languish in the medical system with rare genetic defects, which are so often at the root of House's diagnostics patients. It is, perhaps, a case of life imitating art.

# Words on the Page

## Crafting *House, M.D.*

Dr. Gregory House is fond of metaphors. He has a metaphor for everything from obscure medical conditions to the conditions of the human heart. But *House* star Hugh Laurie isn't too bad at metaphors, either. Describing the series' scripts and writing, Laurie once compared *House* scripts to Faberge eggs, those enameled, intricately designed Russian egg sculptures that open to more surprises inside.

*House* is a writers' show. Layered storytelling merges with character development and rapid-fire dialogue; a magnetic, yet unpredictable central character holds together layers of plot and subplot. So much transpires during an average episode of *House*, it's remarkable the show's creators can carry it off within the typical 43- to 44-minute time frame. Creating the density, the pacing, and the emotional ebbs and flows requires perfect cohesion of script, direction, editing, and acting. Frantic activity is intercut with moments of exquisite soul-searching; witty one-liners are interlaced with intelligent ethical debate. When it works, the results are spectacular. And on *House*, it usually does.

The *House* writers' room is inhabited by a group of immensely creative and talented individuals, churning out some of the snappiest and smartest dialogue this side of cable TV. Most of the show's scribes have been with *House* several seasons: some from the beginning like Shore and Lawrence Kaplow, many of the others since season two. Although the producers insist there is no series "bible" (a detailed document detailing character and story histories and timelines), the writers seem to possess a comprehensive memory of the stories, characters, and character histories. They plant subtle story strands only to harvest them again seasons later (although this particular quirk of the show has occasionally frustrated viewers).

## When It Doesn't "Fit"

Dr. Gregory House is uncomfortable when not quite everything "fits." Likewise, when some element on *House* doesn't fit, it feels off — or just plain wrong. The show's combination of good storytelling, tight writing, and great acting doesn't always work perfectly. It's not often, but the occasional lapses are noteworthy.

Sometimes the show gets bogged down in narrative arcs that seem to go on too long or stretch believability — even within the unbelievable world of Dr. Gregory House. In season one, House meets his first major nemesis, Edward Vogler, the new chairman of the hospital board ("Control," 1.14). The writers' intentions were honorable, trying to insert an irritant from outside House's universe to create conflict and mayhem. But at the time, many fans simply wanted him to disappear. Cartoonish and one-dimensional, there is little nuance: Vogler is the bad guy and House is the good guy — end of story.

On the heels of the Vogler story arc, we are introduced to House's ex-lover Stacy ("Three Stories," 1.21). Back in House's life after five years, their story line is compelling and revelatory. Her presence allows us to view House through a different prism. The writers tried to make the first several episodes of season two into a dance between them: he loves her; he hates her. A step forward, two back. But we only get hints of the conflict, and there are episodes during the story where Stacy is completely missing and not mentioned — as if she didn't exist.

Where was she in "Daddy's Boy" (2.05), a pivotal episode right in the midst of her story line — and featuring House's parents? They would have certainly known of Stacy, yet she's not mentioned at all. By "Hunting" (2.07) and the final two episodes of the story arc ("Failure to Communicate," 2.10, and "Need to Know," 2.11) we finally come to the heart of the relationship, and the writers nail it. Would it have been better, though not to have dragged out the story halfway into season two? Many fans thought so.

The same complaint was registered for the seven-episode "Tritter" story arc in season three. Introduced in "Fools for Love" (3.05), Michael Tritter is a vengeful police detective who goes after House for narcotics trafficking after being treated rudely in the clinic. But the biggest criticism of this story arc was neither for its length nor the unrealistic way the legal aspects of the story unfold (another fan complaint). Fans seemed most annoyed that for all that happens to House during this time — from arrest to overdosing on oxycodone to admitting himself to rehab — there is no discernable effect on him. All that build-up, all that drama — and by the first episode after Tritter's departure, it is as if none of it has ever happened.

Of course, the most controversial move by the show thus far was to jettison House's original team at the end of season three, introducing an entirely new fellowship team in season four. However, instead of making a clean break, the show's producers kept the three former fellows. Foreman returned to House's team after a brief absence, while Chase and Cameron were relegated to significantly smaller roles. This did not sit well with many in the show's fan base who felt the two popular characters had been marginalized. Would it have been better for the producers to cut them entirely, making a clean break? By the middle of season five, the series seemed to find a way to balance the screen time among the larger cast while focusing on House's story. But in season six, when the show's producers decided to cut Cameron's character from the mix, many fans objected to the abrupt nature of her departure. It seemed to be a capricious and unfair way to send off a beloved member of the original team.

### Plucking Threads

During season one, the father of fellow Dr. Robert Chase visits his estranged son unexpectedly ("Cursed," 1.13). He reveals confidentially to House that he has stage-four lung cancer and only a few months to live. The story, which has interesting potential, seems to be dropped as soon as Rowan and Chase say goodbye at the end of the episode — without Chase aware that his father is dying. Hearing nothing further about Chase's father, or his impending death, many fans began to wonder if they ever would. But the story thread wasn't dropped; it was simply woven back into show's fabric. The following season, we learn that Rowan died months earlier — and right on schedule. His death drives events in "The Mistake" (2.08) — a great Chase-centered episode — and becomes the springboard into the next story arc.

Another thread seemingly dropped mid season concerns the brother of House's best friend, oncologist Dr. James Wilson. We learn that Wilson's intense interest in a homeless patient ("Histories," 1.10) is fueled by memories of his younger brother, missing for years. For several seasons to come, Wilson fans expressed frustration about the lack of any news about Wilson's "long lost brother."

However, late in season five, the long-lost Danny resurfaces in "The Social Contract" (5.17). Schizophrenic and homeless, he now resides in a psychiatric ward. This tiny, almost-forgotten season one thread becomes crucial to our understanding of House and Wilson's relationship — and to the remaining episodes of season five. In a 2008 interview, writers Garrett Lerner and Russel Friend noted that the creative team for the series had always planned on picking up this important strand, and had even hoped at one point to incorporate Danny's story into the season four finale. The writers revealed that they had to bring Danny back into the story in a way that made sense for longtime viewers — and for those who might not have recalled the reference to a long-lost brother back in season one. They wanted to "do it right." And they succeeded.

We experience "real life" as a series of moments: significant, inconsequential, tragic, and joyful. They occur and then are eventually forgotten or slipped back into the recesses of our memories only to be picked up again later. This happens in literature all the time: clues, foreshadowing, elements briefly touched upon in Chapter 3 are revealed in greater relief only when we arrive at Chapter 15.

As viewers, we learn about Danny Wilson (as House does) mid–season one; we learn more in season five. How he factors into the future certainly will only be revealed in bits and pieces, "brought up and woven back into the fabric of the series," as executive producer Katie Jacobs has noted. Much like real life.

### A Script Is Born

A writer comes up with an idea — a disease, a "cool" case they'd like to play with, or maybe a character they'd like to explore in a particular way. This is where the episode begins. A few seasons ago, writer Lawrence Kaplow wanted to create an episode where the doctors have to actually kill the patient in order to save her life (neat trick, huh?). He didn't know at the time such a scenario was possible or even existed within medical literature. But it was possible, and from that idea was born "Autopsy" (2.02), which requires House and company to "kill" a young cancer patient to diagnose her. The poignant and dramatic episode won Kaplow a Writers Guild Award.

During season four, *House* scribe Doris Egan thought it might be interesting if House turned up somewhere, without knowing how he got there. At the time, Egan was busy preparing another episode (her Writers Guild Award–nominated "Don't Ever Change," 4.12) so two other writers — Garrett Lerner and Russel Friend — stepped up and created the stunning two-part season finale "House's Head"/"Wilson's Heart."

Writing for *House* is said to be a collaborative process. The starting point of most episodes is the medical mystery, which provides the framework for the character story. Ideas are fleshed out as they pass through executive producers (who are also writers) and back to the original writers, with notes along the way from *House* creator David Shore, the medical consultants, and others.

Commercial drama series typically are created in four acts, with a pre-credits "teaser" to open the episode. The acts are fairly equal in length, separated by commercial breaks. It's a tried-and-true structure, and one that had worked well for *House*.

In season five, the network directed the show's producers to alter its narrative structure from the four-act format to a six-act structure with longer, but fewer, commercial breaks during the show's first half, and more frequent breaks during the second half. This can result in commercial breaks nearly as long as the story segments themselves as the episode moves toward its climax moment.

> "We hate, we hate it, we hate it [the six-act structure]. It's not our choice. We're given no choice. We don't like it all. We beg and plead to go back to a four-act structure. We control content as best we can, but we have no control over this."
>
> **— Showrunner/executive producer/director Katie Jacobs, January 2009 interview**

The change presented the writers with the challenge of working with more acts — and of uneven length. It was a particular challenge for a series that tries to end each act at a crisis point for the patient. The show still times out at 43 to 44 minutes, but trying to balance the requirements of the story and the network's demand for more commercial breaks frustrated the series writers and producers for months.

The longer first-half commercial breaks could wreck the mounting tension and take viewers out of the moment. On the other hand, the shorter acts during the second half could render the narrative overly choppy, breaking the action at odd moments — something especially problematic during a particularly intense episode.

But good writers rise to challenges, and the *House* writers are among the best.

By the end of season five, the writers began to appreciate the new rhythm the structure afforded them. (Either that or they learned to better deal with it.) According to Doris Egan, the writers finally began see the advantages of the longer opening act, which allowed them to establish the story and the emotional beats before going to the first commercial break. But even into season six, the uneven act-breaks tend to give the writers some problems — and frustrate the fans.

### A Flair for Their Characters

Although the writing is collaborative, it does seem that some writers have a particular feel for one or another of the characters and relationships. Fans of the House-Wilson dynamic consider Egan their champion, dubbing her "Saint Doris." Her scripts have taken House and Wilson on some interesting journeys — literally, since she's also the go-to girl for House-Wilson road trips — including "Son of Coma Guy" (3.07), "Birthmarks" (5.04), "Social Contract" (5.17), and the season five finale "Both Sides Now" (5.24), as well as the season six trip up to a medical conference in "Known Unknowns" (6.07).

> "The writers have differing views of all the relationships. We're always hashing them out between us in rather vociferous, lengthy conversations, but I think that makes it better. Part of what makes the writing better is that we push on each other, push to make each other better."
>
> — **David Foster, October 2008 interview**

The writers also have differing takes on the characters. Doris Egan and David Foster noted in a 2008 interview that opposing views fuel a productive creative tension among the writers. Garnett Lerner and Russel Friend likewise pointed out in a 2009 interview, that like the show's fans, the writers also sometimes debate about the characters' actions and motives. For example, does House "care"? Is he fundamentally a good person? Or is he only interested in the puzzles?

> "It's something that's endlessly debated not just by fans but internally here by the writers. Does he have a compassionate streak under it all?"
>
> — **Garrett Lerner, September 2009 interview**

If you examine the episodes created by the various *House* writers, it's even possible to notice some of those differences. Sara Hess tends to write House as more obnoxious, colder than, say, Lerner and Friend do.

David Hoselton has written episodes that seem to feature a lot of tension between House and Cuddy ("Airborne," 3.18; "Lines in the Sand," 3.04; "Joy," 5.06; "Unfaithful," 5.15; and "Ignorance Is Bliss," 6.09). While he was writing for *House*, John Mankiewicz had a feel for House's vulnerability ("Socratic Method," 1.06; "Sports Medicine," 1.12; "Honeymoon," 1.22; and "Who's Your Daddy?" 2.23).

Presumably knowing his creation better than anyone, series creator David Shore has written several episodes that dive deep below House's surface: "Pilot" of course, "Occam's Razor" (1.03), "Three Stories" (1.21), "No Reason" (2.24), "Meaning" (3.01), and "One Day, One Room" (3.12). Although he has stepped back a bit from writing original episodes, with no writing credits at all in seasons four and five, he worked with Lerner, Friend, and Foster on the season six premiere "Broken" (6.01) — and he has a hand in every script before it's final.

### From the Page to the Small Screen

Hugh Laurie has often said that the *House* scripts are so beautifully written, all he can hope to do is read them out and "just not screw it up." Indeed, the scripts are beautifully written. But take a page of random dialogue from *House* and just read it out — then watch the performance on-screen. Magic happens to make the words come alive, the dialogue sing, and the words between the lines resonate. It's called acting.

> "That is one great thing about these shows. You put something like that into a script and Hugh or someone else . . . It's so perfect. It's wonderful to watch. It's like being God [seeing your creation come alive]."
>
> **— Doris Egan on the talented cast, May 2009 interview**

On the printed page, House comes off as a jerk, sometimes so obnoxious, it would be hard to find him at all sympathetic. But take those same lines and put them into an episode — with Laurie "reading out" the lines and everything else he puts into his performance: body language, inflections, rhythm, and perhaps most importantly, those gloriously expressive eyes. The transformation from page to screen is astonishing.

In "A Simple Explanation" (5.20), fellow Lawrence Kutner commits suicide, and House accompanies Foreman and "13" to visit Kutner's adoptive parents. While the two younger doctors are content to sit with the parents, offering whatever comfort they can, House cannot accept the death and is desperate to make rational sense of it.

"It was his name. He was conflicted, didn't know where he fit in, being ripped out of his world and stuck into yours," House accuses Kutner's stunned parents. "All his Anglo name gave him was the illusion that he was someone he wasn't. . . . You didn't understand him."

Harsh, cold, unfeeling: how can you talk like that to the parents of someone who has just killed himself? House is an unsympathetic bastard daring to argue with Kutner's grief-stricken and unsuspecting parents. How could anyone relate to such a jerk?

But watch Laurie's performance, and you get it — you understand. House isn't so much talking to the Kutners, as he is to himself, attempting to make sense of the senseless. He is trying to understand Kutner's isolation and loneliness within an outwardly loving family. But at the same time, you perceive that House may be talking as much about himself and his troubled upbringing as he is about Kutner.

It's in his tone of voice. There is a haunted quality to it that makes you suspect he'll fall apart if he doesn't keep talking through this extremely inappropriate rational analysis. He is deep within himself, even as he accuses the Kutners of their son's death. Yes, he is saying terrible things, but with such pathos, you can't help but feel for him. There are scenes like this in nearly every episode. But if you're not paying attention, they're easy to miss.

Equally important are the scenes that take place between the written lines while House is alone in his office or home, or staring into a patient's room. As the camera simply observes him, we, as viewers, are given an intimate glimpse of House, allowing us to speculate about what's on House's mind or in his heart. These scenes are crucial to understanding — and truly appreciating — the character.

In "Maternity" (1.04), House has identified an epidemic brewing amongst newborn babies. As the episode progresses, he wants to perform a "therapeutic trial" to test two different antibiotics, hoping to save the babies' lives. But doing the trial means probably condemning one of the six sick babies to death. If he performs the experiment, he explains, one baby will likely die; if he doesn't, all six are condemned. The hospital's lawyer and Cuddy oppose the ethically questionable experiment when House goes to them for approval. Frustrated with the choice he's put before them, Cuddy finally tells House "do what you think is best," putting the entire burden on his shoulders as he stalks from her office after flippantly implying that he'll toss a coin to choose "which baby lives."

The next scene finds House sitting alone in his office with the coin. The shooting script for the episode simply has House flipping the coin, with no further direction or note. But as you watch the scene, it is obvious House is not the smug and arrogant doctor who appeared so cavalier in the previous scene. The burden of making this choice is plain on his face and in body language.

If "Maternity" were a novel, this scene would require a page of narration to describe what House is going through. In a television show, it is but a brief moment of seeing into the soul of a character through the actor's craft.

Certainly, the focus of the show is House's journey, and we rarely see any of the supporting characters living lives separate from the hospital — or House. But the supporting actors have also infused their Housian alter egos with depth and vigor. Each has grown over the course of six seasons, and in season six, *House* has featured special episodes with both Wilson ("Wilson," 6.11) and Cuddy ("5 to 9," 6.14) taking center stage.

Robert Sean Leonard's dry sense of humor makes his Wilson a great counterbalance to House's sometimes manic energy. We suspect there is something dark lurking beneath his surface, but we can't quite put our fingers on it — it's something that eludes even House from time to time.

Leonard instills Wilson with layers that render him an enigmatic puzzle. But he's also funny. In a classic moment from "Alone" (4.01), Wilson kidnaps House's brand new — and very expensive — guitar. At one point he threatens the defenseless Gibson Flying V, describing the pain and anguish he's about to inflict on the instrument, mimicking the screeching sound of a dying string to the seriously *unamused* House. It's a brilliant moment, and one of the funniest in the entire series.

Lisa Edelstein brings vivacity to a role that could have easily come off as cardboard. Her Cuddy has made tough choices — sacrificing a conventional personal life for her career. And Edelstein has let us into Cuddy's angst over those choices. But her saucy sense of humor also provides Cuddy the ability to go toe-to-toe with House, trading sarcasm for sarcasm. In "Need to Know" (2.11), she perfectly delivers Cuddy's rant about going against a patient's wishes when House wants her to consult hospital attorney Stacy Warner. Knowing that House and Stacy are involved, Cuddy mimics her perfectly, down to the Southern drawl, talking about House's dreamy eyes and big cane — while making her point. In the final episode of season six, she perfectly sells Cuddy's resignation over her fate to love House.

Likewise, Jennifer Morrison, Jesse Spencer, and Omar Epps have all grown into their roles, their characters evolving from young fellows to veteran attending physicians. Spencer in particular has imbued Chase with a great deal of depth, taking him on a real journey in the six seasons we've known him. And Jennifer Morrison has grown along with her character, taking Cameron from ingénue to the much more skeptical, street savvy emergency room director she becomes. Particularly at the end of season five, Morrison did a fantastic job conveying Cameron's ambivalence in marrying Chase. Many fans were sorry to see her go mid season six, when a creative decision eliminated her role. Her final scenes in "Teamwork" (6.08) are powerful and poignant as she says goodbye to Princeton Plainsboro, but the highlights of Morrison's six years on *House* are her raw final scenes with Chase in "Lockdown" (6.16).

And as we've gotten to know Olivia Wilde and Peter Jacobson better, their individual strengths have helped us see into their characters, who were not universally welcomed by the fan base when they landed on *House* in season four.

Before his departure towards the end of season five, Kal Penn had endeared himself to the fans as the slightly goofy, but creative Kutner, making us wonder if he was a happier version of House. Until, that is, Kutner killed himself in "Simple Explanation" (5.20).

> "On one hand, people react negatively to change. On the other hand we're not *The Simpsons* [where years later, no one has aged a day]. We can't keep the characters fellows forever."
>
> **— Russel Friend, May 2008 interview**

Of course, it's not *only* the performance, but also how the director understands the scene, the episode, and what the writers are trying to say. Several of the *House* directors, have, like the writers, been with the series for years, and have developed a particular look for their episodes. Deran Sarafian loves tight close-ups on House, sometimes so close, they're a bit unnerving. Greg Yaitanes has a good sense of intercutting scenes in a non-linear fashion. He uses this technique in "House's Head" (4.15), "Simple Explanation" (5.20), and "House Divided" (5.22) to lend a disjointed and very off-kilter feeling to the episodes, appropriate for their intense and psychologically difficult stories. In the season six finale, "Help Me," he employed a unique way of filming in close quarters using a high-definition digital SLR camera.

Interestingly, regular *House* director/executive producer Daniel Sackheim, a longtime producer and director on the *X-Files*, directed the "Cane and Able" (3.02), in which the week's patient believes he has been abducted by aliens. Stylistically, the episode has *X-Files* emblazoned all over it. Executive producer Katie Jacobs has, herself, directed several episodes, including "Half Wit" (3.15), "Last Resort" (5.09), and the two-hour season six premiere episode "Broken" (6.01, 6.02). She has a particular flair for getting into the heart of the characters (especially House) and the emotional landscape of the stories.

It's no mystery why *House* continues to be both popular and critically acclaimed. Resonant storytelling, tight writing, densely packed dialogue, brilliant performances, and often-artful editing — it is a Faberge egg, indeed.

Occasionally, the writers make a bizarre turn with the characters themselves. All of the characters have suffered from inconsistent writing from time to time. But it's most notable when House seems to be "off."

For the most part, the writers really nail him and he's been consistently written since the start. But even House's behavior sometimes has us scratching our collective head and heading off to the nearest fan forum or Live Journal or blog to discuss.

We all know House is a jerk. But usually, even at his worst, we get to witness some glimpse of House's humanity, some inkling of his motivations. We *need* to, in order to keep House sympathetic. Because if we completely lose sympathy with him, as unlikable as he can be, we lose our reason to care what happens to him. If we don't care about House, the show is finished.

> "The tricky thing about the character is that we have this sort of misanthropic, drug addicted guy. We want to preserve his edginess. Not betray that. But we always want to see that humanity."
>
> **— Garrett Lerner, May 2008 interview**

On rare occasions, the show's creative team seems to forget that detail, and we are served a cold, bitter, obnoxious SOB, who is impossible to like — and impossible to care about. David Shore has said over and over again that he likes to push the limits of House's unlikability. But there is a line — one that shouldn't be crossed too many times. Because, even at his worst, we should see vestiges of the troubled intellectual ("Distractions," 2.12), the reluctant healer ("Merry Little Christmas," 3.10), or the deeply compassionate man who wants to help a patient recover his normal life ("Social Contract," 5.17).

"Top Secret" (3.16), "Airborne" (3.18), "Whatever It Takes" (4.06), "No More Mr. Nice Guy" (4.14), and "Teamwork" (6.08) all venture into this territory to greater or lesser degrees. This version of House has the additional effect of tending to push the story over the line from a serious show with comedic elements to a comedy about a sarcastic jerk with few redeeming qualities.

Occasionally, the writers also forget that House is supposed to be the smartest guy in the room. When he is easily outguessed by his subordinates with no underlying reason, or appears stupid — even foolish — neither the character nor the viewers are well served. House defines himself and his self-worth by his intelligence, and his greatest fear is losing his intellectual edge.

His genius and intuition are what make his less attractive qualities forgivable, and when the character loses that, he also threatens to become simply a jerk, full stop. If he's not a genius, and he's an ass on top of it, devoid of humanity, why put up with him at all? Fortunately for us all, these episodes are relatively rare, even after six seasons.

# From Bach to Eddie Van Halen

## The Music of *House, M.D.*

*House, M.D.* uses music in several ways. Its dialogue has cadence; Hugh Laurie has noted perceiving his lines in musical terms — possessing both sound and rhythm. Used to underscore the action, the show's music helps to propel the narrative forward; used within the story itself, music sometimes provides escape or solace for Greg House. At times as essential as the hospital clinic or House's whiteboard, the show's music frames and enriches the fabric of nearly every episode.

> "It's a cool part of a show. We use music sort of differently. I think we try to use songs in a more important way. Not just background filler. We aspire to use it more cinematically."
>
> **— Katie Jacobs, January 2009 interview**

At one time or another, we have seen House play most of the instruments in his enviable collection of vintage guitars. He also keeps a banjo at his bedside, as well as several horns resting atop various surfaces in his apartment, including the one given to him by John Henry Giles, the jazz trumpeter whose life he saves in season one ("DNR," 1.09).

House can even repair his own guitar — and no, it is not common for musicians to repair their own guitars! In the season four premiere "Alone" (4.01), Wilson kidnaps House's $12,000 Gibson Flying V, damaging it (oh, the carnage)! House reclaims the expensive electric, repairing it himself during the next episode ("The Right Stuff," 4.02). It's just very cool that House, who is not a trained luthier (although with House, you never know) undertakes such an intricate and complex task. It's one of those wonderful subtle details, easily missed, that enriches our knowledge about him.

### An Emotional Language

Hugh Laurie has suggested that music provides a sort of emotional language for the emotionally inarticulate House. He's a musician, adept at several instruments, and we have seen him numerous times engrossed at the piano or on his guitar pouring his feelings through his fingers onto the keys or strings. What he plays — and when — provides us with clues to what's on his mind, and what's in his heart.

For a man who professes cynicism about God and disdain for religion of all sorts, you have to wonder what prompts him to so wistfully play "Silent Night" sitting alone in his darkened apartment Christmas Eve ("Damned If You Do," 1.05). It's a starkly beautiful arrangement by Hugh Laurie. And in "House vs. God" (2.19), how has House come to possess the sheet music for that bluesy setting of "What a Friend We Have in Jesus," much less play it so passionately?

Playing the piano seems to distract him from his wounds inside and out. One of the series' most heartbreaking moments comes at the end of "Skin Deep" (2.13). Trying desperately to divert himself from escalating leg pain (which Cuddy and Wilson insist is psychosomatic), House sits at his piano, playing Bach's French Suite no. 5. As the camera pulls in, we get the brief sense that it may be working, as House easily scales the trills of the complex baroque piece. But then it hits him; an intense pain causes him to miss a note as he clutches his thigh in agony. The music is a metaphor here for House's resolve, his battle against rising pain and his defeat; he retreats when he can no longer do battle against it.

House's piano playing over the closing montage in "Unfaithful" (5.15) provides a perfect emotional backdrop as Cuddy celebrates her daughter's religious naming ceremony with family and friends. The evocative piece, with motives suggestive of Eastern European Jewish music as well a bit of blues and hints of the *House* anthem "You Can't Always Get What You Want," elaborates on the religious and emotional beats of the scene — and upon House's conflicted feelings about Cuddy (and even God). The song, "Cuddy's Serenade," was composed specially for the episode by series star Laurie.

There are hints here and there throughout the series that at one time, House was more than a gifted amateur. Maybe back in his college or med school days, he played jazz gigs, perhaps sitting in with musicians like Jesse Baker ("Who's Your Daddy?" 2.23), of whom he notes, "I'd give my right hand to have his left."

In scripted (but never-aired) scenes from "DNR" (1.09), House's stab at professional music is more directly addressed when his patient, jazz trumpeter John Henry Giles recalls hearing about House's obsessive personality from his saxophone player who had played with him back in the day. So, when Giles calls House an "obsessive son of a bitch" he's probably not only referring to his medical reputation.

For the first couple of seasons, House keeps a biography of Beethoven sitting on his grand piano; a poster of bandleader Chick Webb first appears in his office at the beginning of the series, and now hangs on his apartment wall. House's interest in both of these legendary musical figures is worth noting. Beethoven, who became totally deaf, was able to overcome serious adversity to be one of the most recognizable and beloved classical composers of all time. Webb was a renowned 20th century jazz drummer and bandleader who also overcame disability to succeed as a musician.

House's personal musical tastes are an eclectic mix of genres from opera to metal and everything in between. In "Autopsy" (2.02) House listens on his iPod to the famous aria from Puccini's opera *Turandot*, "Nessum Dorma" ("None Shall Sleep"). It is a very specific musical choice, considering House has complained throughout the episode of not sleeping as he is plagued by severe hay fever. As House thinks about Stacy, his former lover, now married and back in his life, he plays Blind Willie McTell's version of the traditional blues tune "Little Delia" at the end of "Honeymoon" (1.22). "Delia, Delia, how could it be? / You loved all those rounders, / you never really did love me. / She's all I've got, / is gone." He plays Eddie Van Halen riffs in "Alone" (4.01) and sings Gilbert and Sullivan in "Broken" (6.01, 6.02).

### Musical Diagnosis

House's musicality occasionally fits directly into plot. As we learn in "Half Wit" (3.15), House began a piano composition in junior high school — something never finished. It's something upon which he's probably ruminated often (knowing House), never having been able to find the right way to complete it. When he treats brain-damaged musical savant Patrick, House plays the fragment for him, curious about his patient's gift and what he might do with the composition. Hearing it, Patrick segues into a gorgeous concluding segment, which leaves House moved and nearly speechless. On one level, it's House's way of testing how Patrick's brain works, but on another it's something far more personal.

House uses his highly developed musical ear to help diagnose his patient in "Who's Your Daddy?" (2.23). Detecting a hearing problem in the patient's grandfather (a legendary jazz pianist) by listening to a long-ago recording session, House notes that although the pianist insists the piano is out of tune, it's actually not. An incredibly subtle clue — and one immediately dismissed by Foreman — it sets House on the right diagnostic course.

House's musician's ear also comes into play both in "Autopsy" (2.02) and "The Right Stuff" (4.02). In "Autopsy," House's acute hearing is able to pick up on a tiny irregularity in the recorded heart sounds of a young patient. It's such a minute variance that no one on the team hears it until House points it out. Even then, Cameron is the only one able to detect it.

In "The Right Stuff," House examines his patient for a mass in the chest using only his stethoscope and a very finely tuned ear. He explains to his fellows that a skilled physician with a good ear can literally *hear* a mass by listening in just the right way. It's a low-tech but effective method of diagnosing his patient, an astronaut trying to avoid a paper trail of diagnostic tests.

### The *House* Soundtrack

Because the character of House is unusually guarded and so well hidden, the series soundtrack often expands our understanding of him, of his thoughts and what he feels. Early in the series ("Paternity," 1.02), we observe House standing at the edge of a deserted lacrosse field wistfully reminded of his long-gone athleticism and days gone by. Rickie Lee Jones' wistful and nostalgic "Saturday Afternoons in 1963" underscores the otherwise silent scene, helping us see into House's heart and mind.

Executive producer Katie Jacobs is very much involved with establishing the musical feel of the show and has a strong hand in selecting the *House* soundtrack — the diverse range of songs that underlay the series' signature (usually dialogue-free) montages. The show has developed an extensive music library from which the tracks are chosen. In addition to Jacobs, music supervisors Gary Calamar and Lynn Grossman, Hugh Laurie, and writer/executive producer Peter Blake contribute to the show's music library, Jacobs noted in a 2009 interview.

When trying to get the right feel for an episode, the music editors cut in what they think fits. The director gets a version of this cut to make any needed changes before Jacobs adds her touch. "I come in, and I always like to hear a bunch of different things. I let them sit in my brain for a little bit."

A whole range of genres have been used to catch the right feel for House — from Bach to Ella Fitzgerald to heavy metal. Jacobs points out, however, that the only time she really knew *ahead of time* that she wanted to use a particular song was after getting an advance copy of John Mayer's album *Continuum*, which included the song "Gravity."

"I knew that House would be starting out [season three] not using a cane, and then he goes back to using one," Jacobs said in a 2009 interview. "When I heard the song 'Gravity,' I thought, 'This will work for when House needs to go back to his cane.' That show coincidentally aired the day Mayer's album came out."

Anyone remembering that scene at the end of "Cane and Able" (3.02) is aware of how powerfully that track resonates as House finally succumbs to the returning pain, picking up the old cane.

### Sometimes You Might Get What You Need

"You can't always get what you want," goes the Rolling Stones 1960s rock classic. The song is virtually *House*'s unofficial anthem. The lyrics and melodic line have been referenced throughout the series' run, meaning different things in different situations.

In "Pilot" (1.01), House uses the "philosopher" Jagger's words to explain to Cuddy that he does not intend to fulfill his tedious obligation in the hospital's free clinic, chiding her, "You can't always get what you want."

Later, after she abruptly pulls his privileges, an angry House bursts into her office, but Cuddy immediately disarms him. "I looked up that philosopher Jagger," she zings back at him. "And you know, you're right; 'You can't always get what you want.' But sometimes," she continues, quoting the song's lyrics, "you just might get what you need." Check and mate. Defeated, House has no choice but to give in — for this time, anyway.

The same song evokes a more bittersweet image when it underscores the final scene of season one ("Honeymoon," 1.22) as House vainly tries to take a "normal" step without using his cane. Fueled by the return of Stacy Warner, whom he both loves and resents as the one he holds responsible for his leg, House must wonder if perhaps things have a chance of going back to the way they were "before" — if only he can walk "normally." But he can't. And, when he stumbles, grabbing his leg in pain as it gives out beneath him, House goes for "what he needs" in that little amber bottle of Vicodin. He *wants* Stacy; he *wants* to be "normal." But is that what he *needs*?

The song pops up again in the premiere of season three ("Meaning," 3.01), which has House enjoying the freedom and speed of the successful ketamine pain therapy. He can run, skateboard, and make a gleefully quick getaway. But weeks of living a "normal" life are but "a tortuous taste of the good life," as Wilson puts it, when the pain returns.

After Wilson dismisses House experiencing the simple "pangs of middle age," House's fear gets the better of him, and he steals into Wilson's office to "get what he needs": Wilson's prescription blanks. As the song plays over the scene, it is a harbinger of House's troubles to come.

Jagger's famous lyric puts in another appearance in the fourth season finale ("Wilson's Heart," 4.16). In a coma, House hallucinates that he's on a bus bathed in white light, where he chats with Wilson's recently deceased girlfriend Amber Volakis. As he hovers between life and death, House seems to find the serenity of the bus (possibly an avatar for the "white light" often seen by people near death) comforting and he wants to stay there with Amber. This is a place of no pain — and no wrath of Wilson, whom House believes will blame him for Amber's death. But Amber reminds him gently, "You can't always get what you want," before sending him back to face the harsh reality of living. It may not be what House wants, but it's not his time, and he must return to "what he needs."

"As Tears Go By," a different Rolling Stones classic, frames the season five final sequence ("Both Sides Now," 5.24). First played by a string quartet, the uncharacteristically lyrical melody sets a perfect backdrop for Cameron and Chase's elegant garden wedding. Then the lyrics begin to Jagger's mournful whine, underscoring House's isolation and despair as he and Wilson take the long drive to Mayfield Psychiatric Hospital where House will be a patient for several weeks to come.

# House's Haunts

The next time you watch an episode of *House, M.D.*, hit pause if you can and take a moment to look around at House's office and apartment, Cuddy's office, or Wilson's. Their personal spaces offer more insight to these closed-off, guarded characters than pages of dialogue. Each office and home tells a story. Like House and his team, who invade patients' homes and workplaces to find the hidden crucial details of their lives, we can likewise go inside the characters' lives by entering their individual spaces.

The *House* sets are remarkably detailed, from the equipment in the operating rooms to the half-used bottle of shampoo and rubber duckie on House's bathtub ledge. The meticulous attention paid by the series' art department lends an air of realism. Much of the medical equipment on set *is* real; doctors called to the set to treat cast members for minor injuries have even been able to make use of various "props" to administer on-the-spot treatment!

### House's House

Because most of our time is spent following House, it's only fair to start with him. The look and feel of House's abode is primarily the work of Katie Jacobs. Dark and masculine, it's House's nest, his sanctuary. But star Hugh Laurie also has influenced the look of House's environment, helping to select the musical instruments and many of the little trinkets we find there.

House seems to be something of a pack rat; his apartment is a veritable antique shop, from the vintage record collection to the knickknacks, inlaid wooden boxes, scientific curiosities, and other paraphernalia cluttering nearly every surface. He has an ancient pachinko pinball game propped against his bedroom wall, and sets of antique medical calipers hang from his living room wall between two of his several guitars. Although his apartment is decidedly masculine, it exudes warmth with its muted lighting and large wood-burning fireplace.

House's apartment completely contradicts the image he projects and carefully cultivates. This is not the home of a crude, unabashed "frat boy," nor a cheapskate "scrounger" always begging food and money off everyone. Nothing in House's apartment looks cheap. Old? Yes. Well-worn? Perhaps. Cheap? Not at all.

House's apartment projects lived-in elegance, suggesting that at one time he might have cared more about maintaining an attractive living space. His comfortable, expensive-looking (but worn) leather sofa, the large antique-looking bed and armoire in his bedroom, the art decorating his walls, and the well-appointed kitchen all suggest a life left far behind after the infarction (the arterial blood clot in House's leg).

Until season six, it would have been easy to wonder why House would possess such a well-equipped kitchen. It seems incongruous for a guy who appears to subsist on a diet of peanut butter and jelly sandwiches, beer, and Vicodin. Of course, who could have imagined House displaying an aptitude for cooking? But given the vigor with which embraces his inner chef ("Epic Fail," 6.02; "The Tyrant," 6.03; "Knight Fall," 6.18), House may have (at least a bit) more chef in him than we thought.

Although cooking might serve as a temporary distraction from his problems, House's real passion after medicine is music. And his surroundings reflect that as well. House's baby grand forms the focal point in House's apartment. The beautiful but aged Sohmer, which dominated his living room in the first season, imparted a venerable grace that fit well with House's décor and his personality. It was replaced by another old baby grand, maker unknown, in the second season. And now, the shiny Yamaha (let's hear it for product placement!) sitting in the corner doesn't seem quite at home there. House's piano is more than just a prop. A gifted musician, Hugh Laurie often plays it to relax between scenes, production designer Jeremy Cassells noted in a 2009 interview.

House's vintage guitar collection would make any musician jealous. He owns a Gibson Flying V, a Les Paul, and a Stratocaster electric, as well as three acoustic guitars, including a "dobro" resonator; his oldest guitar was acquired when he was in junior high school. House's art deco poster of jazz drummer Chick Webb is, perhaps, the most interesting of all the artwork decorating House's walls.

Webb, the mid-20th-century jazz drummer and bandleader, overcame spinal tuberculosis, which left him a badly deformed spine. It's easy to see why House, who has occasionally referred to himself a "freak," would gravitate to someone like Webb. Like Webb, House has a gift that enables him to find a place in society. It's an extremely subtle illumination of the character, something most viewers would never notice, but it is exactly the sort of detail that lends richness to House's world.

Hundreds of books line the shelves in every room, and not all of them are medical texts. A biography of Beethoven sometimes lies atop the baby grand; a copy of Rudyard Kipling's *Kim* sat on his nightstand until Wilson's dog, Hector, destroys it ("Resignation," 3.22). In a slightly self-referential bit of prop placement, *The Complete Sherlock Holmes* sits on the end table beside House's sofa.

But, alas, with coming out of Mayfield Psychiatric Hospital at the beginning of season six, House not only gives up Vicodin, he also moves from his apartment to live with Wilson. Recommending that he not live alone, House's therapist believes that House's old environment would be too conducive to familiar isolation and slipping back into old habits. House takes nothing with him from the apartment, and it is weeks before House shows up with boxes of trinkets and a few of his musical instruments ("Wilson," 6.11). It is not until the season's penultimate episode, "Baggage," that he returns to it.

### House at Work

In addition to being the gathering place for differential diagnosis sessions, House's outer office/conference room serves as the bullpen for his team of fellows; it's where they confer, do research, and hang out. It's a large, bright space, uncluttered and modern with glass walls open to the adjacent hallway.

The long hours spent in the office justify the nice kitchenette in the corner, fully stocked with tea, bottled water, animal crackers and other snack foods, and the always-essential coffee pot. Coffee appears to be the lifeblood of House's team, and it must be an extra special blend. If you look closely, you can see that the coffeemaker's label says "Better than Prozac."

The room has a several freestanding bookshelves crammed with medical texts and decorated with anatomical models. Except for the small wall-mounted photographs next to the computer desk in one corner, there are few personal touches anywhere. This is a working office.

During a case, the conference room whiteboard serves as the operations center. House's oracle, it is the repository of the collective wisdom of the Diagnostic Department; symptoms are written, considered, crossed out, and erased. Much of the diagnostic debate takes place in front of it.

House is possessive of his whiteboard, appointing himself (for the most part) sole keeper of its dry-erase markers. Although he's loosened up over the seasons, House still maintains tight control over who does, and does not, get to write on it. It is more than simple territoriality. What would happen if everyone on House's team were allowed to write their theories on the board? Without House filtering and focusing their thoughts, chaos would reign — and patients might die.

For House, the board is more than simply a place to organize his thoughts. He spends hours staring at it during a tough case, using his encyclopedic knowledge to process information and consider tests. He gets frustrated with it, talks to it, and has even knocked it over, upset that it hadn't given him anything but more questions as his young patient lay at death's door ("All In," 2.17). For this part of his process he often drags the board into the dark of his adjoining private office.

Interestingly, the whiteboard vanishes at the beginning of season six when Foreman takes the reins of House's practice ("Epic Fail," 6.03). When House returns after his brief absence, it remains out of sight. It's not until "Moving the Chains" (6.13), that House is really once again fully engaged in the differential diagnosis sessions, it is not until "Open and Shut" (6.19) that we once again see the whiteboard restored to its proper place. But almost as if to show that all is still not quite right with House, it is Chase who wields the dry-erase markers and not House!

---

### The "Ball of Unknown Origin"

You may not be aware of it, but that giant red and white tennis ball on House's desk has a name — or at least it does within the online community of *House* fans. It is called the "ball of unknown origin," or BOUO for short.

There have been a few generations in the BOUO's life. The original ball, prominently featured on House's desk from the first episode on, apparently went missing at the end of season one. It was replaced by a solid red ball (briefly) before an exact replacement could be found (or created by the props department).

Almost as much as House's whiteboard, the BOUO seems to provide him with at least part of his medical mojo. He uses it to think, consider, and ponder as he palms it, tosses it, or simply holds it waiting for it to advise him — a sort of diagnostic divining rod. Others have tried in vain to exact its seemingly magical powers, including Chase and even Cuddy. Only House seems to have the ability to use it properly. In "Known Unknowns" (6.07), House refers to it by the name "Bally."

## House's Inner Sanctum

In contrast to the conference room, House's private office is a darker space, despite the large windows and the metal and glass of his desk. Although the furniture here is modern, House's office is an extension of his home, complete with its own collection of antiques and other trinkets, particularly surrounding his desk.

This is where House goes to think, brood, be alone, do research, and read. From the comfortable corded-fabric Eames chair, necessary for House to prop up his bad leg or take a short nap (when he works a case, he puts in very long hours), to the expensive Akari column lamp, it's a comfortable work space that has strong personal elements.

The area around House's desk suggests an intellectual man of sophistication. Spherical objects — from the gigantic red and white tennis ball to an autographed baseball, metal orbs, and his Magic 8-Ball, the "magic pool hall oracle" — lie within easy reach. These playthings are as much a part of House's method as his whiteboard, his pacing, and his brooding. When he's in physical pain, look for House to hold the tennis ball or one of his other spheres in a death-grip; they seem to help him maintain his cover in front of the team ("Skin Deep," 2.13).

And then there are the scientific antiques — a globe, various mortar and pestle sets, balances, the seemingly ancient beakers and flasks decorating his credenza. When working on a case, House often refers to historical events and medical techniques. His office artifacts also suggest an appreciation for history.

House's other office surfaces are also cluttered with collectibles. Miniature motorcycles, wooden boxes of various sizes, and small sculptures — including a tiny set of "hear no evil, see no evil, speak no evil" chimpanzees — decorate most of his bookcases and his desk. Although these trinkets may hold significance for him, there is nothing we have seen in either House's office or home connecting him to family — or to anyone else; there is not one personal photograph in either place. And considering that he is a world-famous doctor, House's walls and shelves are notably free of any hints of his professional background — unlike Cuddy's and Wilson's offices — no diplomas, certificates, awards, or trophies, although we know he keeps a copy of his high school yearbook at home in his apartment ("Adverse Events," 5.03).

House's desk drawers also give us a few clues about the man. In addition to the typical paraphernalia people stash in their office desk, House keeps a harmonica there, a few medical journals (perhaps containing something he's written sometime in his distant past?), and some old case files ("All In," 2.17). Perhaps that's where he stores his failures, which House feels last forever ("Broken," 6.01). Does he pull them out every once in awhile, wondering late at night about what he might have done differently, still worrying years later about what went wrong?

Of course, it's no surprise that musician House has a high-end audio system in his office. A pricey Sota turntable, iPod dock, and column speakers (which were replaced in season six) are there to provide him with the audiophile's listening experience. Strangely enough, though, for a man who is so particular about his sound equipment, his various televisions are surprisingly primitive. He has three televisions: an old set at home, one in the office, and his handheld (which was most in evidence during the first season).

## The Mutual Admiration of Stephen Colbert and Dr. Gregory House

If you look closely, you might notice that House has a photograph sitting on his credenza along with all of his scientific paraphernalia. It is a framed photograph of *The Colbert Report*'s Stephen Colbert. Why on earth, you may wonder, does the fictional Dr. Gregory House keep a photo of the Comedy Central star? According to production designer Jeremy Cassells, the story goes back a couple of years to when Colbert went on the air.

A big *House* fan, and a big fan of Dr. Gregory House, Stephen Colbert's fictional alter ego proudly displays House's photograph in his gallery of "the best television doctors," along with pictures of "Dr. Heathcliff Huxtable" (Bill Cosby) and "Noah Drake" (Rick Springfield), a doctor on *General Hospital*. During the first couple of seasons of *House*, Colbert would occasionally comment on the week's episode, amusing fans of both shows with the cross-pollination.

During *House*'s fifth season, someone pointed out to star Hugh Laurie that Colbert kept his picture on the set. Laurie wondered why House didn't also have a picture of Colbert, returning the favor, noting that turnabout was fair play. Eventually *House* (and House) was supplied with a photograph, and there it sits on House's credenza: a small inside joke.

### Around the Corner to Wilson's Place

Wilson's office is notably smaller than House's, and is not a suite. Princeton-Plainsboro evidently has a larger Oncology Department somewhere within the hospital's grounds, where Wilson's fellows work ("Wilson," 6.11). But his office is conveniently located so House can easily intrude — and so Wilson can keep an ever-watchful eye.

Until season two, their offices seemed much farther apart, but we learn then that the offices are actually next to each other, although they appear to be in different corridors. The colleagues share a divided balcony, perfect for quick consults and bits of gossip. The wall between the two balconies is low enough for House to manage despite the leg, giving him a direct and convenient route to Wilson's place.

A stark contrast to House's office, with its lack of professional paraphernalia, Wilson's office is decorated with trophies, certificates, and other symbols of a successful doctor's career. The diplomas on Wilson's wall tell us he went to McGill and Columbia Universities. The trophies suggest Wilson is a good golfer and a tennis player, and he is clearly a classic film buff, with posters of Orson Welles' *Touch of Evil* and Alfred Hitchcock's *Vertigo* bracketing his bookcases. Like House, Wilson displays numerous mementos on his shelves and desk, but while House's are antiques with historical value, Wilson's are sentimental gifts from patients: stuffed animals, silly dime-store toys, a miniature Zen garden.

Wilson's homey office is decorated with lots of wood and a comfortable-looking sofa, compared to the ultra-modern glass and metal of House's office. Fitting the more enigmatic Wilson much better, his office is more private, and easy to hide in, lacking the glass walls of House's office suite.

Until purchasing a condo in season six ("Wilson," 6.11), Wilson has had no permanent home. Away from the office, he has always been a bit of a wanderer. Towards the end of season two, after leaving his wife, he lives with House for several weeks ("Sex Kills," 2.14). From there, Wilson moves in with Grace, a terminal cancer patient ("House vs. God," 2.19), and from there to a hotel, where he lives through seasons three and four. And then he meets Amber Volakis, a candidate for a fellowship position on House's team. She doesn't land the coveted spot, but does manage to hook Wilson, and he moves in with her. After she dies ("House's Head," 4.15; "Wilson's Heart," 4.16), Wilson continues living in her condo, unwilling to let go of her memory. A man who has difficulty losing people, Wilson takes until the middle of season five to even bring himself to rinse out her lipstick-stained coffee mug ("The Greater Good," 5.14).

### The Dean's Domain

Cuddy sits in a large office suite directly across from the clinic, off the hospital's main lobby. From there, she presides over the free clinic, staying close to the pulse of the hospital's activity.

Her outer office functions as a small waiting room, with a sitting area for her assistant — when she actually has one; the last time we heard about Cuddy's assistant was in season two ("Distractions," 2.12). Her inner office has bay windows leading out to a terrace, which House uses to consult with Chase about his bleak future in "The Mistake" (2.08).

Damaged by a desperate patient holding several hostages at gunpoint in "Last Resort" (5.09), Cuddy's office is completely remodeled in "Let Them Eat Cake" (5.10). House contributes to the damage by using her walls as a substitute whiteboard during the hostage crisis, and smashing the toilet in her private bathroom in retaliation to her taking over *his* office during the renovation.

Cuddy's office is comfortable, with a cozy sitting area, perfect for chatting up potential donors — or mitigating some new House-related problem. Her bookshelves are lined with medical texts and mementos, including a few items of Judaica, a nice personal touch. She currently works at her restored old medical school desk, which House had retrieved from her mother, anonymously sending it to her while the office was being remodeled ("Let Them Eat Cake," 5.10).

A romantic and surprisingly touching gesture from House, the desk must hold sentimental value for Cuddy — and maybe House — although the desk story has not been mentioned since. (Might it connect to their one-night romance back at the University of Michigan mentioned in "Known Unknowns," 6.07?) Like most of the subtle touches on *House*, what little we know of the desk's origins and significance has been woven back into the fabric of series lore. Who knows when it may come up again?

Cuddy is the only one of the show's main characters to live in a freestanding house. It's a nice touch, and symbolic of her status as dean and chief administrator at a major teaching hospital. Her home is warmly decorated, and like House, she has fully crammed bookshelves everywhere. Her fireplace mantle is cluttered with family photographs, candles, and other knickknacks.

Life is in the minutia. Sometimes it's obvious, but more often, it is barely noticeable: a religious item here, knickknack there, a book left open on a coffee table, a tiny memento. These subtle touches richly illuminate the *House* cast of characters and their surroundings. For every prop — from the prescription blanks used by the doctors to the labels on House's pill bottles — there is a specificity to it all that makes it real, adding yet another layer to the comprehensive telling of House's compelling story.

# God, Religion, and Hypocrisy

For a television series whose central character is an avowed atheist, it's interesting that religion, faith, and God have been such oft revisited themes during the show's run thus far. House loudly decries religion as nonsense, its adherents as fools. He's a scientist, rational to the core, and to him, science is almost a religion itself. Quick to mock and ridicule anything he views as religious hypocrisy, Gregory House has taken on nuns ("Damned If You Do," 1.05), faith healers ("House vs. God," 2.19), a philosophy student ("One Day, One Room," 3.12), his Mormon fellowship candidate Jeffrey Cole (throughout the first half of season four), and a disillusioned priest ("Unfaithful," 5.15). He has ridiculed patients who credit miracles and God rather than Dr. House and science ("Human Error," 3.24; "Here Kitty," 5.18; "Instant Karma," 6.05).

But that's not to say House isn't curious about God, our place here on Earth, or even what the world's religions teach us about human nature; he quotes from the Bible and other religious texts when it suits his purposes. Ironically, some of the most intriguing *House* episodes explore that intersection between House's cynicism, his intellectual curiosity, and religious belief.

Sister Augustine, the sick nun in "Damned If You Do" offers an interesting analysis of House early on in the series when they debate the existence of God. She argues that although she lives in the "real world," she feels that God loves her no matter what she does. Wondering bitterly where God is hiding in the suffering of crack babies and violence against innocents, House admits that he has a problem with belief in general. But noting House's anger, Augustine counters quickly that it's impossible to be angry with God and not believe.

Several seasons later, Daniel, a disillusioned and troubled priest, makes a similar observation in "Unfaithful," suggesting that House wants his cynicism proven wrong. "You want to believe," he accuses House. "You say you don't care about anyone or anything, yet here you are saving lives," observes the priest.

House rejects Daniel's presumption immediately, noting that any lives saved as he feeds his puzzle-solving addiction are purely "collateral damage." But

Daniel disagrees: "I don't think you're hoping for someone to prove you right, I think you're hoping for someone to prove you wrong."

Does Daniel have a point? Or is he projecting his own hope for renewed belief onto House?

Could it be, as "13" suggests to House in "You Don't Want to Know" (4.08), "You spend your whole life looking for answers. . . . You know that when you run out questions you don't just run out of answers . . . you run out of hope."

Hope, perhaps; belief, on the other hand is not something House likely thinks much about. He rants about people putting hope in the "imaginary" and "wanting to believe" in something House is certain does not exist. "Get out of your holes, people," he shouts, frustrated about "people with advanced degrees" taking seriously the teenage faith healer in "House vs. God" (2.19). He can't understand how a well-educated nurse in "Here Kitty" (5.18) can believe that a cat is a messenger of God sent to usher the dying into an afterlife, which in House's worldview does not exist.

House believes that "*this* is it" — there is no "better life" on the other side. Perhaps that is why he so tenaciously and consistently "chooses" life when his own life has hung in the balance, refusing to follow the "white light," even when it might have been easier just to give in to it.

In "Three Stories" (1.21), House describes to a packed auditorium the visions he experienced when hovering between life and death several years earlier. In a courtroom-like exchange, Wilson, Foreman, and Cameron (who have been sitting in on the lecture) debate what those visions mean to him, and how they fit into his cynic's worldview. Wilson wonders whether House thinks "those experiences were 'real.'" House argues that while the experience itself was "real" and something he experienced, the term is subjective. House says that he *chooses* to "believe that the white light people see" is a natural consequence of dying. How you interpret a near-death experience is subjective and a matter of whatever best comforts.

An incredulous Cameron wonders how House can be comforted believing that "*this* is it." House asserts that he can't believe that living is merely a test for some better life ahead. He revisits this assertion in "97 Seconds" (4.03), nearly killing himself trying to prove to his patient that there is no afterlife. He also attempts to "enlighten" a dying patient with a chronic illness that his belief in a better life in the world to come is ridiculous.

Hugh Laurie, who's a master at portraying House as a complex blend of cynicism and vulnerability, believes that House is an "old soul" and someone "who has seen a great deal of human suffering in his life." Through that perspective, House's position — cynical, disillusioned, and so very angry at a God he does not believe exists — is completely understandable.

# ► MAD, BAD, AND DANGEROUS TO KNOW

DR. GREGORY HOUSE

When diagnostics fellow Eric Foreman resigns in season three ("Family," 3.21), House tells Wilson that Foreman wants "not to be me" ("Resignation," 3.22). House knows not even the lure of more money would tempt Foreman to stay. "How much do you think it would cost to make him want to be like me?" he asks. But Wilson insists that Foreman is not afraid to *become* House, "he's afraid to be who he *thinks* you are."

There is, as Wilson suggests, an enormous divide between what Foreman thinks, and what Wilson, Cuddy, and some of House's patients know. Is House simply an arrogant, self-centered jerk with a fondness for medical puzzles, as Foreman believes? Or is he some sort of dark angel with a unique moral code combating disease and death one patient at a time? With a character as complex as House, the answer is probably "both," but finding the "real" House isn't so easy, even for the most ardent fans. You have to grope past the bluster of House's vast verbal defenses and watch him in action — especially when no one's looking.

Series creator David Shore has often maintained that House isn't a "good" person — he has no heart of gold lurking beneath the caustic, cold surface. House would likely agree with his creator, vociferously arguing that any good he does is mere collateral damage to his puzzle solving. As Wilson notes, although many doctors possess a messiah complex, impelling them to save people, House has a "Rubik's complex," a compelling impulse to "solve the puzzle" ("DNR," 1.09). Anytime someone in his orbit credits him for caring or doing something nice, he quickly deflects — or outright denies it. He would insist that there is no humanity involved in his puzzle solving; if a life is saved in the process, it's purely incidental.

If it were really that simple, the series would have died seasons ago, never becoming the worldwide phenomenon it has. As brilliant as House is, after a couple seasons, a brilliant jerk with a possible drug habit would have lost his novelty. And unless viewers had some reason to care about him, *House* and House would have long since faded off into television oblivion.

### A Literary Hero on Prime-Time TV

The series loves to play with the connections between the character of Gregory House and Sir Arthur Conan Doyle's fictional Victorian detective Sherlock Holmes. But House is also descendent to a whole literature of 19th century literary heroes — melancholic, romantic antiheroes who find roots in Lord Byron's 1812 narrative poem *Childe Harold's Pilgrimage*.

Lord Byron's lover Lady Caroline Lamb described the poet (and by extension, all "Byronic" heroes) as "mad, bad, and dangerous to know." Heroes often by default, Byronic heroes possess no overt "heroic" or even altruistic motive, drawing us in with their dark magnetism and charisma.

In his 1962 book, *The Byronic Hero: Types and Prototypes*, scholar Peter Thorslev characterizes "Byronic heroes" as different from "conventional" heroes. Byronic heroes are highly intelligent, cynical, and moody. They tend to brood and are often found struggling with their own integrity and with their pasts.

They are among the darker literary heroes, but that's not to say they can't have a lot of good lurking beneath the surface. But that good is usually submerged — only to surface under very specific circumstances.

Series star Hugh Laurie has noted several times that he sees the Byronic in

House. And if you Google "Byronic hero," you will find Dr. Gregory House right there with Heathcliff (*Wuthering Heights*), Edward Rochester (*Jane Eyre*), Edmond Dantès (*The Count of Monte Cristo*), Humphrey Bogart's Rick Blaine (*Casablanca*), the vampire Lestat from *Interview with a Vampire*, and even Batman. (Think more *Dark Knight*, less Adam West.)

Byronic heroes come in many stripes: some of them are irredeemable, often meeting tragic ends. (John Milton's *Paradise Lost* portrays Satan as a Byronic hero.) Sometimes they are completely redeemable like Rochester in *Jane Eyre*, but even then, often only by the love of a good woman.

Will House be redeemed in the end? Or will he meet with tragedy like Heathcliff who dies? It's anyone's guess, because the *House* writers love their narrative left turns and we aren't likely to know what the ultimate future holds for House until the series' final moments.

So, what exactly makes a House "Byronic" and how does he fit in with such heady literary stars? As House often says, "thanks for playing," and join me at the whiteboard for a Byronic differential on our antihero.

## House's Genius

Almost more than anything, a Byronic hero is distinguished by high intelligence. It is the root of their survival and how they flourish despite the odds.

House's entire self-worth is tied up in his intelligence. He believes it is all he has ("No Reason," 2.24). But House is more than simply intelligent; he is a genius. His unique combination of hyper-observation, deductive reasoning, finely tuned perceptiveness, and highly developed intuition all make House's intellectual gifts nearly superhuman. And, although House is sometimes smug, even arrogant, he holds even his own ideas up to a magnifying lens, with a willingness to discard them quickly when he's wrong. This intense objectivity filtered through his (sometimes coldly) rational prism allows him to see past "being right" to "getting the right answer."

> "I think House, surprisingly — for someone who has a big ego in some ways — never lets that ego get caught up in his theories and ideas. In a way, he's sort of selfless in that sense. He'll look at what the truth is, and if what he's thinking is incongruent, he will throw off what he believes."
> — **Writer/co-executive producer Doris Egan, October 2008 interview**

House seems to know a little something about absolutely everything. His knowledge is broad and deep: music to history, languages to literature, philosophy to physics. (He'd clean up on *Jeopardy* if he ever became a contestant!) His diagnostic skills are so profound that even while in the throes of narcotics withdrawal, without sleep and "puking every hour," he is still able to out-diagnose both Dean of Medicine Dr. Lisa Cuddy and oncologist Dr. James Wilson ("Merry Little Christmas," 3.10).

It isn't too surprising that House has a broad scientific background. After all, his *is* a doctor. But House is some sort of über-doctor, with several sub-specialties, including board certification in nephrology and infectious diseases ("Occam's Razor," 1.03). An early version of the "Occam's Razor" script also refers to a fellowship in rheumatology.

House knows so much about obscure symptoms and odd presentations, it baffles his fellows, who scramble to catch up with where he's headed intellectually. House waits (occasionally, patiently) while guiding them through his clues, cues, and questions before he welcomes them at the "end of the thought process" ("Autopsy," 2.02).

In "Babies and Bathwater" (1.18), Foreman thinks House is insane for asking the team to examine a patient for a drooping eyelid after she chokes on piece of canned pear. Dismissing the choking as a random event, Foreman assumes it's completely unrelated to her other symptoms. Grudgingly he checks it out, however, and the patient's husband confirms that indeed Naomi's eyelid droops exactly as House thought it might. House explains it as Lambert-Eaton syndrome. The nature of her subtle, seemingly unrelated symptoms indicate lung cancer — all deduced from the seemingly trivial piece of soft pear.

House also seems to have an understanding of medical history, able to summon centuries-old science and medicine as needed. In "Distractions" (2.12), House calls upon antiquated medicine, including the use of maggots by Napoleon's Bonaparte's surgeon to clean battlefield wounds, and Einthoven's galvanometer when high-tech methods won't work with a severely burned patient.

But House isn't just "book-smart." He is also a keen observer of people. His sensitivity and perceptiveness are what help elevate his intellectual skills to genius. When these abilities emerge in House's occasional one-on-one encounters with his patients, it almost seems House can see into their hearts and souls. Although his ability to key into people's flaws and problems can make him a wise counselor to his patients and his colleagues, he also uses it to hone in on their deepest fears and insecurities. His unique insight then becomes toxic and destructive. He has used it on both enemies — and friends.

## Is It Luck — Or Is It Memorex?

Foreman, especially, seems to take a particular delight in calling out House's "luck." "You make enough calls, and one of them is bound to be right," he scoffs in "DNR" (1.09). "He's just a lucky, lucky guy," Chase shoots back sarcastically, realizing it's more than luck that has earned House a well-deserved reputation as a diagnostician.

Even Wilson, House's best friend (and presumably the one who knows him best), attributes House's genius more to luck than intellect — at least until mid–season three. "He got lucky," Wilson insists to Cuddy in "Meaning" (3.01), when House is able to stunningly reverse a patient's long-term paralysis with no apparent medical evidence for his diagnosis.

Having taken on the patient, Richard, as a way to "find meaning" after being nearly fatally shot, House asserts he simply wants to help Richard (whose illness provides no medical puzzle) with his pain. Midway through the episode, House hears the brain-damaged and paralyzed Richard grunt. Except House interprets this "grunt" as "talking." Suddenly, he believes that he can find a way to "cure" Richard so he can walk, talk, and make love to his wife again — hope that no other doctor has given him, despite years of treatments and surgeries by dozens of specialists.

The electrons in House's immense brain are sparking, but they haven't yet come together. The fellows think he is on a wild goose chase; Wilson and Cuddy believe House is bored, concocting a puzzle where there is none, giving Richard's family false hope — playing with them for his own amusement.

Late one night, sweating, hot, and thirsty, after a run in the park, House refreshes himself in a nearby fountain. The answer strikes him — an Epiphany!: The pieces suddenly click together, forming a cohesive picture, as they so often do. But he cannot adequately articulate to Cuddy the precise science behind what he simply "knows." His treatment plan is simple and low-risk — an injection of cortisol — but Cuddy refuses. She believes that House must learn that he cannot practice medicine based on whim and luck.

But she also knows House well enough not to completely dismiss him, and the next morning, without his knowledge, Cuddy gives Richard the cortisol. And it works! Wilson is adamant they not tell House. "He could have just as easily killed that guy," he warns. "Next time he may not be so lucky."

Several months later, Wilson finally understands, almost too late, that House's gift is not simple luck ("Merry Little Christmas," 3.10). Under the extreme stress of narcotics withdrawal and an almost certain jail sentence in his future, House is still able put together the disparate symptoms of dying teenager in a way that Wilson and Cuddy are simply incapable of. As Wilson finally sees it in this context, he admits the unqiue good of which House is capable due to his gift, defending him as a "force for good in the universe."

### In the Orbit of House's Energy Field

Whether it's through the sheer force of their intellectual power or something less definable, there is a larger-than-life vibe to all Byronic heroes. Despite their flaws, constant brooding, and frustrating moodiness, they seem to draw people in by sheer force of personality, always at the center of things, even when not interested in being there.

Of course, House seems especially magnetic to women, drawing in those he encounters both in his fictional world and the millions who find the middle-aged, cranky, troubled genius irresistible. Maybe the women in his orbit, like those who watch the show, perceive a wounded spirit within him, and are driven by a natural desire to heal him. That is certainly what House believes attracts Cameron. And that woundedness is a classic literary device to humanize an anti-hero like House. All he needs, like Jane Eyre's Rochester, is the love of a good woman. Right?

> "I think [wounded nobility] is a really good way of phrasing that. And I think that is what Hugh Laurie does so beautifully."
>
> — **Actress Jennifer Morrison (Cameron), April 2009 interview**

But woundedness is not the only thing that attracts women to House. Cuddy is turned on by his intelligence and drive. In "Help Me" (6.22), after an act of tremendous personal courage, Cuddy finally acknowledges to herself that she's in love with House. Cameron is drawn in by what she perceives in House as a somewhat tarnished nobility. Stacy finds House "surprising and sexy" ("Honeymoon," 1.22). And in season six, Lydia recognizes a "nice" person behind his sarcastic façade ("Broken," 6.01, 6.02).

Part of House's charisma originates in his irrepressible energy when the "game's afoot," and perhaps his passion for things important to him. The sheer force of his personality makes him a natural leader. As Chase says in the season six episode "Instant Karma" (6.05), House is in command, even when he's not. Trying to keep up with his thought processes, guided by his use of colorful metaphors and the vivid imagery of his explanations, everyone within earshot can't help but be drawn in. Consider the way in which he captivates students and colleagues alike during the unforgettable lecture that is "Three Stories" (1.22).

We see how effortlessly House commands a large team of experienced physicians in "Autopsy" (2.02) as he orchestrates an experimental and dangerous diagnostic protocol on a young cancer patient with a blood clot in her brain. House literally holds court in the crowded operating room, rehearsing the complex procedure, which requires precision as they must virtually exsanguinate their young patient. Directing a large team of surgeons, anesthesiologists, cardiologists, neurologists, nurses, and technicians, House directs them like a symphony conductor. They are frustrated by his insistence on perfection, yet they seem to understand who's in charge.

House is charming: joking and jocular to break the tension in the room as they rehearse the procedure several times until House is satisfied they've gotten it right. He is meticulous and in complete control as the team finally performs the procedure for real to a standing-room only gallery of observers — captivated by the genius at work.

We know House is a "world-famous" doctor, and we can only speculate as to why. In order for him to be so renowned, and be such a financial asset to the hospital, he would probably have had to publish, lecture, and do endless speaking engagements — all of that likely long before we meet the reclusive House at the start of the series.

He still has enough credibility to be sought after to attend conferences ("Sports Medicine," 1.12), endorse new pharmaceuticals ("Role Model," 1.17), and be asked to speak at an international conference in Singapore ("Airborne," 3.18). People seek his medical advice from all over the world — and don't forget, studying under House is considered one of the most prestigious fellowships in medicine. While negotiating a contract with a major insurance provider, Cuddy reminds the negotiator that Princeton-Plainsboro has the best and "most innovative" Diagnostics Department in the United States ("5 to 9," 6.14), run, of course by Dr. Gregory House!

House's unorthodox methods, his encyclopedic knowledge base, his lack of an intellectual ego, and his personal magnetism all must contribute to the legend. But part of that legend is also fueled by a troubled past.

**House's Troubled Past and Painful Present**

Batman's parents were murdered in front of him. In *Wuthering Heights*, Heathcliff was tormented and degraded by his half-brother Hindley. We know House, too, had a troubled childhood — one that frames his equally troubled present.

In "One Day, One Room" (3.12), he confides in his patient — a young rape victim — that his father made him sleep outside as punishment, and subjected him to baths in ice. House calls it abuse, but it's been debated within the online fan community, and even among the *House* writing staff, whether his father's actions really amounted to child abuse.

By today's standards, certainly, it might have earned a visit from the local child services agency. But it's equally plausible that John House, a colonel in the Marines, might have been just trying to "toughen up" the undoubtedly rebellious young Greg — military style. House also recalls to Wilson a summer when he was 12 years old, during which his father refused to talk to him ("Birthmarks," 5.04).

> "I might refer to his father as abusive. But I can also argue his father's point of view, which was about discipline and helping his son reach his highest potential."
>
> — **Writer/co-executive producer Doris Egan, October 2008 interview**

Describing his parents to Cameron in "Daddy's Boy" (2.05), House talks about his father's attitude towards lying — about anything or to anyone. "Great for police witnesses, terrible for a dad," he observes. His mother hated conflict, according to House; so did she simply allow the brutal John to do whatever he wanted to Greg? One can only imagine the tension in that home as House grew up, especially with Mom knowing and Greg suspecting that John is not Greg's biological father ("Birthmarks," 5.04). But whether or not John's actions actually represented physical abuse, they certainly left their mark emotionally.

> "David Shore likes us to write the characters realistically and have a real perspective. We didn't want to paint [House's father] as some horrible, abusive man. Even as a kid, Greg House was probably not the easiest to be around, either."
>
> — **Writer/producer David Foster, October 2008 interview**

And then there is the leg.

As viewers we sat mesmerized like the medical students sitting in on his diagnostics lecture as House describes the circumstances that led to his life of constant pain, requiring the support of the ever-present cane ("Three Stories," 1.21). An arterial blood clot (infarction), undiagnosed for three days, caused muscle cell death in House's right thigh. The doctors want to amputate; House points out they have already botched the diagnosis, and merely want to cover their asses by taking the easiest route.

He has no intention of allowing the doctors to amputate, insisting they only remove the clot and let nature take its course. He may regain the full use of his leg — or he might die as the built-up toxins flood back into his system. But this is his express wish — his choice. And it is a risk he is willing to take.

House's significant other, Stacy, sits at his bedside, worried for his life, pleading with him to allow the amputation. Cuddy, his doctor at the time, describes a "middle-ground" option to her. It's less radical than amputation, she explains, but won't be as risky as the waiting game upon which House insists.

They try it House's way, but the pain is unbearable. As they wait, he suffers a heart attack, and after being revived — still in terrible pain — he asks to be put in a chemically induced coma to sleep through the worst of it. While he is in the coma, the desperate and worried Stacy uses her medical proxy to overrule House's express wishes. She knows House may never forgive her, and her actions may mean the end of their obviously loving relationship; she does it (as she believes) to save his life.

As we know, the surgery leaves House in chronic pain and physically disabled. Neither House nor we will ever know if doing as he had requested would have resulted in a better outcome for him. In that one defining moment, he had made a deliberate choice to either live a normal life or die, but the choice was irrevocably snatched from him in an act — albeit performed with the best of intentions — that profoundly betrayed his trust. It has left him scarred since, both inside and out. It is not until the season six finale ("Help Me," 6.22), and under extreme stress, that we see House beginning to wonder if his own decision making was faulty. Would he have been better off if he had allowed his doctors to amputate? Would he have avoided the pain and suffering through which he has lived for so many years — years that he now acknowledges have made him "a harder person; a worse person?"

From what little we know of the aftermath, we might presume Stacy's actions and the results of the surgery sent House spinning out of control. He pushed Stacy out of his life and couldn't hold a job. As we learn in "Humpty Dumpty" (2.03), he was fired from four hospitals before Cuddy hired him at

Princeton-Plainsboro. As she asserts in "Top Secret" (3.16), he was a "good doctor who couldn't get himself hired at a blood bank."

Through whatever combination of past relationships, betrayals, and his very real physical pain, House lives life in misery. It's a hole he doesn't even begin to work his way out of until season six, when he begins treatment with psychiatrist Dr. Darryl Nolan. How much of his pain is due to the actual injury, and how much of it is emotional, we do not know. House has described his pain as sometimes "soul-sucking" ("Words and Deeds," 3.11), and there are days he seems to barely manage getting out of bed and standing on his own two feet ("Skin Deep," 2.13; "Who's Your Daddy?" 2.23; "Painless," 5.12). Yet by the time he's at work, he limps along at a pace that could win a foot race. "Patients don't want a sick doctor," House tells Wilson in "Pilot." House never wants to appear too infirm; he doesn't want to be pitied or be defined by his disability. Yet, his steadfast refusal to be defined by it defines him nonetheless.

### The Disillusioned Idealist

When we first meet Rick Blaine in the classic American film *Casablanca*, he's tough, hard-bitten, and cynical. Something in his past eradicated all idealism and trust in humanity. Rick would have agreed with House's maxim, "humanity's overrated," ("Pilot," 1.01). Edward Rochester in Charlotte Brontë's *Jane Eyre* describes himself as "heart-weary and soul-withered after years of voluntary banishment," before Jane happens into his life.

Like his Byronic brothers, House, too, is a pretty hardened cynic — "Everybody lies," his mantra. House believes that all love is conditional, but "we just don't know what the conditions are" ("Son of Coma Guy," 3.07). It's almost as if House lies in wait for someone who cares about him to suddenly abandon ship — perhaps when his need is greatest. He constantly pushes the boundaries of his relationships (especially his friendship with Wilson) looking for the weakest spots, wondering how far he can bend them before they break.

House has a hard time believing in people because he has a problem with the "whole idea of belief" ("Damned If You Do," 1.05). People are always self-serving, and there's always an agenda.

We don't really know what combination of circumstances and native personality has created the cynical, misanthropic Gregory House we meet at the start of the series. We can only surmise that it's a combination of his childhood, the leg, the giant hole left in his heart by Stacy — and a naturally dour and acerbic personality.

But scratch a cynic's veneer and you may discover an idealist lurking there. Although not every Byronic hero has an idealistic or romantic side, many do —

sometimes so deeply buried beneath a lifetime of torment, it only emerges under the rarest of conditions.

> Definitely House has a romantic streak. But it's covered in fear and pain
> and a desire not to make himself vulnerable. As romantic as he is wounded,
> and that's part of the problem.
>
> **— Executive producer/director Katie Jacobs, January 2009 interview**

Cameron perceives in House a good person beneath the cynic's armor, maybe even an idealism not unlike her own. In the early first season episode "Fidelity" (1.07), Cameron is upset over the patient's marital troubles and she flees to the lab, where she busies herself calibrating the laboratory centrifuge.

House finds her in tears, wondering why she is so upset. She reveals that she married her (first) husband already knowing he was dying of cancer. House is sympathetic, gently admonishing her, "You can't be that good a person — and well adjusted, because you wind up crying over centrifuges." But Cameron expertly deflects House's observation back onto him. "Or hating people?" she asks, perceiving a parallel between them.

In "The Right Stuff" (4.02), Cameron, now running the hospital's emergency room, anonymously refers a patient to House: Greta, a young NASA astronaut. Greta is experiencing strange visual and auditory symptoms. She insists being treated "off the books," fearing she will be booted out of the training program if her superiors suspect she's sick.

House takes the case, diagnosing her while he's "auditioning" a roomful of candidates for fellowship positions. After House diagnoses her, the fellowship candidates pressure Greta to inform NASA. Seeing this, House interrupts, coldly informing them all that he's already ratted her out. The new doctors are stunned by House's callousness, and already familiar with his reputation, it's what they would expect. But like everybody else, House lies. More true to what we viewers know of him, House has kept Greta's confidence.

Why lie to his team? That's what Cameron wants to know after House learns that she's the one who referred Greta. He explains that he feared the new fellowship candidates would ignore confidentiality and call NASA on their own. House wanted to forestall them, trying to plug a "few leaky faucets," telling Cameron it was none of their business. But Cameron doesn't buy House's simple explanation. She has a better — and more revelatory — one: "You couldn't kill her dream." She sends Greta to House knowing how he will react — and in the end she is right.

Like his Byronic literary ancestors, from classic outsider Heathcliff, to the vampire heroes Lestat in Anne Rice's *Interview with a Vampire* and Edward Cullen in Stephenie Meyer's novel *Twilight*, House clearly sees himself on the outside society's circle, on the fringes looking in.

In "Son of Coma Guy" (3.07), House describes how a childhood encounter with a hospital janitor profoundly influenced him to become a physician. Living in Japan as a teenager while his father was stationed there, House accompanied an injured companion to the hospital after a climbing accident and met a janitor. When House's friend comes down with an infection that his doctors are unable to diagnose, House encounters the janitor again in a corridor. It turns out that this lowly janitor, an "untouchable" in Japanese society, was also a gifted doctor. And, no matter how much the other doctors disdained or ignored him — no matter how much of an outcast he was — when they needed him, "nothing else mattered; they had to listen to him." No matter how society looked down on him, he could not be dismissed.

The experience clearly resonated strongly with the young House. It's hard to know whether he was always as isolated as he is at the start of the series, but it's clear that he's always been a loner, identifying deeply with the Burkau doctor.

House's off-the-charts intelligence by itself renders him an outsider, lonely and isolated. When House treats a physicist in season six ("Ignorance Is Bliss," 6.09) whose brilliance has made him miserable, House perceives a kindred spirit. They discuss the loneliness and isolation that their unique giftedness brings. When she discovers that the patient has found a measure of happiness in chemically "dumbing himself down" to normal, House understands and sympathizes with him.

Even when he is at the center of a social setting, House is an exile. At Chase's bachelor party ("House Divided," 5.22), which House organizes, complete with music, lights, strippers, and much alcohol, he welcomes everyone as the jovial MC. But when the party gets going, he disappears, locking himself in the bathroom alone with a bottle while everyone else socializes.

House usually doesn't seem to mind his isolation and sometimes revels in his status as an outsider, deriding "circle queens" who would try to force outsiders to conform ("Lines in the Sand," 3.04). "Normal's overrated" is a classic "House-ism," after all. But it seems, given the opportunity, isolation and exile from "the circle" is not a path House recommends to his patients, despite anything he might say.

House has argued vigorously with the families of patients that "normal" is better than "special," and if they have a chance to provide their children with a more "normal" life, they should grab it. That's surprising in someone who seems (at least to some) to revel so much in his differentness.

In "Merry Little Christmas" (3.10), House treats the daughter of a carti-lage-hair hypoplasia dwarf. Like her mom, Abigail has been short of stature all her life, and everyone has assumed that she, too, has dwarfism. She has learned to embrace her uniqueness; it makes her feel "special." But as he diagnoses her symptoms, House realizes that the 16-year-old Abigail is not a dwarf — she has a growth hormone deficiency. Treat that, and she will grow normally again. But Abigail refuses to give up her "special status." And her mother militantly supports her decision, accusing House of trying to force Abigail "to be tall."

Frustrated, House appeals to the mother on their common ground — understanding the hardships that accompany their mutual outsider status. "You and I have found that being normal sucks because we're freaks," he asserts. "Advantage of being a freak is that it makes you stronger. How strong do you really want her to have to be?" he asks earnestly.

Only a few weeks later, House has another opportunity to grant an outsider an all-access pass into the circle of "normal." ("Half Wit," 3.15). This time, he offers Patrick, a brain-damaged musical savant, an opportunity for a "normal," albeit less extraordinary, life — exchanging his musical gift for the ability to button his own shirt and "be happy." It's something House believes would be a more than fair trade. It's a hard choice for Patrick's father to make, but at House's urging, he consents to brain surgery. And as House watches Patrick button his shirt probably for the first time in years, he remarks that his patient "looks happy." It's a state that has probably has eluded House for years.

### Survival 101: Change and Adaptability

As classic outsiders, Byronic heroes need unique, highly developed coping skills. They have to be cunning and adaptable to survive in a world that either dis-misses or scorns them. Faced with adversity, perhaps a family that casts them out or a lover who proves faithless, they go off to war; they get an education. They return, perhaps not triumphant, but stronger for the experience.

Growing up in a military household, a brilliant, isolated, curious, and rebel-lious kid, adaptability and some cunning were probably survival skills that enabled the young Gregory House to reach adulthood. As Foreman speculates in "Daddy's Boy" (2.05), House would have had to have either been a "good fighter or a fast runner."

As an adult, House wages an offensive war, using keen observational powers to hone in on opponents' weak spots and poke at them with biting — and some-times cruel — words. House acquires as much information about everyone as he can with little regard for personal, professional, or legal boundaries. He thinks nothing of invading a friend's privacy — or a stranger's — to maintain an edge in nearly every relationship.

On House's skilled tongue, his words are daggers aimed with precision for maximum effect. House's defensive strategy is to push people away before they can get close enough to harm him. House's psychiatrist wonders in "Broken" (6.01, 6.02) why he insists on keeping people away, putting them off. "Why do you think that people would treat you worse if they knew the truth?" he asks. It is doubtful even House knows the answer to that question. As he admits to Wilson in "Detox" (1.11), "I've been alienating people since I was three."

House also copes with his issues chemically, using drugs not only to dull the pain in his leg, but to escape from his emotional pain as well. However, his coping skills completely give way at the end of season five, triggered by the suicide of Diagnostics Department fellow Lawrence Kutner in "Simple Explanation" (5.20).

On emotional overload with all losses he has experienced during the year, House's mind retreats into a delusion: a pretty fantasy about getting off Vicodin and making love to Lisa Cuddy. "A nice story," Kutner taunts from the great beyond. "Too bad it isn't true."

In season six, House has tried again to adapt and change, more afraid of returning delusions and hallucinations than any physical pain. Coming out of Mayfield Psychiatric Hospital, House moves in with Wilson, takes up cooking, tries to pursue a relationship with Cuddy — and stays off Vicodin. At this point, he is the only one who can save himself from being trapped again in the quicksand of his life thus far. The battle may be too much for him as the people in his life try to move on while he is emotionally stuck.

But House keeps coming back, keeps "choosing life." He knocks at death's door several times over six years: gets shot, overdoses on narcotics, is nearly killed in a bus crash, undergoes a dangerous brain procedure, and goes off the deep end. It might seem the easier choice to give up, quit, commit suicide, or allow himself to be carried off gently in the night. But he keeps coming back, which speaks to his resilience and adaptive ability. As he reminds Cuddy in "Simple Explanation" (5.20), "It's slightly better to live in misery than to die in it."

For all his other survival skills, House is hopelessly inept at office politics, and has no professional survival instinct whatsoever. When Cuddy suggests to him in "Living the Dream" (4.14) that he's unlikely to cut his own throat by making trouble for her with a hospital inspector, House is shocked. "Yeah, that sounds like me," he counters sarcastically.

## Rebel with a Cause: The Maverick of Princeton-Plainsboro

There's a line in the 2008 film *The Dark Knight* spoken by Bruce Wayne's servant and protector, Alfred: "You're the one who can be the outcast and do the things that no one else can. . . . A watchful protector; a dark knight." Wayne's alter ego Batman is described as the necessary evil to combat the greater evil. House is the doctor who doesn't care about medical protocol or rules, yet he alone can save patients when no one else is willing to take the legal or professional risk. He does what he has to do — convention and medical standards be damned.

You might almost say that conventional medical thinking is House's biggest enemy, particularly given his personal experience. After all, conventional medical thinking misdiagnosed his leg ("Three Stories," 1.21).

House is unquestionably a rebel; he is an iconoclast, smashing the idols of medicine as obstacles in the way of saving lives. He even looks the part, refusing to wear a white "doctor coat" — preferring his uniform of rumpled dress shirt and jeans (with an impeccably tailored jacket — except in season one) to symbolically thumb his nose at the medical establishment. He refuses to attend lectures and fill out forms, accept speaking engagements or solicit donations for the hospital.

Foreman has called him a medical anarchist ("Deception," 2.09). But is House an anarchist or a hero? By the time patients cross his threshold, they've gone the mainstream route. They've seen all the doctors who follow protocol and have memorized every standard operating procedure and ethical guideline. House is unique — a medical court of last resort. He doesn't care about protocol or proper procedure — all that matters to him is getting to the answer in time to save the patient's life. And usually there is little time to spare.

House's Department of Diagnostic Medicine was created to make use of his particular intellectual gifts — and his fearlessness in breaking the rules that would hinder him from saving patients. As dean, Cuddy understands what House has to do to make his practice work; she also understands the liability he poses to the hospital. She monitors his practice carefully either herself or by proxy (usually Wilson or Foreman), ensuring that he doesn't venture too far off course.

But does Foreman have a point in calling House an anarchist? "He is not [famous civil rights pioneer] Rosa Parks," Foreman points out after House breaks ethical rules before venturing upon the correct diagnosis. "He is not a hero" ("Deception," 2.11).

Foreman views the way House practices medicine as ultimately toxic, and by all rights, this patient "should have died." But the same might be said about most of House's patients. His willingness to throw out the rulebook and most copies of the ethical guidelines, including the Hippocratic oath, saves many more lives than it costs. As House says, he can "do the math" ("Detox," 1.11).

There is a downside, of course, with House's peculiar brand of medicine. His colleagues (even beyond his usual foil Foreman) often worry that his methods might just as easily kill as save a patient as he plays a dangerous game of medical brinkmanship. But House seems to know the feel of the fine line between doing exactly enough — and not too much — to eventually get at the right answer and cure the patient. And he's "almost always eventually right" ("No Reason," 2.24).

House would likely argue that many of medicine's guidelines are there to protect "doctors' lifestyles" and minimize the hospital's risk, not to save lives ("Three Stories," 1.21). Rules like these, House might say, are made to be broken!

### The Fine Line Between Right and Wrong

The struggle between right and wrong, the inclination to do good or evil, to yield to better angels when tempted, or to go the other way — this is what makes Byronic heroes so compelling. And we're never quite sure upon which side they'll land.

House has said that the one thing he would have wanted to hear from his father, now deceased, is "You did the right thing" ("Son of Coma Guy," 3.07). But House's better angels and his darker side are sometimes at odds. And sometimes his less honorable nature prevails, exposing him as petty ("Distractions," 2.12; "Joy," 5.06), manipulative, even dishonest and self-serving ("Insensitive," 3.14; "Last Resort," 5.09; "Teamwork," 6.08).

But House walks a very fine line between right and wrong. He is guided by a set of principles so idiosyncratic that it would be nearly incomprehensible to anyone outside his sphere. Even when his career is on the line, he rarely compromises these principles, but the struggle is often there. He may seem capricious and morally ambiguous in his medical decisions, but his ethical choices are not usually resolved without a lot of soul searching and brooding.

Lie about a patient's condition to get her into a lifesaving clinical trial? So be it ("Babies and Bathwater," 1.18). Surreptitiously shrink a tumor by injecting it with ethanol to put it within surgical guidelines? No problem ("Socratic Method," 1.06). Blackmail a transplant surgeon into doing a high-risk liver transplant? Why not? ("The Mistake," 2.08). Help a man commit suicide to save the life of his dying son? Sure ("Son of Coma Guy," 3.07).

What about lying to the transplant committee to get a heart for a dying patient? Hmm. Here's where the line begins to blur — and where House's virtuous focus on the patient runs into some greater ethical questions.

In "Control" (1.14), House's patient Carly needs a transplant, but her mental health issues disqualify her. She does not meet the hospital's transplant criteria because she has bulimia, which is "right up there with suicide." House considers lying to the transplant board, and not disclosing what he alone knows about her psychiatric issues. He visits her, hoping to understand the "right" thing to do.

If he lies, he could lose his medical license — and medicine is all (he believes) he has in his life. If he doesn't, a young woman will die because of a seemingly arbitrary rule. In the end, he decides that he cannot bring himself to forfeit her life. A pretty noble thing House is doing, risking his career for a stranger. Right?

But what about some theoretical "other guy" — a legitimately qualified transplant candidate — the one who *didn't* get his heart while Carly got hers? Did he die waiting? It's not something House would have spent much time thinking about because *he's* not House's patient. Yes, House saves Carly's life, but has someone else's life been forfeited in the process?

Later in season one, House struggles once again with a decision that has consequences for others when hospital board chair Edward Vogler forces House to make a choice between giving a speech that violates his personal ethics and having to fire one of his fellows. House struggles with "selling his soul" to keep the department intact, but ultimately he cannot bring himself to make the five-minute speech ("Role Model," 1.17).

House's conflict with his better angels seems to intensify when it involves his pain. He has admitted that pain — and fear of pain — are powerful motivators ("Euphoria, Part 2," 2.21). He has forged prescriptions for Vicodin ("Meaning," 3.01) and falsified his medical records to qualify for a cancer study that would involve implanting a drug in the pleasure center of his brain — while allowing his friends to believe he had cancer ("Half Wit," 3.15). These are both instances when House is willing to sacrifice integrity to serve a personal agenda. He may be able to rationalize it; we as viewers may be able to understand that these are desperate measure to deal with his pain and sympathize with him, but House often leaves collateral damage in his wake, affecting everyone around him.

The forged prescriptions become a weapon used against both House and Wilson later in season three by Detective Michael Tritter, the vindictive cop in hot pursuit of House for narcotics trafficking. And the brain cancer adventure upsets everyone who cares about him; whether House believes it or not, people do care about him. He also risks the study itself, which would have affected anyone involved — from the researcher to the patients.

Although some might argue that House never serves any agenda but his own, his integrity usually stays more or less intact. But sometimes House needs Jiminy Cricket to sit on his shoulder and whisper in his ear when he ventures too far astray. That job often falls to his best friend Wilson.

In "Insensitive" (3.14), House has been doing a lot of reading about nerve transplantation as a way to deal permanently with his leg pain. Coincidentally (not really, since this *is*, after all, a scripted television show — and nothing is ever coincidence) Hannah, a teenager with congenital insensitivity to pain (CIPA) happens into his orbit after a car accident.

When it appears that Hannah needs a nerve biopsy to diagnose her condition, House sees an opportunity to obtain a needed spinal nerve fiber for transplantation — and from a person who cannot feel pain. The lure is too great and House advocates for a *spinal* nerve biopsy, although it is riskier than a biopsy taken from a peripheral nerve. House is insistent until Wilson pulls him back, wondering if he's being objective about the patient. Realizing Wilson may be right, House recuses himself from the decision, leaving his team to decide how to proceed with the needed biopsy. His integrity remains intact, albeit with a little help.

"Insensitive" aside, most of what House does for his patients is out of a passion for his "one thing" — medicine.

### A Sacred Calling: House's Passion for Medicine

Passions often drive Byronic heroes: a passion for revenge, like Edmond Dantès in *The Count of Monte Cristo*, or sexual passions, like Heathcliff and his love for Cathy. In House's case, it's a passion for medicine.

You may argue whether his passion derives from a driving need to "solve the puzzle" and "be right" as Wilson defines House's "Rubik's complex" ("DNR," 1.09) or whether it derives from a "sacred calling," similar to the way in which House describes his father's military career ("Birthmarks," 5.04). But unquestionably, House is passionate in the extreme about his "one thing," as patient John Henry Giles puts it "DNR."

House's dedication to find the answer sometimes drives him beyond all reason, and long after everyone else — sometimes even the patient — has given up. He'll risk his career, and even his physical well-being, in the interest of saving a life ("Control," 1.14; "DNR,"1.09; "Hunting," 2.07; "Sex Kills," 2.14; "The Right Stuff," 4.02; "Living the Dream," 4.14, etc.).

Even sick or strung out, he can't stop working the diagnosis, pushing through pain or narcotics withdrawal ("Detox," 1.11; "Skin Deep," 2.13, "Merry Little Christmas," 3.10; "Wilson's Heart," 4.16). Why go to those extremes? If it's all about the puzzle, then why risk his career long after the puzzle has been solved? Why risk his career to get a needed heart transplant for Carly in "Control" (1.14)? He knows the diagnosis already — and he's been proven "right." Isn't that what it's all about for House? Carly wonders the same thing. But all House quietly responds is "You're my patient."

In "All In" (2.17), House's residual passion for an old case helps him save the life of six-year-old Ian, who suffers from the same rare illness as an elderly patient 12 years earlier. If House hadn't pushed on long after Cuddy threw him off the case, Ian would have died.

House seems to be a passionate practitioner no matter what he takes on, even beyond medicine. He is dedicated to music as a listener and musician. And then there is his love life. We know House takes love seriously — enough that it terrifies him. He obviously had a passionate, loving relationship with Stacy, continuing to carry a torch for her long after he pushed her out of his life and she remarried. Even his short dalliance with Lydia ("Broken," 6.01) seems intense and — on House's part — deep. When she leaves, House feels "lost." And then there's Cuddy. We don't yet know how that will play out in the end, but it's clear that House's feelings for her run deep and have been present for more than 20 years ("Known Unknowns," 6.07).

### When House's Objectivity Fails Him

What happens when House's famous objectivity fails him? Keeping himself as distant as possible from his patients, House would argue people lie and are useless in the diagnostic process. It's much better to snoop around their homes and interview their co-workers. Part of House's modus operandi of avoiding patients "like the plague unless it's the plague" ("Three Stories," 1.21) is to maintain his objectivity. Getting involved with a patient and "caring" about them won't make them well, House might argue. It might make them feel better, which is useless if they still die. But even House's renowned objectivity fails him occasionally.

In "Honeymoon" (1.22), House agrees to treat Stacy's husband, Mark Warner. Trying to keep his objectivity is not easy when his feelings of love and resentment for her conflict with his ability to remain dispassionate and cure his patient. House receives a fax late at night; it's Mark's test results — he's not responding to the treatment. But House is more stunned to realize that he feels happy about it. Distressed by his own reaction, he calls Wilson away from a dinner party to talk about it. "He's my patient . . . and some part of me wants him to die." But the power of his own feelings disturbs him enough that his attitude towards the case dramatically changes, and in the next scene, you see him conciliatory and humbled.

Something similar happens in "Insensitive" (3.14) with House's CIPA patient. For much of the episode, House sees her as an opportunity to obtain spinal nerve cells by doing a biopsy. Taking the spinal nerve would serve House's purposes, but could prove debilitating to his patient. When Wilson questions his objectivity, House immediately removes himself from the decision making, realizing that he's not serving the patient's best interest, but his own.

When Foreman gets sick after breaking into a patient's home, House's objectivity is challenged in quite another way ("Euphoria," 2.20, 2.21). It's the first time someone close to House has become a patient, and it's interesting to observe him in this unique situation. Feeling responsible for sending Foreman to the patient's apartment, House is unable to distance himself from the case. His first instinct is to forbid anyone else from going back to look for more clues.

House is suddenly more cautious in his approach, unwilling to risk Foreman's life in pursuit of an answer that, ironically, might cure him. When Foreman demands that he perform a deep brain biopsy, House is reluctant, knowing the procedure might render Foreman either physically or mentally disabled. The entire team, including Wilson and Cuddy, notices this aberration in House's behavior and tries to urge him back to the more reckless, but more effective, doctor he normally is. Wilson calls House on it directly, mocking House's inability to push ahead as he normally does. He accuses House of being "common," refusing to take risks while "the gun's pointed" at Foreman's head.

Obviously shaken, House is furious with Wilson. "How many of your guys have caught cancer from their patients? Let me know when that happens. Then we can have this conversation."

Up until the very end, House cannot risk Foreman's life, and he tries the best he can using more conventional medical thinking, trying to minimize the risk. Ultimately, Cameron, to whom Foreman has given his medical proxy, decides the risk is worthwhile and she becomes the more aggressive doctor, insisting on the deep brain procedure. It's interesting to observe House in this reversal of roles pleading with Cameron for more time to use conventional methods before risking Foreman's future.

### Feeling Too Little — Or Too Much?

In House's worldview, there is little room for human emotion. Emotions rip away objectivity, lead to mistakes. House avoids them when he can, even going so far as to deny them completely. He insists he doesn't care — full stop. House maintains that his heart is "three sizes too small" ("Instant Karma," 6.05). This is something we know isn't true, but like his closest associates Wilson and Cuddy, we also know that House has difficulty with his feelings. They are hard to manage and impossible to control. You can't quantify feelings or rationalize them — or explain them. And that makes House uncomfortable.

He fights a preventive battle against emotions that would threaten his rational, quantifiable world. His defense is to numb himself by overusing Vicodin. He reacts to emotional conflict by acting out in the worst way he can, pushing everyone as far away as possible, and then brooding alone, tormented by feelings he can't quite get rid of.

When Cuddy is about to adopt an infant ("Joy," 5.06), House sees the baby as an intrusion. He knows she has wanted a child for several years, and has even helped her in her efforts ("Who's Your Daddy?" 5.23).

Confronted with unwelcome, but clearly strong, feelings fueled by his deep attraction for Cuddy, House expends huge amounts of energy playing juvenile pranks on her to prove she'd be a terrible mother. He breaks a lamp, douses her with baby spit up, and makes a general nuisance of himself. As Wilson observes, the emotionally stunted House is act like an adolescent boy pulling the pigtails of the girl he likes.

But when Cuddy loses her chance to adopt the baby, it devastates her, and House visits her at home, suddenly sympathetic and supportive. Trying to comfort her in a way that is probably truer to his real feelings, he tells her she would be "a great mother." But instead of accepting House's comfort, Cuddy turns on him, furious, calling him on his behavior of the past several days. "Why do you always have to negate everything?" she asks him.

This is one thing for which House doesn't have a ready answer. Cuddy has completely disarmed him and he is at a loss. With his defenses stripped, House's emotions surface, and he pulls her into a passionate embrace. The emotionally inarticulate House has found his voice, albeit temporarily.

But House's continued struggle to maintain tight control over his emotions is lost in the face of personal losses, and guilt over the suicide of diagnostics fellow Lawrence Kutner. Amber Volakis harasses him from beyond the grave, plaguing his every waking moment ("Saviors," 5.21 through "Both Sides Now," 5.24). The final blow is yet to come, as his mind retreats to the comfort of an imagined night with Cuddy helping him detox from Vicodin and making love. As the realization dawns that it wasn't real, House's long-defended façade crumbles under the immense emotional weight and crushes him from within. It is simply too much, and at the end of season five, House admits himself to Mayfield Psychiatric Hospital afraid he has lost his mind.

But at Mayfield, we finally come to a truth about House's emotional inner-workings ("Broken," 6.01). When House's misguided but kind actions towards a fellow patient end in near tragedy, his psychiatrist, Dr. Darryl Nolan suggests that House apologize and allow himself to move past it. But to House, apologies are meaningless; they do nothing — they cannot right a permanent wrong, cannot bring back someone who has died.

It's suddenly clear why House finds it impossible to apologize to Wilson for Amber's death in "Dying Changes Everything" (5.01). "It's meaningless," House tells Cuddy in that episode, explaining why he won't. It's easy to misinterpret House's refusal as stubbornness — or that he really does feel guilty about her death. But that's not it at all. He feels words are cheap and hollow: "Only actions have meaning — can change things."

House believes that his failures are "forever" and that no words can right his wrongs. So he keeps them locked inside, the toll mounting, while any success is dismissed as fleeting. "Is that it?" wonders Nolan. In a just world, does House believe he doesn't deserve to be happy — something both Stacy ("Three Stories," 1.24) and Wilson ("Son of Coma Guy," 3.07) have mentioned?

Yet in season six, House tries to apologize to someone he believes he wronged in the past ("Remorse," 6.12). Safer than expressing remorse to someone emotionally close to him like Cuddy, House selects a medical school classmate — someone with whom he swapped a final paper. Later in the season he is confronted by a man on his deathbed, someone whose case House refused to consider ("Lockdown," 6.17) and the consequence of his cavalier approach to selecting cases. In the end, when all he can do is to make the patient comfortable as he dies, House apologizes to him for not having looked into his case. As Wilson might say, "baby steps."

But in the season six finale ("Help Me," 6.22) House has no words for his dying patient, watching her slip away despite his Herculean effort to rescue her from a disaster site. He has connected with her on an elemental level, and with nothing left to do — nothing left to save her — House is inconsolable. He has opened himself up to save her, exposing himself, only to have her die. And her death is almost enough to push him over the edge. Yes, indeed House feels.

## Mad and Bad . . .

We like to think of heroes as . . . heroic — noble and good, kind, and forthright. But Byronic heroes are antiheroes, a heroic class set apart. They are haughty and arrogant, dismissive and sometimes cruel — "mad and bad," as Lady Caroline Lamb so aptly noted. House is no exception. He can be real jerk: arrogant, self-centered, jealous, petty, and vindictive. As David Shore has often said, House is not a "nice" person.

He seeks revenge on an old medical school adversary in "Distractions" (2.12), punches Chase in the jaw ("Finding Judas," 3.09), outs Taub's financial woes and "13's" health problems and bisexuality. In season six he creates a deep wedge between Chase and new bride Cameron — apparently, just because he can. It eventually leads to their breakup ("Teamwork," 6.08). The list goes on.

But House is seldom a jerk just to be a jerk (although that does happen). Even Cuddy admits he (almost) always has a reason even for his worst behavior ("Finding Judas," 3.09). He likes to push people's buttons, provoking them to some sort of action, like in "Hunting" (2.07), when House provokes the patient's father into hitting him. The provocation leads to the diagnosis, without having to risk surgery on the already physically compromised patient.

House has also been accused of being cruel and even of torturing patients from time to time. In "Distractions" (2.12), he wakes his patient Adam, a burn victim, out of a chemically induced coma so he can interview him. Another doctor is horrified at House's request and argues that it is torture to wake him because Adam will wake up in excruciating pain from his severe burns. But House insists, incurring the wrath of Adam's parents, who bar him from further contact with their son. But House is able to elicit a crucial piece of information from Adam, which eventually leads House to the diagnosis. Had he not woken the patient, he might have died — undiagnosed.

Because House's patients are always on the brink of death, House would argue that the shortcuts he takes may sometimes inflict pain, but not taking them can be much, much worse.

He is usually pretty confident that whatever he does is in some way justified and necessary, always believing he can control the seeming chaos of his diagnostic process.

"I recognize self-confidence is not my short suit," he tells Wilson in "Damned If You Do" (1.05). House believes completely in his ability to get the right answer, and he has pretty good reason to feel that way. That self-belief, however, sometimes ventures into smugness and arrogance, which has the potential to turn toxic and destructive. Most of the time it doesn't cost lives, though it can lead him down wrong diagnostic paths. But, in "97 Seconds" (4.03), a patient dies as an indirect result of House's arrogance while he is busy auditioning potential diagnostic fellows.

With more than 20 candidates under his direct responsibility, House believes he can manage the large group, although Cuddy is skeptical. He pits fellow wannabes against each other in two teams to diagnose a spinal muscular atrophy patient with a new medical problem. Turning the diagnosis into a game with these young, ambitious, and competitive doctors creates chaos as the teams try to one-up each other. Although House already knows the answer to the diagnostic puzzle, confusion among the doctors in the patient's room distracts fellowship candidate "13," who fails to watch the patient take his medicine.

When House sees that the prescribed treatment hasn't worked, he discards his original assumptions (and what he thought was the correct diagnosis) and goes down a new — and incorrect — diagnostic path. By the time he realizes what happened, it's too late and the patient cannot be saved. Had there been less chaos — had House kept more control — it would have proved a more straightforward case. Instead, they have a dead patient for whom House bears substantial responsibility.

For someone as arrogant as he is though, House is amazingly self-critical and introspective — and if you think about it, probably more than anyone else within his circle. Of course, these are probably not the most obvious things that come to mind when thinking about the smug Dr. Gregory House.

In the final analysis, House's considers his ideas are no more sacrosanct to him than Foreman's or Chase's, Taub's, or anyone else's. Although he always starts from the premise that he knows best, if someone else's theory fits better — it fits better. House shocks his fellows in "The Softer Side" (5.16) by doing an about-face as he walks into an elevator, dismissing his own idea to irradiate the patient's body in favor of Taub's less radical, but more logical, suggestion.

House is self-aware enough to understand he's not always right. "I have a gift for observation," he tells a filled auditorium of fellowship candidates in "Alone" (4.01). But he confesses as well, "I make mistakes."

In "Games" (4.09), House fires fellowship candidate Amber Volakis, although she "played the game better than anyone," because she doesn't know how to accept being wrong. "If you're gonna work for me," he explains, reluctantly letting her go, "you have to be willing to be wrong, willing to lose."

House has also acknowledged the necessity of being constantly challenged by gifted doctors for his practice to work — for his mojo, magic, genius, whatever you want to call it, to really kick into high gear. Since we've known him, he has never surrounded himself with fawning sycophants, preferring the company of people who will challenge his every word — even going over his head, if they feel it necessary. In "Frozen" (4.11), House sets up an elaborate game to show his team of new fellows that they must challenge him and learn when to refuse — to simply say "no!"

It's why in "Forever" (2.22) he is so upset when Foreman suddenly becomes agreeable following his brush with death ("Euphoria" 2.20, 2.21), refusing to engage House and challenge him. He needs and craves it, and mourns its loss when it's gone. So, while House can be both smug and arrogant, it is usually tempered by his introspection, extreme objectivity, and self-criticism.

Sometimes, however, House is an ass simply because he can be. And when there's no emotional conflict, no discernible reason, no motivation for his behavior, House becomes a truly dark character. This is House at his most unlikable — a flat-out (and even pompous) bastard. His victims have been clinic patients, colleagues, patient families, and, on rare occasions, patients who come under his care. He has even used his disability to take advantage of a situation. As he boasts to Wilson in "Autopsy" (2.02), "I'm not terminal; I'm merely pathetic, and you wouldn't believe the crap people let me get away with!" It's something of which he's keenly aware, and as much as he tries hiding from his disability, he is not above using it when it suits.

### . . . And Dangerous: House's Self-Destructiveness

A death wish, chronic recklessness, a simple ambivalence about whether you live or die — Byronic heroes usually have a self-destructive streak. Sometimes it leads to tragedy; sometimes our antiheroes have too much survival instinct to actually allow themselves to die.

After Kutner commits suicide in "Simple Explanation" (5.20), House begins to lose himself, sinking deeper and deeper into an emotional black hole, trying to make sense of a senseless act. As House obsesses over identifying the one clue he may have missed, Wilson believes House is afraid of losing his "one thing" — his intellectual gift. The sum of House's self esteem — his entire being — is wrapped up in it. And Wilson is afraid of what House will "do then."

House's self-destructive streak is especially evident in "Merry Little Christmas" (3.10). Pursued by the vindictive Detective Michael Tritter, House finds himself backed into a corner (largely, but not completely, of his own making). Wilson and Cuddy have abruptly cut off his pain meds to force him into a deal that will send him to drug rehab instead of jail. Detoxing from Vicodin and in terrible pain, House steals a bottle of oxycodone from the pharmacy, and out-of-his-mind desperate, he pops pill after pill of the powerful drug.

Declining an invitation from Wilson to spend Christmas Eve together,

House goes home; the medical case is solved. By now at the end of his emotional rope, House places a call to his mother, leaving a halting and emotional "Merry Christmas" message on her voice mail. Hanging up the phone quickly, he swallows the few pills remaining in the bottle, which had only hours ago contained 30. He chases them with a full tumbler of Bourbon — a toxic and potentially deadly cocktail.

Is House actively suicidal in this scene? It's hard to tell for certain. But his anguish is so intense, he probably doesn't much care whether he lives or dies. He simply wants the pain — in his leg and in his soul — to be finally over.

In "Ignorance Is Bliss" (6.09), when asked if he's ever tried to kill himself, House responds "not quickly," acknowledging his self-destructiveness. But no matter how self-destructive, House has always chosen life in the end. Nearly succumbing to despair in "Merry Little Christmas," Wilson finds him hours later on his floor barely conscious, but alive, having vomited all those ingested pills. It would have been so much easier for him to simply give into the warm cocoon of numbness that surely surrounds him by that point.

At the end of "No Reason" (2.24), House hovers between life and death as he bleeds on his office floor after being shot at point-blank range. We witness House's hallucinatory journey as he ponders his life, ultimately hanging on to it as he craves meaning. And once again at the end of "Wilson's Heart" (4.16), he wills himself back to life, knowing he has to face Wilson — and Amber's death. As House says, "Living in misery is slightly better than dying in it" ("Simple Explanation," 5.20).

### House the Linguist

House's familiarity with several foreign languages comes in handy when diagnosing "stupid American daughters" ("Sleeping Dogs Lie," 2.18) and taking revenge on an old medical school rival ("Distractions," 2.12). Just how many languages are at House's disposal with which to snark and insult?

**Mandarin Chinese** — In "Sleeping Dogs Lie" (2.18) House eavesdrops on a mother and daughter in the clinic as they argue in rapid Chinese about birth control pills. House surprises them when he responds — in their own language. In "Epic Fail" (6.03) House's cooking school buddy is a Chinese woman. They converse in Mandarin as they cook.

**Spanish** — In "Humpty Dumpty" (2.03) House is able to gain an important clue to the medical mystery by understanding a heated argument between the patient and his brother. In "Remorse" (6.12) he has an entertaining conversation with Wilson's clinic patient — made more entertaining because Wilson doesn't understand a word.

**Portuguese —** In "Fidelity" (1.07) House has researched African Sleeping Sickness in a Portuguese medical journal, and in "Whatever It Takes" (4.06), House is familiar with the Brazilian (Portuguese) name for Brazil nuts.

**Hindi —** He may not be fluent, but in "Distractions" (2.12) House is able to translate an article from an East Indian medical journal written by an old medical school rival. He needs a dictionary, but still!

**Italian —** In "House vs. God" (2.19) House refers to an obscure article in a 19th century Italian journal on the effect of the herpes virus on cancer cells. Although it's never stated, there is no doubt he could have read it in the original language.

**Yiddish —** House uses Yiddishisms all the time. "*Mazal 'toff'*" (the way he pronounces it) is a much-used expression; he also gets all "*gemutlicht*" over Cameron's newfound cynicism in "Failure to Communicate" (2.10), and recognizes a "*shanda*" (a shame) when he sees one ("Autopsy," 2.02).

**Hebrew —** Although he doesn't use it as often as he uses Yiddish, House has shown he knows an "*aleph*" from a "*bet*" (the first two letters in the Hebrew alphabet). He translates bits of the Sabbath prayer "*Eishet Chayil*" in "Don't Ever Change" (4.12), and in "Unfaithful" (5.15) his pronunciation of "*simchat bat*," the Jewish ceremony Cuddy has for baby Rachel, is spot on.

**Greek —** House shows his competence in Greek when he explains the symptoms aphasia (inability to speak) and syncope (fainting), but no more so than most doctors. However, he also tells his about-to-be-married patient he has "*kryo podia*" (cold feet) in "The Choice" (6.20).

**Latin, etc. —** House has used Latin phrases at least twice ("Needle in a Haystack," 3.13; Don't Ever Change," 4.12). And no one would be surprised if House at least understood some Arabic (from his time spent in Egypt as a kid) and Japanese (from when he was a child there with his military dad).

### . . . Yet Vulnerable

As much as House tries to completely guard himself with high fortress walls manned by armed centurions, he occasionally lets his associates see inside and behind his those tragic eyes. A heartfelt conversation with Foreman in

"Euphoria, Part 2" (2.21) about the effect of pain on judgment, an awkward confession to Cameron about his relationship with his dad at the end of "Daddy's Boy" (2.05), his shyness with Cuddy the morning after their passionate kiss in "The Itch" (5.07) are rare the glimpses he allows. As viewers we are privy to much more. We observe the vulnerability when he stares yearningly into a patient room, sits isolated in his darkened apartment at the piano, or when he's in soul-sucking pain as he tries to get out of bed. We understand the loneliness that threatens to drive him to despair when he thinks he might lose his closest friend Wilson on the operating table ("Wilson," 6.11). We even see it in his somewhat misguided acts of kindness fueled by a surprising sentimentality lying nearly dormant beneath his misanthrope's skin.

> "No matter how difficult he can be or rough around the edges he may appears, there's a glint in his eye all the time, when he finds the solution, or he sees someone saved, or he sees someone have the life they've always wanted to have."
>
> **— Jennifer Morrison on the character of House, March 2009 interview**

David Shore and the House writers have indeed drawn a well-rendered Byronic hero, worthy of his ancestors and their travails. But Dr. Gregory House is a one-of-a-kind. He is a many-faceted crystal, and depending upon the part of the prism through which you happen to observe him, he can be angel or devil, noble or an unrepentant bastard. The true colors you see may vary greatly.

# Broken

## House, Pain, and Drugs

Is Dr. Gregory House a drug addict? It's a question that's been hotly debated in the fan community almost since the start of the series. In "Detox" (1.11), Cuddy challenges House to go a week without Vicodin in exchange for a month off clinic duty. A week later, the victorious House admits to Wilson, "I'm an addict." But he adds, "It's not a problem." He can function: pay his bills, prepare meals, and make it into work each day.

The word "addict" has pejorative connotations. It suggests someone who can't function, and whose life is built around and defined by his or her addiction. So, is House an addict? He is obviously dependent on Vicodin. When he goes off it, he suffers withdrawal symptoms, indicating a physical dependence on the drug. He has needed larger and larger doses of the drug, as Cuddy indicates in "Detox" (1.11) doubling his dose from 40 to 80 milligrams per day from the time she hired him several years earlier. But that doesn't necessarily prove addiction. Physical tolerance to painkillers is common, and the longer you're on a medication, the less effective it becomes. Larger doses are often required.

Addiction, on the other hand, is a different matter. Addiction indicates a psychological dependence. Addicts often resort to extreme measures to obtain their drug of choice, including stealing, "doc shopping," and forgery, all of which House does in season three, particularly after Wilson and Cuddy deny him Vicodin in an effort to manipulate him into rehab. Is House looking for a "high" — or is he simply looking for pain relief?

House, himself, often clouds the issue with comments about "jonesing" for his pills, flaunting his drug use, and referring to himself as an addict. But is House doing himself (and other pain medication users) a disservice? Is it possible that House isn't an addict — but is instead a "pseudoaddict?"

Pseudoaddicts exhibit some of the same behavior as addicts: they watch the clock, gauging the amount of time until the next dose; they may hoard pills, or do other things that seem to indicate addiction. But they are not trying to "get high"; they are trying to achieve adequate pain relief.

They're not genuine addicts, according to the American Pain Foundation. Their addict-like behavior is related to under-treatment of underlying pain. Once a pseudoaddict's pain is properly managed, the "addict" behavior stops.

The times we've seen House's pain being adequately managed over the seasons, his interest in Vicodin seems to vanish. When he is pain free for a while after the ketamine treatment in season three, he is off Vicodin for months. In "The Softer Side" (5.16), House gives up Vicodin, trying methadone. It's risky, and can kill him if he even accidentally misuses it. But it completely eliminates the pain. For the brief time he's on it, House seems fine. He even shaves. He seems to neither miss nor crave the Vicodin.

House has always made a distinction between needing drugs and wanting to use them. In "Broken" (6.01, 6.02), when his psychiatrist, Dr. Nolan, offers House antidepressants, House is reluctant to try them, believing they may affect his medical edge. Although Nolan reminds him that he seems to have no difficulty taking drugs of another kind, House quickly reminds him that those drugs are for physical pain — not to alter his reality. And the Vicodin doesn't dull his edge.

There is no doubt that House's relationship with pain — and with drugs — is extremely complicated. And while House insists he takes Vicodin for physical pain, there is some suggestion that the Vicodin has also treated his emotional pain, numbing him to feelings that run too deep or wounds from past internal hurts. But whether that makes him an addict or not, the drugs have been an occasional source of difficulty for him going back to long before we ever meet him, perhaps even before the infarction that left him disabled.

In "Three Stories" (1.21), House reveals that when he first came to the hospital emergency room suffering pain in his leg, he was originally dismissed as a "drug seeker" by the doctors and sent home. He didn't help matters by grabbing a syringe of Demerol and injecting himself. Of course we never learn whether House was actually a drug seeker — or was only perceived that way by the ER doctors who treated him.

As House says during his lecture in that episode, there are much easier ways (especially for a doctor like House) to get his hands on drugs should he so desire. And there is no indication that House was a hardcore drug user before the infarction.

By the time we meet House, however, his closest associates, Cuddy and Wilson, are both concerned enough to manipulate him into proving their point. And though sorely tempted when Foreman brings him a bottle of pills so he can function better during the case, House is also trying to prove his point. So he toughs it out, preferring to suffer withdrawal symptoms.

If he were really an addict, would House have been able to ignore temptation? Or is it that his stubbornness trumps his need for a fix?

In season two, House's leg pain seems to intensify after his briefly rekindled affair with Stacy Warner, the woman with whom he had been involved at the time of his infarction ("Skin Deep," 2.13). Wilson believes his increased pain is psychosomatic: a result of Stacy leaving. After a placebo shot administered by Cuddy, House feels better and is able to complete work on the case, which leads Cuddy to agree with Wilson's assessment. But are they really right, or is House's relief caused by the "placebo effect?" The placebo effect is a cure of the mind, where the expectation of relief is great enough that the patient experiences measurable, real relief. Clinical pain research has revealed that it can be very effective in chronic pain management, especially of the sudden intense "breakthrough" pain House seems to experience in "Skin Deep." So Cuddy's experiment proves nothing about the nature of House's pain. But House is unnerved enough when she finally tells him that he, himself, begins to doubt, what he's feeling.

Through the remainder of season two, House's leg is visibly worse. He limps more, grips his thigh more often. Finally in the season's penultimate episode ("Who's Your Daddy?" 2.23), the pain in House's leg is so severe, he cannot seem to rest. He paces relentlessly trying to find relief in movement, but nothing seems to distract him — not even the current case. Eventually digging out a morphine stash hidden the far reaches of his bookshelves, House finally finds relief in the powerful narcotic painkiller.

House doesn't resort to this extreme measure lightly. And after he is shot in the season finale ("No Reason," 2.24), House hallucinates while unconscious on his office floor. During the hallucination — a harsh self-examination — House processes his morphine use (among many other things). His subconscious in the guise of Lisa Cuddy berates him for embarking on the road to "becoming a junkie."

Obviously, House survives the shooting and over the summer between seasons two and three undergoes risky experimental pain treatment. The risk pays off. House starts season three pain free and enjoys his newfound mobility, taking pleasure in running and doing skateboard tricks. But when House's leg pain suddenly makes a brief comeback, Wilson dismisses it as the "pangs of middle age," showing House little sympathy when it's clear that House is worried and afraid the treatment is wearing off.

As we observe House, blown off by his friend and concerned about the pain as he sits in his office brooding and considering his options at the conclusion of "Meaning" (3.01), his words to Foreman late in season two ("Euphoria, Part 2," 2.21) come to mind. "Pain makes us make bad decisions," he told Foreman, who was suffering intractable pain from a mysterious and deadly infection.

"Fear of pain," he continues "is almost as big a motivator."

But now, it is House feeling boxed into a corner, about to make a terrible decision based on fear of his pain returning. Sneaking into Wilson's office, House steals prescription blanks, a desperate act that will come back to haunt him in the not so distant future.

Enter Detective Michael Tritter. With the pain returned and the experimental procedure now a distant memory, House pisses off the wrong clinic patient — Detective Michael Tritter, a police detective with a big chip on his shoulder and a vendetta against drug addicts ("Fools for Love," 3.05). Noting that House pops a Vicodin during the exam, Tritter puts two and two together and comes up with "addict." And when he later stops the doctor for speeding, he finds "probable cause" to search House, whose pockets are filled with pills.

After Tritter finds hundreds of Vicodin bottles stashed around House's apartment, he wonders whether House is dealing or just wants to spend every waking minute stoned out of his mind ("Que Será Será," 3.06). If House is always in so much pain, Tritter wonders, how is it that House never misses a day of work? House responds that it's the pills that take the edge off his pain and allow him to function. They let him do his job, as he so often asserts.

As Tritter continues his investigation over the next several episodes, collateral damage follows House in his wake. Everyone in House's circle is now suspect, and the police pursue drug fraud charges, involving Wilson and the fellows in the investigations. Wilson becomes a "person of interest," and the DEA yanks his license, leaving him unable to write prescriptions. His car is impounded, and the fellows' bank accounts are also frozen (except for Chase's). As Tritter continues his relentless pursuit, House's Vicodin supply dwindles, and everyone is reluctant to write prescriptions for him.

Either House needs the pain medicine or he doesn't. If he doesn't, Tritter is right; if he does, and his medicine is being withheld, what does that say about how House is being treated by everyone in his circle? Everyone from Wilson to Foreman has defended House to Tritter, acknowledging House's legitimate reason for taking Vicodin. But Tritter believes this is actually part of the problem. He insists to Cuddy that the medical establishment has failed in its duty and should not protect impaired physicians like House. "You have failed," he accuses, which is why he believes it's time for the police to become involved ("Finding Judas," 3.09).

Whether or not she believes House's Vicodin use is legitimate, Cuddy begins to ration his pills, cutting him back abruptly and dramatically, which is not the way to take someone off narcotics. Strung out and in agony, if he wasn't impaired before, he is by the end of "Finding Judas." His rash medical decision nearly maims a patient for life, and he punches Chase in the jaw for blocking his way, as the fellow tries to advocate an alternative diagnosis.

Now concerned that Chase will cooperate with Tritter, Wilson preempts him, making a deal that will get House off the legal hook in exchange for a stay in drug rehab. At this point, is anyone in House's orbit treating him fairly? Or are they covering for him when they should be cooperating with Tritter? If they believe House legitimately needs Vicodin, they should be unafraid to defend him. But in their defense, they would each be taking a substantial professional risk.

The DEA has put physicians in a difficult position. According to the American Pain Foundation, pain management specialists are under incredible pressure to minimize the amount of narcotics given for pain relief. And with the threat of license revocation and jail terms, chronic pain patients are often severely under treated.

When House refuses the deal, Wilson conspires with Cuddy to cut off his supply entirely, removing him from his current case and sending him home ("Merry Little Christmas," 3.09). Beginning to suffer withdrawal symptoms, House exhibits some classic "addict" symptoms. He doc shops, going to a nearby emergency room to connive the doctor into prescribing Vicodin (unsuccessfully). He begins "cutting" himself to release endorphins, which might provide him some relief. Cameron visits at one point, urging him to take the deal, reminding him that he had been "clean" for months after he was shot. But House pointedly counters that he hadn't been in pain then — reminding *her* that his relationship with drugs is about pain, not addiction. His friends believe they are helping him, but are they instead helping him cut his own throat?

At a particularly fragile moment, House steals a bottle of oxycodone. Sick from the forced withdrawal and nearly out of his mind with pain, he downs pill after pill of the stolen narcotic. House is desperate, and the pounding his life has taken since having been shot seems to come crashing down around him. Sentenced to a life of relentless pain, House must constantly justify his drug use — even to his best friends — and has to wonder at this point if it's all worthwhile. After leaving a halting message on his mother's voice mail, he downs the remainder of the 30 pills — with a bourbon chaser. Wilson finds him barely conscious, hours later, but, disgusted, leaves him to lie in his own vomit.

Of course the debate in the fan community raged for weeks (and probably still does) as to whether House was actually intending to commit suicide with the potentially lethal combination of drugs and alcohol — and the despondent-sounding call home. Is he actively suicidal, or simply past the point of caring? All we do know is he survives his "dark night of the soul," waking up to take

Tritter's deal. But it's too late, and he has to go to court.

In a move to impress Tritter — or the judge hearing his case — House admits himself to the hospital's drug rehab program. But instead of complying, he hustles Vicodin off one of the aides and rants about the constant platitudes and the uselessness of group therapy. This is where the Tritter story line might have made an interesting statement about House, his pain, and his drug use. But David Shore and company want (or perhaps need) to keep the issue as ambiguous as possible. So, after Cuddy lies to the judge, House is off the hook — and seems to have learned nothing at all from the experience. By the next episode, he is back on the Vicodin and we are left to wonder what the encounter with Tritter actually accomplished.

But as the series headed into the latter part of season three, it became apparent that maybe something had sunk in. In both "Insensitive" (3.14) and "Half Wit" (3.15), House seems to be once again exploring alternatives to painkillers, researching nerve transplant protocols and clinical trials that deal with the brain's pain centers. Perhaps he's beginning to worry about the physical effects of long-term narcotics use. As he notes to his patient in "Insensitive" (3.14), he checks himself for jaundice by examining his eyes every morning, which would indicate the Vicodin has finally trashed his liver.

With the series' heavy subject matter in season three, House's relationship with drugs is touched on only mildly in season four, when he and his team of fellowship candidates treat a heroin addict ("Games," 4.09). Connecting the patient's illness with his drug use, the fellow wannabes dance around House's constant pill popping. Amber Volakis, who is the most obviously judgmental of the patient's drug use, excuses House's Vicodin as necessary, assuring him that she doesn't view him as an addict.

But once again in season five, we see House trying to address his pain and drug use in several episodes. It's an issue the show doesn't deal with to any great degree during the first half of season five (despite the amount of emotional pain House suffers through the first several season five episodes). But mid season, he treats a chronic pain patient ("Painless," 5.12), whose life resonates. The patient, who is intent on suicide, is an avatar for House's future. Beyond hope, the patient has tried everything to alleviate the terrible physical pain he suffers. After several more suicide attempts and no diagnosis to explain his pain, the patient wants to go home and finally end his life there. "Can you tell me you would want to live this way?" the patient's wife asks House, noting the cane, the limp — and the obvious pain. House has no answer for her.

Whether fueled by his encounter with this patient or his growing attraction for Cuddy, House again contemplates alternatives — no longer willing to live a life in pain. In "The Softer Side" (5.16) he tries methadone, which eliminates his pain, but dulls his mental edge, and in "Locked In" (5.19), therapy — before an act by fellow Lawrence Kutner triggers an emotional collapse for House that is years in the making.

But with each decision, House's friends question or distrust his motives. In "The Softer Side," Cuddy threatens his job if he refuses to stop taking methadone — a dangerous, but effective painkiller. "Heroin without the high," House calls it. Yet throughout the episode he's "high." Being pain free lightens House's mood considerably — just as it had at the start of season three.

In "Locked In" (5.19), Wilson confronts House about why he might be seeing a psychiatrist. Although Wilson thinks this is a good thing, and House can certainly use professional help in dealing with his emotional and physical issues, his interference alone causes House to back off (as it so often does).

Vicodin seems for House to be the only recourse he has: it's effective, yet doesn't dull his thinking. But after House's emotional collapse at the end of season five, he has no choice. Vicodin is no longer an answer.

In an interview, clinical psychologist Dr. Robert Spector suggested that perhaps the losses House suffers over the course of season five combined with overdosing on Vicodin may have been the tragic combination to cause his final crash, landing him in Mayfield Psychiatric Hospital. "Was he feeling lost? Was the Vicodin finally no longer enough to blunt the feelings?" Spector wondered. "Or was is it as simple as drug-induced psychosis?"

After going through supervised Vicodin withdrawal at Mayfield ("Broken," 6.01, 6.02), House is ready to leave, but the facility's director, Dr. Darryl Nolan isn't so quick to let him go. House spends two months under Nolan's care before he's released, diagnosed with depression.

House leaves Mayfield on a regimen of therapy, antidepressants, and non-narcotic pain relievers. During his delusion about Cuddy his subconscious (as Cuddy) assures him that Vicodin may have been deceiving his brain into thinking he has more pain than is actually present. And once off the narcotic, a milder pain reliever might be effective. In the months that follow his release from Mayfield, we can observe ebbs and flows in House's pain level: he limps heavier, he rubs more often at his right thigh, and he has a harder time keeping up. But through it — and through the emotional pain he suffers through some of the season — he manages without narcotics.

Is the cycle for House finally "broken"? In the season six finale, House sits on his bathroom floor, seemingly for hours, in terrible, agonizing physical pain, racked by the torment of a tragic patient death — and feeling as isolated and hopeless as we've seen him. He wills himself not to take the Vicodin caplets that sit in the palm of his hand. It would be so easy and, he says, there's little "downside" to tossing them back; the pain in his leg and in his soul would fade away, lost in a Vicodin haze. It is an incredible moment, but what propels it? Is it the hard work he has done with Nolan? Or is House's fear of losing his mind still stronger than his fear of the pain?

# Doing the Right Thing

## House and Ethics

In "Son of Coma Guy" (3.07), the father of House's patient, Gabe Wozniak, asks him what last words he'd like to hear from his own father. House hesitates, but answers honestly, "I'd like him to tell me that I was right; that I did the right thing." What does it mean to do the "right thing"?

"Being right" sounds like our Dr. House. He likes to be right, and he often goes to a lot of trouble to be proven right. "Doing the right thing" is something else. That doesn't sound like the manipulative, sarcastic, verbally abusive House — at least not to most people outside his immediate sphere.

Admittedly, House has done things to warrant the less praiseworthy aspects of his reputation. His colleagues, hospital lawyers, and even patients must sometimes wonder if House operates under any sort of ethical framework at all. House has lied to the transplant committee ("Control," 1.14) and has induced a migraine in a coma patient to test the efficacy of an anti-migraine drug ("Distractions," 2.12). He has shot a cadaver in the head to test how the MRI machine would handle a live patient with a similar gunshot wound — breaking the machine in the process ("Euphoria, Part 1," 2.20). He has assisted one patient's suicide ("Son of Coma Guy") and applauded another ("Informed Consent," 3.03) — and kept silent when Chase killed a patient intentionally ("The Tyrant," 6.04). He has provoked any number of patients into physically attacking him (albeit all for a greater medical good). Doing the right thing? Seriously?

But House has a highly defined sense of medicine, ethics, and medical justice that goes beyond much of common medical practice. It is a complex moral code. It is sometimes subjective, but it is is very consistently applied.

"You are aware of the Hippocratic Oath, right?" diagnostics fellow Dr. Eric Foreman asks Dr. Gregory House in "Damned If You Do" (1.05). House isn't impressed. "You mean the one that begins 'first do no harm'? Then goes on to tell us: no abortions, no seductions, and definitely no cutting of those who labor beneath the stone?"

If doctors "first do no harm," House might argue, many of his patients would not survive, much less get needed medical attention. Drugs, diagnostic tests, and medical procedures all carry with them a degree of risk, sometimes small and sometimes great. And when patients finally get to House, most have gone through all of medicine's tests and procedures that "first do no harm."

When House lectures a roomful of medical students in "Three Stories" (1.21), he warns them there is always right and wrong, even if "right" is unknowable. A misguided, well-intentioned wrong has the same consequences as a malicious wrong. Intention doesn't matter to the victim. And sometimes, especially in medicine, there's no way to make it right again. This idea weighs heavily on House and is an important part of who he is — and contributes to his misery ("Broken," 6.01, 6.02).

The nature of right and wrong, doing the right thing, being "right" — these are all underlying themes that play into many episodes. You can be the kindest doctor in the universe, but if the patient dies, what meager recompense does all that niceness buy? So House continually poses the question: is it more "right" to be less "nice," to even hurt the patient if it means the patient lives?

Who has the moral high ground? The doctor who colors within the lines following the rules, allowing a patient to die because "there was nothing more we could do," or a doctor like House, who ignores medical conventions and ethics, only to save that same patient's life? Of course most doctors are not House, who is a fictional character with cognitive superpowers. In real life, he would not exist. But many people would agree that if you're on the verge of death, House would be the physician you'd want on your team.

Whether House admits it or not, his experiences, both his personal tragedies and his experiences as a physician, have had a profound effect on him, and on how he views the practice of medicine. He is skeptical of conventional medical wisdom, and the hypocrisy he sees in it. He believes that blind adherence to standards of medical practice often comes into conflict with patient care.

In the season one episode "Socratic Method" (1.06), House argues with Cuddy about the ethics of temporarily shrinking a tumor to put it within the surgical guidelines. Cuddy argues that medical guidelines have a purpose that should not be disregarded.

"I know," he counters. "To save lives — specifically doctors' lives, and not just their lives but their lifestyles." He ends his rant telling her, "You do what you think is right."

Is House right to temporarily shrink the tumor to trick the surgeon into operating? Or should he have let the patient die because the tumor fell 10 percent beyond the surgical guidelines? Wilson, the oncologist, agrees with House, and ultimately so does Cuddy. But it's the sort of ethical dilemma that House (and *House*) tackles all of the time.

### House's Influence

House's colleagues, though influenced by him in one way or another, also have their own independent ethical guiding principles. House rarely criticizes his fellows for doing what they believe is "right," even if that means ratting him out to a higher authority (usually Cuddy).

Foreman has done it practically since the start of the series ("Damned If You Do," 1.05). Cameron, too, has gone to Cuddy when she has believed House has gone too far or not done enough. In "Skin Deep" (2.13), she reports him to Cuddy when he fails to call social services on a child-molesting father. When Taub believes House is wrong in "Ugly" (4.07), he goes to the patient's father and tells him that he will get his boss thrown off the case. Although House's instinct is to fire Taub, he doesn't — even later in the episode when he has the chance. Doing what he believes to be right has earned Taub House's respect (at least for the moment).

Although Cameron often understands and even approves of House's actions — sometimes when no one else would — and has herself euthanized a patient ("Informed Consent," 3.03), her rigid morality renders her occasionally judgmental. And when Cameron harshly judges a patient, she sometimes purposely inflicts physical pain (as in "Sleeping Dogs Lie," 2.18).

Foreman, too, has a judgmental streak. Most often his target is House, whom he believes operates with no moral code whatsoever. Foreman is all too willing to kick a patient to the curb with a drug abuse diagnosis — even before assessment ("Histories," 1.10; "House Training," 3.20). Foreman has stood by while a patient crashes, doing nothing to save his life ("Acceptance," 2.01). Yet at the end of that episode, Foreman is willing to testify on Clarence's behalf and also asks for House's opinion. And in typical Housian fashion he says, "You'll do what you think is right — on your own time."

In season six, especially, we see the effects of House's philosophy of doing the right thing — consequences be damned — when Chase assassinates genocidal dictator Dibala ("The Tyrant," 6.04) and Wilson risks his career to bring a controversial subject out in the open light of the medical community ("Known Unknowns," 6.07).

In "Teamwork" (6.08), Cameron's rigid morality contributes to the breakup of her marriage to Chase — and her saying goodbye to Princeton-Plainsboro Teaching Hospital. Blaming House for "poisoning" Chase so he can no longer tell "right from wrong," Cameron cannot forgive either of them for the dictator's death.

### The Case of Ezra Powell

Renowned physician/researcher Dr. Ezra Powell calls on House in "Informed Consent" (3.03) with heart and lung symptoms after collapsing in his lab. He has sought out House knowing that he would "have the guts to do what had to be done." Powell assumes House will have no misgivings about injecting him with a lethal dose of morphine — if it comes to that point, which Powell thinks is imminent.

But House refuses to honor Powell's request. In his opinion, they have not yet exhausted the diagnostic possibilities, and there is still a chance at this point for Powell to be diagnosed and cured. Is House drawing an ethical line — making a moral statement — or is he driven solely by the challenge of diagnosing Powell to the endpoint?

Even Wilson wonders why House is reluctant to do as Powell requests. He reminds House that he's done it before (and we get the impression Wilson has too, which is confirmed in "Known Unknowns," 6.07). But, explains House, only "to patients that I knew were terminal." In House's medical opinion, they have not yet reached that threshold.

House and Powell are at a standoff; Powell refuses consent to more tests, and without the tests, he'll certainly die. So, either House kills him, or he dies a slow and painful death. This puts House in an interesting quandary, but one with which he seems more comfortable. He is compelled to continue testing to save Powell's life (or, you might argue, to solve the puzzle of Powell's illness). Telling Powell he'll help him die, House sends his fellows from the room so they will not be tainted with assisting in House's illegal act. Foreman and Cameron want no part of it anyway, and they leave. Chase stays behind; his experience in critical care medicine may lend him a different perspective. The doctors he has worked for in the past have all done it, he explains.

But it's not morphine in House's syringe; it's something to simulate death and put Powell into a coma, allowing the team to continue working towards a diagnosis. Chase is shocked at House's deception, but as House explains: lying, while bad, is "way further down the list than murder." How much of this is driven by House's "need to know" what's wrong with Powell, and how much by House's internal ethical compass, we never really know.

Although House argues that Powell could have any number of treatable conditions, Cameron counters that there are just as many that are not. House is frustrated with her. She's opposed to euthanizing him but won't participate in the tests necessary to save his life. House demands she take a stand, arguing that they can't just stand there, hope for the best, and watch the patient die while they debate the ethics of the case. (This hits on the familiar *House, M.D.* theme of action versus words. Words are meaningless; action is the only thing that matters. What you do counts; what you say is useless when your patient is dying by the minute.)

Ultimately House diagnoses Powell with untreatable amyloidosis; he will die. But when Powell mysteriously dies overnight after being reported in stable condition, Cuddy confronts House to ask what he knows of the suspicious death. House asks in return: "If I did, would you want to know?" It's a question to which they both know the answer.

It is Cameron, not House, who actually euthanizes Powell. Her decisive action earns House's respect for taking a stand and mercifully ending Powell's life.

House is not opposed to ending a life under certain circumstances. In "Son of Coma Guy" (3.07), House helps Gabe, condemned to life in a vegetative state, commit suicide in order to save the life of his son. As House sits vigil outside Gabe's hotel room, waiting for him to die, you can see the toll this decision has taken on him. And when Cuddy confronts him about it in a parallel to their scene in "Informed Consent" (3.03), there is no doubt about what happened and why. House's actions are neither ethical nor legal in any conventional sense, but it's clearly not something he's done cavalierly. But is it the "right thing" to do, given the circumstances?

All doctors help patients hasten their own deaths, but it's all in the dark, Wilson asserts in his conference paper, arguing that the discussion should commence — within the medical establishment. House knows that a paper on this taboo subject is dynamite, and if Wilson actually delivers it, his career will explode, rendering him unemployable.

But Wilson has learned a dangerous yet important lesson from House; sometimes doing the right thing means ignoring the consequences in the service of a greater good or quality of care.

# ▶ BOY WONDER ONCOLOGIST

DR. JAMES ("JIMMY") WILSON

"Sometimes I feel like Wilson is House's conscience and Cuddy is his heart. But I think Cuddy and Wilson have a great camaraderie. There is an unspoken understanding between them in regards to House and all things House-related. They know the other's piece of the puzzle, and they both use and support each other through it."

— **Actress Lisa Edelstein (Cuddy), October 2008 interview**

Successful doctor, and tenured faculty member at a major teaching hospital, Dr. James Evan Wilson sits on the hospital's board and is profiled in *Who's Who* ("Babies and Bathwater," 1.18). Psychiatrist Cate Milton describes him in

"Frozen" (4.11) as "responsible, nice, human." However, she quickly adds that "indiscriminate niceness is overrated." This being *House*, no one is ever quite who he or she seems — and everyone is pretty screwed up. Wilson is enigmatic in ways House can only dream, and beneath his affable, open, good-guy persona lurks hidden layers not even House has viewed.

Whereas Wilson projects a "nice guy" image, House seems a perfectly uncaring jerk. Wilson attracts people and House pushes them away. Neither image is entirely accurate, but both are successful at their respective charades — except with each other. Cate wonders why House and Wilson are best friends, since Wilson is so "nice," and House is so "not." It's not until season five ("Birthmarks," 5.04) that we learn their "origin story."

House and Wilson met at a medical conference in New Orleans shortly after Wilson finished medical school. In the midst of his first divorce, he caught House's attention among the conference's 3,000 attendees. When Wilson became involved in a bar fight, causing the establishment considerable damage, including a broken antique mirror, House came to his rescue, bailing him out of jail.

But what draws these outwardly very different characters towards each other beyond that one incident? Both Robert Sean Leonard and Hugh Laurie have commented on what makes the House-Wilson dynamic unique among all of House's other relationships. Theirs is a relationship of choice, unlike the obligatory relationships of student-teacher between House and his fellows, or his employer-employee relationship with Cuddy.

Early in season one ("Damned If You Do," 1.05), House and Wilson discuss the yin and yang of their relationship. "As long as you're trying to be good, you can do whatever you want," House submits. Wilson counters, "And as long as you're not trying, you can say whatever you want." Together, they can rule the world — or so they believe.

As long as Wilson tries to be good — a nice guy, accessible, kind, and caring, no matter if it's an act or sincere — he can get away with pretty much anything. He cheats on his wives, runs DNA tests on Cuddy's saliva without her consent (and knows House will be blamed if she ever finds out), and he has an ongoing bet with House collecting every time that he can deliver bad news to a patient and have that patient thank him for it. To House, Wilson is the master of manipulation.

### Wilson's Defining Moment

If he were to describe Wilson in fewer than five words, House would say he "needs to be needed." His relationships feed on the neediness of others, whether his cancer patients, the women in his life, or House. Is this needing to be needed a part of Wilson's genetic makeup, or does it originate in something that happened to him long before even House met him?

Wilson has a younger brother Danny, whom he never mentions to House before the mid–season one episode "Histories" (1.10). House tracks Wilson to the same bleak, deserted corner in Princeton where Danny was last seen. It is here Wilson reveals that his brother disappeared and was presumed homeless nine years earlier.

Wilson's "long lost brother" (as he has been dubbed in the online fan community) isn't mentioned again until season five, in "The Social Contract" (5.17), when we finally learn that Danny is schizophrenic, diagnosed at age 16. Wilson reveals that when he was in medical school Danny, an undergraduate, would call incessantly, keeping him on the phone for long periods of time, something for which med student Wilson had little time. One day Danny called while Wilson was studying for exams, and with no time to listen to his brother's ranting, Wilson hung up on him and fled to the library. It was soon thereafter that Danny disappeared without a trace, leaving his psych meds behind.

More than 13 years pass without a word, and then in "The Social Contract," Wilson learns that Danny has been admitted to a psych ward in a New York hospital. That one event, years earlier, the simple act of hanging up a phone — understandable in an overworked and under-slept med student — gives context to Wilson's relationships with House and others who cross his path.

Wilson once said that his friendship with House is an "ethical responsibility" ("Control," 1.14), but he has never elaborated on why — at least not for us viewers to witness. At the time, it sounded like an important bit of information contained in what seemed to be a throwaway line. Why would their friendship be an "ethical responsibility?" Does it somehow tie back into Wilson's experience with his brother? If he never "hangs up the phone" on House — never abandons him as he feels he did with his brother — will Wilson somehow be redeemed? Will House be saved?

When House is at his neediest at the end of season five "Under My Skin" (5.23) and "Both Sides Now" (5.24), Wilson is there for him. And in "Both Sides Now," when House's world completely comes apart, Wilson accompanies him to Mayfield Psychiatric Hospital, being there for him, but letting House walk that final mile alone, as he must, up the stairs and into treatment.

As House is in treatment at Mayfield, Wilson once again must "hang up the phone" as he did with Danny ("Broken," 6.01). This time the person on the other end is House, wanting to involve Wilson in a scheme to get out of Mayfield long before he is ready. Eerily reminiscent of that fateful phone call with Danny, Wilson hangs up the receiver not to help himself — but to help House. It may be one of the most difficult moments of his life, as he is still haunted by the night Danny disappeared.

After House is discharged from Mayfield, he moves in with Wilson. After weeks of inpatient treatment House is still fragile and should not be living alone. But Wilson is no longer blindly supportive, and maybe that's what's required at this point, treating House more like a wayward adult child who risks being thrown out of the house if takes one wrong step. And House nearly does — through no fault of his own ("Epic Fail," 6.03).

But Wilson continues to be there for House throughout the season, even buying a larger condo (well, he really had to move out of Amber's old digs) to accommodate both him and House ("Ignorance Is Bliss," 6.09). Ultimately, however, Wilson wants to move on with his life, and that includes ridding himself of House — at least from the constant companionship of their condo ("The Choice," 6.21).

### Symbiosis or Codependence?

The sheer force of House's personality would suggest that *he* would dominate any relationship. But it's easy to argue that Wilson is the "alpha" in his relationship with House.

"Mirror Mirror" (4.05) establishes this dynamic when House treats a man with a rare disease that causes him to mimic the dominant personality in any group of people. When the patient encounters House and Wilson together, he mimics Wilson — much to Wilson's glee (and gloating).

In season two, we learn that House avoids inviting Wilson to his weekly poker game ("House vs. God," 2.19). And it's not until Wilson worms his way in that we understand why. Although House seems to be an expert poker player, running rings around his marks . . . er . . . competition, Wilson, we learn, is able to read House's "tells" as well as House reads everyone else's. The hyper-observant House sees through anyone and everyone, but not Wilson — one of the few people who can both easily lie to him and manipulate him.

Of course, Wilson's motives are pure, or at least that's how he perceives them, as he manipulates House strictly for his "own good." Wilson ever seeks opportunities for House to "change," be less miserable, and perhaps even grab a little happiness. But too often these manipulations backfire, causing more damage than any possible good they might have done.

One of Wilson's biggest failures occurs after House undergoes an experimental pain treatment using the veterinary anesthetic ketamine ("Meaning," 3.01). No longer needing narcotics — or the cane, the elated House is pain free for the first time in years. Wilson concludes that House has become too arrogant, infallible even. To try to teach House a little humility, he withholds information, leading House to believe he has missed a diagnosis. Wilson's plan backfires spectacularly by the end of the next episode ("Cane and Able," 3.02) when House becomes increasingly depressed over his failure. His leg pain returns with a vengeance, and by the end of the episode he can barely walk. When Cuddy ultimately tells him the truth about the diagnosis, House sees the hand of Wilson at work.

But does Wilson have a point? Has House begun to feel omnipotent with his newfound physical freedom? "I was afraid your wings would melt," he explains to a furious House, referring to the story of Icarus from Greek mythology. In the myth, Daedalus crafts a set of wax wings for his son Icarus. Energized and set free with the newfound ability to fly, Icarus ignores his father's warning not to fly too high. Fascinated by all he sees in this newly discovered world, he flies too close to the sun, which melts his wings. He falls into the sea. But as House points out, it's hard to feel omnipotent when you can barely walk. "God doesn't limp," he bitterly reminds Wilson.

But as much as House resents Wilson's interference in his life, he also craves the intrusions, moralizing, and guidance. When Wilson feels the need to distance himself from House at the beginning of season five, House is upset and hurt. And by "Birthmarks" (5.04), when Wilson returns, House acknowledges he doesn't mind if Wilson is only attracted by "the shine" of his neediness.

When he feels Wilson is not interfering enough, House will seek him out on his own, pining for the absent lecturing ("Emancipation," 5.08). House trusts Wilson as much as he trusts anyone, and a perverse part of that trust is in knowing Wilson will manipulate and lie to him — but only with his best interests at heart.

At the same time, House constantly pushes at their relationship, looking for proof of it, edging ever closer towards the conditions under which it will bend or break. And House has come close several times in six seasons, especially towards the middle of season three (during the story line involving Detective Michael Tritter), and at the beginning of season five after the death of Wilson's girlfriend, Amber Volakis. Perhaps House best explains why he and Wilson are friends to his psychiatrist, "I can say anything to him and he won't leave" ("Baggage," 6.21).

## Amber and House

In the season four episode "97 Seconds" (4.03), House takes a calculated risk when he inserts a knife into a live electrical outlet. Calling for help before he does the deed to ensure he will be found and revived quickly, House dials Amber Volakis, a new fellowship candidate. Why call her? Why not Wilson? Why not Cuddy? Why not one of the several other fellows House is auditioning for a coveted spot on his team? Is there something about Amber that draws House to her — even early in season four when he barely knows her?

Dubbing her "Cutthroat Bitch," House admires her willingness to do anything and everything it takes to "be right," but he's less of an admirer of her tactics. In "Games" (4.09), House ultimately fires her, observing that for as well as she plays "the game," her inability to lose — to be wrong and accept it — is a detriment on House's team. But for all her outward lack of caring, House knows she does. Is it a reflection of himself that he sees: someone who cares more than they can possibly let on, couching vulnerability behind a wall of ambition and selfish indifference?

When Amber becomes involved with Wilson, at first House is stunned. She is so unlike Wilson's previous partners that House cannot believe it will last — until he realizes that Wilson is finally dating a female version of his best friend. And as Wilson asks, "Why not?" House competes with Amber for Wilson's affections, and he loses. And when he drowns his sorrows in "House's Head" (4.15), House is bitterly angry that it's Amber who comes to give him a ride home, and not "dial-a-Wilson."

On their fateful bus ride home, House observes Amber taking flu medicine — amantadine. In the hours after the crash, although his short-term memory is shot, he holds on to the thought that he saw someone do something — saw a symptom in someone — and nothing can distract him from mining his subconscious and his memory to save that person's life. Finally recalling the crash in vivid detail, House remembers grabbing for Amber's hand and then trying to save her leg before losing consciousness himself. But it's the image of seeing her carried off by the paramedics that seems emblazoned into his memory — even when he can't recall that it's Amber. There is more than mere antagonism between them — at least in House's mind, although he's unlikely to admit it.

Throughout "Wilson's Heart" (4.16), Amber is House's muse, helping him through his memories as he dreams, fantasizes, and hallucinates. She seduces and snaps, haunts, and taunts House with a soft, seductive voice, moving with a weightless grace around him in "Wilson's Heart" (4.16) and throughout the last part of season five when she reappears as a hallucination. She is House's rational side, devoid of emotion, giving him the straight-on ugly truths about himself as his mind slowly crumbles.

### Wilson in Love

Wilson has been married three times; he seems to have a penchant for becoming involved with needy women only to abandon them for the next best thing once they've become too independent ("House vs. God," 2.19). Wilson's season one assertion "I love my wife" ("Fidelity," 1.07), seems to ring a bit false with House as he points out: "You certainly love saying it. I'm sorry. I know you love your wife. You loved all your wives. Probably still do. In fact, you probably love all the women you loved who weren't your wife."

In fact, the marriage to which House refers falls apart only a year later, but throughout season one and into the first part of season two, Wilson refers to the less than heavenly aspects of his marriage to Julie. We never actually meet her, but we do meet wife number two, Bonnie, in season three. Wilson's first marriage broke up just after he finished medical school and before he met House ("Birthmarks," 5.04).

We do meet the first ex–Mrs. Wilson, Sam Carr, towards the end of season six. After Wilson encounters her online, they begin dating ("Knight Fall," 6.18), and although House does his best to break-up the happy couple, they move in together, trying to make another go of it.

Wilson seems to have a history as a serial adulterer, and in "House Training" (3.20), second wife Bonnie explains how Wilson's attention is like a "silky trap." She points out to House that Wilson calibrates "his level of protectiveness for your individual needs." Appearing to be a "knight in shining armor," Wilson is always there "until he's not." Whether he grows resentful, as House suggests in "House vs. God," or simply grows bored after his wives are "healed," Wilson can't stay faithful. And perhaps that's why he stays close to House, who is, after all, the king of neediness.

In season four, however, Wilson seems to have met "the one" in Amber Volakis. Dubbed "Cutthroat Bitch" by House, Amber is cut from House's team of fellowship candidates. She and Wilson begin dating somewhere between "Games" (4.09), when Amber is dumped from House's team, and "Frozen" (4.11), when House discovers they've been seeing each other.

Amber is vastly different from the needy women Wilson has had in his life. She seeks to break his relationship cycle, refusing to be caught in the same trap as his wives.

When they try to buy a mattress in "Living the Dream" (4.14), Amber tells Wilson to buy the mattress he wants, but instead he buys the one she had chosen — simply to please her. Rather than make her feel loved and cared for, as Wilson had intended, the gesture frustrates and angers Amber. "I can take care of me. I need you to take care of you," she reprimands. With no intention to become the fourth ex–Mrs. James Wilson, she will not allow Wilson to repeat the behaviors of the past only to grow resentful and bored. She tears into him, saying that he can't always let her get away with winning.

At first, House doesn't understand why Wilson would be attracted to the aggressive, intrusive, and annoying Amber. But then he gets it. "You like that she's conniving. You like that she has no regard for consequences. You like that she can humiliate someone if it serves . . . Oh, my God. You're sleeping with me," he suddenly realizes.

When it becomes clear that Amber is there to stay, House (somewhat grudgingly) finally gives the couple his blessing — but not before some territorial game playing within their bizarre little love triangle. House and Amber fight over Wilson like a divorced couple haggling over weekends with their child ("No More Mr. Nice Guy," 4.13), but in the end, the perceptive House notices a profound difference in their status: Amber has usurped House's role as the most important person in Wilson's life. In "Wilson's Heart" (4.16), this point is made clear when Wilson asks House to risk his life to save Amber's. The expression on House's face as he agrees to undergo the dangerous procedure confirms it for him.

But his risk is to no avail; Amber is doomed to die from injuries sustained in a fatal bus crash after going to a bar to pick up an inebriated House. A random set of circumstances cause her death, but linking it back to House's phone call for a ride, Wilson finds it impossible to forgive House — or himself. He blames himself for exposing Amber to House, and House for being who he is.

### The Impact of Amber's Death: A Closer Look at "Dying Changes Everything"

"Obviously, House does not have another friend who's even comparable to Wilson. There's no replacing Wilson in House's life, and no replacing House in Wilson's. But the rift between them and the damage it causes are very real."

**— Eli Attie, September 2008 interview**

Wilson resigns his position at the beginning of season five ("Dying Changes Everything," 5.01), saying he needs a change and a fresh start in the face of Amber's death. House is terrified at the prospect and makes a desperate effort to get him to stay. But in the devastating final scene of the episode, Wilson severs their ties. House has finally and tragically pushed their relationship past the breaking point. Although Wilson has tried to blame House for the circumstances leading to Amber's death, he can't. It is as if Wilson can't blame House for Amber any more than one can blame a wild animal for biting. House is who he is; Wilson has concluded that House is simply too toxic. But the cut has to be clean and sharp as a scalpel's incision. And Wilson makes it sharp as he possibly can.

"You spread misery because you can't feel anything else," begins Wilson's litany of House's human failings. Had Wilson not been sucked into House's orbit, Amber would still be alive. She was on the bus — involved in the crash — because she answered House's call. Momentarily ignoring that House had risked his life to save Amber ("Wilson's Heart," 4.16), Wilson delivers the knockout punch. "We're not friends anymore, House. I'm not sure we ever were."

Watch House's entire universe come crashing down during Wilson's soft-spoken but harsh tirade. House says nothing in his defense. Doesn't argue with him; doesn't push back. He just stands there, not saying anything, not moving. Lost.

House doesn't want Wilson to hate him, and Wilson doesn't hate him. Wilson is telling him something else. Wilson is telling him that he no longer cares, that he's indifferent, that he's immune. The finality of Wilson's words suggests a marriage long-festering that finally breaks, leaving one of the partners beyond caring. For Wilson, that one last phone call pushes his friendship with House one phone call too far, finally breaking it.

Fortunately, this dire state of affairs doesn't last long, and Wilson returns after four episodes, realizing that for all his issues with him, he has fun with House and being in his "vortex of insanity." But throughout season five, there is a tension in their relationship. Wilson is more reserved and less willing to play House's games. On the other hand, he does manage to coach House on his relationship with Cuddy throughout the remaining season five episodes. Wilson continues to mourn Amber for months — living in her apartment, not even washing out her lipstick-stained coffee cup until late in the season.

## It's Not *All* About the Neediness

In the season five episode "Birthmarks" (5.04), Wilson returns to his friendship with House, not for House's neediness, but because of the fun and the challenge of their relationship (when it's not emotionally draining). It's what makes the relationship a delight to watch, and the chemistry between Hugh Laurie and Robert Sean Leonard makes it soar.

From the start of season one, there is playfulness between them, despite Wilson's occasional self-righteous preachiness and House's intermittent exploitative behavior. A chapter on Wilson would not be complete without a look at some of the most delightful moments of their unique relationship:

**"Damned If You Do" (1.05):** The bookend scenes framing this episode give us House and Wilson discussing Dante's circles of Hell. The episode's final scene shows a rare moment of kicking back and relaxing, as House and Wilson share a Christmas feast of Chinese food from cartons. This episode defines them as close friends who enjoy each other's company.

**"Poison" (1.08):** Wilson does a very public reading of a love poem written to House by an elderly clinic patient, whose syphilitic brain damage has caused her to fall head over heels for the much younger doctor. Wilson finds this amusing and is pleased with House's embarrassment when the poem is read aloud in the hospital lobby.

**"Love Hurts" (1.20):** As the extremely nervous — and very out of practice — House readies himself for a date with Cameron, Wilson coaches him from the sofa, giving him "panty-peeling" advice and offering condoms pre-treated with antibiotics! But he is also reassuring when House thinks the corsage he's bought for the occasion might be a bit lame. "I think she likes lame," Wilson reminds gently.

**"Skin Deep" (2.13):** Wilson puts House through an MRI after his leg pain suddenly worsens. House looks worried as the test begins, but Wilson relaxes him by pretending to be the booming voice of God coming over the MRI speakers. The moment takes House's mind off his anxiety for a moment — until Cuddy breaks into their fun.

**"Sex Kills" (2.14) through "Safe" (2.16):** After Wilson leaves his wife, who has cheated on him, he moves in with House. These episodes show a lot of great moments between the two, but it's in the final episode "Safe," that we really get the payoff. House plays a series of frat boy pranks, but they have a point — to get passive-aggressive Wilson to get some of his buried feelings out. Wilson finally does react, eventually pushing back by partially sawing through House's cane. It breaks while he's walking, but House appreciates it nonetheless.

**"All In" (2.17):** Every scene between them crackles in this episode framed within a hospital poker benefit. Trying to distract Wilson from concentrating on the game, House harasses him with references to barnacles and testicle size and sly digs about his separation. Then he effectively manipulates Wilson's game by phone in several amusing coded exchanges.

**"Top Secret" (3.16):** Wilson and House discuss the Village People in an early scene. It's a great moment between them, leaving House to wonder why Wilson knows so much about the group, which appeals particularly to gay men. It's not the only time that House teases Wilson about his sexuality.

**"Act Your Age" (3.19):** There is a playfulness between House and Wilson that had been missing during most of this tense season. House gives theater tickets to Wilson, who then takes Cuddy with him. During the rest of the episode, House sends Wilson flowers (from Cuddy), and screws with his mind in other ways that suggest Cuddy wants to deepen their relationship. Wilson isn't really fooled, but it makes for a very entertaining series of exchanges.

**"Alone" (4.01):** Wilson "kidnaps" House's guitar to blackmail him into hiring replacements for the recently departed Cameron, Chase, and Foreman. As cruel as it seems, there is such an evil glee in Wilson's guitar-napping scheme that it's hard to be angry with him, even though he damages a $12,000 instrument in the process.

**"97 Seconds" (4.03):** House declares his love for Wilson. (Okay, it's because Wilson is upping House's Vicodin dosage, but still!)

**"It's a Wonderful Lie" (4.10):** Wilson gets very silly when he's drunk. And here he is that at the Princeton-Plainsboro Teaching Hospital annual Christmas party, wearing a reindeer hat with movable antlers. House thinks this is ridiculous: "It's a moose on a Jew," he mocks. Wilson doesn't care; he just waggles the antlers at House, who can only roll his eyes — but it does lead to a House medical epiphany.

**"Birthmarks" (5.04):** After his dad's funeral, House provokes Wilson to hurl a liquor bottle through a stained glass window. Writer Doris Egan called it an iconic moment in the history of their relationship. House quipped, "Still not boring," referring to the first time they met many years earlier.

**"Lucky 13" (5.05):** Wilson is back and ready to prank House, who wonders what his friend has been up to in the four months since Amber's death. Wilson fakes House out, making him believe he is dating a hooker — and that he's shooting heroin — all because he wants to assure House that things are finally back to "normal."

"House Divided" (5.23): Wilson is drunk (again), this time losing his trousers at Chase's bachelor party. Although Wilson had insisted he wouldn't attend, House has arranged the party in Wilson's apartment to ensure his presence. After the party ends, Wilson gets arrested for wandering around pantless, trying to walk home from a party held in his own home. Good times!

"Epic Fail" (6.02): House and Wilson taking cooking classes together is a great riff on their relationship after the intensity of the previous episode ("Broken," 6.01). With House now sharing Wilson's apartment until he's ready to return home, they make quite a domestic couple. House's psychiatrist, Dr. Darryl Nolan, suggests to House that he join Wilson in something he enjoys. When House attends cooking class with his new roommate, he discovers a whole new hobby and takes to it with gusto.

"The Down Low" (6.12): Now moved in together, House and Wilson are fascinated by Nora, who resides in apartment 3B. Both pursue her, but she thinks they are a "couple" and has no romantic interest whatsoever. Each uses his own tactics to win her over, to great comedic effect.

# ▶ SMART, FUNNY, AND FULL OF SASS

DR. LISA CUDDY

"I think when an actor has been playing a character for long enough, the way you end up inhabiting the character has an effect on the way the stories unfold in the writers' minds. It would be a different Cuddy with a different path if someone else were playing her."

— **Lisa Edelstein, October 2008 interview**

A typical day in the life of Dean of Medicine Lisa Cuddy ("5 to 9," 6.14): up at five, a little power yoga, tend to baby Rachel, get dressed and out the door by 7:30 a.m. Power meetings, approve a radical procedure requested by House, fire-fight a hospital crisis, manage House, play power games with the "big boys" (whether the board or some corporate insurance carrier), manage House, defend herself against charges of favoritism (to House), followed by lunch (maybe with Wilson). Deal with personnel crises. Deal with House (or his staff). Home by 9 p.m. Such is a typical day in the life of Lisa Cuddy. Who knew?

*Fact:* Without Lisa Cuddy there would be no House. She hired the untamed diagnostic genius after four other hospitals fired him, when he was a "good doctor who couldn't get a job at a blood bank" ("Top Secret," 3.16). Noting the seemingly constant friction between them, Cameron asks Cuddy why she's never fired House. But to Cuddy, Cameron is asking the wrong question. The more relevant question is, "Why did I hire him?" ("Humpty Dumpty," 2.03).

Deciphering House and Cuddy's relationship is like plucking roses from a particularly thorny bush. Of course there's snark, and name-calling, but there's also affection and caring. We see it from the start — the very first episode — as they quote the "philosopher Jagger" to each other. He thrusts; she parries.

House and Cuddy have known each other for years. We know that Cuddy already knew him at the University of Michigan ("Humpty Dumpty," 2.03), although we will not learn more about those early interactions until season six ("Known Unknowns," 6.07). She understands his genius, and although he's always a risk to the hospital, she is also uniquely aware that House's diagnostic ability probably results in a lot of very grateful patients. His reputation brings recognition to the hospital and donors through the doors. Other doctors (including Wilson, occasionally) resent her favoritism and don't understand why she would bother. Few others would be willing to take such a risk; House is a lawsuit waiting to happen. But Cuddy smartly has set aside $50,000 per year specifically to deal with any legal matters that may arise ("DNR," 1.09).

Cuddy sees the hidden gem beneath House's defensive barriers. Where he projects laziness, she sees the dedication in his relentless pursuit of "the answer" — and another saved life. Where he projects indifference towards his patients, she sees a deeply buried humanity that emerges only when absolutely necessary. She knows that when a life is at stake, his patients could want for no better doctor ("Fetal Position," 3.17).

House sees Cuddy as an idealist, especially for putting her faith in him. He believes she sees the world as it is and as it might be, but is blind to the "gaping chasm that lies between." And he is certain that's why she hired him — when no one else would take the chance.

But her idealism extends beyond House. If you look closely around her office, you might notice photos of her taken with children from the third world, suggesting, as *House* production designer Jeremy Cassells noted in a *Blogcritics* interview (August 2009), a stint or two with a group like Doctors Without Borders.

"He came to her when he had his infarction," Lisa Edelstein said about the characters of House and Cuddy (*Blogcritics*, 2008. "After that, his anger and pain melted his career away, and it was Cuddy who believed in him enough to hire him, despite himself."

As House's doctor at the time of his infarction ("Three Stories," 1.21), it was Cuddy who recommended to House's significant other (Stacy) that they go ahead with the medical procedure that would eventually leave him disabled and bitter — and unemployable. Does her guilt over House's disability play a role in how she relates to him — and explain why she protects him, sometimes beyond all reason? Cuddy has gone to enormous lengths to protect "her hospital's biggest asset," even perjuring herself to prevent House going to jail for drug fraud ("Words and Deeds," 3.11).

While House believes idealism and guilt drive Cuddy's motives, he also believes she can lose her objectivity — too closely identifying with her patients. In "Fetal Position" (3.17), House treats Emma, a middle-aged woman, who, like Cuddy, is trying to have a baby using a sperm donor. When House diagnoses a fetal condition that is killing both mother and child, he wants Emma to abort the pregnancy, which will save her life. But Emma defiantly refuses; she insists on waiting, no matter the risk, although, as House explains, not aborting will likely lead to both their deaths.

Cuddy takes a very personal interest in the case. She identifies with Emma's situation and unyieldingly supports her position, much to House's chagrin. Eventually chasing House from the case, Cuddy tries to go it alone. But everyone, from the diagnostics team to Wilson, disagrees with her medical choices.

With no one on her side, Cuddy tries to conjure House's medical magic for herself. She goes into his office, tosses his big tennis ball, stares at his whiteboard — even tries to bounce ideas off Wilson, explaining the situation via elaborate metaphor. She tries to *be* House. It works. She comes up with an idea that might kill both mother and baby, but if it succeeds will save them both — and it does.

### Managing Dr. House

After training as an endrocrinologist, at the age of 32, Cuddy became the youngest dean of medicine in the United States ("Humpty Dumpty," 2.03); according to the series' canon, she is one of only four female deans in the country. It's a massive undertaking to run a teaching hospital, but it appears to be a challenge at which she's accomplished. Even House has acknowledged her skills in several episodes, including "Humpty Dumpty" (2.03), "Games" (4.09), "No More Mr. Nice Guy" (4.13), and "5 to 9" (6.14). But by far, her toughest mission is to manage Dr. Gregory House. We get a taste of that in "5 to 9," which takes us behind the scenes at Princeton-Plainsboro through Cuddy's point of view.

Not only does she have to approve (or disapprove) House's innovative, but usually dangerous diagnostic procedures, she also has to defend herself against charges by other doctors that she runs the hospital to satisfy House's whims, not the hospital's (and their) best interests. She brushes off such accusations as false (although House's colleagues probably have a good point), likely wondering why they don't see House as the asset she does.

Because he's always brilliant — even when being a jerk, a petulant brat, or strung out on drugs — she can never dismiss House entirely, even when part of her believes he's wrong. She must know the line between genius and recklessness very well, and with House it's not always easy to tell. Much to her dismay, she realizes in "Big Baby" (5.13) that she has the singular ability to know when to say no — and when to let him do what he thinks is best, even when every administrative bone in her body tells her it's a lawsuit in the making. By employing a doctor who has no fear of breaking medical rules to save a life, she has something that few other deans possess. But it's a double-edged sword. And he can go too far.

House is like a genie in a bottle, and in order to exploit his abilities, Cuddy needs to be able to control him. So she spends a lot of time managing her star player — the hospital's best doctor. And like a good poker player, she has learned when to hold — and when to fold.

Cuddy succeeds best at managing House when she is straightforward, appealing to his sense of right and wrong — and to their long-standing friendship. When she manipulates and threatens, she rarely gets far. As House has told her, she should never threaten him unless she's willing to follow through ("Lines in the Sand," 3.04). He relies on the limits she sets, which are usually flexible enough either to give him the range he needs or pull him back when necessary. As much as he struggles against the boundaries she sometimes imposes on his practice, he craves them. And he's disappointed when she doesn't do "her job" ("Living the Dream," 4.14).

Skilled at breaking down his defensive walls, Cuddy knows House well enough to understand that there is a heart and soul beneath the well-guarded persona. Her modus operandi is to ignore his deflections and cut right through to uncover what he's actually saying through his actions, expressions, or body language. Cuddy gets into House's personal space like no one else can, and effectively shatters his emotional barriers, if only temporarily. And when she does, she uncovers his truths.

By "Cane and Able" (3.02), the experimental pain treatment House has undergone between seasons two and three is quickly wearing off. Cuddy and Wilson have allowed House to believe that he failed in his first case back after surgery. After discovering the deception, Cameron informs them that House is losing his confidence — and they need to come clean to him. Cuddy wants to scan House's brain first and rule out a physical cause for the returning pain. But House is in no mood to talk about it when she visits.

At first, House deflects with the obligatory lewd remarks about her breasts and maternal ambitions. But Cuddy simply ignores him, refusing to take the bait. She moves closer until she's perched on his desk and deep within his personal space. She presses him about the leg, and when House realizes that the deflections aren't effective, he drops his defenses enough to let her see into him. Although he lies to her that he's fine, the worry in his eyes says he's not. But there is really nothing more she can do for him. He lets her in enough to see that he's lying — granting her (rather obliquely, but this is House were talking about) access.

Because so much of what House says to Cuddy is couched in leering, sexist innuendo, it may appear that House doesn't respect her as a doctor, administrator, or as a human being. But it's clear that he does. At the end of the sixth season episode "5 to 9," as Cuddy victoriously announces she has bested a corporate giant of an insurance company, his smile of pride is genuine and heartfelt. But the innuendo and sexual commentary are so much a part of their odd relationship, if he suddenly stopped, Cuddy would probably wonder if there's something wrong between them.

House thinks of Cuddy sexually, even, or perhaps especially, in his dreams and fantasies. But from what we have seen as viewers, he never considers her on purely sexual terms. In "House's Head" (4.15), Cuddy is both sexual object and brilliant diagnostic partner. As House fantasizes her performing an erotic pole dance, she enticingly strips while debating the patient's symptoms. Is she arousing him through her dancing or the intellectual debate — or both in equal measure? Ultimately, she must be his medical muse as House's intellect overrules his libido. The fantasy diagnosis continues without the sexual overtones.

But Cuddy is more than House's fantasy diagnostic partner. She is also his fantasy redeemer. In "Under My Skin" (5.23), House imagines Cuddy as the only one tough enough to help him kick his Vicodin habit, and it is she who sits by his side, bringing him ginger and holding his hand through the worst of his withdrawal symptoms. From within that fantasy, he also believes that even at his absolute worst, Cuddy is still sexually attracted to him, wanting him physically. And in his imagination, their sexual encounter after he detoxes from Vicodin is passionate and loving.

"I think House is well aware of what Cuddy made possible in his life. I think he has a deep trust in her, something a person like that has a hard time finding elsewhere."

— Lisa Edelstein, October 2008 interview

But their sexual attraction is not only reserved for fantasy. For several seasons House and Cuddy have been engaged in the sort of unconventional pas de deux that would be at home in a Victorian novel. They are antagonists, but nearly every confrontation is edged with a barely concealed sexual energy. Both might admit to tension between them — but never admit that any of it is sexual.

During the first four seasons, there was flat-out denial. Any move forward was strictly coincidental. "She's evil." "He's a moron." Yet as early as "Occam's Razor" (1.03), Wilson perceives the sparks between them, noting the famous thin line between love and hate. House quickly snaps back that "there is not a thin line between love and hate. There is, in fact, a Great Wall of China with armed sentries posted every 20 feet."

His fervent rebuttal to Wilson's simple curiosity suggests that were House not in perpetual denial, he would wonder the same thing. House is too curious about Cuddy for nothing to be there. It's not until season six ("Known Unknowns," 6.07) that we begin to understand their history, which goes back 25 years to a one-night sexual encounter when they were both students at the University of Michigan.

"Hugh and I are pretty much on the same page about the relationship. We've talked about it before, though I don't dig too deeply. There is something nicer about letting House be nearly as mysterious to me as he would be to Cuddy. That way, it's kind of exciting."

— Lisa Edelstein, October 2008 interview

Of course, House's jealousy speaks louder than anything he might say. Throughout the series' six seasons, whenever there has been even the hint that Cuddy might be interested in anyone else, House becomes territorial and jealous. When she goes on a blind date in season three ("Insensitive," 3.14), House seeks any reason possible to crash her fun. Like a hovering older brother, he quizzes her date, who — much to House's chagrin — might pose a real threat.

House interrupts them using his current medical case as pretext, until Cuddy finally puts an end to it by confronting him. Pushing into his personal space, she challenges him to express his feelings. Of course, her assertiveness terrifies House, and he immediately backs off, denying any interest at all. But Cuddy's date hasn't missed the intensity of the exchange, noting their obvious attraction even as they argue.

Several weeks later, House obsesses over his latest patient: a soldier who appears to him in a dream just moments before Cuddy hands him the case file. Cuddy appears in House's dreams as well, telling him he needs her and that she is always there. House finally realizes he had observed the soldier at a benefit, making out with Cuddy — ages ago. She is amused that the brief encounter has left such an impression, flattered (but unwilling to admit it) by House's apparent interest. She tells him to stop fantasizing about her and lusting from afar. As she sashays away coquettishly, she instructs him to get over her: "That ship sailed a long time ago." House's delighted smile at the mild rebuke suggests that he is unlikely to either "get over her" or stop fantasizing about her.

Several of the remaining third season episodes appear to set up a deeper exploration of the House-Cuddy relationship. Little things: a glance, a throwaway line that takes on greater significance if you're watching through that particular lens. (Admittedly, not everyone views the series through that lens.)

Although little time was available to explore their relationship in greater depth during the strike-shortened fourth season, House does assesses Cuddy's needs, wants, and desires as only he can in "No More Mr. Nice Guy" (4.13) — couched in a bogus performance review. "You're desperate to have someone jump on you and tell you they love you one grunted syllable at a time," House tells her. "What you want, you run away from. What you need, you don't have a clue."

### Enter Rachel

Cuddy's motherhood wish is finally granted in season five, and from House's point of view the prospective baby is the biggest interloper yet. But nothing on *House* is easy. Just as she's all set to adopt in "Joy" (5.06), Cuddy loses her chance when the birth mother changes her mind.

During the process, House has been obnoxious to Cuddy, badgering her for days about the tribulations of parenthood and belittling her preparedness.

When the adoption falls through, House visits her, his attitude transformed. No longer gloating and mocking, he tries to be supportive in the only way he knows how. He assures her that there will be other opportunities and that she will be a good mother after all (sure, now that prospective little interloper is no longer a threat).

> "Cuddy is in so much pain that in a way, they can see each other eye to eye for a moment. Absolute clarity . . ."
>
> — Lisa Edelstein, October 2008 interview

Furious, Cuddy wheels on him, stunning him with a visceral (albeit verbal) slap across the face. "Why do you always need to negate everything?" she demands. And with Cuddy deep into his personal space, he suddenly has no answers. Caught up in a moment of emotion, all House can think to do is embrace her, leading to a passionate kiss. It is full of meaning: regret, affection, passion, and desperation — maybe even some history between them — leaving them both shell-shocked in the aftermath. It awakens something in both of them.

In the episodes between "Joy" (5.06) and "Joy to the World" (5.11), their dance heats up. She flirts; he makes tentative moves to get closer to her. But House can't quite bring himself to actually knock on the door ("The Itch," 5.07). Instead, he makes a grand, romantic gesture by restoring her medical school desk, sending it to her anonymously from her mother's house. But Cuddy backs away when she sees him with another woman in what may or may not have been a compromising position ("Let Them Eat Cake," 5.10). Another missed opportunity?

Finally in "Joy to the World" (5.11), Cuddy gets her three season-long wish to become a mother when she rescues a baby girl, left for dead by a teenage mother. But motherhood does not come naturally to Dr. Lisa Cuddy. Having read "all the books" and done everything right, she is at a loss trying to bond with baby Rachel.

She feels like a failure. But in reality, she is not unlike many new mothers (biological or not) who — much to their surprise — don't form insta-bonds with their new babies. They miss the excitement of adult problem solving, of being at work with the big kids, and not tending to the every whim of a tiny being who does little but sleep and eat. Eventually, Cuddy does what she should have from the beginning; she hires a nanny.

With the new baby, Cuddy has less time to engage House in his elaborate game playing. She's not sure she wants him at Rachel's religious naming ceremony ("Unfaithful," 5.15). Her hesitance hurts House, who is too enmeshed within his own barriers to tell Cuddy how he really feels. So, while everyone else gathers to welcomes Rachel into the world, House sits alone at home pouring out his feelings onto the piano keys, playing an evocative melody evoking the warmth and joy of her moment — and the resignation and poignancy of his.

Rachel is Cuddy's priority, and although she fades into the background for much of the remaining season five episodes, she hovers there — a serious consideration in any future relationship. As much as she clearly cares for House, Cuddy has to think like a mom now. And House, never the most stable person, may not be the most reliable suitor for her at this stage of her life — something he realizes by "Known Unknowns" (6.07). Cuddy has by now become involved with Lucas Douglas, House's friend from early season five.

Although House tries to break them up at first, he backs off realizing that at this point, any efforts will be fruitless. He confesses drunkenly to Lucas in "Ignorance Is Bliss" (6.09) that he's in love with Cuddy. Although House later admits to Wilson he was playacting a drunk routine, there is probably at least some truth to House's confession. Lucas is probably good for Cuddy — and a much more stable relationship in which to nurture baby Rachel — at least that's what she tries to tell herself.

For much of the remainder of the season, Cuddy is barely there, much to the consternation of her (and Lisa Edelstein's) fans. What there is of a relationship with House is mostly chilly, although House (true to his character) essentially leaves Cuddy and Lucas in relative peace. But there is a reason for Cuddy's absence, only evident as season six draws to a close.

Far from secure in her feelings about Lucas, Cuddy cannot sever her deep romantic feelings for House. It makes sense that Cuddy would allow herself within House's orbit as little as possible, and when she does, it is only with full protective armor round her heart. She cannot let him in — full stop. But it is telling when we catch a glimpse of Cuddy's day in "5 to 9." It is House she turns to for advice during a grueling battle with an insurance provider. And, despite his hurt over Lucas and their more contentious relationship during this time, House supports and advises her constructively and seriously during her trying day.

But when Lucas proposes ("Help Me," 6.22), Cuddy accepts — until she witnesses both in word and deed a side of House she rarely sees. As she observes him at a disaster site caring for a patient in the direst circumstances — his dedication, passion, skill, and compassion — she realizes that as much as she would like to resist, she has no choice. For all his flaws, for all his baggage, she cannot help but be in love with him.

# ▶ AN OVERCAPACITY FOR CARING

DR. ALLISON CAMERON

"You married a man who was dying," notes Dr. Gregory House in the first season episode "Fidelity" (1.07) when trying to define Dr. Allison Cameron. House expends much energy over the series trying to understand what motivates the young immunologist (turned emergency room director in season four). "You can't be that good, and not be screwed up," he continues, "or you end up crying over centrifuges . . ." But Cameron has her own ideas about House. "Or you wind up hating people?" she astutely replies.

It's an interesting conversation, and one that characterizes the lens through which each sees the other during much of *House, M.D.*'s first three seasons. House has always viewed Cameron as someone who cares far too deeply about everyone who ventures within her orbit. She especially, according to House, gravitates towards "damaged" people: anyone emotionally or physically wounded.

When the series premiered in 2004, Morrison's character Cameron was a naive ingénue. In "Pilot" (1.01), the insecure young doctor wonders why House hired her for the prestigious fellowship, when Foreman went to a better school and had better grades than she managed.

"I hired you because you're pretty." House's overt sexism is completely inappropriate — until we understand just why he says it. And like a lot of what House says, the line is layered with meaning.

Cameron imagines House "wants to get into [her] pants," an understandable interpretation of House's statement. And how is she to know at this early point that little of what House says reflects what he actually means? Of course, House does think Cameron is *pretty*, but as he subsequently explains, it's not the primary reason why he hired her. No. House actually hired her not because she's like a good piece of art in the lobby, as he quips, but because her good looks would have been an automatic free pass into success without all the hard work required to become a top-notch doctor. But because she "worked [her] stunning little ass off," she intrigues him and can only be an asset to the team.

> "[Cameron] is a woman who had worked very hard to get to where she is. She is very smart and always at the top of her class. But she still hadn't had an opportunity to prove herself."
>
> **— Jennifer Morrison, March 2009 interview**

Working under someone as hostile and abrasive as House "brings out your insecurities rather than your confidence," according the Jennifer Morrison, who plays Cameron in the show. It's not exactly an easy environment for Cameron to overcome her vulnerabilities. As the only female on the diagnostics staff, Cameron has had to learn to be assertive, so over the years, she has grown from an ingénue to a capable, mature, and even tough doctor. Mid–season one, concerned that people dismiss too easily her because she's "pretty," Cameron begins to assert herself by trying to get a handle on "soft positional bargaining" (as House puts it in "Control," 1.14): "How to get to 'yes' in five easy steps." But Cameron's attempts to manipulate are too obvious, and it only leads to big-brotherly teasing from both Chase and Foreman.

In the very early episode "Occam's Razor" (1.03), Cameron's potential for power over the males in her environment is firmly established in one of the series' most unforgettable scenes. Seductively eating a big red apple, she has

Chase completely flummoxed as she earnestly explains the clinical realities of the sex act. Chase is so distracted, that he completely loses his composure and pours hot coffee all over himself, missing the cup completely!

Little ingénue Cameron knows exactly what she's doing, and it isn't seducing Chase, but showing she's able to play with the big boys in their testosterone-laden office. However, at this point in the series, she has a long way to go.

> "I think one of the fears going into a TV show [is that] you don't know how long the show's going to run, and if it does run for a long time, I wanted to make sure that the character would grow just like a normal person would over the years. Not just stay the same week after week."
>
> **— Jennifer Morrison, March 2009 interview**

### Cameron's First Husband

Cameron married her first husband knowing he was dying because she could not let him die alone. Losing him to cancer soon after marriage has shaped how she relates to people: whether they're patients or colleagues. This early, tragic experience seems to have ingrained in her reluctance — perhaps a fear — of relaying bad news to patients and their families. She doesn't believe that disclosing bad news will help the healing process for the family, or soften a later blow. She would rather give the family a day or a week more of hope and peace before the reality of a loved one's death becomes all too real.

House and Wilson know this is a liability because giving bad news — especially as often as they deal with dying patients — is part of the job. In "Maternity" (1.04), Cameron argues her point from experience: telling the parents their baby is likely to die will do nothing but cause them to lose hope. And hope is the one thing she can give them. But Wilson explains to her that it's only "false hope." She retorts that it's the only kind available to her at the moment. If the baby lives, then she's done no harm; if he dies, then it doesn't matter what she told them.

House tries to force the issue, insisting that Cameron relay the news of a baby's death to his parents, and "do her job." Like pulling a bandage from an old wound, she needs to deal with her fear. To House, it's the only way to move past it and move on.

From Wilson's perspective as an oncologist, telling patients and their families gives them time to emotionally prepare for the inevitable, but Cameron disagrees. Nothing can prepare you for the death of a loved one. No matter how prepared you think you are.

### Cameron's "Insane Moral Compass"

In the second season episode "Daddy's Boy" (2.05), House reveals a similarity between Cameron and his father, with whom he had a difficult relationship. As with his father, House perceives an "insane moral compass that won't let you lie to anybody about anything." There's an important distinction, though — unlike his father, hers is tempered by occasionally overzealous caring and protectiveness. But it is via Cameron's moral compass that we navigate the treacherous waters of House's idiosyncratic ethical code. It is her job to challenge House on his more dubious ethical choices, and House respects and values her opinion, whether he shows it or not.

A less admirable aspect of Cameron's moral sensibilities occasionally rears its head when someone has breached her bounds of right and wrong; her sense of justice may turn harshly judgmental. In "Acceptance" (2.01), Cameron calls House's death-row patient a "piece of garbage," furious that he would diagnose and treat him over her more-deserving and dying clinic patient, Cindy (who, House argues, is beyond his help).

And when House treats a champion cyclist in "Spin" (2.06) who has been using illegal performance enhancing methods, her instinct is to rat out the cyclist to the *New York Times* and spill the beans. It is only Wilson's intervention, when he intercepts the newspaper's phone message to her, that spares Cameron from violating patient confidentiality and committing a career-damaging ethical breech.

Later in season two, the team treats Anica after she suffers a seizure in an off-track betting joint ("Deception," 2.09). Cameron insists that Anica is faking to seek attention, suffering from Munchausen's syndrome, a mental illness.

Although she's right, her treatment of Anica borders on the abusive. "I'm not giving you what you want?" Cameron snipes. "Hopefully for you, whatever you injected yourself with won't wear off before you get the fun of a caring and concerned doctor cutting into your head." (Even if Anica has Munchausen's, it's not her fault; it's a mental illness.) But Cameron's moral hackles have been raised and her "diagnostic test" for Munchausen's (the antibiotic rifampin) masks the cause of Anica's symptoms. Cameron is also not above causing pain to patients who cross her moral line in the sand ("Sleeping Dogs Lie," 2.18; "Informed Consent," 3.03).

Cameron rightly turns her moral compass on Wilson and Cuddy when they lie to House about a case after he returns to work pain free at the start of season three. Concerned that House will feel invincible, they lead him to believe he's blown a diagnosis. Cameron warns them that he's become depressed and the leg pain, eliminated over the summer, is creeping back. She threatens to tell House the truth, if they don't ("Cane and Able," 3.02).

Cameron also takes on the role of House-protector later in season three during his ordeal fighting drug fraud charges. Wilson has made a deal with the vindictive Detective Michael Tritter to drop the drug charges if House enters drug rehab ("Merry Little Christmas," 3.10). Wilson believes he is doing the right thing for his friend. But Cameron questions his motives, noting that the deal has also meant the restoration of Wilson's impounded car and his DEA privileges (both casualties of the drug investigation). House's situation, on the other hand, has been made "much worse," she angrily maintains.

By the next episode, "Words and Deeds" (3.11), she learns that the increasingly desperate House (now completely denied access to Vicodin) has used Wilson's name to steal a bottle of oxycodone. She is equally judgmental of House, refusing him any words of comfort until she also learns he's apologized to Wilson.

> "She has this deep-rooted sense of wanting to do good for others, and House has given her a lot of crap over the years for that."
>
> **— Jennifer Morrison on her character, March 2009 interview**

"Informed Consent" (3.03) presents the greatest challenge to Cameron's sense of right and wrong to that point in the series. Their patient, researcher Ezra Powell, believing that his illness is terminal, has asked House to end his life. House won't agree until he's certain they've ruled out any treatable cause for Powell's symptoms. When Powell refuses to submit to any more tests, House "agrees" to inject him with a lethal dose of morphine. But instead, ignoring the patient's wishes, House refuses to give up on the patient and puts him in a coma so they can run more tests. During an earlier heated ethical debate about euthanasia, Cameron equivocates, unable to decide for herself what is right, but when House pulls his stunt, she refuses to participate in using Powell like a lab rat, running tests without his consent.

However, when she learns that Powell's groundbreaking research has included inducing irradiating babies without their parents' consent, her attitude towards Powell immediately changes. She becomes outraged at what he has done, especially after he suggests to her that informed consent would have interfered with his research. She takes delight in slicing off a piece of his skin for biopsy (with no anesthesia), without his consent, telling him that his informed consent interferes with their diagnosis. Powell applauds her assertiveness in finally taking a stand.

In the end, after House decrees Powell's condition terminal, Cameron euthanizes Powell, ultimately unwilling to see him suffer until his inevitable death. She has taken a stand, guided by her own morality and caring that trumped judgmentalism. Whether legal or not, to her, it is "the right thing to do," which earns her House's admiration and respect.

By the time Cameron resigns from House's team at the end of season three, she is tougher, more cynical, and more seasoned than when she first comes onto the team. As she says in "Ugly" (4.07), she is a "doctor who has learned to be a doctor from House." She has learned his unique way of looking at a case and understands the potential good that his methods can yield.

In the fifth season episode "Big Baby" (5.13) Cameron is put in the unique position of playing House's boss. Cuddy has taken time off to be with her new baby Rachel, and has put Cameron in charge, both of her administrative duties, and, more importantly, House.

> "Like in the episode with the agoraphobic patient and the morphine. She knows how to anticipate the way [House is] going to operate, which I think, in diagnosing, gives her a hand up [by extension]."
>
> — **Jennifer Morrison on her character, March 2009 interview**

Of course, House challenges Cameron from the start, and she believes she knows House well enough to beat him at his own game. She actually does — to an extent — getting House to go along with limitations on his procedures, and requiring that he closely supervise his staff during procedures. But she realizes that in the long run, she can never really say no to House (medically).

"I trained under House; he's in my head," she tells Cuddy, explaining why she cannot be House's boss. She will always understand House's motivations; as insane as his theories may be, they always have at least some merit.

In some many ways, even by the end of season five, Cameron is still defined by many of the same characteristics as at the series' start: intense caring, highly tuned morality, and — despite a stable relationship with Chase — the ghost of her dead husband. But she has also grown, learning to be much more assertive than when she first came under House's influence, and much less needy of House's approval and affection. Likewise her attraction for him is now seen through wiser eyes, although she still views him as someone with latent nobility that most others seem to miss.

Cameron is sorely tempted to take another life in season six when the team treats African dictator President Dibala ("The Tyrant," 6.04). But as tempted as she is, she cannot bring herself to make that sort of voluntary life and death decision, despite — or perhaps because of — the dictator's goading. And when Chase does what she had decided she could not, Cameron cannot forgive him.

In the end, Cameron leaves the circle of House's influence and the hospital, blaming him for creating a toxic environment in the Diagnostics Department. It is his influence, she believes, that has poisoned Chase's morality to the point that he is able to murder without regret. And it is more than she can take.

### House and Cameron

"[House] and Cameron both want the same thing, they just have a different way of going about it. I think she recognizes that similarity in him. It's kind of hidden inside and far away."

— Jennifer Morrison, March 2009 interview

Cameron's relationship with House has always been a complex mix of attraction to both his wounded spirit and the nobility she sees within him. Unlike House's other fellows and colleagues, old and new, she has always appeared to be able to see past his façade and into his humanity.

Her attraction begins to emerge after House takes her to a monster truck rally in "Sports Medicine" (1.12). Having been stood up by Wilson to attend the event, House diffidently approaches Cameron, suggesting she go with him. "Like a date?" she asks. "Except for the date part," House counters.

They seem to have a great time, and although we only glimpse them after the big event, they are joking with each other as they watch couples arm in arm all around them. Cameron has brought out House's usually buried playfulness as he grabs for her cotton candy and she teases him.

Her feelings for him growing, and perceiving that the feelings are mutual, Cameron is confused and unsure of where she stands with House. She finally asks him outright in "Control" (1.14). "Do you like me? I need to know," she pleads. But House's response is ambiguous: a simple "No." Is he responding to her question — or to whether he wants to answer it? House probably has no idea of whether he "likes" her at this point.

But he does seem to hang around her and solicit her advice as he comes under fire from the new board chairman Edward Vogler, who would like nothing better than to get rid of House — and his department. Initially ordered to cut his department by one fellow, House is unable to decide who to cut. He doesn't want to cut anybody, but he asks Foreman and then Cameron what they think ("Heavy," 1.16).

When Cameron suggests he cut no one and instead slice the salaries of all three fellows to make up the difference, House accuses her of seeing the world too idealistically, trying to find a solution where no one gets hurt. But then House proposes exactly what Cameron suggests — and one ups her, suggesting to Vogler he cut the salaries of all four them, including himself to minimize everyone's losses.

House comes back to her "Do you like me?" question in "Role Model" (1.17) — weeks after she first asks it. Under pressure to deliver a speech that would violate his personal ethics, House visits Cameron in the lab, now wondering why *she* "likes" *him*.

Does she admire his idiosyncratic ethical code (which prevents him from giving the speech)? Or does she see a "nice guy" beneath the surface, who would sacrifice his beliefs to "help" his subordinates? Perhaps a more important question for their relationship is why he cares what she thinks at all. The bewildered Cameron confronts him directly, asking why he wants to know. But direct questions seldom yield the desired answer from House — as we viewers are already aware. In any case, it scares him off and he leaves without either of them getting their answer.

In the final scene of "Role Model" (1.17), Cameron finally does express, beautifully, why she "likes" House. Because what he does — even skirting the rules or inflicting pain — is not to "help people," she explains, as she resigns from his staff, sacrificing herself. He does it "because it's right."

Once Vogler becomes history, House can reassemble the team, but Cameron is coy, disinterested in coming back with House's ambiguous feelings in the way. She strikes a bargain with him. She'll come back — if he'll go out with her on a date, which they have in "Love Hurts" (1.19).

Clearly attracted to his young fellow, House cannot conceive how she would find him at all appealing — except for the fact he's like some sort of stray, wounded puppy dog, just waiting to be healed by a good woman. House is endearingly awkward and nervous as he prepares for their date at Café Spiletto, even buying Cameron a corsage — slightly embarrassed that it's a "lame" gesture. Wilson, smiling at that sappiness of the gift, suggests that Cameron "likes lame."

Unfortunately, Cameron's attraction to House's woundedness, combined with her direct and aggressive pursuit, ultimately ruins her chances (if ever she had any to begin with). When House challenges her during dinner about her attraction to him, she hits him with a direct request: "I have one night . . . I want to know how you feel about me." She hasn't known him long enough to understand that House never approaches anything directly, preferring oblique and obscure metaphors rather than literal conversation. So he strikes back bluntly, deflecting anything he might actually feel for her, observing only that she views healing his spirit as her next "project."

She comes away from their dinner devastated and in tears, understanding that House is really too messed up to have a relationship. But by "Honeymoon" (1.21), seeing how he responds to Stacy, even after all they've been through, Cameron realizes that he is quite capable of love. Although House may be *attracted* to her, he does not *love* her — and probably cannot even if he wants to. The attraction is certainly mutual, and perhaps had they met at a different time or under different circumstances things might have worked out better.

### Cameron and Chase

"So here's this woman who keeps saying 'no' to him. Of course it sort of sucks him in more and more while working so closely together on the team. But I think it is interesting for us to show how often Cameron does have her guard up with Chase — and how hard it is for her to just be at ease in the relationship."

— **Jennifer Morrison on Chase and Cameron, March 2009 interview**

Starting out with a "friends with benefits" casual sex agreement mid–season three, their relationship evolves into a marriage by the end of season five. Even as Cameron and Chase become more deeply involved through seasons four and five, Cameron is still haunted by her husband, long ago deceased. In "The Itch" (5.07), we learn Cameron has still not made room in her apartment for Chase to stash his clothes for an overnight stay; he still feels like a stranger when he spends time with her there. But even after she clears out a drawer for him, she keeps part of herself off limits. Once they're engaged towards the end of season five, Cameron reveals she still has a vial of her dead husband's sperm. She'd had it frozen rather than getting rid of it because she couldn't bear the finality of her losing the last remaining vestige of him. Initially this proves too much for Chase to deal with and ironically, it is House who steers Cameron in the right direction, which helps Cameron put her relationship with Chase in perspective.

And in the midst of all the sadness at the end of season five — with Kutner's suicide still hanging in the air and House unable to distinguish fantasy from reality — Cameron and Chase marry in a beautiful and joyous ceremony intercut with House's journey towards his own uncertain future at Mayfield Psychiatric Hospital.

It is poignantly ironic that House, understanding Cameron's fears and advising her to take a chance on happiness, saves her relationship with Chase as his own possibility for happiness evaporates like a mirage in the desert.

But their happiness is fleeting after Chase takes it upon himself to deliver justice to the genocidal dictator in "The Tyrant" (6.04). At first unable to tell Cameron about it, Chase eventually confesses to her — and she forgives him because she assumes he only feels shame and remorse for his actions ("Teamwork," 6.08). When Cameron learns that he doesn't necessarily regret it, and that he considers killing dictator Dibala may have been the right thing to do, she immediately blames House for poisoning Chase. "You ruined him; he doesn't know right from wrong." Determined to get as far away as possible from Princeton-Plainsboro, she leaves Chase and her marriage behind.

Cameron's abrupt departure from Chase's life and the show left many fans upset and angry. Neither Chase nor the show's fans got closure on this significant story line in the series. In "Lockdown" (6.17), Cameron returns briefly to serve divorce papers on a hesitant Chase who wonders if Cameron ever really loved him. Being locked in an exam room for the duration of the episode allows the two characters to talk honestly about their relationship and bid a proper farewell (while leaving the possibility open for another return appearance by this much beloved character).

# ▶ HIS FATHER MADE A PHONE CALL

DR. ROBERT CHASE

A blond, pretty rich kid is probably the last person you would think House would hire for his elite team of fellows — unless we're talking about a blond, pretty female doctor. But Dr. Robert Chase was the first person hired for House's original team — hired, so House says, because "his father made a phone call" ("Pilot," 1.01). Chase, who has worked for House long enough to see him obsess over old cases ("All In," 2.18), is there for six months before Cameron joins the team. Both of them precede Foreman. "His father made a phone call" doesn't begin to explain why House hires Chase in the first place, or keeps him on after betrayals and mistakes — only to fire him with no apparent cause at the end of season three.

It's understandable why House would take a call from Chase's father, Rowan, a world-famous rheumatologist, who literally "wrote the book" on the subject ("Cursed," 1.13). Once onboard, Chase's specialty of critical care medicine is useful to House in his diagnostics practice. As an intensivist, Chase would understand both what to do in the operating room and how to deal with the critically ill patients who come under House's care. Given the way many of the show's scripts progress, at some point during the diagnostic process, House's patients always "almost die," so having an intensivist on the staff is a real plus.

While it's conceivable that House hires Chase on his father's recommendation alone, or even because of his medical specialty, House generally has more complex reasons for his actions, especially professional decisions. Does House see in Chase a son, like himself, being pushed by a demanding father, or a son trying to please a father who abandoned him? Does that make Chase damaged and therefore interesting to the chronically curious House?

### The Transformation and Redemption of Robert Chase

We learn early on that Chase was at one time, a seminarian, drawn to the priesthood. And it is easy to see Chase in the role of priest in episodes like "Forever" (2.22), as he serenely prays over an infant's body while performing its autopsy, and as he trades favorite parables with Sister Augustine, his patient in "Damned If You Do" (1.05). There is a strong suggestion in "Damned If You Do" that Chase's career in medicine was more to please famous-doctor Daddy than to follow his dream career path.

However, by the time we meet him, Chase is a lazy, spoiled rich boy, uninterested in medicine and much more interested in his social life — and what being a doctor can do to enhance it. Foreman pegs Chase early on as someone who really doesn't want to be there and who doesn't deserve to be on an elite team like House's.

From the beginning, House notices Chase's laziness and wastes no opportunity to goad the young doctor, attributing every idea Chase comes up with to Rowan or to some other, smarter doctor.

Chase will do almost anything to ensure his continued employment, and as a result, is a bit of an ass-kisser, generally liking to be on the side where the power resides. Until Edward Vogler comes on the scene as the new hospital board chairman in "Control" (1.14), Chase is House's obedient servant, very seldom disagreeing with him, and always quick to defend his actions — something that earns him Foreman's disdain.

But in "Control," Chase makes a critical mistake while performing a scan of the patient's leg. Distracted by a pretty resident, he MRIs the wrong leg. Because the leg in question is the right leg, and because they're looking for a clot — something about which House is extremely sensitive, given his history — House is furious. Chase, fearful for his job, seeks a way to cover himself against anything House may do to punish him.

Finding evidence that House has lied to the transplant committee to get the patient a heart when she was ineligible, Chase secretly informs Vogler, which sets up the first major confrontation between House and the new board chairman.

As the story arc progresses and Chase settles in as Vogler's snitch, House eventually asks Chase how it will be possible for the two of them to work together ("Role Model," 1.17) under these circumstances. Protected by the evil Vogler, Chase tells House that he has no choice in the matter. It's an arrogant statement, and eventually, Chase's betrayal earns him a reputation that lasts well into season three ("Finding Judas," 3.09).

Interestingly, although it would be completely justified, House doesn't fire Chase over the incident. House understands that Chase is "only trying to protect his job" ("Kids," 1.19). He doesn't like what has happened, but he won't hold it against Chase long-term. For a short while, House torments him, making him do grunt work while letting Foreman have all the diagnostic fun, but eventually, he lets it go.

Like most characters on *House*, Chase is far more complex than first meets the eye, something we discover only gradually over several seasons. As we've seen layers of Chase's personality get peeled away, he has emerged from a sycophantic brat to a bright, creative doctor struggling to "do the right thing."

By season two, we begin to perceive that there is a lot more to Chase than we thought in season one. Actor Jesse Spencer imbues his character with some depth, and we're led to wonder about what lurks beneath the bratty exterior. In "Autopsy" (2.02), House's dying, young cancer patient is attracted to the cute, blond Aussie doctor. The nine-year-old girl convinces a very reluctant Chase to give her what may turn out to be her only kiss. Although he endures a lot of teasing from all ports when House figures it out, the bond he forms with his young patient is undeniable, as we see when he gives her tickets to see a butterfly exhibit when she victoriously leaves the hospital.

Of all House's fellows, old and new, with the possible exception of the now-deceased Lawrence Kutner, Chase is the one who is most willing to cast aside assumptions and look at a problem from all directions. This sort of lateral thinking is evident in "Pilot" when House is frustrated that his patient needs proof of her final diagnosis, even when there is none to be had. Chase's fast, creative thinking saves the day — and the patient's life — when he recalls a low-tech method he had studied as a student. It works and the patient lives.

By the end of season three, Chase's creative thinking earns House's respect. But it also ultimately leads to a boot out of the Diagnostics Department when House feels he's ready to leave the nest and fly on his own.

### Family Matters

We learn in "Cursed" (1.13) that when Chase was young, his world-famous father abandoned him and his alcoholic mother. Chase was left with the task of taking care of his mother until she died when he was 15, which explains much of why Chase has little tolerance for patients whom he thinks may have drunk themselves into illness ("Socratic Method," 1.06).

When Chase's dad shows up unexpectedly in "Cursed," ostensibly to attend a systemic lupus erythematosus (SLE) conference, House is curious about why Chase seems so intent on avoiding his father, especially since he's made the trip all the way from Australia. Chase hides out anywhere but in the same room as Rowan, and resents it when House includes the rheumatologist in the differential diagnosis, even though the case falls within the elder Chase's specialty. The two men barely speak.

Of course this little personal drama piques House's insatiable curiosity. He refuses to stop prying until learning that Rowan is actually in the States to visit a famous cancer facility, stopping in Princeton to visit oncologist James Wilson. Rowan has stage 4 lung cancer — and only a few months to live. Rowan asks House to keep quiet about his condition and not tell Chase. House believes it's a mistake to keep him in the dark ("I'll have to be the one to watch his face as he reads your obit"), but House honors Rowan's request.

Chase and Rowan do part ways on better terms after Chase realizes that Rowan is still his father, no matter what he may have done. It's an awkward moment that gives way to genuine affection, made tragic by our knowledge (but not Chase's) that this may be the last time he sees his father.

When Chase's father succumbs, dying early in the second season ("The Mistake," 2.08), the shocked Chase is distracted by the news, and he neglects to ask a critical question of his patient. As a result, the patient dies.

Later in season two, we discover (although the other characters don't) that Chase's father has left him little or none of what we are led to believe was a substantial estate. Whatever comfortable lifestyle Chase may have envisioned for himself is no longer a possibility.

### Chase and Cameron

Chase has had a thing for Allison Cameron almost since the series' start ("Occam's Razor," 1.03). While Cameron holds forth on the topic of sex, Chase is clearly turned on by her provocative dissertation on the subject. He tells Foreman that "of course she's hot," but that he doesn't want to "jump her bones." At least not then. But by mid–season two, Cameron seduces him while she is stoned on crystal meth ("Hunting," 2.07). Both admit the sex was good, but neither wants a repeat performance. At least not then!

In season three ("Insensitive," 3.14), Cameron abruptly suggests that she and Chase commence a "friends with benefits" relationship: sex for convenience and pleasure with no strings attached. Chase is the perfect man for this, she presumes: in it for himself and easy sex. If he wants something more than that, she's not interested. The couple seems to have an insatiable appetite, and seek new and exciting places to have sex: the janitor's closet, while running a study in the sleep lab ("Top Secret," 3.16), and even in a patient's home ("Airborne," 3.18). But Chase does want more from their relationship than sex, even if Cameron doesn't, as he finds himself surprisingly in love. Who would have thought that *Chase* would be the one to get romantic and spoil things?

As a result, Cameron ends their relationship, not wanting to commit to anything deeper. But Chase is more of a romantic than he would seem, and he pursues Cameron through a series of rejections. Romantically (and humorously) courting her, he delegates Tuesdays to telling Cameron "I like you." In "Act Your Age" (3.19), he even gives her a large bouquet of flowers, not expecting anything more. "I know you like flowers," he explains simply. Cameron continues to reject Chase, insisting she wants nothing more than a superficial — no emotional attachment — relationship.

Eventually, Chase's devoted courtship pays off and by "Human Error" (3.24), when Chase is fired from House's service (in the en masse exodus at the end of season three), the chilly Cameron, seeing the wounded boy — or maybe the mature Chase — finally reconciles with him. They are together throughout season five, and after House's fellow Lawrence Kutner commits suicide, Chase proposes. After a few more bumps in the road, they finally marry in the season five finale.

The biggest bump for Chase comes at the beginning of season six. Confronted with a patient whose genocidal actions have led to, or will lead to, the deaths of thousands, Chase medically assassinates President Dibala, dictator of a small African nation. Although he is not found out, except by Foreman and later on House, his action haunts him. House advises him to seek professional help, but Chase turns towards his faith, seeking a priest instead, who then refuses him absolution. As the finality of his action eats away at him, it begins to affect his marriage to Cameron, and he finally confesses to her "Known Unknowns" (6.07).

Believing that House is more to blame than Chase, Cameron initially accepts that Chase killed Dibala. But Chase insists that the decision was his and that although it may have been the worst act he has ever committed, it may also have been the right thing to do. He explains that the moderates in Dibala's country are talking and peace is on the horizon there. But Cameron believes that House has poisoned Chase's mind irrevocably with his "damn the consequences" attitude. She leaves their marriage (and the hospital) at the end of "Teamwork" (6.08).

A guarded character, Chase doesn't want to discuss his feelings — or Cameron — with anyone. In "Ignorance Is Bliss" (6.09), Chase slugs House in the jaw primarily to get everyone in his circle to back off. But House protects Chase from disciplinary action by refusing to accuse him of the violent action.

As season six progresses, Chase begins to doubt whether Cameron ever really loved him, wondering if her attraction was merely physical. When Cameron returns briefly in "Lockdown" (6.17), Chase and Cameron make their peace, but do not reconcile.

# ▶ LIKE HOUSE, BUT NICER

DR. ERIC FOREMAN

Although he is the last to come onto House's original team of fellows, Dr. Eric Foreman is the most experienced — in so many ways. He is neurologist with a straight A record at Johns Hopkins School of Medicine. But his impressive academic accomplishments notwithstanding, House claims he hired Foreman because he wanted someone with "street smarts." Someone who could as easily have been a savvy, smart gangbanger as a doctor. On the verge of a gang-centered life along with his older brother Marcus, Foreman experienced the wrath and profound disappointment of his mother when he was 14 ("Moving the Chains," 6.13). Bailing Foreman and Marcus out of jail, her glare and words forestalled Eric's criminal future, according to Marcus. Eric vowed then and there never again to so disappoint their mother.

Foreman's relationship with his brother is contentious, and even when Marcus is out of jail and on parole in "Moving the Chains," Foreman refuses to grant him yet another chance. It is only through House's manipulation and interference that the brothers finally reconcile.

Somewhere within Foreman, House sees a kindred spirit, an outlier who overcame whatever he had to, but in the process emerged numb. He seems ever running to escape his past: a past that has less to do with his family, and more to do with his own self-image. Ever since we have known him, Foreman has always been tightly controlled, almost as if he is afraid to slip up, make a mistake, and give himself away as the juvenile delinquent he once was.

He seems to come from a stable working class family; his parents have been married a long time. His father a is a "God-fearing" Christian, who believes that everything good in his son's life is attributable to Jesus, and everything bad is attributable to the flawed human being that is Eric Foreman ("Euphoria, Part 2," 2.21). Foreman seems to have given up any ties to his past life, not having been home since he'd left for college years earlier. When his parents visit in season three ("House Training," 3.20), he has little interest in seeing them. But when he does spend time with them, his mother only fleetingly recognizes him; she has Alzheimer's disease. She dies sometime mid–season six, something that Foreman never mentions — to anyone, including girlfriend "13." "It's no one's business," he argues defensively after Marcus tells House — and House, naturally blurts it to the rest of the team ("Moving the Chains").

### Looking Out for Number 1

Having survived some tough odds, Foreman tends to look out for himself above anyone else. He is extremely ambitious and has set his sights on taking over House's department since he first had a taste of command in season two ("The Mistake," 2.08). He's "taken over the reins" several times, each time with the belief that he is as good and as smart, but nicer and more efficient. But it takes more than running a department to make a leader. We've seen him attempt it several times over the seasons, only to fall short each time.

The first time Foreman is in charge comes after a family sues Chase over a patient death ("The Mistake," 2.08). Part of the fallout is that House's practice is to be supervised by "another doctor." Cuddy appoints Foreman, who is the only one who hasn't realized it's all for show. There is no real power in his command because House's department isn't about who's running it, it's about the genius with the answers — the genius who saves lives.

House starts out mildly amused and revels in besieging his fellow-turned-supervisor with all manner of long-overdue administrative paperwork. But House quickly learns that Foreman takes this "boss" thing far more seriously than House does, and isn't amused for long.

When Foreman orders House to take a routine medical history on a patient, House goes straight to Cuddy, insisting to her that Foreman's mandate is "a formality to get past the suits in legal." Cuddy reminds House the hospital peer review board issued the decree. That makes it official, and he'll just have to live with Foreman supervising the diagnostics department for four weeks.

Foreman can barely contain his glee, ordering House to be in early for grand rounds and to wash his car. It's a stupid and arrogant slap in the face, especially in front of Cuddy, who reminds Foreman that being in charge means total responsibility for the department. Any screwups will be his, not House's. Foreman has it all figured out and plans a bloodless coup that would allow House to continue playing mad scientist and enable Cuddy to have a well-run department. But it is not to be.

In "Deception" (2.09), House effectively works around Foreman's supervision to treat a Munchausen's patient after Foreman forbids House from running any more tests on her. And when the patient's life is saved, Cuddy sides with House. Confronting Cuddy, Foreman argues that House is an anarchist, not some heroic rule breaker. He doesn't break bad rules to prove a point; he breaks them simply because he can. Foreman insists the patient should have rightly died; maintaining established medical standards is worth the death of a patient, something that both House, and the many patients whose lives he's saved would surely debate.

Cuddy disagrees with Foreman, understanding why she hired House the first place. She dismisses the notion that House is in the wrong. But Foreman feels exploited; Cuddy has undermined his interest in running the department to serve her own agenda in satisfying the disciplinary board.

In the following episode ("Failure to Communicate," 2.10), Foreman still runs the Diagnostics Department — nominally. House is out of town and Cuddy allows Foreman to take the case, knowing the real boss is only a phone call away. Despite Foreman's belief that he can manage the case on his own, the team is pretty lost without the mad scientist, whose force of personality via telephone manages to keep the controlled chaos working, despite his absence.

Foreman realizes that the burden of command isn't all it's cracked up to be when you've got all the responsibility as well. "What happened to the Foreman who always has an answer?" badgers Chase. "The guy who practically wears a sign saying, 'I'm as good as House, but I'm nicer.'" Foreman agrees that it's different, but the experience doesn't dampen Foreman's desire to eventually really run House's department. And he keeps trying, even into season six.

In the late season two episode "Sleeping Dogs Lie" (2.19), Foreman's self-interest takes another turn when he steals Cameron's idea for an academic paper. Cameron is upset that he would steal her paper in this way and is disappointed that their friendship means so little, especially after Foreman points out that they're "just colleagues." Any collegiality is purely coincidental; they are not friends. All's fair in love and academia.

By the next episodes, "Euphoria" (2.20, 2.21), Foreman ups the nastiness factor even further when he's infected by a highly contagious but unknown agent picked up in the patient's home. Concerned about the team's safety, House refuses to allow either Chase or Cameron to return to the contaminated apartment to further investigate. But Foreman, taking matters into his own hands, coldly makes Cameron a stakeholder by stabbing her with a potentially tainted needle, which motivates her to ignore House's order.

### A Welcome Thorn in House's Side

When Foreman comes back to work after nearly dying, he is content and agreeable — happy to be alive ("Forever," 2.22). His new, changed attitude drives House crazy, annoying and frustrating him. Every agreeable comment and every missed opportunity to challenge and disagree grates obviously on House.

You might assume that a doctor as arrogant as House would want to surround himself with fellows who hang on his every word as if made of gold. But he doesn't. Just as House challenges all of the fellows, Foreman included, he needs his team to challenge him — on everything. It's an integral part of House's process. And when that's gone, House misses it. House wants his old antagonistic Foreman back. And if he's not coming back, House says, he needs to replace him.

Foreman has a love-hate relationship with his boss. He views House as brilliant but reckless — the "best doctor I've ever worked with," Foreman tells his father ("Euphoria Part 2," 2.21). However, Foreman feels that House lacks humanity — and humility, *yet* when he has a chance to leave House's team early in the series ("DNR," 1.09), he doesn't take it.

That chance comes by way of Foreman's old mentor, Dr. Marty Hamilton, an easygoing California doctor who has been treating jazz trumpeter John Henry Giles for ALS (Lou Gehrig's disease) with an experimental protocol. In New York for a recording session, Giles suddenly has difficulty breathing. Hamilton refers him to Foreman to treat for pneumonia. But when House gets wind of the case, he wants in, setting himself into conflict with Foreman and Hamilton, who eventually arrives on the scene.

146

When Hamilton offers Foreman a partnership in his practice on the West Coast, Foreman is lured, not only by the perks of Hamilton's practice, but because he sees Hamilton as humble and forgiving — compassionate in ways House doesn't even pretend to be. While House violates the patient's do not resuscitate (DNR) order and insists on doing tests on Giles without his consent, Hamilton by contrast adheres to Giles' wishes, kindly willing to "pull the plug" on him, allowing him to die. House refuses to give up on the patient; Hamilton is satisfied to simply know he's done the best he can.

But Giles doesn't die after the Hamilton pulls the plug, and House goes back to the drawing board, continuing to press for an alternative diagnosis to ALS. Of course, House is right, and they treat him, freeing Giles from his wheelchair and a death sentence. Foreman eventually realizes (albeit temporarily) that had House not kept driving forward, criminal charges and ethics violations be damned, Giles would be dead. The case gives Foreman reason to ponder who is the better doctor and teacher. And in the end, Foreman stays on House's team to continue being a doctor trained in House's unique style.

He is drawn to House's manner of practicing medicine, even as he is repelled by it. But when Foreman really decides to leave House's practice ("Family," 3.21), it is because he fears that to be a doctor like House means to become like him as a person — all rationality untempered by humanity.

He looks for work elsewhere, grabbing a diagnostics position at New York's Mercy Hospital, where he tries to live up to his self-image of "as smart as House, but nicer." (It's fun to watch him snark at his team in excellent imitation of House and retract his words, forcing himself to speak kindly and patiently.)

But he breaks hospital protocol when he treats a patient without firm proof of a diagnosis, saving her life in the process. He is proud of his daring, and indeed the patient would have otherwise died. But his dean at Mercy doesn't see it quite the way Cuddy might have and he is fired for saving a life.

Returning to Princeton-Plainsboro only because no other hospital will touch him, he blames House. He asks for more money and other perks, which Cuddy refuses to grant. Feeling he has no choice (actually he does — he can return to neurology), he rejoins House's team as Cuddy's spy ("97 Seconds," 4.03). But by "Mirror Mirror" (4.05), Foreman realizes he is reasonably satisfied where he is — on House's team, as second in command — for the moment.

### Ready for Prime Time?

When Foreman resigns at the end of season three, House believes he's not ready yet to fly the nest and be out on his own. Foreman needs to accept responsibility for what he does — and to know when to trust his own instincts more than those above him in the pecking order. In "The Jerk" (3.23) House proves his point, keeping Foreman in the lab frustrated and running tests to prove House's original (and incorrect) theory even after they have a final diagnosis — and despite Foreman's insistence that they are on the wrong track. But rather than listen to his own counsel, he continues to do House's bidding. House argues that he's correct in his belief that Foreman's simply "not ready" to run his own diagnostics practice. He argues: "You could've defied me. But you didn't. Because you still trust my judgment more than your own." And in many ways, House is right.

A year and a half later ("Emancipation," 5.08), Foreman asks House's permission for time away from diagnostics to do clinical research. He argues that he can do both jobs; House summarily refuses. Brooding and angry, Foreman tries to go over House's head to Cuddy. She declines to insert herself into the dispute and overrule House, but she does allow Foreman take a separate case on the sly to show House he can do both jobs.

The diagnosis goes poorly and Foreman almost loses the patient. He seeks out Chase and Cameron for their advice, but they insist he admit that he's stumped and consult House. House refuses to get involved, reminding Foreman that he wanted a case on his own, and now he's got it — with all the concomitant responsibility. Foreman complains to Chase and Cameron that the patient might die, blaming House for playing games with his patient's life. But Chase reminds him that he can't blame House for refusing to interfere; the case is Foreman's responsibility — not House's.

Eventually Foreman is able to diagnose and cure the patient without House. His confidence bolstered, Foreman goes back to his boss, telling him — not asking — that he's going to work on clinical trials, like it or not. House responds with a simple "Okay," which baffles Foreman, who wonders what's different now. "You didn't ask. If you don't ask, there's no reason to say no," House explains. What Foreman doesn't know is that House has set up the entire thing, giving Foreman a much-needed shove out of the nest.

Not until now does Foreman really understand what House is seeking in him: someone who no longer asks, someone who no longer does only what he's told, gnashing his teeth and whining about it like a self-made martyr. House wants Foreman to trust his own instincts well enough to do what is right, whether or not someone in authority agrees with him. Although Foreman did that at Mercy and it got him fired, by now he should know that the same thing would not happen under House, who craves independent thinkers on his team.

## House's Fellows: Imprinting on the Daddy Doc

If you've ever watched a mother duck walk across the street or a field, or swim in a local pond, you might have noticed the small flock of ducklings trailing behind, trying to keep up, but always slightly behind mama duck. This is how baby ducks learn how to be adult ducks. It's called imprinting.

It's an image that comes to mind in nearly every *House, M.D.* episode as we watch of the fellows trailing behind their mentor, smaller, slower and always a step or two behind him: ducklings. Coined by fans noticing the similarity to actual ducks, the name has stuck, even on the official *House* fan site. (Even *House* creator David Shore has noted the term.)

It's possible to refer to both the new and old teams of diagnostic fellows by the term, and the newer fellows do seem to have learned the correct method for walk-and-talk differential diagnosis, but it just doesn't quite seem to fit them. Maybe Ducklings 2.0 would be more descriptive.

### The Love Doctor

There is a scene in the season one episode "Love Hurts" (1.20) in which Foreman advises House on an upcoming dinner date with Cameron — explaining how to brush her off. House sarcastically calls him "The Love Doctor." But in six seasons, we've seen Foreman involved only three times: first a dalliance with a pharmaceutical rep ("Sports Medicine," 1.12), then with a pediatric nurse, with whom he is involved for months before he breaks up with her when it gets too intimate ("Fools for Love," 3.05 through "Insensitive," 3.14), and finally in season five, Foreman falls for Dr. Remy Hadley, also known as "13," one of House's new team of fellows. Whether he's drawn to her by her troubles (she has Huntington's disease), her great beauty, or the fact she's bisexual — or something just clicks — they are together through much of season five and into season six.

As Foreman begins working on a clinical study to test a new Huntington's drug ("Last Resort," 5.09), he urges "13" to get into the trial. When he learns she is on a placebo in the "double-blind" study ("Painless," 5.12) his protectiveness takes over, and he wants to violate the study's protocol, by switching her to the real drug ("Big Baby," 5.13).

Everyone thinks it's a bad idea: a career-ending move, as he seeks advice from his colleagues. When Foreman finally asks House his opinion, he hears a typically rational explanation. But as Foreman is about to leave, House stops him cold. "Do you love her?" he asks. Because if he does, counsels House, "You do stupid things." Foreman follows House's counsel, and it ends disastrously. Hadley is angry when she finds out what Foreman has done without regard either to her feelings, the clinical trial itself, or his career — especially so early in their relationship. It's something she cannot quite handle.

But the relationship survives and by the end of season five Wilson notes that Foreman and "13" are "good together" as he and Foreman observe the bisexual "13" sip drinks from between a female stripper's breasts ("House Divided," 5.22). But no relationship on *House* stays happy for long. When Foreman becomes head of Diagnostics after House resigns at the beginning of season six ("Epic Fail," 6.03), he fires "13," unable to be both her boss and her lover. Stunned, "13" views the unilateral move as selfish and self-serving. Foreman loses her — and, shortly thereafter, the leadership of the department when House returns.

# ▶ THE ENIGMATIC, UNLUCKY 13

DR. REMY HADLEY

Remy Hadley, otherwise known as "13," begins her career at Princeton-Plainsboro Teaching Hospital rather inauspiciously when she neglects to watch a patient take his pills. It's a small error, made in the chaos of half a dozen doctors all trying to diagnose this lone patient at the same time. The patient dies, and although she bears some responsibility (House bears at least as much for creating the chaos in the first place), House doesn't fire her ("97 Seconds," 4.03).

Hadley has "enigmatic" practically written all over her from the time she first appears in "The Right Stuff" (4.02), and maybe that's why House hires her. She is smart and cynical, wary and aloof. But she possesses a wounded quality that gets to House in a way he probably can't quite define. It's not romantic, but he's clearly intrigued by her. Her medical specialty is diagnostic radiology, although there's been no reference to it on series.

She has been called "13" since her first appearance in "The Right Stuff" (4.02) when House assigned his fellowship candidates numbers rather than use their names. She refuses to give her real name to fellow fellowship candidate Henry, telling him she doesn't want to get invested. Unwilling to exchange names with anyone, the name just sticks.

She and fellowship candidate Amber Volakis do not get along well during the fellowship tryout. Amber, with her well-deserved nickname of "Cutthroat Bitch," takes on the quieter "13" no-holds-barred. In "Guardian Angels" (4.04), which aired just after "13" makes a mistake that costs a life, Amber sets out to shake her using the slightly spooky patient (who speaks with dead people) and several props, leading "13" to believe she is being tormented by the ghost of her dead patient. It is simply Amber having fun, trying to unnerve "13," and win at all costs.

Yet "13" prevails and becomes part of House's team; she is tough, secretive, and angry. But her dour personality covers her real fear: contracting Huntington's chorea, a devastating and fatal genetic disease, from which her mother died when she was a young girl. Goaded by House after he learns the possibility that she might have the genetic marker ("You Don't Want to Know," 4.08), she finally tests herself in "Wilson's Heart" (4.16), motivated by Amber's death and the tragic events of that episode.

Learning she has Huntington's and will likely die in 10 to 15 years, "13" embarks on a trip to the wild side during the early half of season five. But she also searches for meaning during what will likely be a much shortened life. She wants desperately to have an impact ("Dying Changes Everything," 5.01), but at the same time seems on a downward spiral that will likely remove her from that path.

We learn that "13" is bisexual and in "Lucky 13" (5.05), her self-destructive streak goes into high gear as she we learn that she has been cruising gay bars in search of one-night stands. Coming into work hungover, House saves her career by refusing to force her to have a drug test, but then fires her for her recklessness. His harsh wake-up call helps her only briefly as she allows herself to briefly connect with a patient (with whom she also happens to be sexually involved). But she quickly slips back into her downward spiral.

By "Last Resort" (5.09), "13" has fallen into a pattern where she values her own life very little. She has no interest in taking action to maintain motor function, which she knows will soon begin to deteriorate from the early effects of

Huntington's. She refuses to learn about a promising clinical study when Foreman suggests that she might be a candidate. But by the end of the episode, during which her life has been put in real peril, she decides to fight the disease and not be a passive bystander to her own demise. She decides to pursue the study.

Foreman has a thing for "13" that begins in "Lucky 13" (5.05), but their relationship intensifies as "13" participates in the Huntington's clinical trial. Foreman is a researcher on the trial, and as the study seems to be going well, they draw closer. But after they share a kiss ("Joy to the World," 5.11), "13" withdraws, unwilling to commit to a relationship given her limited future.

Thirteen's view of her future is tainted by her own experience with her mother, who died of the disease when she was a teenager. As she meets other, more advanced Huntington's patients, she recalls in flashback that she refused to say goodbye to her mother as she left home for a final time to be placed in a home to die. She sees her mother in her future. The other trial patients are too near a reminder to her of what lies ahead, and her first instinct is to draw back and not allow herself to open up to anyone.

Eventually, "13" and Foreman have an affair, which seems to progress nicely. Foreman seems unfazed by "13's" bisexuality and seems to revel in it, as they are tasked by House to hire a stripper for Chase's bachelor party before he and Cameron marry ("House Divided," 5.22). Wilson remarks how good they are together as she sips drinks from between a stripper's breasts.

As Foreman takes over House's practice at the beginning of season six, he cannot handle both supervising "13" and dating her. To keep their relationship viable, he fires her without discussing other options. Incensed about it, "13" resigns from the hospital and plans to travel to Thailand. Wilson tries to persuade her not to leave, suggesting that not only is her fellowship with House worth keeping, but House needs her equally, as she is one of the few in his orbit not able to be swept into his "vortex of insanity."

When House returns, he convinces "13" to rejoin his staff ("Teamwork," 6.08), and throughout season six, she seems to find her niche on the team and with her patients, even connecting with House, who at times seems unnerved by her ability to see into him — even when no one else can. But as the season draws to a close, her health seems to take a downward turn ("Help Me," 6.22).

# ▶ "SOME PEOPLE TAKE PILLS; I CHEAT"

DR. CHRISTOPHER TAUB

Taub's backstory is that he was a successful and wealthy plastic surgeon in private practice, until he was caught having an affair with one of his partner's daughters. Big no-no! Caught between his partners ratting on him to his wife or leaving the practice — with a non-compete agreement — Taub decided to leave plastic surgery to protect his marriage. But what brings him to House? It's an interesting question as Taub's quick disdain for his new boss places him in a power struggle he cannot win.

In "Ugly" (4.07), Taub defies House, undermining his authority with the patient Kenny and his family in ways that would get him fired by another physician. Taub sees treating Kenny, a teenager with a terribly disfigured face, as a way to distinguish himself. The team is being filmed for a documentary about the young man who is about to undergo a life-changing surgery. Taub sees the potential publicity as a way to get back into his career — and away from the unorthodox House. Defiantly and on camera, Taub attacks his boss as wrong and irresponsible, assuring boy's family that he can get House kicked off the case.

Taub is out of line, and House wants him gone. But Cuddy is reluctant to get rid of anyone while the cameras are rolling. So House digs into Taub's private life to uncover dirt on him. He discovers Taub's philandering background and the fact that he hushed up his affair by signing a non-compete agreement with his former partners.

House confronts Taub, but doesn't use it against him — at least not to fire him. And Taub's defiance ultimately wins him House's respect. House generally doesn't punish anyone for having the courage of their convictions if it's for the good of the patient. In this case, Taub thinks House is flat-out wrong, and does something to address it. And he risks losing his job to defy House; these are two things that usually win House's respect.

Taub seems to be intended as Foreman's replacement: someone who will not let House get away with anything. Not especially creative, afraid to take many risks outside his comfort zone, but not easily intimidated by House, Taub always has the potential for, being a good foil and a potentially difficult adversary. With his many more years experience, he's an even a bigger threat than Foreman. He is cynical, but his cynicism doesn't seem as ingrained as House's. Taub also seems more pragmatic than anyone else on House's team: willing to compromise to meet an end, whether it involves his own career or his personal life. His marriage works because he and his wife "don't do storybook." They live their lives with no illusions ("Adverse Events," 5.03).

We don't know much else about Taub's personal history, but in the episodes leading up to Kutner's suicide, there is much hinting that Taub and suicide are not strangers. It's never made explicit who in Taub's life has committed suicide, or whether it Taub himself has attempted it, but his attitude towards the senselessness of it strongly suggests something has happened. It's further reflected in how Taub initially reacts to news of Kutner's death.

Taub is more angry than sad in the aftermath, considering he and Kutner have gotten close over the year they have worked together. He is angry with Kutner, maybe angry with himself for not seeing the signs. Showing no effects at all during the episode, distancing himself from Foreman's and "13's" obvious grief, Taub shuts down emotionally. He throws himself into the case, unable to bring himself to even attend the funeral. But he finally breaks down, in the corridor outside House's office, allowing his grief to surface in the episode's final moments. His breakdown in the closing sequence of "Simple Explanation" signals something more profound in how Taub is processing the death of his colleague.

Taub is Jewish (don't let the decidedly non-Jewish given name "Christopher" fool you), but he's completely non-practicing. "I'm not going to become Hasidic; I'm not even going to become slightly more Reform," he assures Kutner in "Don't Ever Change" (4.12), explaining he'd have to go some distance to belong to even the most liberal of Jewish denominations. But Taub is certainly intrigued by the structure and matter-of-fact belief system of his deeply religious Jewish patient in the episode.

Through the middle episodes of season five, we see Taub struggle with his self-worth and his marriage — and how both are withstanding the blow taken to Taub's financial worth after leaving his plastic surgery practice. He feels trapped by House, but at the same time, he's invigorated and challenged by the type of medicine they practice in diagnostics. He wants more money; he hates House; but for the first time professionally, it matters to Taub what he is doing and why. This is the lure, and why, in the end, he can't leave ("Locked In," 5.18).

Interestingly, when Foreman briefly takes command of House's department at the beginning of season six, Taub resigns, telling Foreman that he signed on to work with and learn from House. With his non-compete agreement presumably expired, Taub goes back into private practice ("Epic Fail," 6.03).

But when House returns to his rightful place in "Teamwork" (6.08), he convinces Taub to return to diagnostics. In addition to lure of working for the most brilliant mind in diagnostics, Taub seems to miss the challenge and meaning he can obtain from helping the helpless that come across House's threshold. As a plastic surgeon, Taub has done a lot of cosmetic surgery to feed people's vanity. On House's team they're saving lives, and that's something Taub seems to have missed along the way during his more lucrative days as a plastic surgeon doing nose jobs and face-lifts.

We learn that at one point in his career, before financial success hit him, Taub worked with Doctors Without Borders. He was accomplished with a potentially brilliant career ahead of him. He confesses to Foreman that at one point he wanted to "be" House: a legendary genius of a doctor ("Lockdown," 6.17). But somewhere that short-circuited and he "settled" for a more ordinary life. Perhaps that's part of the lure for Taub in working for House.

# ▶ THE TRAGEDY OF LAWRENCE KUTNER

DR. LAWRENCE KUTNER

In many ways, Kutner might have been House's heir apparent. A creative thinker like House, but without his corrosive cynicism, Kutner seems even less risk-averse. In his first year on House's team, Kutner sets a patient on fire ("The Right Stuff," 4.02), and nearly electrocutes another patient, shocking him while wet ("Mirror Mirror," 4.05). His recklessness leaves him unafraid to take risks if it means saving the life of a patient.

As he puts together his new team in season four, House needs someone who can replace Cameron's optimism and Chase's creativity. In Kutner he has a bit of both. But late season in season five, Kutner commits suicide — an act with no warning, no note, and no reason. (Actually, Kal Penn who plays Kutner had plenty of reason — the politically active actor joined Obama's administration in the White House.)

Kutner's life has been framed by tragedy. His parents were shot in front of him in their store when he was six years old. Although he seems serenely accepting of it the few times he discusses the event with his colleagues, it is something that must have haunted him.

In "Joy to the World" (5.11), we learn Kutner was once a bully. He goes to apologize to his victim, and we are shocked, because "bully" is the last thing we think of when we observe the geeky, sci-fi teddy bear of a fellow. We are more prone to think of Kutner as a victim, bullied as an outsider. But as he stands in doorway of his victim's home, you have to wonder if that's how Kutner dealt with life as a child, by tearing people down before they could hurt him.

Somewhere along the line, he learned to internalize the anger and when we get to know him, of course, he is nothing like that. He's a "fanboy," and an Internet-surfing science fiction geek, who likes Dungeons & Dragons and *Star Trek* Classic. As House notes to Wilson in "Simple Explanation" (5.20), Kutner "had his passions," having searched eBay for months to find a particular piece of sci-fi memorabilia. To all, Kutner is just a very bright, slightly untamed sweetheart with a gift for medicine and pushing boundaries.

Without a note, without any apparent cause, the outgoing, creative Lawrence Kutner kills himself with a gunshot wound to the head. "Simple Explanation" asks the question "why?" Why would an apparently content, almost Zen-like character — gregarious and friendly, fun and with an almost childlike enthusiasm for medicine, especially as practiced by House — suddenly commit suicide? The answer is: there is no answer. There is no explanation. And, as "13" points out in the episode, 25 percent of suicides occur with no apparent reason, with no explanation, simple or otherwise.

Kutner's death happens not as a cliffhanger to the season (as Amber's did in season four), not even at the end of an episode in which we (the audience) get the clues that Kutner's colleagues cannot. It happens abruptly, without warning. And that's the point. It is the trigger pulled literally and metaphorically to explore not Kutner, but his survivors.

Many of us have had friends or colleagues who have ended their own lives, leaving us wondering what we might have done differently. What did we miss? Were there warning signs? Could we have helped? The senselessness of the act leaves the surviving circle of associates with nothing but questions, guilt, and anger. But no amount of soul-searching, wondering, or rationalizing can illuminate a reason or diagnose a cause.

And for the lovable Kutner to commit suicide was a shock, not only to the people at Princeton-Plainsboro Teaching Hospital, but to the series' millions of fans. The evidence poured out all over the Internet in chat rooms, in discussion forums, on blogs, and on Twitter. Fans were shocked, angry, upset. Even Fox put up a memorial site for fans to place their thoughts, although many fans felt that the move was cloying and rather silly.

Each of Kutner's colleagues searches for answers, though none are forthcoming. Taub, arguably the one closest to Kutner, is angry. In "Painless" it is suggested that Taub may have once attempted suicide earlier in his life. Having survived it, he believes that suicide is a coward's way out, and he has no sympathy for anyone who tries it.

Perhaps House is right to suggest that Kutner's early life — being abruptly transplanted from the familiar to the unfamiliar after his parents' murder — created a loner. Grateful to his adoptive family, the Kutners, he buried his pain deeply, so deeply that even he may not have even been aware of it most of the time. He became a man who hid from everyone, and became so good at hiding that no one had a clue about the pain he was in for so many years.

It's not the Kutners' fault; it's no one's fault. Each person in Kutner's circle — from his closest friend Taub to House — wonders if there was something they missed, something they might have done. Each person in Kutner's circle has a way of dealing with the loss, anger, and frustration of losing someone so senselessly.

# Guide to the Guide

This six-season episode guide requires a bit of explanation. The entries are part summary and part commentary. I've tried to highlight the best each episode has to offer, while keeping the entries a reasonable length. In-depth analyses of many episodes can be found at *Blogcritics Magazine* (Blogcritics.org) in my "Welcome to the End of the Thought Process" feature.

Introduced by an overview of the season's main character and narrative arcs, the guide summarizes each episode, followed by a series of episode highlights, intended to add meaning and enjoyment to your viewing (or re-viewing). Not intended as exhaustive or encyclopedic, I've tried to hit what I think are each episode's most memorable moments. Your mileage may vary, of course!

**Zebra of the Week:** Each week House and his team chase down the week's "zebra" — an unusual or rare medical condition. Here's where you'll find the patient's final diagnosis.

**Epiphany!:** House's (usually) "lightbulb moment." The final piece of the diagnostic puzzle falls into place.

**Iconic Moment in *House* History:** The episode's most memorable moment (or moments).

**Clinic Duty:** Did House treat someone in the clinic? Present in nearly every episode during seasons one through three, clinic duty went nearly AWOL by season four. Often providing comic relief during very intense episodes, it returned in season five, but not as regularly as in the first few years the series was on the air.

**Manipulative Wilson:** Wilson is one sneaky doctor, and is especially adept at out-maneuvering and manipulating his best friend, House — usually "for his own good." Sometimes he's in cahoots with Cuddy, sometimes he's solo, but here's where you'll find Wilson's efforts to get House "to change."

**A Fine Bromance:** "Bromance" refers to heterosexual male friends who are especially close. Most episodes include at least one "bromantic" moment (especially if you look hard enough).

**House Is a Jerk:** Irredeemable, bad, or obnoxious behavior by House. Yes, House is a jerk at least once an episode. Sometimes more than once, and sometimes so much so that he's rendered a completely unsympathetic . . . jerk.

**Judgmental Fellow Alert:** Anyone guilty of being judgmental in the episode — not necessarily one of House's diagnostics fellows, it can be any fellow (or female) in the main cast of characters.

**Patients Know Best:** House's patients love to pick him apart. Whether out of a sense of kinship, transference, or projection of their own ills on him, they're often right. House really hates it, but it makes for some of the series' best moments.

**Housian Ethics:** Ethical dilemmas, controversial medical decisions, and other questionable acts.

**Shipper Alert!:** What's afoot in this episode's relationship game, whether "Huddy" (House-Cuddy), "Hameron" (House-Cameron), or some other combination with or without House.

**Gross-out Warning:** If you feel a sudden urge to cover your eyes or look away, that's what this warning's for.

**Classic Rant:** One of House's vigorous oral dissertations about society or medicine. Or both.

**Metaphorically Speaking:** House often uses colorful metaphors to explain medicine — and even non-medical concepts. Some of the series' most memorable instances are highlighted.

**Did You Know?:** Trivial facts and points of interest, including self-referential bits.

**Pop Culture References:** Books, movies, television, music, celebrity culture. The series is filled with these references. It's impossible to list them all, but this section notes some of the major nods. Advance apologies for missing anything obvious (or subtle)!

**Lost in Translation:** House speaks several languages, from Latin to Hindu to Yiddish.

**Musical Notes:** Noteworthy underscoring, soundtrack tunes, musical interludes, and other things of a musical nature.

**Props Department:** Interesting new item on House's desk? New cane? Noteworthy prop appearances are listed here.

**Plot Hole:** Something that doesn't jibe with what we know about the series timeline and facts.

**World-Famous Doctor Moment:** References to House being a "world-famous" doctor.

**Casting Call:** Think you've seen that guest actor somewhere before? Here's where.

**House Doing "Doctor Stuff":** It's sometimes hard to remember that House is a skilled medical practitioner beneath the snark and the goofiness. These moments remind us that he is.

***House* Canon:** A new established fact in the series.

**Title Tale:** The episode title usually serves as a metaphor for the episode.

**Why It's a Classic:** Every episode of House is worth watching; many are worthy of multiple viewings. My appreciation of the series is always enchanced by re-watching an episode. But some episodes are simply "must sees" even if you don't plan to watch every episode. These episodes reveal important information about the characters, their medical and personal philosophies — or are just beautifully written. Classic *House* episodes are marked with an asterisk (*).

### Cast of Characters

If you are new to *House*, you may not yet be familiar with all the characters. You may know Chase as "that cute Australian guy," or Remy Hadley as the "bisexual female doctor," or Wilson as "House's friend, the oncologist." The *House* cast of characters isn't huge, but can be confusing — especially if you don't know the show well. But it's hard to watch the game without a scorecard. So without further ado, I present the "*House, M.D.* Cast of Characters."

*House and His Inner Circle*

**Dr. Gregory House (Hugh Laurie):** The main character usually known as "House," and occasionally as "Greg" — he's the one with the cane. House runs the hospital's Department of Diagnostic Medicine. He is a genius with the ability to make associative intellectual leaps using disparate bits of information to diagnose his patients. Long before we met him, House's significant other betrayed his trust, which is why he needs the cane. This book is about him and his world.

**Dr. James Wilson (Robert Sean Leonard):** House's best friend, the head of oncology. We often find Wilson and House trading zingers, and giving each other (usually unwanted) advice about life and love. After three failed marriages, Wilson finally finds the love of his life in Amber Volakis in season four.

**Dr. Lisa Cuddy (Lisa Edelstein):** Everyone's boss. Sassy, smart, and beautiful, she is the dean of medicine and hospital's chief administrator. Her toughest job is treading the line between giving House free rein and saying "no" to him, usually while ignoring his lewd remarks about her body.

*House's Fellows: Classic Version*

**Dr. Robert Chase (Jesse Spencer):** An Australian intensivist (specialist in critical care medicine). After House fires him (for no real reason) at the end of season three, he joins the surgical staff, only to come back onto House's team early in season six. He is the first of the three original fellows hired by House, and has evolved over six years from a spoiled and selfish rich kid into a creative, principled physician. However he may carry his principles too far sometimes.

**Dr. Allison Cameron (Jennifer Morrison):** Cameron begins the series as an immunologist, moving from the diagnostics team to the emergency room at the end of season three. She briefly rejoins House's staff at the start of season six. The ingénue of House's original team of fellows, she is defined by her strict moral code.

**Dr. Eric Foreman (Omar Epps):** Foreman is an African-American neurologist, constantly at odds with House. The last to join his team when the series first premiered, his default position is that House is wrong — and insane. At the same time, Foreman is afraid of becoming too much like his boss. He is generally considered House's second in command on the team, and has directed the department from time to time.

*House's Fellows 2.0*

**Dr. Christopher Taub (Peter Jacobson):** Taub is a plastic surgeon who gave up a lucrative plastic surgery practice after getting into ethical hot water with his former partners. Starting over with House, Taub tends to think of House as an out-of-control mad scientist. But he also knows that the work they do is more significant than liposuction and nose jobs. And he seems to respect House's genius and leadership in their pioneering work.

**Dr. Remy Hadley (Olivia Wilde):** More commonly known as "13," Hadley is a young, cynical internist. In the very early stages of Huntington's chorea, she lives life a bit on the wild side. A bisexual and occasionally self-destructive, she spends the beginning of season five picking up random women in bars and partying — even coming into work hungover or drunk. Learning to cope with Huntington's has sometimes been difficult for her, having witnessed the terrible toll the disease exacted from her mother when she was younger.

**Dr. Lawrence Kutner (Kal Penn):** A creative and out-of-the box physician, he shares House's view of medicine. He seems to be the calmest of souls with a childlike enthusiasm for all things geeky. But Kutner witnessed his own parents' murder when he was a six-year-old child, which clearly stayed with him all these years.

*Significant Guest Characters*

**Edward Vogler (Chi McBride):** Donating $100 million to the hospital earns him a spot as the hospital's board chairman. But his major-league money comes with major-league strings attached: total control. His immediate dislike for House sets Vogler on a mission to rid the hospital of him.

**House's Parents — Colonel John House (R. Lee Ermey) and Blythe House (Diane Baker):** Appearing for the first time in season two, it becomes quickly apparent that House has a troubled relationship with his father, John, a marine pilot. Although they seem nice enough when first we meet them, we eventually learn that House's father was (at least) emotionally abusive to his son. Blythe makes a second appearance in season five after John's death.

**Stacy Warner (Sela Ward):** Stacy was the love of House's life — years before we ever meet him. She first appears in "Three Stories" (1.21) appealing to House, asking him to treat her husband, Mark. In season two, she's hired by the hospital, putting her and House in close proximity once again.

**Detective Michael Tritter (David Morse):** House pisses off the wrong clinic patient early in season three. A vindictive cop with a chip on his shoulder about doctors, drugs — or both — Tritter pursues House full throttle, arresting him for possession and bringing him up on drug fraud charges.

**Amber Volakis (Anne Dudek):** A fellowship candidate in season four, she competes for a position on House's team, only to win the heart of his best friend, Wilson.

**Lucas Douglas (Michael Weston):** House hires the quirky private investigator at the beginning of season five to help him diagnose cases and spy on his friends and colleagues. He returns in season six with attentions focused on dean of medicine Lisa Cuddy.

# SEASON 1

**Patients Make Us Miserable**

The first season of any television series is going to be heavy on exposition, details, and reveals to bring viewers up to speed on the main characters and plotlines. Unlike later seasons, where one story line flows into the next, season one of *House* has the disadvantage of having been created in pieces, lending it a bit of a patchwork quality. The network initially ordered 10 episodes, and soon after ordered another three. The series became a surprise mini-hit mid season when *American Idol*'s fourth season premiered as the lead-in to *House*. As more people discovered the show, Fox ordered additional episodes in two more batches for a total of 22 episodes.

Although both Hugh Laurie and the producers seemed to nail the character House — and the tone of *House* — right from the pilot, the series only began to really find its footing in the second half of its inaugural season. By then, the show's star began to garner critical and popular attention for his nuanced, sensitive portrayal of the series' misanthropic, snarky, and very idiosyncratic main character, Dr. Gregory House.

Most of the season's first half is characterized by "stand-alone" episodes. You don't need prior knowledge of the series to jump in and understand what's going on. But by later in the season, there is more focus on the characters, and the stories begin to form a narrative arc that threads through the episodes — and leads naturally into season two and beyond.

Episodes marked with an asterisk (*) are those I consider *House* classics.

## * 1.01 "Pilot"

**Writer:** David Shore **Director:** Bryan Singer

**Patient of the Week:** Rebecca Adler (Robin Tunney)

"You can't always get what you want," goes the Rolling Stones classic. "But sometimes, you get what you need." In the series' first case, House treats Rebecca, a kindergarten teacher who collapses in front of her classroom speaking in gibberish. Wilson talks House into taking the case, claiming that the patient is his cousin. But as Rebecca gets sicker and sicker, she gets frustrated with House's trial and error approach. She ultimately refuses to submit to even one more test or treatment just as House thinks he's hit on the right diagnosis. She simply wants to go home and die with a "little dignity." But Chase saves the day with a low-tech idea.

Emerging from years of eluding patients (and the dean of medicine) has its costs for House, including making up for years of avoiding clinic duty. As House runs his tests, we begin to become familiar with the language of diagnostics — and House's sometimes unconventional modus operandi (including "breaking and entering"). As he sends his young fellows off to run tests and break into Rebecca's apartment in search of clues to the medical mystery, we also begin to get a picture of House, his team, and his friends.

**Zebra of the Week:** A dying tapeworm in the brain (cysticercosis).
**Epiphany!:** Foreman and Cameron break into Rebecca's apartment, where Foreman discovers ham in her refrigerator. Eating undercooked pork can lead to cysticercosis, a tapeworm infection. House makes the obscure connection between Rebecca's ham, her symptoms, and a dying tapeworm.
**Iconic Moment in *House* History:** After being run through House's diagnostic mill, Rebecca wants no more tests, although House is now certain it's a tapeworm infection. House visits Rebecca to convince her that he's right, but she's not buying. But, when she tells him she just wants to go home and die with dignity, House argues passionately about how we can only live with dignity — we cannot die with it.
**Clinic Duty:** There are several patients in this first episode, but the most humorous is a major hospital donor who has eaten *way* too many carrots and has turned orange. House deduces that his wife is having an affair because — had she been paying attention — she would have noticed her discolored husband.
**Manipulative Wilson:** Wilson manipulates House into taking the case, lying to him that Rebecca is his cousin.
**House Is a Jerk:** We learn that House has somehow discovered Foreman's past as a juvenile criminal, although the court records have been sealed. But not much obstructs House when he wants to invade someone's privacy.
**Shipper Alert!:** House tells Cameron he hired her because she's "pretty." But as with much House says, the real meaning lies beneath his words. Although Cameron could have taken it easy and lived off her looks alone, she took a more strenuous route, becoming a physician. And this is what really intrigues.
**Plot Hole:** House notes that Foreman's teenage criminal past involved breaking into people's homes at 16 years old. The season six episode "Moving the

Chains" (6.13) contradicts that assertion entirely.

**House Canon:** Wilson is Jewish. Foreman went to Johns Hopkins Medical School (which is also the alma mater of House and Lawrence Kutner, another of House's fellows).

**Casting Call:** Robin Tunney (Rebecca Adler) stars as Teresa Lisbon in *The Mentalist* (2008–present) and starred in the Fox series *Prison Break* as Veronica Donovan (2006–2007).

**Why It's a Classic:** This is where it all begins. This episode still stands as one of the series' best. All the elements that make this series great were there from the beginning: Wilson manipulating House to take on a patient (and lying to do it), House making a soul-to-soul connection with a patient, House and Cuddy bantering with all the wit and spark that characterizes their relationship. The humor is perfect, serving as a balance to the main story's intensity. We first hear House's axiom "Everybody lies," a simple phrase laden with many meanings revealed over the series' history.

## 1.02 "Paternity"

**Writer:** Lawrence Kaplow **Director:** Peter O'Fallon
**Patient of the Week:** Dan (Scott Mechlowicz)

House treats Dan, a teen suffering from night terrors who collapses on the field while playing lacrosse. House isn't interested in Dan's case until he learns that Dan suffers from night terrors — and he notices a myoclonic jerk in Dan's leg as he sits on the exam table. At first thinking he has multiple sclerosis, House changes his mind after Dan is found about to leap off the hospital's roof. The night terrors are actually a "confusional state," leading House towards diagnosing a brain infection.

A humorous side story unfolds when House guesses that Dan is adopted and everyone is interested in betting on Dan's paternity. As amusing as it is, Dan's paternity becomes the crucial missing piece of the diagnostic puzzle.

**Zebra of the Week:** Subacute sclerosing panencephalitis caused by a mutated measles virus lying dormant for years.

**Epiphany!:** House tests Dan's DNA without consent to resolve the bet, and discovers Dan is adopted — neither of his parents is biological. His biological mother may never have been vaccinated for measles. Although Dan had been, he may have acquired the virus before receiving his vaccination. House realizes that the symptoms point to a rare measles side effect.

**Iconic Moment in *House* History:** In the episode's final scene, House stands on the sidelines of a lacrosse field as he cheers on the players, holding his cane like a lacrosse stick. Suddenly the field is empty. House stands there alone thinking of days gone by when he was healthy and whole.

**Clinic Duty:** House lectures an "earth mother" who only feeds her infant "yummy mummy" (breast milk) and believes vaccines are a corporate scam. Playing with the baby's cute all-natural fiber frog, House coos to the baby sweetly about the natural immunity in "yummy mummy" while warning the mom about the much less cute "teeny, tiny baby coffins" that may be in store for her newborn once that immunity wears off. He also attends a litigious man who seems to make a habit of suing doctors.

**House Is a Jerk:** House swipes the parents' coffee cups to grab a DNA sample for the paternity bet while being condescendingly sweet to them.

**Housian Ethics:** House runs a DNA test on Dan without his parents' consent — for a bet.

**Shipper Alert!:** Cuddy and House share a delicious scene as she buys into the paternity bet. Then there is the follow-up scene, in which she forces him to pay for the expensive DNA test — with his winnings. Both scenes crackle with chemistry.

**Gross-out Warning:** While undergoing a sleep study, Dan suffers a night terror featuring mad scientist House, gleefully about to cut off Dan's big toe — without anesthesia. He also undergoes a treatment that requires sticking a needle in the eye, which is always cringe-inducing to watch.

**Pop Culture References:** House wonders if *General Hospital* is playing on a diagnostic monitor.

**Musical Notes:** Rickie Lee Jones' "Saturday Afternoons in 1963" during the episode's final scene provides a wonderful commentary on House's inner life.

**Props Department:** We see House's apartment for the first time as he answers the phone late at night. Notable are the grand piano and an ashtray with half-smoked cigars. This is also the first time we see House sucking on a red lollipop, something we will see him doing often over the years.

**House Canon:** House smokes cigars.

**Casting Call:** Scott Mechlowicz starred in the 2004 Dreamworks movie *Eurotrip*.

**Title Tale:** It's all about Dan's paternity.


## 1.03 "Occam's Razor"

**Writer:** David Shore **Director:** Bryan Singer
**Patient of the Week:** Brandon Merrell (Kevin Zegers)

Occam's razor, a basic principle of scientific investigation states that the simplest explanation is usually the correct one. House and the team diagnose twenty-something Brandon, who passed out during a night of intense sex. No single explanation seems to define his constellation of symptoms, which include abdominal pain, nausea, low blood pressure, and a fever, in addition to a cough (for which he's been taking a cough medicine).

In House's world, the simplest explanation is "somebody lied" or its corollary: someone screwed up. And as Brandon's symptoms worsen, House wonders if it isn't the cough medicine — which does nothing to cure Brandon's cough — causing all of his problems.

**Zebra of the Week:** Colchicine poisoning. The cough medicine is actually colchicine, a gout medicine: a mistake made when Brandon's prescription was originally filled.

**Epiphany!:** Believing Brandon's symptoms are caused by a cough medicine mix-up from nearly the start, House seems to be proven wrong after further investigation. But when Brandon develops two new symptoms in the exact order as colchicine poisoning would have, House realizes he should never doubt himself.

**Iconic Moment in *House* History:** House introduces himself to a roomful of clinic patients in an attempt to convince them to choose a different doctor: "My name is Dr. Gregory House. I am a *bored* [board] certified doctor in infectious diseases and nephrology . . ."

**A Fine Bromance:** House doubts himself after being (temporarily) proven wrong on his elegant colchicine/cough medicine diagnosis. Wilson visits his office to offer his support and encouragement.

**House Is a Jerk:** He tells a clinic patient that she is very bad at her job (as he deduces that she's gotten herself fired).

**Shipper Alert!:** Wilson asks House if he and Cuddy have a thing for each other, since they're always at each other's throats, suggesting that there is a "thin line between love and hate." House replies, "There is not a thin line between love and hate. There is, in fact, a Great Wall of China with armed sentries posted every 20 feet." **Shipper Alert #2:** There is a fantastically funny scene about sexual power between Cameron and Chase, foreshadowing the chemistry between them over the course of the series.

**Casting Call:** Alexis Thorpe, who plays Brandon's girlfriend, was a regular (Cassie DiMera) on *Days of Our Lives*, the long-running NBC soap opera, from 2002 to 2005. Brandon's mother is played by Faith Prince, a Tony Award–winning actress, having won best actress Tonys for *Guys and Dolls* (1992) and *Bells Are Ringing* (2001).

**House Canon:** House has board certifications in nephrology and in infectious diseases.

**Title Tale:** Occam's razor — House is right; the simplest explanation is the correct one.

## 1.04 "Maternity"

**Writer:** Peter Blake **Director:** Newton Thomas Sigel
**Patients of the Week:** Six sick infants

The team tries to diagnose six newborns that have become critically ill in the hospital maternity unit after House finds what appears to be a brewing epidemic. They race against the clock to identify the bacteria or virus — and determine the appropriate treatment.

As the situation becomes dire, House proposes testing two antibiotics on two of the sick babies, knowing that only one of the drugs will work. It's likely that one of the infants will die in the process, but there seems to be no alternative. Cuddy and the legal department are uncomfortable when House insists it must be done without trying to get the parents' informed consent. Ultimately, she leaves it in House's hands to do what he thinks is "best." House decides to run the trial, but it leads only indirectly to the ultimate diagnosis.

**Zebra of the Week:** Echo 11 enterovirus spread by a hospital volunteer with a cold. Echo 11 can cause aseptic meningitis and is extremely serious in infants. It is hard to diagnose because its symptoms often mimic other common viruses and bacterial infections.

**Epiphany!:** Testing the babies' blood, House notes the presence of several virus antibodies, which makes no sense until he suddenly realizes that infants share their mothers' immune systems. He only has half the picture and knows they can complete the puzzle by testing the mothers' blood as well.

**Iconic Moment in *House* History:** When House argues with Cuddy and the hospital attorney about the therapeutic trial, he uses cold rationality about sacrificing one baby for the many, knowing that only one of the antibiotics will work, and that one of babies will likely die. But House's cold demeanor is more than offset when we see him later in his office agonizing alone over the choice he must make. When one of the treated infants predictably dies, House chooses himself to perform the autopsy, sparing the exhausted and dispirited team from the grim task.

**Clinic Duty:** House diagnoses a dippy young woman with a parasite — one for whom she can eventually set up play dates: she's pregnant.

**Housian Ethics:** Is House's therapeutic trial ethical — or even legal? House argues that asking the parents' consent would be fruitless as they are unlikely to grant it. But if he can't run the trial, surely all six babies will die.

**Shipper Alert!:** House is curious about why Cameron has difficulty delivering bad news to the parents of one of the babies. He tries to her ask about it at the end of the case, but handles it badly.

**Classic Rant:** House lashes out at the medical establishment for overprescribing antibiotics, thereby creating antibiotic-resistant superbugs. **Lesser Rant:** Cuddy yells at a medical resident for failing to wear a tie clip, using his tie as a virtual petri dish in the midst of an epidemic.

**Casting Call:** Sam Trammel, who plays the father of one of the babies (Rob Hartig), is a series regular as Sam Merlotte on the HBO hit *True Blood*.

**Title Tale:** An obvious title choice, with most of the medical focus in the maternity ward — and with House's maternal clinic patient.


## 1.05 "Damned If You Do"

**Writer:** Sara B. Cooper **Director:** Greg Yaitanes

**Patient of the Week:** Sister Mary Augustine (Elizabeth Mitchell)

Sister Augustine, a nun, comes to the clinic with a supposedly simple rash. House treats her for contact dermatitis, but she's allergic to the antihistamine and goes into anaphylactic shock. When House injects her with epinephrine to counteract the anaphylaxis, however, she has a heart attack. Cuddy accuses him of grabbing the wrong syringe in his haste, and overdosing her on epinephrine. House insists he didn't make a dosing mistake and there's another cause to the nun's symptoms. But even he begins to wonder.

Realizing his original diagnosis of severe allergy was correct, House places Augustine in an allergy-free clean room, but she impossibly goes into anaphylaxis.

**Zebra of the Week:** As House says, "You know how it is with nuns: you take out their IUDs and they bounce right back." A copper IUD, the vestige of her wild, pre-convent past remained in place after she had become pregnant and tried to self-abort. Her job of washing the convent's new copper pots kicked her allergy into high gear, and she is fine after they remove the IUD. Her heart attack is caused by a combination of the correct epinephrine dosage and the stimulant-containing figwort tea, consumed religiously by all the nuns.

**Epiphany!:** Wilson wonders if Sister Augustine is allergic to God, which she insists she has "inside her." House orders a full body scan to find what he's looking for — a "copper cross" IUD.

**Iconic Moment in *House* History:** Bored doing paperwork ("condemned to acts of useless labor"), House and Wilson discuss Dante's circles of Hell, reprising the discussion at the episode's end.

**Clinic Duty:** House treats a department store Santa for inflammatory bowel syndrome using . . . wait for it . . . cigarettes!

**A Fine Bromance:** House and Wilson share a Christmas feast of camaraderie and Chinese food.

**House Is a Jerk:** He mocks the self-righteous infirmarian nun, asking her about her sins and wondering if she should enroll in the "Cath-Olympics."

**Judgmental Fellow Alert:** Chase confesses that he "hates nuns" when they learn they are treating a cloistered sister.

**Patients Know Best:** Augustine tells House that no one can be as angry with God *without* also believing, and as she pointedly notes, that includes self-described atheist House. Although she's not a patient, the convent's infirmarian notes that House hides his gifted intelligence behind a veil of sarcasm and humor, refusing to take anything seriously, to mask his vulnerability.

**Housian Ethics:** House orders the team to put Sister Augustine in a hyperbaric chamber to treat her against protocol. Foreman objects, ratting him out to Cuddy, and she pulls House off the case. House recollects reading the Hippocratic Oath once, noting to Foreman that he "wasn't impressed."

**Shipper Alert!:** Cameron gives House a Christmas gift. He seems slightly embarrassed by the gesture, especially when Chase intrudes on them. But when Cameron finds a gift on her chair at the end of the episode, her smile suggests that it's from House.

**Classic Rant:** House wonders about the existence of God in crack-addicted babies and domestic violence.

**Musical Notes:** House sits alone on Christmas at the piano in his apartment drinking whiskey. He serenades himself with a wistfully elegant "Silent Night" on his baby grand.

**Casting Call:** Elizabeth Mitchell starred as Dr. Juliet Burke on ABC's hit TV series *Lost* (2006–2010) and as FBI agent Erica Evans on *V* (2009–present).

***House* Canon:** Chase is a former seminarian; his mother has been dead for 10 years. Wilson has marital problems.

**Title Tale:** Dante's circles of Hell, religious themes, and Christmas.

## * 1.06 "Socratic Method"

**Writer:** John Mankiewicz **Director:** Peter Medak
**Patient of the Week:** Lucy Palmeiro (Stacy Edwards)

The Socratic method is "the best way of teaching anybody about anything," according to House. However, some scholars have speculated that Socrates was a schizophrenic, just like this week's patient, Lucy.

Lucy hears voices, landing at Princeton-Plainsboro after collapsing at the state unemployment offices. She has a blood clot in her leg, but House doesn't buy the pat explanation from the ER doctor that the clot results from a combination of schizophrenia and alcoholism. Lucy's teenage son, Lucas, has been caring for his mom, keeping careful notes on her medical care, and he insists that it's neither alcohol nor mental illness causing her symptoms.

Taking the case, House stuns his staff by strongly connecting with both Lucy and her son Luke. He reads to her, listens, and tries to understand what she says between her psychotic ravings. When it appears that Lucy has a tumor in her liver, House wants to operate, but the tumor is too large according to surgical guidelines. (When has a mere guideline ever stopped House?) By ignoring conventional wisdom, House realizes that Lucy's not schizophrenic after all, and suffers from a completely treatable condition.

**Zebra of the Week:** Wilson's disease, a genetic disorder, produces the psychiatric and neurologic symptoms as well as Lucy's liver problems.
**Epiphany!:** Someone has called social services to report that Lucy's minor son is essentially on his own, and House realizes it was Lucy, herself, who made the call in a moment of complete clarity. He believes that it's too sane an act of self-sacrifice for a schizoprhenic, and forges ahead to find an alternative explanation.
**Iconic Moment in *House* History:** House reads W. B. Yeats to Lucy from her poetry book. It's but one moment among numerous memorable scenes in this classic episode.
**Judgmental Fellow Alert:** Chase assumes Lucy's symptoms are all due to alcoholism. It's his personal experience talking; as we learn, his mother was an alcoholic.
**Housian Ethics:** When Wilson determines that Lucy's liver tumor is too large according to the surgical rules to operate, House uses ethanol to shrink it. Although Cuddy questions his actions after she finds out, she doesn't rat him out to the surgeon and allows House to complete the ruse — and get Lucy her needed surgery.
**Shipper Alert!:** Cameron notices House's birthday. House tries not to care.

**Shipper Alert #2:** Cuddy tracks House into the men's room; House is completely unfazed.

**Classic Rant:** When his interest in Lucy surprises Wilson, House rants about how poorly medicine has dealt with schizophrenia. He concludes with a long list of famous schizophrenics beginning with Socrates and ending with Pink Floyd's guitarist (Syd Barrett, although House never names him directly).

**Musical Notes:** Through his apartment window, we hear House playing a baroque piece on his piano, followed by a plaintive "Happy Birthday," as he ponders the case.

**Plot Hole:** The episode takes place in December and Cameron notes that it's House's birthday. But at the end of season two when House is hospitalized ("No Reason," 2.24), his hospital bracelet reveals his birthday as June 11, the same as Hugh Laurie's.

**Casting Call:** Stacy Edwards (Lucy) played Evan's mom in *Superbad* (2007).

***House* Canon:** House likes Reuben sandwiches; he dislikes pickles.

**Title Tale:** Socrates might have been a schizophrenic like Lucy — and House is a super-adherent of the Socratic method of teaching.

**Why It's a Classic:** The episode features an interesting case and patient along with some important character reveals about House — and Chase. For the first time, we see House involved with a patient right from the beginning, and it's rarely happened since. His obvious connection to Lucy and Luke stuns even his own team and Wilson. We witness a different side of him; House is caring, even compassionate — and willing to break the rules to help his patient.


## 1.07 "Fidelity"

**Writer:** Thomas L. Moran **Director:** Bryan Spicer
**Patient of the Week:** Elise Snow (Myndy Crist)

What causes Elise to sleep for days on end? The simple answer is African Sleeping Sickness. But Elise has never been to Africa. Concerned about her extreme lethargy, Elise's husband brings her to House for diagnosis. As always, House believes the answer ultimately leads back to someone's lie. The team considers all possible alternatives, coming up empty as Elise's condition worsens and she slips into a coma.

House speculates that either Elise or her husband has had an affair with someone who's traveled to Africa, through which Elise might have been exposed to the disease, but neither admits to an affair. Finally, House asks the husband to consider the remote possibility that the now-comatose Elise might have been unfaithful — and allow them to do a dangerous, but effective treatment. If it works — which it does — it proves that Elise has been unfaithful. Elise's life is saved, but her husband walks out, unable to forgive his wife for her infidelity.

**Zebra of the Week:** African sleeping sickness, a parasitic disease that causes extreme lethargy — hence the name.

**Epiphany!:** There are no other possible explanations, and her symptoms are classic. It's an obvious answer obscured when she and her husband insist they've been completely faithful. House first comes upon the idea while treating a well-endowed clinic patient.

**Iconic Moment in *House* History:** Still upset with Elise's husband, Cameron seeks refuge in the lab calibrating a centrifuge. House walks in on her, noting her tears, and they discuss her first marriage to a man dying of cancer — and how being good and idealistic can leave you damaged.

**Clinic Duty:** House shares his voluptuous (and artificially enhanced) clinic patient with an equally lecherous Wilson.

**Judgmental Fellow:** Cameron judges Elise's husband harshly, telling him she hates him for leaving his wife without a second chance.

**Gross-out Warning:** We observe Elise's point of view as she hallucinates bugs bursting from her skin and scratches her arm. Ick.

**Lost in Translation:** House tells the fellows that he'd read an article in a Portuguese medical journal.

**Casting Call:** Australian actor Dominic Purcell (Elise's husband) starred as Lincoln Burrows on Fox's *Prison Break* (2005–2009).

**Title Tale:** Obviously, this is a tale of infidelity and its consequences.


## 1.08 "Poison"

**Writer:** Matt Witten **Director:** Guy Ferland
**Patient of the Week:** Matt Davis (John Patrick Amedori)

A high school boy collapses during a calculus test. House believes it's due to pesticide poisoning, but the very protective and highly skeptical mom insists her son has never been exposed. When another teenager from the same high school is also admitted with the same symptoms, it reinforces House's theory.

The mom refuses her consent until the Centers for Disease Control (CDC) confirms House's diagnosis. This is also the first time comparisons are drawn between Foreman and House, noting their similarities, down to identical running shoes.

**Zebra of the Week:** Organophosphate pesticide poisoning.

**Epiphany!:** Two sick teenagers are eventually brought into the hospital. Their only commonality is their new, but made-to-look-old jeans, purchased from the back of a truck contaminated with the pesticide. The pesticide is absorbed from the fabric, through the skin and into the bloodstream.

**Iconic Moment in *House* History:** Georgia writes love poetry to House, whom she thinks resembles Ashton Kutcher. Wilson intercepts Georgia's love poem and reads it loudly in the clinic waiting room, much to House's embarrassment.

**Clinic Duty:** The episode features one of the series' best clinic patients, the elderly Georgia, who develops a syphilis-induced crush on House.

**House Is a Jerk:** House is particularly smug with the mom, and Foreman's attitude isn't any better. Although House usually believes he's correct about every diagnosis, he's rarely this aggressively condescending. He mocks her repeatedly for failing to implicitly trust him.

**Casting Call:** John Patrick Amendori (Matt) was in the *Butterfly Effect* (2004), playing the main character, Evan (Ashton Kutcher), as a boy. Maybe House should have introduced Georgia to Matt.

**Title tale:** The teenage patients are being poisoned.


## * 1.09 "DNR"

**Writer:** David Foster **Director:** Fred Keller

**Patient of the Week:** John Henry Giles (Harry J. Lennix)

Is it ever permissible to violate a "do not resuscitate" (DNR) order? That is but one ethical dilemma of this brilliant episode — one of the series' best. The patient, John Henry Giles, a world-class jazz trumpeter, collapses unable to breathe at a New York recording session. Referred by Foreman's old mentor, Marty Hamilton, Giles has ALS (Lou Gehrig's disease). He is admitted to the hospital, but as Foreman's — not House's — patient.

House, a big fan of Giles' music, wants in on the case. Knowing ALS is a death sentence, House plans to investigate other possibilities, but Foreman has been instructed by Hamilton to simply treat Giles' pneumonia. Is House onto something, or is this just wishful thinking? Giles has a DNR order, but when he stops breathing, House revives him and is charged with assault. But even that doesn't stop House from continuing his pursuit of a diagnosis less dire than ALS.

**Zebra of the Week:** An arteriovenous malformation (AVM) in Giles' spine. An AVM is an abnormal connection between veins and arteries causing a tangled mass of blood vessels. The AVM is concealed by swelling in Giles' spine, and only revealed after House treats him with steroids.

**Epiphany!:** The AVM is discovered by the team after House requests another scan of Giles' spine, proving Dr. Marty wrong and giving Giles a new lease on life.

**Iconic Moment in *House* History:** While Hamilton is at Princeton-Plainsboro he offers Foreman a partnership in his Los Angeles practice. As Foreman ponders whether to accept his old mentor's job offer, he and House argue the difference between Marty's laid-back conventional approach and House's.

**A Fine Bromance:** Wilson attends court to support House when he is charged with assault for intubating Giles against his wishes.

**Judgmental Fellow Alert:** Foreman harshly judges House throughout the episode as arrogant, indifferent, and unethical, but in the end decides to stay with House, rather than return to his old mentor in a cushier position.

**Patients Know Best:** Giles immediately sizes up his doctor, noting that he's not married and obsessed. Seeing a kindred spirit in the gifted, lonely House, Giles notes that they both have "one thing." But when that gift is gone, "it's over."

**Housian Ethics:** House violates Giles' DNR, intubating him after he stops breathing. House is charged with assault, but does he have a point? The breathing issue was a reaction to medicine that House ordered, and from this vantage, he is only reversing the reaction he caused. It has nothing to do with Giles' underlying illness — or the reason he signed the DNR.

**Pop Culture References:** Wilson says that House has a "Rubik's complex" referring to the 1980s puzzle craze.

**Casting Call:** Harry Lennix (John Henry Giles) starred as Boyd in Joss Whedon's (*Buffy the Vampire Slayer*) Fox science fiction series *Dollhouse* (2009–2010). Pop singer Brandy plays herself in the teaser, which takes place at a recording session.

**Why It's a Classic:** "DNR" synthesizes all the elements that make *House* unique and wonderful: the series' take on medical ethics, the conflict between House and his colleagues, plus a glimpse at what really makes House tick. The episode ends on a poignant note as Giles, now healed due to House's persistence, presents him with a priceless gift — his beloved trumpet. The gesture deeply moves the usually unflappable House.

## An Odd Sort of Humility: A Closer Look at "DNR"

As Foreman suggests in "DNR" (1.09), does House lack humility? Foreman (and we) get an up close opportunity to compare a good, but mainstream physician to House. Dr. Marty Hamilton (Foreman's old mentor) is called in from California to pull the plug on his ALS (Lou Gehrig's disease) patient, the jazz trumpeter John Henry Giles.

Hamilton and House are as different as two doctors can be. Hamilton's casual, easy affability contrasts starkly to House's dark, brooding intensity. Hamilton is humble, self-deprecating, and a team player. Foreman is tempted when Hamilton offers him a partnership in his practice on the West Coast. But House wonders if Foreman sees in Hamilton "genuine humility" (with its accompanying self-doubt and introspection) or an "aw shucks" humility (more a self-deprecating politeness).

Their argument elaborates on the stark difference between Hamilton as an avatar for mainstream medicine and our antihero. We get some insight into how much medicine really means to House, not simply as a puzzle to amuse and forestall boredom, but as near-sacred calling. "He believes you do the best you can, and what will be, will be," he explains to Foreman. But House believes that doctors can make an impact, noting why he never gives up long after doctors like Hamilton have closed the case file.

As viewers, we often get to observe what House's colleagues do not. While working a case, he is tireless, often going late into the night, driven by his passion and dedication. He operates from a position that he will be able to get at the diagnosis eventually; that he will "be right." But the process he uses to get to "right" is self-critical and hyperobjective. It's not arrogance when House readily discards his own theory for someone else's better idea — quite the opposite.

House argues that Hamilton "sleeps better at night" and wonders how that's possible with a dying patient in the balance. How is it humble to turn off the life support of a patient — giving in to the seemingly inevitable — when there are still alternative diagnoses to be explored? Hamilton is satisfied in knowing he's "doing the right thing." House is never satisfied until the final puzzle piece fits. It's no wonder that after really comparing Dr. Marty Hamilton and Dr. Gregory House, Foreman rejects Hamilton's offer to join his practice as a partner.

## 1.10 "Histories"

**Writer:** Joel Thompson **Director:** Daniel Attias

**Patient of the Week:** Victoria (Leslie Hope)

An unidentified homeless woman suffers a seizure at a rave while she seeks someone named James. Wilson asks Foreman to examine her for neurological problems, but Foreman, who believes she's faking, wants nothing to do with her and plans on sending her back out on the streets. Wilson appeals to House, who takes the case despite Foreman's protests. During the episode, Foreman begins to understand and sympathize with her, and we learn why Wilson is so interested in the case. They go together to unlock Victoria's past: she lost both her husband and young son in a car crash she survived. They are unable to save her, but Foreman helps her die in peace.

**Zebra of the Week:** Rabies from bats that share Victoria's cardboard box of a home.

**Epiphany!:** Victoria escapes from the hospital and is tasered by a police officer. But she barely feels the jolt. To House, it suggests localized numbness. Combined with her other symptoms, it adds up to rabies.

**Iconic Moment in *House* History:** Victoria has a moment of redemption when a chastened Foreman helps her win absolution on her deathbed.

**A Fine Bromance:** Curious about why Wilson is so passionate about this particular case, House follows him out to a deserted street corner in a Princeton slum. It is the last place Wilson saw his presumed-homeless brother nine years earlier. They sit in silence as the episode fades to credits.

**House Is a Jerk:** He snoops into Wilson's private personnel files to find out why he's so interested in the case.

**Judgmental Fellow Alert:** Foreman wants to kick the homeless Victoria out of the hospital, assuming she's faking it to find a place to sleep.

**Housian Ethics:** What good is compassion when it's doled out only to the "deserving"? As in other episodes like "Socratic Method" (1.06) and "Acceptance" (2.01), we see House's ability to ignore a patient's past and consider only his or her medical best interest. It doesn't matter to him whether the patient is a homeless drug addict or a death row inmate, they still deserve treatment. Foreman would have disdainfully thrown this week's patient to the curb.

**Casting Call:** Leslie Hope (Victoria) played Jack Bauer's wife in the first season of *24* (2001–2002) on Fox.

***House* Canon:** Wilson has two brothers, only one of whom House has met to this point in the series.

**Title Tale:** It's impossible to judge people without knowing their history. When they visit the apartment shown in Victoria's comic drawings, Foreman and Wilson discover a very different person than the broken homeless woman they are now treating. The mystery of Wilson's brother — and their history — is not resolved until late season six.

## * 1.11 "Detox"

**Writers:** Lawrence Kaplow, Thomas L. Moran **Director:** Nelson McCormick
**Patient of the Week:** Keith (Nicholas D'Agosto)

After teenager Keith and his girlfriend crash his dad's sports car, he suffers unremitting internal bleeding. The team thinks it's lupus, but House insists it can't be — his symptoms are progressing too fast.

At the same time, House gives up Vicodin for a week to win a bet with Cuddy. As Keith's symptoms continue to suggest lupus for everyone but House, the team wonders if his judgment has been compromised by a combination of pain and withdrawal symptoms. When Keith suddenly begins to talk about his dead cat, no one thinks it's significant. The team thinks it's just a hallucination. But House persists, ordering the team to dig up the buried cat. Sick, hands trembling, House autopsies the cat, trying to hang on long enough to find the answer before Keith is scheduled undergo a potentially unnecessary liver transplant. Of course House is correct; the answer is in the cat, and Keith is saved.

**Zebra of the Week:** Naphthalene poisoning from termites. The chemical is produced during termite infestations and can be accumulated in human fat. As Keith's appetite fails during his hospital stay, the poison is released into his bloodstream — causing his symptoms.
**Epiphany!:** House wonders if Keith is dying from whatever killed his cat. The diagnosis is confirmed upon autopsy, when House finds dead termites in the cat's innards.
**Iconic Moment in *House* History:** After House has won his bet, he and Wilson argue intensely about whether years of Vicodin use have changed him. It's one of the few times we hear House raise his voice in anger. **Iconic Moment in *House* History #2:** Desperate to relieve the agony in his leg, House smashes his fingers to redirect the pain to the more severe injury — the "gating mechanism," as Wilson explains.
**Manipulative Wilson:** Wilson has manipulated the entire bet as a means to get House to admit narcotics abuse. He tells Cuddy that House would never believe it was him.

**A Fine Bromance:** To help with his pain, Wilson buys House an hour with Ingrid, a Spanish-speaking masseuse.

**Judgmental Fellow Alert:** Wilson has judged House as an addict, without considering his need for pain relief. A whole list of other conditions besides "drug addict," might fit House's relationship with drugs. Wilson's attitude, always "for House's good," is condescending and potentially destructive (and will nearly destroy House in season three). It is a major source of conflict between the two characters for the entire series.

**Gross-out Warning:** After House diagnoses naphthalene poisoning, he sends Chase and Foreman to check out Keith's home, where they find swarms of termites crawling around in the walls of the kid's bedroom. Ick.

**Housian Ethics:** Is it ethical to allow House to continue practicing while in withdrawal?

**Casting Call:** Nick D'Agosto (Keith) starred as Sean Colfax in the 2009 teen movie *Fired Up*. Amanda Seyfried (Keith's girlfriend) played Sophie in the 2009's *Mamma Mia!* and Sarah Henrickson in HBO's hit television series *Big Love*.

**Title Tale:** This multitasking title describes the bet between Cuddy and House as we observe him withdraw from long-term Vicodin use. It also describes Keith's condition. Naphthalene from the termites has poisoned Keith; detoxing will cure him.

**Why It's a Classic:** A tour-de-force performance by Hugh Laurie pits House's stubbornness against his team — and his need for narcotics. This is the first time the series addresses House's drug versus pain issues, raising the question of whether House is an addict. House admits to Wilson that he is addicted to the Vicodin, but says, "It's not a problem." He can't give them up because "they let me do my job; they take away my pain."


## * 1.12 "Sports Medicine"
**Writers:** David Shore, John Mankiewicz **Director:** Keith Gordon
**Patient of the Week:** Hank Wiggen (Scott Foley)

House treats Hank Wiggen, a major league baseball pitcher trying to make a comeback after drug rehab. Wiggen breaks his arm while lobbing a soft pitch during the filming of a public service announcement. Is the star slipping back into his old drug-user days?

House thinks it's steroid abuse, but Wiggen and his protective wife insist that he is completely drug free. Initially, House diagnoses Addison's disease, but that, too, fails to complete the picture. Wiggen's wife Lola holds the key to the diagnosis — and Hank's lie.

In an elaborate side plot, House has scored a pair of tickets to big monster truck rally — for $1,000 each. He invites Wilson, but he has other plans. Foreman becomes involved with a new female drug rep. But does she have a hidden agenda?

**Zebra of the Week:** Cadmium-tainted marijuana. Hank has slipped big time.

**Epiphany!:** House realizes Hank's wife has lost her sense of smell after Hank spills urine on House's clothes and she fails to detect the odor. House combines Lola's inability to smell and Hank's symptoms to arrive at the diagnosis. Chase gets an A for guessing correctly from House's clues.

**Iconic Moment in *House* History:** House can have fun! Cameron accompanies him to a monster truck rally after Wilson turns him down. They share cotton candy, small talk, and House makes a rare disclosure about his past after Cameron asks if he's ever been married. He tells her that he lived with someone "for a while." We are left to wonder if that woman might be mysterious Stacy.

**A Fine Bromance:** Wilson lies to House about why he can't attend the monster truck event. When he discovers the lie, House asks, "Did we break up or something?" Wilson is actually trying to spare House's feelings, by concealing his dinner date with someone named Stacy, who clearly means something to House.

**Housian Ethics:** House lies on Hank's medical record, omitting his final diagnosis of cadmium-tainted marijuana, knowing that drug finding will end Hank's career. He argues that no one deserves to have his life destroyed for one mistake.

**Shipper Alert!:** House has a "non-date" date with Cameron, taking her to the monster truck rally when Wilson declines the invite. Watching them relaxed and genuinely enjoying each others' company suggests an intriguing mutual attraction.

**Props Department:** House breaks out a fancy silver-tipped black cane to use on his non-date.

**World-Famous Doctor Moment:** A female pharmaceutical representative sleeps with Foreman to get access to House and maneuver him into attending a medical conference. ("That's how the groupies get to Mick," reminds rock-star doc House.)

**Casting Call:** Scott Foley (Hank) played Bob Brown in David Mamet's gritty CBS television series *The Unit* (2006–2009) and starred as Noel on teen drama *Felicity*. *House* executive producer/director Bryan Singer makes a cameo in the teaser as — you guessed it — a director.

**Title Tale:** A convergence of sports — and medicine. A ballplayer patient, a sports fan doctor, add in the dubious sport of "monster trucks," and stir.

**Why It's a Classic:** A densely packed episode, exploring House's relationships with Wilson and Cameron, it also hints at his previous relationship with "Stacy" that may have ended badly. We see several rarely revealed sides of House: caring about a patient, being vulnerable, and having fun.

## 1.13 "Cursed"

**Writers:** Peter Blake, Matt Witten **Director:** Daniel Sackheim
**Patient of the Week:** Gabe (Daryl Sabara)

After an Ouija board predicts his death, pre-teen Gabe suddenly becomes afflicted with a variety of increasingly weird symptoms, including a strange rash and a week-long fever. The symptoms suggest everything from anthrax to lupus (it's nearly never lupus).

As often happens on *House*, the key to the puzzle is hidden in someone's lie — this time Gabe's father.

Chase's estranged dad, Rowan, a renowned rheumatologist, visits from Australia, and Chase takes great pains to avoid him. While enlisting Rowan in the differential diagnosis, the ever-curious House wants to know to what's going on between father and son. When House learns that the elder Chase has stage 4 lung cancer and only a few months to live, he can't understand why Rowan refuses to tell Chase, but promises to keep his secret.

**Zebra of the Week:** Leprosy. Gabe's dad contracted it years earlier while not being a fighter pilot, as he has told both (ex) wife and son. Instead of being a fighter pilot, he spent time on an East Indian ashram following a guru who left him penniless. Humiliated by the experience, he concocted a more awe-inspiring history for his family.

**Epiphany!:** House notices that the father's wrist is painful and stiff even after surgery for carpal tunnel syndrome. He speculates that the dad has lied about something in his past, especially since the father incongruously wonders whether Gabe has been afflicted with an exotic tropical disease. When the dad finally confesses, House places the final puzzle piece.

**Iconic Moment in *House* History:** Chase and his father reconcile as Rowan heads back to Australia, though without telling him about the cancer. Rowan's omission comes back to haunt his son in season two ("The Mistake," 2.08).

**Casting Call:** Daryl Sabara (Gabe) played Juni Cortez in the Spy Kids movies. Nestor Carbonell, who plays Gabe's lying dad, was the mayor in the 2008 hit movie *The Dark Knight*.

**Title Tale:** Believing the Ouija board, Gabe thinks he's cursed. His only curse is a lying father who gave him leprosy.

## * 1.14 "Control"

**Writer:** Lawrence Kaplow **Director:** Randy Zisk
**Patient of the Week:** Carly (Sarah Clarke)

Carly, a young female CEO, is afflicted sudden severe thigh pain. House thinks it may be colon cancer, which killed her mother. But when Wilson wants to perform a colonoscopy, she prefers to die rather than submit to the embarrassment inherent in the procedure.

Surprised, House wonders why, and begins to consider Carly's emotional state after she goes into respiratory arrest. Noting her physical symptoms on the whiteboard, he wonders if he should add control and shame to her constellation of symptoms. Examining Carly as she sleeps, House observes that she "cuts" herself, and discovering a bottle of the emetic Ipecac in her purse, he realizes that Carly is also bulimic.

Meanwhile, Cuddy introduces the board to new chairman Edward Vogler, a pharmaceutical industry billionaire who has just donated $100 million to the hospital. House immediately distrusts him, and the feeling appears to be mutual.

**Zebra of the Week:** Carly's heart has failed due to long-term Ipecac abuse. She will only survive with a heart transplant.

**Epiphany!:** When House finds the Ipecac in her purse, he realizes she needs a transplant before the team does its confirming tests. House tells no one of his find, knowing she would never be approved for a transplant if the transplant committee were made aware of the bulimia and the cutting.

**Iconic Moment in *House* History:** Vogler visits House's office to introduce himself after Carly has her transplant. With his patient recovering, House enjoys himself playing "air" piano and drums to the Who rock classic "Baba O'Reilly." Vogler interrupts just as he is about to start his big drum solo. It's an amusing start to a deadly serious confrontation between the power-hungry Vogler and the iconoclastic House.

**Clinic Duty:** House treats the son of a mute patient for strep, but also cures the dad, treating him with Botox.

**Housian Ethics:** House lies to the transplant committee, risking his medical license to save Carly's life. He knows that bulimia will exclude her from the transplant list, and he tries to avoid an outright lie by omitting the relevant facts from his presentation. But directly challenged by Cuddy, he has no choice: either lie or watch his patient die. On the surface it seems a noble act, but is another patient denied while Carly gets her heart?

**Shipper Alert!:** Vogler wonders why Cuddy is so protective of House. "You sleeping with him?" he inquires pointedly. **Shipper Alert #2:** Cameron needs to know if House "likes" her.

**Musical Notes:** House has the "Hava Nagila" on his iPod. One can only imagine why.

**Casting Call:** Sarah Clarke (Carly) played Nina Myers in the first three seasons of Fox Network's *24*. Edward Vogler is played by Chi McBride, known for his starring role as Steven Harper in the Fox series *Boston Public* (2000–2004) and as Emerson Cod in the 2007–2009 ABC series *Pushing Dasies*.

**Title Tale:** A power-hungry CEO is in charge of the hospital, a young CEO tries to control her own high-powered life, and House plays God. Meanwhile Cameron tries to learn to control people through manipulation. She has read a book on "soft positional bargaining, 50 ways to get to 'yes.'"

**Why It's a Classic:** The start of the Vogler story arc, House is pitted against someone from "outside" his universe. We also observe House's complex moral code in action. He will risk his career, even crossing ethical boundaries to save a patient's life. House would say that he's only concerned about "doing the right thing." But is what he does "right," or only right for his patient?

## 1.15 "Mob Rules"

**Writers:** David Foster, John Mankiewicz **Director:** Tim Hunter
**Patient of the Week:** Joey (Joseph Lyle Taylor)

Mobster Joey Arnello is about to enter the Witness Protection Program, but collapses after eating a steak dinner preceding his appearance in front of a grand jury. House treats him, as his brother (a mob lawyer) hovers menacingly nearby making sure that House does his job as he sees it: diagnose Joey and make sure he never enters the Witness Protection Program.

House believes Joey has hepatitis C, contracted during gay sex, which infuriates the brother, who denies even the possibility that Joey is homosexual. As Joey goes in and out of comas, his liver begins to fail, and he tests for high levels of estrogen. House is stumped; nothing seems to explain the full range of symptoms.

Vogler continues his crusade against House and his department, eventually demanding that he fire one of the fellows.

**Zebra of the Week:** Joey has ornithine transcarbamylase deficiency, a genetic condition that prevents digestion of the proteins found in beef. It flares when Joey is given steak to eat — once at the beginning of the episode and again towards the end. But it only fits if Joey's elevated estrogen is being caused by using the female hormone directly.

**Epiphany!:** Everything fits the diagnosis except the elevated estrogen levels. This anomaly is explained by Joey's use of an herbal aphrodisiac marketed to gay men. It's the simplest explanation: two different conditions causing the symptoms. House realizes it while in with his clinic patient trying to figure out why the young patient keeps sticking small toys up his nose.

**Iconic Moment in *House* History:** House uses a live pig to filter Joey's blood, insisting that it's "kosher."

**Clinic Duty:** A teenager brings his toddler brother to the clinic several times as the little boy continues shoving a series of small toys up his nose.

**A Fine Bromance:** Joey's brother gives House a vintage Corvette as thanks for helping Joey. He and Wilson waste no time — they are soon tooling down the streets of Princeton together.

**Shipper Alert!:** Cameron confesses to Foreman that she "likes" House, who teases her unmercifully. **Shipper Alert #2:** Vogler can't understand why Cuddy continues to protect House.

**Casting Call:** Joseph Lyle Taylor has had guest roles on numerous television series in the 1990s and 2000s, including *Law & Order*, *CSI*, *Grey's Anatomy*, and *Dexter*.

**Title Tale:** Joey is a mobster.

## 1.16 "Heavy"

**Writer:** Thomas L. Moran **Director:** Frank Gerber
**Patient of the Week:** Jessica (Jennifer Stone)

Nine-year-old, overweight Jessica has a heart attack on the playground during gym class. With her mother insisting that her symptoms have nothing to do with her weight, House and the team try to determine what caused her heart to stop. As her symptoms worsen, they learn she's been taking diet pills on the sly. But when the skin on her chest begins to necrotize and the only solution seems to be amputating her breasts, House insists on looking deeper.

Vogler's pressure continues to ratchet up as he insists House cut one fellow from the team. House is at a loss, not wanting to cut any of the fellows, and after consulting both Foreman and Cameron, he endeavors to keep the entire team intact by offering to slash everyone's salary. But House soon realizes Vogler's issue has never been about money, but about hegemony. Further pressed, House finally chooses to cut Chase. But with Chase firmly in place as Vogler's snitch, his position is safe. And by the episode's end, House must choose either Foreman or Cameron — or risk losing the entire department.

**Zebra of the Week:** A small tumor on the pituitary gland.

**Epiphany!:** The team wonders if Jessica's weight is a symptom — not a cause.

**Iconic Moment in *House* History:** Cameron confronts House after he's told the team that Jessica's necrosis is due to her mistake. If she has screwed up, it would give House an easy excuse to fire her, thus solving his Vogler problem and allowing him to avoid his feelings about her. But Cameron knows he's far from sure of his diagnosis.

**Clinic Duty:** House treats a zaftig woman with "heartburn" that turns out to be a very large benign tumor. There is much snap and sass as they argue about the tumor, which she doesn't want removed for fear of becoming disfigured from the surgery.

**Judgmental Fellow Alert:** Chase has a major thing against overweight people, which will carry over into future seasons.

**Shipper Alert!:** House seeks Cameron's advice about who to cut from the team. They spar, with Cameron accusing House of running away from the problem by stalling, and House accusing Cameron of suggesting a solution in which no one is hurt. But House takes her advice, which is to cut the fellows' salaries across the board, and proposes it to Vogler, including himself in the pay cuts.

**Plot Hole:** The episode's final scene with Jessica is clearly weeks, if not months, later. All three fellows are there. Does it foreshadow the resolution of the Vogler arc with House's team intact, or is it simply a plot hole?

**Casting Call:** Jennifer Stone (Jessica) played Harriet in the Disney Channel movie *Harriet the Spy*.

**Title Tale:** Both Jessica and House's clinic patient are heavy, and House is placed a very heavy situation with Vogler.

## * 1.17 "Role Model"

**Writer:** Matt Witten **Director:** Peter O'Fallon
**Patient of the Week:** Senator Gary Wright (Joe Morton)

Senator Wright, an African-American presidential candidate, collapses while giving a speech on the campaign trail. Wright tests positive for the parasite toxoplasmosis, leading House to suspect AIDS, which is confirmed by initial blood tests. After Wright insists he can't have AIDS, House uncharacteristically retests him. The results come back negative, but it's little comfort, because now they're back at square one with the diagnosis. As Wright's symptoms continue to worsen, House recalls the scar he noticed on Wright's tongue when first examining him and wonders if there's a clue there.

While House puzzles out Senator Wright, Vogler gives him a last chance to keep the team intact. House must publicly endorse his company's new "wonder drug" in a speech during a medical conference. Reluctantly agreeing to give the speech for the sake of his department, House's team is stunned that he would deign to do something "nice" for them. But as House prepares the speech, his personal ethical code vigorously nags at him. Wrestling with his integrity, House finds guidance from his patient, who believes that taking a stand is sometimes more important than actually winning.

**Zebra of the Week:** Combined variable immunodeficiency (CVID).

**Epiphany!:** After realizing the scar on Wright's tongue resulted from biting it during a childhood epileptic seizure, House wonders if he was treated with phenytoin as a child.

**Clinic Duty:** A woman exhibits a variety of rashes and abrasions. House's diagnosis: sexsomnia (sex while sleeping).

**House Is a Jerk:** He removes Wright's oxygen mask until he confesses to having had childhood epilepsy. It's nearly torture, but necessary for the final diagnosis. However, as soon as Wright tells House what he needs to know, he replaces the mask, gently reassuring him.

**Housian Ethics:** House agonizes over the speech, knowing it will keep his team intact, but understanding that his endorsement comes with at a high cost to his principles.

**Shipper Alert!:** Although his colleagues and fellows are frustrated and angry with House for failing them, Cameron alone understands why House couldn't give the speech: "I figured everything you do, you do it to help people. But I was wrong. You do it because it's right." Cameron decides to sacrifice herself and resign. House can neither look her in the eye nor even shake her hand when she offers it. **Shipper Alert #2:** Wilson insists to House that Cameron seems to have quite an effect on her mentor, with House reacting strangely to Wilson's suggestion that perhaps he's "put the moves" on Cameron. House also comes back to Cameron's earlier confession ("Control," 1.14) that she "likes" him. Approaching her in the lab, House wants to understand why, but when she turns the tables wondering why he wants to know all of a sudden, he walks away.

**Classic Rant:** House rants about the pharmaceutical industry practice of making trivial improvements to drugs whose patents are about to expire. The "new and improved" versions of the drugs are invariably much more expensive (but not necessarily more effective) than the generic version of the original.

**Metaphorically Speaking:** In one of House's best metaphors, he explains how to find hairy cell leukemia without doing a biopsy on the liver. He notes that when the Inuit fish they can't see the fish, so they look for herons circling the waters and deduce the fish in the water. He also offers not one, but two sports metaphors.

**Musical Notes:** At home after giving the speech, House plinks out "High Hopes" on his piano: a most appropriately ironic song for the moment.

**World-Famous Doctor Moment:** Vogler introduces House at the conference as a doctor with a well-known reputation for integrity; his endorsement of the product would be very meaningful to Vogler's company.

**Casting Call:** Joe Morton played Henry Deacon on the Syfy Channel series *Eureka* (2006–2009).

**Title Tale:** What sort of a role model is House for his fellows? He has always taught them to do "the right thing," consequences be damned (a lesson that resonates deeply even into the sixth season of *House*). But Wright also teaches something to House when he tells him that you don't have to win every fight to make a difference. It is at that moment House realizes he really cannot give the speech. Gary Wright, too, is seen as a role model for a whole generation — with the potential for being the first African-American president in U.S. history. (But, apparently Barack Obama beat him to it!)

**Why It's a Classic:** Viewers are given a rare glimpse at the way House struggles with his integrity.

## Struggling to Do the "Right Thing":
## A Closer Look at "Role Model"

"Dr. Gregory House has a reputation for integrity," says Princeton-Plainsboro board chairman Edward Vogler introducing him to a roomful of doctors about to hear House extol the virtues of Vogler's not-so-brand-new heart drug ("Role Model," 1.17). Coerced into giving the speech, it is the only way Vogler will allow House to keep his department intact.

House believes that the supposedly improved drug has no discernible advantage over its predecessor, which is about to lose its patent, and is notable only for its expensive price tag. When the patent runs out, the drug will become available as a generic, so to stay ahead of the competition, Vogler's pharmaceutical company has made a minor adjustment to the formula, adding an antacid, re-patenting it, and jacking up the price.

House's endorsement of the new drug is only meaningful because of his reputation for integrity, but House just can't bring himself to do it, even though he has been given an ultimatum: deliver this one short speech or lose his department.

House tries, struggling with it, fully intending to make the speech, and understanding the consequences if he does not. Throughout the episode, we see him agonizing, complaining to Wilson that by giving the speech, he's selling his soul. Wilson counters that by giving the speech, House has chosen to save the jobs of the people on his team, and therefore House is doing something nice by sacrificing a small piece of his soul. Which is the "right thing" to do? Keep his department intact, or refuse to give a speech endorsing a product he cannot, in good conscience, endorse?

Before the big event, Cameron thanks him, grateful for the gesture; Foreman is skeptical, believing House too self-centered to do anything that nice. But in the final analysis, House cannot bring himself to promote the new drug, which will bilk money out of people who could just as easily use the new generic. When he gets to the podium to give the ill-fated speech, he can't seem to help himself. At first he offers a few unremarkable words in favor of the product. It's safe and it works: enough for a press release, but no ringing endorsement. But, pressured by Vogler to say more, House snaps and launches into a tirade against Vogler and the entire pharmaceutical industry.

House's colleagues are disappointed in what they see as his refusal to give a simple speech. And, after it's all over, only Cameron really understands.

## 1.18 "Babies and Bathwater"

**Writers:** Peter Blake, David Shore **Director:** Bill Johnson
**Patient of the Week:** Naomi (Marin Hinkle)

A pregnant woman, Naomi, comes to House after becoming ill while driving. She has had several previous miscarriages and is determined to carry this baby to term. House has his diagnosis unusually early: she has small cell lung cancer, an aggressive disease that gives her only a few months to live. She refuses to deliver the baby prematurely to treat the cancer, which gives both mother and child a small chance of survival. House tries to get Naomi into a clinical trial that will increase her chances of survival, but they are too late for her.

In the aftermath of "Role Model" (1.17), Vogler now wants House's tenure immediately revoked, threatening to leave and take his millions with him. Firing a tenured faculty member like House requires a unanimous board vote, and Wilson refuses to cooperate. Vogler forces Wilson to resign, presumably removing the final obstacle. Eventually, Cuddy and the rest of the board understand the danger in someone like Vogler. At what point, Cuddy wonders, do the strings attached to funding begin to compromise patient care?

**Zebra of the Week:** Small cell lung cancer; internal bleeding.
**Epiphany!:** Naomi chokes on a small piece of canned pear, leading House to have the team check for a drooping eyelid, much to Foreman's disbelief. However, the drooping eyelid confirms Lambert-Eaton syndrome, a sign of small cell lung cancer.
**Iconic Moment in *House* History:** As Naomi bleeds into her abdomen during the procedure, the obstetrics team wants to save the baby, knowing there is nothing more they can do for Naomi. To delay means death for both mother and baby. House decides to speak to the grief-stricken husband himself, convincing him to allow a caesarean section, though it will hasten Naomi's inevitable death. House's calm, honest, and earnest words help the husband make the difficult

but necessary choice. **Iconic Moment #2:** Cuddy convinces the board to vote against Vogler and as the team celebrates in House's office, the hero of the day downs a full glass of champagne in one gulp, impressing even House.

**Clinic Duty:** House treats an infant who is losing weight. Are her vegan parents endangering their child by failing to give her enough protein to thrive, or are they just misguided, as House believes? But when the parents assure him they are caring properly for their new baby, House runs more tests, concluding that baby Olive has DiGeorge syndrome, which has caused her failure to thrive. Cuddy, moved by his dedication — continuing to work the case even as the board prepares to fire him — is reminded of House's unique value, perhaps more valuable than Vogler's millions.

**A Fine Bromance:** Wilson resigns rather than be booted off the board for refusing to betray House. Frustrated with House for his intransigence, Wilson confronts him: "Only two things mattered to me: my job and our screwed up friendship. Neither of them meant enough to you to give one lousy speech."

**House Is a Jerk:** In House's first encounter with Vogler after the speech, he tells the board chair that he's fired Cameron as commanded. He's more a coward than a jerk in this slightly uncharacteristic bit of attempted self-preservation, since Cameron sacrificed herself.

**Housian Ethics:** Cuddy has Olive's parents arrested for child neglect after House declines to do so, believing that the parents are simply inexperienced. Although Olive's failure to thrive has a medical cause, should House have reported the parents after his initial exam? **Housian Ethics #2:** House lies to get Naomi into the clinical trial.

**Shipper Alert!:** House tells Wilson that Cuddy "only has thighs" for him.

**Casting Call:** Marin Hinkle is best known for playing Judith Melnick, Alan Harper's ex-wife on the CBS hit television series *Two and a Half Men* (2003–present).

**Title Tale:** Along with ousting Vogler, the hospital loses his $100 million: the baby out with the bathwater. The title also refers to Naomi's nearly losing her own life and that of her baby.


## 1.19 "Kids"

**Writers:** Lawrence Kaplow, Thomas L. Moran **Director:** Deran Sarafian
**Patient of the Week:** Mary (Skye McCole Bartusiak)

In the midst of a meningitis outbreak from a nearby swim meet, House tries to convince Cuddy that Mary, a 12-year-old diver with meningitis-like symptoms, suffers from something else entirely. However, in the aftermath of Vogler, and the loss of his money, Cuddy isn't feeling especially charitable to House's theories, seeing it as his way of getting out of meningitis triage duty. She orders House and his team (minus Cameron, who resigned last episode) to join the other doctors working the crisis, leaving the team to puzzle out Mary's problem while examining the hundreds of exposed patients crowding the foyer.

After Cameron declines House's invitation to come back on the team, Cuddy orders him to hire a new fellow. He indifferently interviews three candidates before deciding he really wants Cameron back on the team. She decides to return to work — under one condition.

**Zebra of the Week:** Mary has a thrombotic thrombocytopenic purpura (TTP), which destroys red blood cells. It's a condition sometimes related to pregnancy.

**Epiphany!:** House realizes that, since none of the male swimmers have visited Mary in the hospital, they must be avoiding her. The discovery leads House to consider that she might be pregnant; blood tests confirm TTP — she needs to end the pregnancy.

**Iconic Moment in *House* History:** The expression on House's face when he realizes Cameron wants a date is a look of shock and wonder — he is completely flummoxed by the request!

**House Is a Jerk:** House is obnoxious to all of the fellowship candidates, particularly to Dr. Petra Gilmar as he tries unsuccessfully to push all of her buttons.

**Housian Ethics:** Wilson suggests that House fire Chase for his betrayal during Vogler's reign as board chair. However, House disagrees saying that Chase was just trying to preserve his job and doesn't deserve to be fired. **Housian Ethics #2:** House's patient asks him not to tell her parents when he diagnoses pregnancy. She prefers to go through the treatment (an abortion) alone. As much as he'd like to, he follows the law and protects her privacy, but he's clearly relieved when she tells them herself.

**Shipper Alert!:** When House visits Cameron a second time, willing to give her anything she wants to come back on the team, she demands a dinner date.

**Pop Culture References:** "That's our Hitler," cries Wilson, quoting Mel Brooks' *The Producers*, after interviewing a tough female fellowship candidate.

**Props Department:** Cameron notices that House has a new cane.

**Casting Call:** Skye McCole Bartusiak got her break playing Susan Martin in Mel Gibson's 2000 movie *The Patriot*.

**Title Tale:** Mary, a kid herself, believes she is mature enough to handle the trauma of an abortion alone.

## 1.20 "Love Hurts"

**Writer:** Sara B. Cooper **Director:** Bryan Spicer
**Patient of the Week:** Harvey (John Cho)

The team treats Harvey, a young man who has a stroke after House yells at him in the clinic. Reviewing Harvey's brain scan, the team (with Cameron now returned to the fold) notices a metal plate in Harvey's jaw, which leaves some of House's favorite diagnostic toys off the table (the MRI with its giant magnet could badly injure him).

Harvey has also suffers nominal aphasia (he has difficulty remembering nouns), and, according to his friend Annette, he has seen several New Age health practitioners, from "shen balancers" to acupuncturists to naturopaths, with no luck. When the team catches Annette strangling Harvey, they learn that she's a dominatrix and Harvey has a sadomasochistic fetish for suffocation. As his condition worsens, he eventually lapses into a coma, and Harvey's old-school Korean-born parents refuse to become involved, even to give their consent for a procedure, citing their shame at Harvey's sexual lifestyle. House threatens to blackmail them to save Harvey's life.

Cameron and House prepare for their dinner date. Each receives unwanted advice from friends and colleagues. But the most unexpected advice is Wilson's to Cameron, urging that she be very certain before becoming involved with House: "It's been a long time since he's opened up to anyone. If he gets hurt, there may not be a next time." The dinner date is far from a success as Cameron dives right in, asking House how he feels about her. House is brutally honest, and can imagine no reason for her interest in him other than a driving need to heal him like a wounded puppy. But his scathing words say more about his self-esteem than her motives.

**Zebra of the Week:** Harvey has a jaw infection from a pervious surgery.
**Epiphany!:** Chase has been popping breath mints taken from Harvey's apartment since the start of the case. This resonates with House when he notices his elderly clinic patient and her boyfriend using breath freshener as they're about to smooch. After Chase tells him that Harvey has tons of the mints, House wonders why — and then takes a whiff of his breath.
**Iconic Moment in *House* History:** At the end of the episode, House digs through his wallet, finding an old photograph (presumably) of Stacy, whom he clearly still thinks about.
**Clinic Duty:** House treats Ramona, an elderly woman with vaginal tearing. She's having an affair with a man on Viagra, who's a bit too virile for both of them. Their lovey-dovey behavior leads House to his diagnosis.

**A Fine Bromance:** While House nervously prepares for his date, the much more experienced Wilson offers him "panty peeling" advice and antibiotic-coated condoms.

**House Is a Jerk:** House does his Archie Bunker best to insult the ethnicity of Harvey's Korean parents.

**Shipper Alert!:** The socially awkward House reveals a bit of his slightly sappy romantic side, consulting with Wilson about whether a corsage he has bought for Cameron is "lame." Wilson responds supportively, "I think she likes 'lame.'"

**Shipper Alert #2:** Although he sarcastically tells her to "wear Lycra" and suggests they're going to a paintball tournament, House takes Cameron to very classy Italian restaurant — and wears a tie. House's suggestion of attending a paintball tournament simply seems like sarcasm, but we learn in season three that House and Stacy met at a "doctors versus lawyers" playing paintball years earlier, so maybe there is more to the remark than immediately meets the eye.

**Casting Call:** John Cho plays Harold in the popular *Harold & Kumar* movies. (Of course, Kal Penn, who plays Kumar, joins the cast in season four as fellow Lawrence Kutner.) Veteran actor Peter Graves plays Ramona's elderly boyfriend Myron. Graves has had a distinguished career in film and television, playing Price in *Stalag 17* (1953) and Jim Phelps in the original CBS *Mission Impossible* television series from 1967 to 1973 and its remake in the 1980s. But he may be best known as the pilot in the classic comedy/satire *Airplane!* (1980).

**Title Tale:** Harvey is a sadomasochist, whose love is all wrapped up in hurt. We also learn that House was badly hurt in his last relationship — something that's affected him ever since.


## * 1.21 "Three Stories"

**Writer:** David Shore **Director:** Paris Barclay

On his way to deliver a diagnostics lecture to medical students, House is startled by a familiar voice. The voice belongs to Stacy, the woman with whom House lived for five years. Although they broke up years ago, she now seeks his help to diagnose her husband, Mark. Though shaken by her presence, House is disinterested in her plight, coldly refusing to treat Mark.

Now sitting center stage in a sparsely populated lecture hall, House begins to weave together the diagnoses of three hypothetical patients with a common symptom: leg pain. The patients are a teenage girl, a farmer, and a 38-year-old golfer. As House guides the students through each diagnosis, pressuring, badgering, and challenging them along the way, the room fills, and it is soon clear to us, if not the students, that the golfer is an avatar for House.

Initially (and wrongly) dismissed as a drug seeker, the golfer returns later, still in pain and with his kidneys shutting down. Three days have been lost in his diagnosis.

House slowly reveals the story behind his own disability to the now standing-room-only auditorium; students, colleagues, and his fellows listen spellbound. Although it's never mentioned explicitly, this may be the first time House is speaking about what happened to him, albeit anonymously.

We begin to understand how this single, life-altering event might have affected House physically, emotionally, and professionally. "Three Stories" gives us a context through which we can understand why House is such a fierce patient advocate: why he believes in a patient's right to choose (once the diagnosis is made), and why his ethical code has more to do with "doing the right thing" than being "by the book." But we also understand why he thinks so little of the medical establishment, standards, and rules — and perhaps what fuels (at least part of) his bitterness and trust issues. In the end, this revealing self-exploration causes him to rethink treating Mark.

**Iconic Moment in *House* History:** The entire episode is an iconic moment in the series as House reveals his own story. Perhaps the most memorable scene is a flashback in which House and Stacy argue about whether House should allow the doctors to amputate his leg. Stacy argues that "it's just a damn leg," and amputation is something that House would readily advocate for a patient in similar straits. House cannot do it. Not even to save his own life. At this point, he would rather die than risk living the life he believes lies ahead for him — disabled and in chronic pain.

**House Is a Jerk:** He flatly refuses to consider taking Mark Warner's case.

**Housian Ethics:** The main ethical issue concerns Stacy's fateful decision to ignore House's wishes regarding his treatment. It may have saved his life, but was that what he really would have wanted given the outcome?

***House* Canon:** Cuddy was House's doctor at the time of his infarction.

**Casting Call:** Sela Ward, who is introduced in "Three Stories" as House's former girlfriend Stacy, won Best Dramatic Actress Golden Globe and Emmy Awards for her role in the 1999–2002 ABC series *Once and Again*.

**Title Tale:** House lectures a class on the diagnosis of three pain patients. But the title may also refer to the three people involved with the procedure done on House's leg: Stacy, House, and his doctor, Cuddy. We see House's story unfold here strictly through his point of view, but is he a reliable narrator? He probably has all the facts, but his interpretation of the events may be clouded by his still-strong feelings about what was done to him. There are two other stories we have not heard. What would Stacy and Cuddy's accounts suggest?

**Why It's a Classic:** A brilliantly rendered story, it is a pivotal episode, giving us the history of House's leg, and unlocking several doors to the mystery of Dr. Gregory House. With its unusual narrative structure and powerful emotional impact, the episode won David Shore the Emmy for writing in 2005, as well as the Humanitas Award.

"The writing staff unanimously holds up 'Three Stories' as the series' gold standard."

— **Garrett Lerner, May 2008 interview**

---

### Before the Leg

When we first meet House, several years have passed since his leg injury. In "Detox" (1.11), as Wilson and House argue about whether House's Vicodin use is a problem, Wilson insists that the narcotics have caused House to fundamentally change. At first House denies that he's changed, except to have gone through the normal pangs of "getting older"; he notes that he's been "annoying people since I was three."

Wilson presses that he's known House long enough to know he's changed drastically. "You are not just a regular guy who's getting older — you've changed! You're miserable, and you're afraid to face yourself." Turning away from Wilson, House slams his cane on the credenza in a rare display of losing his usually tight self-control, and he admits bitterly that "of course" Wilson's right.

So what was House like before the disability? Do we have any clues at all? Perhaps he was a much more social creature *before*, active and involved in sports. We've seen golf clubs in his hall closet ("Cane and Able," 3.02) and we know he's played lacrosse ("Paternity," 1.02 and "Adverse Events," 5.03); he met Stacy at a "doctors versus lawyers" paintball tournament ("Son of Coma Guy," 3.07). None of these is a lone athletic pursuit, and none of them is any kind of sport we might associate with the reclusive, isolated Dr. Gregory House — although he apparently does still bowl now and then as we see in "No More Mr. Nice Guy" (4.13).

House has known both Cuddy and Wilson since before the infarction. He met Wilson at a medical conference ("Birthmarks," 5.04), which tells us there was a time he did attend them, perhaps even willingly. But the last American conference he attended before "Known Unknowns" (6.07) was 15 years earlier, around the time he was with Stacy. He's known Cuddy since they were briefly at the University of Michigan together — and where he danced with her at a university social event.

But it's doubtful House was ever a completely social creature. As Wilson describes House's probable childhood, he was a "brilliant, socially isolated" kid ("Birthmarks," 5.04). This is not so different from the person we've come to know — still brilliant and still isolated, but perhaps even more alone than he was before.

In "Who's Your Daddy?" (2.23), we meet an old friend of House's, Dylan Crandall. Can we gain any insight from what we know of their relationship? They hung around together around back in House's college days. We get the impression that House was pretty streetwise even then. Although he betrayed Crandall back in the day, allowing himself to be seduced by his flaky girlfriend (maybe even to prove a point about her), House also seems to have been somewhat protective of the gullible Crandall as well. He has apparently felt guilty about the incident ever since.

We get a small but significant glimpse of pre-infarction House in the flashback sequences of "Three Stories" (1.22). We learn he trusted Stacy enough to give her his medical proxy, although he certainly would not have trusted anyone that much since. A medical proxy is not something one easily assigns, and House, who, as we have known him these six years, has both serious trust and intimacy issues; he would not have given his medical proxy lightly even then.

We observe House as much less guarded than we know him now. He doesn't blink an eye when Stacy asks whether he would give up a leg to save her life. "Of course," he replies, confused that she would even have to ask such a question. And yet, the House we know would never admit to being self-sacrificing ("Don't Ever Change," 4.12) . . . even if we know that he actually is ("Wilson's Heart," 4.16). In "Three Stories," House easily and sincerely tells Stacy that he loves her — and even lightly jokes with her as he's about to be put under anesthesia. He has no problem allowing Stacy to physically touch him and comfort him, something that the post-infarction House generally rejects, only allowing contact with great difficulty. The House we know practically jumps when anyone touches him — especially in the first several seasons.

Looking hard enough, we are still treated to occasional flashes of House's considerable romantic streak. In "Let Them Eat Cake" (5.10), he restores, and has delivered as a surprise, Cuddy's medical school desk; in "Need to Know" (2.11), he writes Stacy a "prescription" for her "heart condition," which is a sweet moment, and the kind that is rarely present in the current Greg House. In "Love Hurts" (1.20) he buys Cameron a corsage for their date. Critics (and some fans) sometimes call these flashes "uncharacteristic." It's not that they're out of character, but only very deeply hidden within House's many layers — and maybe more clues to pre-infarction House.

## * 1.22. "Honeymoon"

**Writers:** Lawrence Kaplow, John Mankiewicz **Director:** Frederick King Keller
**Patient of the Week:** Mark Warner (Currie Graham)

Although House is now willing to treat him, Mark insists there's nothing wrong. Stacy disagrees, and House slips him knockout drops to get him into the hospital. As House's team diagnoses Mark, it becomes apparent that House still has strong and complicated feelings for Stacy.

After several theories are discarded, House is still at a loss about what's ailing Mark. Stacy has not considered that House might not be able to diagnose her husband, and seeing her in tears, House's instinct is to comfort her. But as they embrace, Stacy pulls back.

Although House eventually figures out what's wrong, Mark refuses consent to a risky confirming test. With Mark paralyzed and getting sicker, the insistent Stacy presses House to ignore Mark's wishes. Closely mirroring the decision Stacy made for House five years earlier ("Three Stories," 1.21) her plea here resonates deeply. "He'll never forgive you," warns House. "*He* will," Stacy fires back, pointedly noting the difference between the two men.

Later, as House sits alone in his office, Mark cured, Stacy visits to thank him. She admits that House will always be "the one," but that it's not enough for her. When Cuddy wants to hire her back as hospital attorney while Mark recovers, House feigns indifference. But back in his apartment, House ponders the past and thinks about the future, wondering if he can even attempt to push back the clock as he tries to take a single normal step without the aid of his cane. The attempt is vain, as his leg gives out from under him and he collapses into his chair. We feel his anguish as he pops a Vicodin, ending season one on decidedly down note.

**Zebra of the Week:** Acute intermittent porphyria (AIP).
**Epiphany!:** House recalls Mark's assertion that he took Stacy to her "dream city"

Paris on their honeymoon. Stacy denies taking the trip. But Mark's not lying; he actually believes they went. House has another symptom for the whiteboard, and combined with Mark's other behavioral changes — and physical symptoms, it all fits.

**Iconic Moment in *House* History:** There are many indelible scenes in this episode, but one of the most revealing takes place after House gives Mark the AIP trigger. Initially the test on Mark's urine specimen seems to prove House wrong as it fails to turn positive. Refusing to give up, facing the skepticism of his team, he adds light to the reaction in the test tube. Relief pours off him; he practically collapses onto the lab bench. He has saved Mark's life — but knows he has also likely lost Stacy forever.

**A Fine Bromance:** When House gets the results of a test, he is disturbed by his own reaction, partly hoping that Mark is incurable. He is so upset by his conflicted feelings he calls Wilson away from a dinner party. "He's my patient," House confesses, "and I don't know if I want him to live."

**Housian Ethics:** House spikes Mark's drink with chloral hydrate to get him to the hospital. Later, Stacy pressures House into giving Mark a "cocktail" of substances to trigger an attack that will confirm Mark's illness when he refuses consent.

**Shipper Alert!:** House gazes yearningly into Mark's room watching him cuddle with Stacy after he's been cured. Cameron approaches, observing that she has been wrong about House, believing that he is too "screwed up" to love anyone. "You just couldn't love me," she acknowledges, realizing how deeply he still must love Stacy. No matter how he may feel about Cameron, House is not in a position to act upon those feelings. **Shipper Alert #2:** Unable to diagnose Mark, House flees to the hospital rooftop where Stacy finds him. He gives her a comforting embrace, which obviously means as much to him as it does her.

**Did You Know?:** An early draft of the "Honeymoon" script ends season one with House drowning his sorrows in a bar, getting badly beaten up in a brawl.

**Casting Call:** Currie Graham (Mark) may look familiar from his appearances on several hit series, including *NYPD Blue*, *CSI*, *Suddenly Susan*, and *Desperate Housewives*.

**House Canon:** House and Stacy lived together for five years; they've been apart for five years at this point in the series. The question still remains: how long did Stacy stay with House after the infarction?

**Title Tale:** Mark and Stacy's honeymoon that wasn't is the key to Mark's illness.

**Why It's a Classic:** "Honeymoon" gives us a lot of information about House and his unresolved feelings for Stacy, the woman who betrayed his trust so many years earlier. The poignant end of the episode shows us how much House would like to turn back the clock to before "everything changed" for him.

# SEASON 2

## Settling into the Story

As much as season one set the tone for the series and began to explore the inner life of its central character, season two further developed all the characters, giving them direction and growth — letting the viewer get to know them all. We also learn that House is quite capable of love and is more romantic — and more easily hurt — than we might have suspected; that his objectivity seems to vanish when confronted with the illness of one of his own staff; and that he is pretty good at keeping secrets.

Season two picks up on several story threads from season one, including that of Chase's father Rowan, who was dying of cancer when last we saw him in "Heavy" (1.16). We meet Foreman's father Rodney and learn more about his family, and we learn a little bit more about Cameron's life with her now-deceased husband.

Stacy's presence during the first half of the season continues to reveal hitherto unexplored territory of House's personality — not all of it attractive. No other character on the show has been able to get to House in quite the same way by this point in the series. She enables House's considerable romantic nature to emerge. We see into House's heart, understand how it was broken and why it has never quite healed. But Stacy also brings out House's pettiness and selfishness.

We learn more about the show's other characters as well. Foreman gets his chance to *be* House for several episodes. But he's not really up to the task. Foreman proves to be judgmental, arrogant, and ambitious (and even nasty) — traits that play out over the rest of the season.

Cuddy's awareness of her biological clock goes into overdrive as she begins a three-season quest to become a mother. It's a subplot not resolved until season five. And Wilson is not quite as good a guy as he lets on, committing a huge ethical breach as the season winds down and his third marriage falls apart. But nothing prepares viewers for season two's finale.

There were several stellar episodes, including "Autopsy" (2.02), "The

Mistake" (2.08), "Failure to Communicate" (2.10), "All In" (2.17), "House vs. God" (2.19), "Euphoria" (2.20, 2.21), "Forever" (2.22), and the surreal exploration of House's mind, "No Reason" (2.24). But the season started out with some fairly mediocre episodes as well: "Acceptance" (2.01) wasn't quite the bang-up season premiere one might have hoped for on the heels of the powerful first-season finale episodes. Other early episodes, "TB or Not TB" (2.04) and "Spin" (2.06), were heavy on the medical mystery without really furthering the character drama, which the best episodes do well.

Starred (*) entries are (subjectively considered) *House* classics.

## 2.01 "Acceptance"

**Writers:** Russel Friend, Garrett Lerner **Director:** Dan Attias
**Patient of the Week:** Clarence (LL Cool J)

House treats Clarence, a death row inmate. He suffers hallucinations, haunted by the victims of his past murders. His heart beats so fast, according to House, that "it pumps air." Bringing him to Princeton-Plainsboro to get appropriate medical care, House treats him over Cuddy's objections and Foreman's disdain — and while grappling with Stacy's presence back in his life and at the hospital.

Cameron treats Cindy, a young woman with a mild cough. But when Cindy's tests confirm lung cancer, Cameron refuses to accept her patient's death sentence and tries to badger House into taking her futile case instead of Clarence's.

**Zebra of the Week:** Pheochromocytoma (a small adrenaline-secreting tumor) causes rage attacks — and possibly enraged Clarence enough to commit his several murders.
**Epiphany!:** House considers the motivations behind each of Clarence's murders. They all had clear motives but one. He wonders if that one murder, at least, had no motivation other than blind and unexplainable rage.
**Iconic Moment in *House* History:** Cuddy insists that Clarence is ready to be discharged, but House disagrees and keeps him over her objections. Confiding this to Stacy, House tests whether she can be trusted (as she has assured him). She quickly rats him out. "I trusted you," he discloses, disappointed, but not surprised.
**A Fine Bromance:** Wilson gives House advice on dealing with Stacy, telling him that, since she's the hospital attorney, he has to get along with her.
**Judgmental Fellow Alert:** Neither Foreman nor Cameron wants to treat Clarence. Cameron is furious that House prefers to diagnose Clarence over her lost cause, Cindy, and refers to the death row convict as a "piece of garbage."

However, when House diagnoses a physical cause to Clarence's rage attacks, Foreman sympathizes and volunteers to testify on his behalf.

**Housian Ethics:** The team argues with House over whether a convicted murderer on death row is worthy of treatment. Frustrated, House challenges the team to create a priority list of worthiness. Do pedophiles outrank murderers? Do car thieves outrank rapists? At one point, Foreman refuses to revive Clarence when he goes into cardiac arrest, standing idly by until House appears on the scene to revive him. But does Foreman have a point? If Clarence is cured, he goes back on death row. They cure him only to see him killed by the State. On the other hand, if he dies, Clarence would be denied the chance of his final appeal. By refusing treatment, Foreman is being judge and jury, circumventing the legal system.

**Shipper Alert!:** Cameron tells House she's completely over him.

**Pop Culture References:** House refers to Clarence as a "dead man walking," a reference to the Sean Penn movie of the same name.

**Casting Call:** Well-known rapper/actor LL Cool J guest stars as Clarence.

**Title Tale:** Should the team accept the case of a death row inmate? Is he an "acceptable" patient? Cameron, who continues to have difficulty telling patients bad news, cannot accept that a lonely young clinic patient with "only a cough" has advanced lung cancer. House disbelievingly accuses her of going through the "stages of dying" on behalf of her patient, jotting them down on a light box: denial, anger, bargaining, depression, and finally, acceptance. But House has his own issues with acceptance as Stacy, whom he both loves and resents, has returned to the hospital staff after an absence of several years. In the final scene, we see House erasing the light box, but pausing contemplatively at "acceptance."

## * 2.02 "Autopsy"

**Writer:** Lawrence Kaplow **Director:** Deran Sarafian

**Patient of the Week:** Andie (Sasha Embeth Pieterse)

Andie is an extraordinarily brave nine-year-old cancer patient of Wilson's who begins suffering hallucinations. Taking her terminal condition in stride, knowing she's going to die, Andie is determined to do everything possible to stay alive as long as she can.

House takes her case while he's suffering from severe hay fever. He is skeptical, asserting that *no one* can be *that* brave. As he looks for clues about what may be causing her new symptoms, he wonders whether Andie's stoicism is also a symptom. The contrast between the courageous Andie and the overly dramatic anguish of House's stuffy nose is stark.

The team runs its usual tests, and Andie develops a special relationship with Chase, eliciting from him a gentle kiss (on the lips) — much to horror of the team when they find out.

House thinks Andie's latest health crisis is a tiny clot in her brain, but they can't simply open up her brain and poke around to find it. They can only definitively locate the blockage at autopsy. So, House finds (or concocts) an elaborate, experimental procedure that will "kill" Andie temporarily, remove her blood, and then "reperfuse" it so they can observe the blockage as the blood flows back into her brain. Although Wilson obtains the mother's consent, House believes that Andie has earned the right to have a say in her own future.

In the end, Andie's life is saved. At first, House refuses to join the rest of the hospital staff in sending her home victorious as she leaves the hospital on her own two feet. But, in the end, House relents, and standing off from the crowd, allows her to hug him — and give him an important life lesson.

**Zebra of the Week:** A small blockage in Andie's brain.

**Epiphany (but not quite)!:** House believes Andie's bravery in the face of cancer indicates a clot in a specific area of her brain. The diagnosis is correct, but her bravery turns out to be real — and not a symptom. The clot is nowhere near where the bravery "symptom" suggests.

**Iconic Moment in *House* History:** House has a heart-to-heart conversation with Andie, explaining the risks of the procedure and telling her that she has a right to refuse — giving her an "out" if she doesn't want to go through with it. **Iconic Moment #2:** As House and the entire team of specialist physicians rehearse his experimental procedure on a corpse, we observe House in complete command of the elaborate operation. Decisive and in control, meticulous and demanding, he is king of the operating theater. **Iconic Moment #3:** The hospital staff gives the little girl a send-off, but House stands apart from everyone, refusing to cheer her on. Undeterred, Andie hugs House, and his eyes tell us that he is more moved by her than he admits. She tells him to live a little and rise above his pain. He actually listens to her — in his own way. Going out into the beautiful afternoon sun, House test drives a motorcycle, something we suspect he hasn't done in many years.

**Clinic Duty:** House treats a man who tried to circumcise himself. The usually unflappable House is horrified at the sight of the man's handiwork.

**House Is a Jerk:** Thinking her bravery is only a symptom, House coldly insists on watching while Wilson tells Andie and her mother that her cancer is untreatable — just to observe her reaction.

**Housian Ethics:** How proper is it that the dying nine-year-old is able to persuade Chase to give her a (quick) peck on the lips?

**Shipper Alert!:** Cameron makes House special tea for House's hay fever. He really likes it.

**Metaphorically Speaking:** House describes Andie's tumor as Al-Qaeda and the blood clots it throws off as sleeper terrorist cells.

**Lost in Translation:** House speaks a little Yiddish.

**Musical Notes:** Elvis Costello recorded this cover of the song "Beautiful" specifically for this episode.

**Casting Call:** Sasha Embeth Pieterse, only nine when she appeared as Andie, is already a television veteran, with a recurring role in the 2009–2010 season of NBC's *Heroes*.

**House Canon:** House has hay fever. He also likes motorcycles.

**Title Tale:** House's diagnostic procedure requires the girl to be "dead" in order to work; it's an autopsy.

**Why It's a Classic:** From Chase's relationship with Andie to the little girl's sage advice to House, it's a brilliant, award-winning episode.


## 2.03 "Humpty Dumpty"

**Writer:** Matt Witten **Director:** Daniel Attias
**Patient of the Week:** Alfredo (Ignacio Serricchio)

Cuddy's asthmatic handyman falls off her roof, but as they rush him to the hospital, she notices his hand is turning dusky. Taking the case, House contends he was ill before he fell. He believes Cuddy's guilt has affected her objectivity as she tries to insert herself into the case, pushing House to take risks with Alfredo's treatment that would make even *him* think twice. As Alfredo gets sicker, showing signs of severe, atypical pneumonia, Cuddy blames herself for pushing the young man to continue working when he wasn't feeling well.

When it appears Alfredo's hand has become infected and gangrenous, Cuddy refuses to allow an amputation, worried about the young man's future. It is only when House overhears Alfredo conversing in Spanish with his brother that he begins to figure out the medical mystery. Alfredo's life is saved, but it's too late to save his hand.

**Zebra of the Week:** Psittacosis, a serious bacterial infection from handling certain types of birds. It is exacerbated by Alfredo's asthma.

**Epiphany!:** House overhears Alfredo talking in rapid Spanish to his young brother about work. Realizing it could be psittacosis, he sends "the Scooby gang" to the local bird-fighting establishment to check it out. Sure enough, Alfredo's brother is working with birds.

**Iconic Moment in *House* History:** House reveals what he really thinks of Cuddy, calling her an idealist who sees things as they are and how they might be, but not the "gaping chasm" between. "If you had, you never would have hired me," he acknowledges. **Iconic Moment #2:** House, Chase, and Foreman search Cuddy's home for clues about Alfredo's illness. House is as delighted as a teenage boy exploring the inner sanctum of Cuddy's bedroom.

**Clinic Duty:** Foreman and House treat an elderly African-American man for high blood pressure. When Foreman wants to put the man on medication targeted at African-Americans, the patient refuses it, suspecting it's part of a racist agenda.

**Shipper Alert!:** Chase, Cameron, and Stacy are all curious about what may or may not have gone on in the past between House and Cuddy. House has more than a passing interest in his boss; he knows where she keeps her spare key, while deflecting all questions about whether they have ever had an intimate relationship. **Shipper Alert #2:** House and Stacy trade barbs in Cuddy's office about their past love life.

**Pop Culture References:** House calls upon "the Scooby gang" to investigate Alfredo's bird activities — a reference both to the television series *Buffy the Vampire Slayer* and the animated series *Scooby-Doo* (which is the original reference).

**Lost in Translation:** Who knew House was fluent in Spanish?

**Casting Call:** Ignacio Serricchio played a streetwise Mormon missionary in the critically acclaimed 2005 film *States of Grace*. Veteran film and television actor Charles Robinson, who guest stars as House's clinic patient, is perhaps best known for his role as court clerk Mac (1990–1992) on the long-running CBS comedy *Night Court*. (He also directed several episodes of the comedy.)

**Title Tale:** Cuddy's handyman has a great fall off her roof, and the team tries to put him back together again.


## 2.04 "TB or Not TB"

**Writer:** David Foster **Director:** Peter O'Fallon
**Patient of the Week:** Dr. Sebastian Charles (Ron Livingston)

House treats Dr. Sebastian Charles, a renowned TB specialist/advocate. He collapses while soliciting a pharmaceutical company to send supplies to the third world. Charles assumes he has TB, but House suspects something else is also at play. He does have TB, and as Cameron rightly asserts, it's interfering with whatever else afflicts him.

But Charles flatly refuses to take the expensive, but necessary, antibiotics. Instead, he sees an opportunity to make a political statement on the need for TB drugs in the third world. And unless Charles is cured of TB, the team cannot diagnose what's really wrong.

Cameron is attracted to the "do-gooder" doctor and the feeling seems mutual. But House sees hypocrisy in Charles' colorful life, complete with photo ops in desolate and disease-ridden hellholes.

**Zebra of the Week:** TB *and* nesidioblastoma, a tiny growth in the insulin-producing glands of the pancreas.

**Iconic Moment in *House* History:** House barges into Charles' hospital room and, incensed by what he views as a publicity stunt, turns up the heat in the room and throws out vestiges of civilization to simulate the African environment in which Charles spends so much time. "You are not like them," House yells. "You cheapen what they go through by pretending to be like them."

**Clinic Duty:** House treats a woman with an allergy to the cat she just inherited from her dead mother. He offers her several alternatives, none of which she likes. Finally, he snarkily offers a bag and a rock to get rid of the feline once and for all. Also, Foreman (using House's name badge) treats Cecilia, a woman who thinks she has breast cancer. When she believes "Dr. House" is dismissive, she complains to Cuddy, who insists House apologize.

**House Is a Jerk:** House is a bigger jerk than usual in this episode, particularly to Charles. He also plays the "cripple card" to manipulate Foreman's angry clinic patient and get them off the hook.

**Judgmental Fellow Alert:** House views Charles' refusal to take TB meds as arrogant and hypocritical.

**Shipper Alert!:** House is perturbed that Cameron is interested in Sebastian.

**Shipper Alert #2:** House discovers that Cuddy supports Sebastian's decision to martyr himself to his cause. He tries unsuccessfully to reason with her just before Sebastian holds a major press conference; the scene between them gives off lots of sparks.

**Pop Culture References:** House tests Charles' circulatory system on a tilt table. In order to push the boundaries of the test, House "cranks it up to 11," a reference to the rockumentary *This Is Spinal Tap*. This is a favorite House's catchphrase and he uses it often over the series' run.

**Casting Call:** Ron Livingston played Carrie's love interest Jack Berger on HBO's *Sex and the City* from 2002 to 2003. He also played Captain Lewis Nixon in the critically acclaimed HBO miniseries *Band of Brothers* (2001) for which he received a supporting actor Golden Globe nomination.

**Title Tale:** Yes, Sebastian has TB, but as House explains, it's not a surprise — and not the cause of current symptoms. But you can draw a comparison between House and Charles using Hamlet's "To be or not to be" soliloquy: "whether 'tis nobler . . ." to be a rare disease diagnostician who saves 50 lives a year that would otherwise be forfeit or a single disease specialist who saves many more but ignores other illnesses ". . . that is the question."


## 2.05 "Daddy's Boy"

**Writer:** Thomas L. Moran **Director:** Greg Yaitanes
**Patient of the Week:** Carnell (Vicellous Shannon)

What causes a young man to experience electric shocks without any outside stimulus? House and the team treat Carnell, a new Princeton graduate, as his father hovers close by. Carnell's symptoms worsen as he suffers convulsions and a lowered white count. Finally, they discover he has a tumor in his spine.

But it is not until House learns that Carnell's father has lied (he runs a scrap metal yard and not a construction company as he had claimed) that House is able to put together the puzzle.

Meanwhile, House's parents drop by for a visit, but House would rather do almost anything (yes, even clinic duty) to avoid seeing them.

**Zebra of the Week:** Radiation from a piece of scrap metal that Carnell's dad gave to him as a keepsake to "remember where he came from."

**Epiphany!:** Carnell's friend is brought to the hospital exhibiting signs of mild radiation poisoning. He mentions that Carnell's dad owns a scrap metal yard and House immediately wonders if the problem might be radiation from the memento — something that Carnell always keeps nearby on a keychain. Carnell, his friend, and his father have all been exposed.

**Iconic Moment in *House* History:** After House's parents have gone, he sits in his office brooding over their visit. Cameron stops by, and House thanks her for backing off her dinner scheme. Confiding in her, House reveals that he hates his father because his rigid moral code does not allow for anyone else to lie for any reason. "Great for police witnesses. Terrible for a dad," he bitterly recalls.

**Iconic Moment #2:** It is also hard to forget the episode's final scene as House leaves for home on his new bike, trying to shake off his emotions from his parents' visit. There is more to this complicated relationship than we can know at this point in the series.

**A Fine Bromance:** House buys a motorcycle with $5,000 borrowed from Wilson.

He reveals that he has been borrowing money from his friend in increasingly greater amounts to test the limits of their friendship. Concerned about the potentially deadly combination of House's disability, his drug use, and a motorbike built for speed, Wilson asks him to return it.

**Shipper Alert!:** Cameron is aggressively curious about House's parents and tries to make their private dinner a very public affair. House is clearly uncomfortable with this attention, and in the end, she backs off, respecting his privacy.

**Casting Call:** Vicellous Shannon (Carnell) also played Keith Palmer, the son of presidential candidate David Palmer in the Fox television series *24* from 2001 to 2002. R. Lee Ermey, who plays House's father Colonel John House, has made a career of playing tough military men. Perhaps his most famous role was in *Full Metal Jacket* as Gunnery Sergeant Hartman, for which he received a Golden Globe nomination. Ermey's voice is also famous for the Pixar animated *Toy Story* movies as — you guessed it — "Sarge." Veteran actress Diane Baker, who plays House's mother, has received critical acclaim for her many roles over the years, but in 1967, Baker had the honor of playing Dr. Richard Kimball's love interest in the two-part finale of the classic 1960s television series *The Fugitive* (ABC).

**Title Tale:** A tale of two guys with serious daddy issues.


## 2.06 "Spin"

**Writer:** Sarah Hess **Director:** Fred Gerber
**Patient of the Week:** Jeff Forster (Kristoffer Polaha)

House treats Jeff, a professional bicyclist who collapses at a race. He admits up front to illegally using performance-enhancing drugs and other illegal procedures, including "blood doping," and sleeping in a hyperbaric chamber to increase endurance. But these measures have not caused Jeff's symptoms. After several false leads and some interactions with his manager, it turns out his performance-enhancing activities have been actually masking his illness.

While diagnosing Jeff, House is also preoccupied with Stacy. Her husband Mark has been attending group therapy sessions at the hospital to deal with the emotional issues of his illness (acute intermittent porphryria — see the entry in season one for "Honeymoon," 1.22). House insinuates himself into the group to goad Mark and find a way to drive a wedge between Stacy and her husband.

**Zebra of the Week:** It's a thymoma, a (usually) benign tumor on the thymus gland, often associated with the disease myasthenia gravis.

**Epiphany!:** House realizes that the blood doping and other performance enhancers coincidentally treated his illness, masking the real cause of Jeff's symptoms.

**Clinic Duty:** A flight attendant comes in with diarrhea, which started when he quit smoking. Cause: gum-chewing overdose (sugar free gum is sweetened with xylitol, a laxative *and* a sweetener!).

**House Is a Jerk:** House's self-interest inspires him to violate Stacy's privacy by breaking into her therapist's files. It's a reprehensible act. Also indifferently letting Jeff fall to the floor after a diagnostic test is pretty heartless no matter what House thinks of his patient personally.

**Judgmental Fellow Alert:** Cameron is offended by Jeff's cheating, which presents a false image to all the kids who emulate and adore him. She calls the *Times*, intending to violate Jeff's confidentiality and rat him out to the press. Wilson stops her before she can actually talk to anyone at the paper, thus preventing her from committing a major ethical breach.

**Housian Ethics:** As a physician, what do you do with information proving your patient is a cheat? Medical ethics protect patient confidentiality and privacy, but Cameron sees a greater good in outing their patient to the media. **Housian Ethics #2:** After Jeff's story is leaked to the press, Cuddy suspects it's someone on House's team. She assigns Stacy to watch over the case and House insists he cannot practice medicine under such close legal scrutiny.

**Shipper Alert!:** House visits Stacy in her office, wondering how they can work together feeling as they do. Stacy lets slip that her therapist says "it will get easier," which makes House aware that Stacy has been discussing him during her sessions. It gives him the idea to steal her files. **Shipper Alert #2:** Cameron tells Wilson she nearly cheated with her husband's best friend years earlier. But her strict moral code would never have let her live with herself. Wilson, who is beginning to have marital problems of his own, admits to her, "You'd be surprised what you can live with."

**Casting Call:** Kristoffer Polaha (Jeff) has appeared in supporting roles on several series, including *North Shore* and *Mad Men*. House's clinic patient is played by Tom Lenk, who played Andrew Wells on *Buffy the Vampire Slayer* from 2000 to 2003 (one of several *Buffy* alums to guest on *House*).

**Title Tale:** The patient is a champion cyclist and his manager tries to "spin" the cyclist's illness into a cancer scare for sympathy and lots of publicity. Also, Stacy's husband is still in a wheelchair — spinning his wheels.

## * 2.07 "Hunting"

**Writer:** Liz Friedman **Director:** Gloria Muzio
**Patient of the Week:** Kalvin Ryan (Matthew John Armstrong)

Kalvin, a young homosexual man with AIDS, has been stalking House, trying to get him to diagnose his new symptoms, which Kalvin insists have nothing to do with AIDS. Initially, House has no interest in the case, but when Kalvin goes into anaphylactic shock after playing tug-a-cane with him, Cuddy gives him no choice. While Cameron attends to Kalvin, he coughs blood onto her face, exposing her to HIV and leading her to reassess her priorities in the face of the potentially fatal disease.

House tries to endear himself to Stacy — and perhaps get into her bed, using the information found in her therapist's files at the end of "Spin" (2.06), helping her wash dishes and get rid of a rat that has moved into her attic. But the plan backfires when Stacy eventually realizes that he has coldly violated her privacy.

**Zebra of the Week:** Echinococcosis, a parasite infesting foxes, which causes liver and heart cysts — and an anaphylactic reaction.
**Epiphany!:** Kalvin's estranged father grudgingly makes a visit to his son, and House observes symptoms consistent with the infection. Dad refuses to undergo a simple confirming blood test, and House resorts to provoking Dad to take a swing at him, which gives him leave to hit back. House takes a swing with his cane, bursting one of the dad's cysts and producing the same reaction Kalvin experienced.
**Iconic Moment in *House* History:** House and Stacy finally apologize to each other for past hurts. It's a moment of closure, each acknowledging the pain and misery they have caused each other. **Iconic Moment #2:** The stoned Cameron meets House in the elevator on the way up to the office. House observes her, noting her condition — and she notes House carrying Stacy's rat in a cage. It's a quick, but memorably amusing moment between them.
**House Is a Jerk:** Using a bit of info from Stacy's files, House intentionally leaves the toilet seat up in Stacy's house, knowing she'll be annoyed with Mark for it. Actually, it's pretty obnoxious all the way around, the way House uses the information from Stacy's files to manipulate her feelings.
**Housian Ethics:** House uses Stacy's pilfered psychiatric records to worm his way into her good graces. **Housian Ethics #2:** House wonders about the ethics of Chase sleeping with a "drugged-out colleague," which does, to say the least, seem a bit exploitative.
**Shipper Alert!:** Somewhere in the midst of House's manipulation of Stacy's

feelings, it stops being a game for him as he helps her locate and capture the elusive rat. They talk, guard down, probably for the first time in years about the final days of their relationship. **Shipper Alert #2:** Foreshadowing the next several seasons, Chase and Cameron have a night of wild sex when she takes crystal meth in a brief walk on the wild side after being exposed to AIDS. She easily seduces her stunned colleague.

**Pop Culture References:** We learn that House lives at 221B — Sherlock Holmes' famous address on Baker Street. Also, House adopts the rat captured at Stacy's and names him Steve McQueen, after the actor known for playing daring anti-heroes in numerous films.

**Casting Call:** Matthew John Armstrong (Kalvin) was a regular on NBC's *American Dreams* (2002–2005) and played Ted Sprague in the 2006–2007 season of *Heroes* also on NBC. Wings Hauser, who plays Kalvin's father, has appeared in numerous films and television series, including a long running stint in the late '70s to early '80s as Greg Foster on the CBS soap *The Young and the Restless*.

**Title Tale:** Everyone seems to be hunting in "Hunting." Kalvin's illness is due to fox hunting and Kalvin is a party animal, always on the hunt. House and Stacy hunt for a rat in her attic. House is setting his bait to capture Stacy's heart. Cameron stalks Chase fairly well too.

**Why It's a Classic:** The episode is a significant milestone in the relationship between House and Stacy as House's manipulation turns to something else.


## * 2.08 "The Mistake"
**Writer:** Peter Blake **Director:** David Semel
**Patient of the Week:** Kayla (Allison Smith)

Using flashbacks and differing points of view, the episode examines the circumstances surrounding a patient's death. Chase makes an error of judgment when Kayla comes into the clinic with joint and stomach pain, and forgets to ask a basic question about symptoms. He is about to follow up when Kayla returns to the hospital, this time with massive bleeding from a perforated ulcer. Now septic, Kayla has significant liver damage; she needs a transplant, which her brother offers. But, unbeknownst to anyone, the brother has hepatitis C and cancer, which he passes on to Kayla.

She needs a second transplant, but due to the hepatitis C and liver cancer, there is little anyone can do. Kayla dies, and Cuddy appoints Stacy to prepare both Chase and House for the hospital's internal investigation. Still angry about House's invasion of her privacy, Stacy is hardly in the mood to defend him. Chase, feeling guilty about his role in the patient's death, makes no effort to defend himself when he is charged with gross negligence. But it is revealed that he was distracted by his father death, which he learned of during Kayla's initial visit.

**Zebra of the Week:** Hepatitis C, liver cancer, and rejection of the liver transplanted from the patient's brother.

**Epiphany!:** House notices symptoms in Kayla's brother, which lead him to suspect cancer.

**Iconic Moment in *House* History:** After Chase claims that he was hungover when treating Kayla, House pulls him aside, understanding the real reason why Chase was distracted. He advises him to tell the truth and save his career, although a finding of gross negligence would get House off the hook. Chase finally tells the truth and House pays the price by having his department put under Foreman's supervision for four weeks.

**Clinic Duty:** While treating a young man for a cough, House scares him into getting health insurance.

**Shipper Alert!:** Stacy tells House that her feelings for him are "not all bad."

**Casting Call:** Allison Smith (Kayla) is probably best known for her role on the CBS comedy *Kate & Allie* (1984–1989), in which she played Allie's daughter Jennie Lowell. The transplant surgeon is played by Broadway, film, and television star John Rubinstein, whose son Michael Weston plays House's friend/rival Lucas Douglas in seasons five and six.

**Title Tale:** The entire episode revolves around Chase's mistake. House also acknowledges his mistake in letting Stacy know he'd stolen her private files.

**Why It's a Classic:** Complex storytelling and tight writing make this nonformulaic episode compelling. It is also the jumping off point for the next major narrative arcs: the intensification of the House-Stacy relationship and Foreman's takeover of House's practice.

---

### House and Medical Mistakes

House's attitude towards medical mistakes has been clearly defined throughout the series, especially because he owes his disability to a missed diagnosis. He is always angry about mistakes — and at the people who make them, but he accepts that mistakes are part and parcel of medical practice. "You are going to kill somebody," he tells a lecture hall full of medical students in "Three Stories" (1.21). He tells them either to "accept that or find another career."

By observing how House reacts to mistakes and other infractions by his team, we can discern what matters most to House professionally. And what angers him in his own staff and about medicine. But also what he accepts as inevitable.

In season one ("Control," 1.14), Chase mistakenly x-rays the wrong leg of a patient because a pretty young resident distracts him. House is furious because Chase allowed himself to be distracted from the task, not even signing the report. With Chase fearful of his position on House's team, he allies himself with the new, power-hungry board chairman, Edward Vogler, becoming his snitch. But two episodes later, with House's department in danger of being shuttered unless he fires one of his fellows, House asks Foreman who he thinks should get the axe. When Foreman suggests "Chase," House is surprised. "Because of one mistake?" he asks, referring to the error in "Control." House had not considered that the mistake should cause Chase to lose his job.

In the season two episode "The Mistake" (2.08), Chase is again distracted, and this time his mistake is fatal. House is justifiably angry about the screwup, reprimanding Chase for failing to ask a basic question during his examination of the patient, especially after he attempts to blame the patient for failing to mention subtle symptoms. "Mistakes are as serious as the results they cause! This woman could die because you were too lazy to ask one simple question!" House rants.

But House understands the reasons behind Chase's distraction here. He has just learned that his father is dead, and it's a shock to Chase. He hadn't known his father was even ill. In his own way, House mentors Chase through the crisis, which could have resulted in the loss of his medical license.

Likewise in season four, fellowship candidate Remy Hadley ("13") tragically fails to watch as a patient takes his medication, an oversight that costs the patient his life in "97 Seconds" (4.03). House reacts, angry as he explains the consequences of her oversight, but does not fire her. House recognizes that making a mistake has little to do with whether or not one is a competent doctor.

## 2.09 "Deception"

**Writer:** Michael Perry **Director:** Deran Sarafian
**Patient of the Week:** Anica (Cynthia Nixon)

Tony winner Cynthia Nixon guest stars as Anica, a woman with Münchausen's syndrome. Although Anica has caused most of her own health problems, House insists that something other than Münchausen's is causing her current symptoms. But his is the lone voice on this, and House (no longer in control of the department) has to plead with Foreman not to "kick her to the curb" with a Münchausen's diagnosis. Unfortunately, Foreman's not listening, so House resorts to desperate, questionable measures to make sure Anica is treated — while making life miserable for his new boss.

**Zebra of the Week:** Clostridium perfringens, a bacterial infection.
**Epiphany!:** House notes the characteristic fruity aroma of the bacterial infection on her pillow while resting in Anica's room as the team prepares her to undergo an unnecessary bone marrow transplant.
**Clinic Duty:** One of the best clinic patients of all time, she is known as "Jelly Girl" by the Internet fan community. Coming into the clinic with vaginosis, she reveals to House her unique "jelly" contraceptive: strawberry preserves!
**House Is a Jerk:** House orders MRIS for the entire maternity unit to provoke Foreman. He tells Foreman one of the MRIS is actually necessary, so he can't simply rescind the entire order.
**Judgmental Fellow Alert:** Cameron correctly calls the Münchausen's diagnosis but disputes that another illness is involved. She and Foreman just want to get rid of her.
**Housian Ethics:** Cameron leaves a bottle of rifampin on Anica's bedside table with a false label on it to lure Anica into taking the drug to induce her desired symptoms. In the short term, it proves Cameron's point, but ultimately, the antibiotic rifampin masks her clostridium infection, significantly delaying the diagnosis.
**Housian Ethics #2:** To prove a point and buy Anica an extended stay, House follows Anica after Foreman discharges her and injects her with a chemical cocktail to mimic the symptoms of aplastic anemia, which House believes she has at this point (she doesn't).
**Shipper Alert!:** When Foreman orders Cameron and House to break into Anica's home, House insists they take his motorcycle. Sitting behind him on the bike, Cameron is shy about holding onto House. Smiling delightedly, House emphatically places her arms around him, quite content at her closeness. His satisfied smile tells the entire story, even though they have a heated argument about

Anica once they arrive at their destination.

**Pop Culture References:** Confirming Anica's infection, House proclaims that he "love[s] the aroma of pus in the morning; it smells like victory." It's a line ripped (more or less) from the film *Apocalypse Now*.

**Casting Call:** Tony and Emmy Award–winning actress Cynthia Nixon plays Anica. Nixon is probably best known for her role as Miranda Hobbes in the hit HBO series *Sex and the City* (and its ensuing movies).

**Title Tale:** Lots of deception in "Deception." Münchausen's is a psychiatric disorder of deception. House deceives Foreman by giving Anica an injection to mimic aplastic anemia. The Münchausen's diagnosis, while true, deceives Foreman and the rest of the team (except House) into thinking there's no other ailment. Cameron deceives Anica into taking the rifampin, and Cuddy deceives Foreman into thinking he's actually in charge of House's department.

## * 2.10 "Failure to Communicate"

**Writer:** Doris Egan **Director:** Jace Alexander
**Patient of the Week:** Fletcher Stone (Michael O'Keefe)

House leaves the Princeton-Plainsboro confines to defend his Medicare billings to the Feds, taking Stacy with him as the hospital attorney. Cuddy reluctantly gives Foreman, still in charge of the Diagnostics Department, a new case: Fletcher Stone, a famous journalist with aphasia. Fortunately, House is only a cell-phone call away. But when he and Stacy become snowbound for the night in a Baltimore airport, Foreman and the team must make sense of Fletcher's incomprehensible speech. Cameron's smart (and cynical) thinking provides a clue when she realizes Fletcher only tries to communicate when his wife is out of the room — he must have a secret from her. Once Fletcher's wife is conveniently distracted, House eventually makes sense of Fletcher's aphasic communication.

Meanwhile, House is alternately annoying (like an adolescent boy) and endearing towards Stacy as they continue their awkward courtship dance. Snowbound, Stacy has reserved a hotel room, aware that House would have difficulty sleeping on one of the airport cots. But he wonders whether she has an ulterior motive, especially since she's just had an argument with her husband. When they get to their room, House questions her agenda.

**Zebra of the Week:** Malaria, rampant in Fletcher's brain, had been undetectable using standard computerized testing. The team correctly confirms the infection after House insists they use low-tech microscopy.

**Epiphany!:** House understands enough of Fletcher's aphasic communication to guess correctly that he's bipolar, which he had hoped to keep from his wife. A secret trip to the third world for treatment exposed him to malaria.

**Iconic Moment in *House* History:** Alone in a hotel room, House and Stacy finally kiss. Slightly hesitant at first, it deepens quickly into a gentle passion that made a million female (and probably more than a few male) hearts flutter.

**Clinic Duty:** House diagnoses an airport full of people to impress the annoyed Stacy.

**A Fine Bromance:** Wilson nags House about his dying cell phone battery and lack of "call waiting."

**House Is a Jerk:** Stacy calls him one as she prepares to kiss him. He simply shrugs. He is who he is.

**Shipper Alert!:** Stacy describes her relationship with House as "Vindaloo Curry," something she has missed in the years since their breakup. In a revelatory scene, suggesting an intimacy between them beyond sex, Stacy seeks out House late at night as he contemplates the case in a secluded corner of the airport. She brings him a phone charger, and then simply keeps him company while he works.

**Pop Culture References:** Stacy's remark to House about the messiness of relationships at the episode's end refers to a similar sentiment expressed in Woody Allen's classic film *Annie Hall*.

**Lost in Translation:** House again demonstrates his fluency in Yiddish, as House is "all *gemutlicht*" over Cameron's newfound information (about the patient). Also, House seems to have at least an abridged version of the "aphasic dictionary."

**Casting Call:** Michael O'Keefe (Fletcher) received a Best Supporting Actor Oscar nomination for his role in the 1979 film *The Great Santini*. Erica Gimpel, who plays Fletcher's wife, starred in the 1982–1987 ABC television series *Fame* as Coco Hernandez, and has also had regular roles on *ER* (NBC), *Boston Legal* (ABC), and *Veronica Mars* (UPN).

**Title Tale:** Fletcher has a literal "failure to communicate." Fletcher and his new bride also seem to have a communication failure, since he has kept a bipolar condition from her. Stacy and House aren't communicating their feelings either — until she puts hers into a metaphor — something House understands very well.

**Why It's a Classic:** This episode marks the beginning of House and Stacy's reconciliation.

## * 2.11 "Need to Know"

**Writer:** Pamela Davis **Director:** David Semel
**Patient:** Margo Dalton (Julie Warner)

The team treats Margo, a super mom on fertility drugs, who suddenly starts flailing uncontrollably. The team thinks her symptoms suggest drug use, especially after they find Ritalin hidden in her automobile glove box. But when House realizes that it's really a secret she's keeping from her husband that's making her sick, she is uninterested in hearing about the easiest cure.

Meanwhile, House and Stacy address the "day after" their Baltimore encounter, with House seeking advice from Wilson. (Yeah, *he's* the expert!) Although they only shared a kiss in "Failure to Communicate" (2.10), both are deeply affected as they consider "what next?" Stacy is ready to go home, back to her life with Mark — and away from House. But House begs her not to go, and it's impossible for her to resist her strong attraction to him.

**Zebra of the Week:** Birth control pills in combination with Margo's fertility meds can be deadly. But worth the risk to Margo, who's trying to fool her husband into thinking she wants more children. When she learns that simply stopping the birth control pills can reverse her symptoms, she refuses, opting instead for an unnecessary and risky surgery to maintain her deception.

**Epiphany!:** Staring at the whiteboard, House realizes that the constellation of symptoms cannot be explained by one condition — but they can by two.

**Iconic Moment in *House* History:** House has a great little (and very insightful) conversation with Margo's young daughter when she intrudes on him watching television and brooding about Stacy. She asks him why he's so sad. "I'm not sad, I'm complicated," responds House. "Chicks dig that."

**A Fine Bromance:** House visits Wilson to talk about his relationship with Stacy and finds him rolling a marijuana cigarette for a patient. House tries to pocket the joint for himself, but Wilson demands he give it back. Also, Wilson warns Stacy that House is probably taking their relationship more seriously than she is, revealing that he has pined for her during the five years since she left him.

**House Is a Jerk:** Trying to run away from a conversation with Stacy's wheelchair-bound husband, House leaves him lying in a deserted stairwell. (On the other hand, what could House do to pick him up? Hopefully he went to get a nurse.)

**Judgmental Fellow Alert:** Wilson finds House on the rooftop brooding and upset after sending Stacy back to Mark. He accuses House of sending her away because he wants to be miserable since it makes him "special."

**Housian Ethics:** Should Wilson really have been rolling that cigarette? **Housian Ethics #2:** Should House be sleeping with a married woman? **Housian Ethics #3:**

Margo asks Foreman to perpetuate her lie and tell her husband that her illness has rendered her unable to have children. He refuses to collaborate.

**Shipper Alert!:** House and Stacy spend the night (or at least part of it) together in bed. House takes their rekindled relationship as a signal that she is prepared to leave Mark and spend her life with him. He sends her a "prescription for her heart condition," asking her to meet him on the hospital rooftop at dawn. But on the roof, House senses Stacy's ambivalence. When she eventually decides she's prepared to leave Mark for House, he sends her back to her husband, certain he cannot make Stacy happy long-term — and unwilling to put himself through the torture he suffered after she left him the first time. **Shipper Alert #2:** House is concerned that Cameron has avoided her follow-up AIDS test after the events in "Hunting" (2.07). He forces the issue, telling Cameron "I love you," and when she opens her mouth to respond, swabs the inside of her cheek to get a sample for testing.

**Pop Culture References:** House refers to the film *Driving Miss Daisy*; Cameron calls Ritalin "Mother's Little Helper," referring to the Rolling Stones classic.

**Musical Notes:** House sings an aria from the Sigmund Romberg operetta *The Student Prince* after his night with Stacy. We've learned since that House often sings when he's pleased with himself or genuinely happy.

**Casting Call:** Julie Warner (Margo) is probably best known for her roles in *Doc Hollywood* (1991), *Mr. Saturday* (1992), and *Tommy Boy* (1995).

**Title Tale:** Does Margo's husband need to know she's been taking birth control pills *and* fertility meds? Does Mark need to know Stacy slept with House? What does House need to know about Stacy's feelings for him? And really, does House need to be lectured to by Wilson on his misery and unhappiness?

**Why It's a Classic:** "Need to Know" is the finale of the long House–Stacy arc, with House finally achieving some closure when he sends her back to her husband. We catch a fleeting glimpse of House the romantic as he sings and sends sappy love notes.

## 2.12 "Distractions"

**Writer:** Lawrence Kaplow **Director:** Daniel Attias
**Patient of the Week:** Adam (James Immekus)

The team treats the teenage Adam, severely burned after crashing his all-terrain vehicle. Unable to perform conventional diagnostic tests due to the extent of the burns, the team must instead resort to antiquated techniques. They use a galvanometer to test Adam's heart and maggots to clean out the wounds sufficiently to perform a lumbar puncture without the risk of serious infection.

But House is missing a crucial piece of the puzzle — Adam's own story. In a chemically induced coma since his arrival due to the intense pain he would suffer if awake, Adam is unable to tell House exactly what happened to cause the accident. It is only after waking up the young man that he begins to put together the clues.

Meanwhile, House exacts revenge on a former medical school rival after inviting him to speak at the hospital. Dr. Philip Weber, whom House calls "von Lieberman" (because "it sounds 'eviler'") once ratted him out for cheating on a math test at Johns Hopkins, getting House expelled and causing him to lose a prestigious internship. Now a migraine expert, Weber is running a clinical study on a new preventative migraine drug of which he claims astounding results. House tries to discredit the study by testing the drug on himself — after self-inducing a killer migraine.

Of course, Weber's medicine doesn't work. House eventually treats his migraine with an unusual choice (LSD, which was, in fact, invented to treat migraines) combined with antidepressants (which mitigate the psychedelic effects of the LSD).

**Zebra of the Week:** Adam is a smoker trying to quit. He's been taking mail-order anti-smoking drugs, which contain antidepressants. The antidepressants in the drugs caused a seizure leading to the accident and Adam's symptoms.

**Epiphany!:** Taking antidepressants to help counteract his migraine leads House to consider the effects and whether they might be causing Adam's problems. But the parents insist that Adam isn't depressed. Not believing them, House visits his patient a second time, noting a cigarette burn among the thousand other burn marks on his body.

**Iconic Moment in *House* History:** After House takes LSD for the migraine, he experiences the psychedelic effects of the drug. He "sees" music as he watches droplets of water drip from his body as he sits in the locker room. After Cameron examines him, she leaves, disgusted that House would get high when his patient is dying. But by the time he returns to the diagnostics office he is thinking clearly due to the antidepressants he takes to counteract the LSD.

**A Fine Bromance:** House attends Weber's lecture on his new migraine remedy, planning to harass him from the audience. Wilson, stunned that House has deigned to attend a hospital lecture, is even more surprised to see him in disguise: fatigue jacket, shades, and a large baseball cap. Realizing what House plans to do, he begs him to get a hobby — even a hooker will do!

**Housian Ethics:** House insists on waking Adam from his barbiturate coma to speak with him, although another physician considers it torture. But waking

Adam eventually saves his life. Is it more ethical to let the boy die comfortably, or inflict pain (torture, even) to save his life? **Housian Ethics #2:** House also induces a migraine in his favorite coma patient to test Weber's migraine drug, prompting Cuddy to ask, "Have you ever read an ethical guideline?" **Housian Ethics #3:** When did it become legal to use LSD for a migraine?

**Shipper Alert!:** Foreman gives House an injection to help with his headache (it doesn't work). When he tells House it can cause heart problems, House assures him (in the aftermath of Stacy) that nothing "can break my heart."

**Lost in Translation:** House reads a journal in Hindi (with the aid of a dictionary, but still)!

**World-Famous Doctor Moment:** House is able to halt Weber's trial simply by emailing the pharmaceutical company sponsoring it. House must have an awful lot of credibility to stop another doctor's clinical trial so easily.

**Casting Call:** The young James Immekus (Adam) has already made a name guesting in a variety of hit television series including *Mad Men* on AMC and *Cold Case* on NBC. House's old medical school nemesis is played by Dan Butler, known for his recurring role on *Frasier* as Bulldog Brisco (1993–2004). He directed one episode of the hit show in 1998.

**Title Tale:** House's big distraction now that Stacy's gone? Revenge on an old medical school adversary. Wilson tells House he needs a distraction and House takes Wilson's advice, but not without a lot of angst.


## 2.13 "Skin Deep"

**Writers:** Garrett Lerner, Russel Friend, David Shore **Director:** James Hayman
**Patient of the Week:** Alex (Cameron Richardson)

House treats Alex, a teenage supermodel who collapses after a taking a swing at another model on the catwalk. With heroin and other drugs in her system, House rapid-detoxes her, revealing new symptoms, including twitching. After they learn she has had sex with her father, who also serves as her manager, House believes it's post-traumatic stress disorder (PTSD). But it's not until his encounter with a whiny clinic patient that House hits on the correct diagnosis.

While diagnosing Alex, House is also trying to deal with a serious upsurge in pain; he is barely able to get out bed, practically collapsing as he tries. The team believes he's letting the pain affect his decision-making, rushing the diagnosis and jumping to conclusions. And when House explains to Alex's father that the symptoms of PTSD can be so severe they can kill, it's impossible not to wonder if House, too, suffers from a sort of PTSD.

After an MRI reveals nothing physically changed in his leg, House goes to

Cuddy, asking her for a shot of morphine in his spine. Both she and Wilson believe the problem is more in House's head than in his leg, and to prove the point, Cuddy agrees to the morphine but substitutes a placebo. The injection mitigates the pain temporarily. When House returns after the case is solved, Cuddy admits to using a placebo, leaving House shocked and wondering whether she and Wilson are right.

**Zebra of the Week:** The supermodel is really a "he." The hermaphroditic Alex has testicular cancer in testicles that never emerged.

**Epiphany!:** House treats a male clinic patient with sympathetic pregnancy. He suffers all the symptoms his pregnant wife suffers due to an excess of estrogen. That leads House to consider that perhaps Alex is "all estrogen" — a hermaphrodite.

**Iconic Moment in *House* History:** Cuddy dismisses House's intense pain as psychosomatic. However, House reminds her that his pain is quite real as he drops his pants, revealing the terrible surgical scar on his leg. It is the first time we see House's disfigured leg.

**Clinic Duty:** House treats a man with sympathetic pregnancy. He not only has the usual morning sickness, he actually grows breasts (much to Cuddy's amusement).

**A Fine Bromance:** Wilson administers an MRI on House's leg. Wilson tries to relax the visibly nervous House by playing God in the control room. The amusing game goes on until Cuddy interrupts their fun.

**House Is a Jerk:** House pushes his sexist image more than usual as he leers at magazine photos of Alex. He seems preoccupied with the gossip rags and her physical attributes, earning the disapproval of Foreman and Cameron. However, House is actually more interested in revealing Alex's sexually abusive father and uses the magazine coverage to confront him. Once he has confirmed his suspicions, his interest dries up, and his disdain becomes obvious.

**Judgmental Fellow Alert:** The whole team is disgusted with the child-molesting dad. **Judgmental Fellow Alert #2:** Foreman calls House out on letting pain affect his work.

**Housian Ethics:** After learning that Alex and her father/manager have had sex, House fails to report him to social services. He insists that he needs the father nearby in case he needs more information about Alex. Cameron reports House to Cuddy, who then calls the child protection agency. Cameron fears that House will be angry and punish her somehow, but he tells her that he knows she only did what she thought was "right."

**Musical Notes:** After House learns he's been treated with a placebo, he returns home, trying to distract himself from (what he now believes may be) psychosomatic pain by playing Bach's French Suite no. 5. It doesn't distract him for long.

**Casting Call:** Cameron Richardson (Alex) co-starred in the 2007 movie *Alvin and the Chipmunks*.

**Title Tale:** Beauty is only skin deep, especially when underneath the beautiful blond hair and ultra-feminine skin you are really a guy. Also, is House's pain real or simply imagined? That scar is certainly real, but is the pain physical (in the skin) or masking deeper problems?

## 2.14 "Sex Kills"

**Writer:** Matt Witten **Director:** David Semel

**Patient of the Week:** Henry Errington (Howard Hesseman)

What happens when a heart-transplant candidate is rejected by the committee because of age? If House is your doctor, you get the fiercest of advocates, who believes that a rejected donor is better than no donor at all. After the transplant committee refuses to grant a heart to 60-something Henry, House goes "dumpster diving" to find an organ donor whose organs have been rejected and are of no use to anyone else. Laura is a crash victim whose physical condition precludes her from being a donor, and House aggressively tries to persuade the woman's husband to donate her heart. Eventually he succeeds, but the now brain-dead woman is suffering heart problems and a fever — both of which the team needs to resolve before transplanting her heart into Henry.

**Zebra of the Week:** Henry has brucellosis, exacerbated by his regular use of antacids, which created a fertile environment for the bug. Organ donor Laura has gonorrhea.

**Epiphany!:** When the team finds pictures of Laura's male teenage students in her desk drawer, they consider that she might have a sexually transmitted disease (STD). But it's actually her husband, Ron, who exposed her to gonorrhea.

**Iconic Moment in *House* History:** Wilson calls it quits with wife number three after learning she's having an affair. He turns up on House's doorstep at the episode's end, suitcase in hand. As "Honky-Tonk Woman" plays on House's stereo, he offers Wilson a beer and the use of his sofa. *That's* being a friend.

**Clinic Duty:** A young man shows up in the clinic professing his love for cows. He asks for medication to suppress the urge to mate with them. It turns out not to be bovine love, but a sexually aggressive stepmother creating a bit of a physical problem for the young man.

**A Fine Bromance:** Wilson moves in with House at the end of the episode. Oscar, meet Felix.

**House Is a Jerk:** House insensitively dismisses Wilson, who is experiencing marital problems and needs a friend. House reminds him that he is not *that* kind of friend, ignoring the number of times Wilson has been there for him. House is also at his manipulative best in trying to get Ron to consent to the transplant, provoking the grief-stricken husband to knee him in the groin.

**Housian Ethics:** Is it ethical to go "dumpster diving" in search of a transplantable organ among the rejects?

**Casting Call:** Howard Hessman (Henry) came to fame starring as the burned out has-been DJ Dr. Johnny Fever on the CBS hit comedy *WKRP in Cincinnati* (1978–1982). Greg Grunberg (best known for recurring roles on *Heroes* and *Felicity*) plays Ron, the donor's husband, a fortuitous bit of casting that introduced musician Grunberg to musician Hugh Laurie. Soon thereafter they formed the charity rock band, The Band From TV.

**Title Tale:** Sex kills the heart transplant donor. Actually, sex kills quite often on *House!* Henry contracts an STD after having sex with his ex-wife. Henry's search for a sexual mate at a church social leads him to contract brucellosis, which nearly kills him.


## 2.15 "Clueless"

**Writer:** Thomas L. Moran **Director:** Deran Sarafian
**Patient of the Week:** Bob (Eddie Mills)

After a rape-fantasy sexual encounter with his wife leaves the Bob gasping for air, House and the team try to diagnose him. His symptoms indicate heavy metal poisoning to House, but when tests of the usual suspects (lead, cadmium, and other common metals) come back negative, the team begins to doubt him. As Bob's symptoms continue to worsen, House begins to suspect that the wife is deliberately poisoning him. But she has not left Bob's side, hovering and seemingly distraught over her husband's condition. Eventually House relies on his trusty old chemistry set to prove his point.

**Zebra of the Week:** Bob's wife has been poisoning him with a gold compound.
**Epiphany!:** House realizes the couple took a trip to Mexico, where a gold compound (gold sodium diamylate) is a readily available arthritis treatment.
**Iconic Moment in *House* History:** House frantically searches for his prized chemistry set after his apartment has been cleaned and organized by Wilson's housekeeper. **Iconic Moment #2:** House munches down Wilson's macadamia nut pancakes, which he calls "little slices of heaven." He slaps away Chase's hand

when he tries to steal one.

**A Fine Bromance:** Wilson and House continue to live together, but Wilson's fastidious early morning routine is a bit much for the late-to-rise House. But when he tastes Wilson's macadamia nut pancakes, House rethinks his position.

**House Is a Jerk:** House can't stand Wilson's morning hygiene rituals (which keep him from sleeping) and kicks him out — that is, until he tastes Wilson's home cooking. Realizing a good thing when he tastes it, House then sabotages Wilson's plans to move into a condo.

**Pop Culture References:** The episode's title is a reference to the classic Parker Brothers board game *Clue*.

**Casting Call:** Samantha Mathis (Bob's wife and would-be murderess) appeared in the 2000 film *American Psycho* as Courtney Rawlinson.

**Title Tale:** It's a game of *Clue* as House tries to find out who poisoned Bob and how: the wife in the hospital with the gold dust. The episode makes several references to the popular game. House is clueless about Wilson's abilities as a chef. The team is pretty clueless throughout the episode, as the fellows refuse to listen to the master game player as he keeps insisting that it's metal poisoning. When will the children ever learn?

## 2.16 "Safe"

**Writer:** Peter Blake **Director:** Felix Enriquez Alcala
**Patient of the Week:** Melinda (Michelle Trachtenberg)

The team treats Melinda, a teenage heart transplant patient with severe multiple allergies. At first, House believes Melinda's symptoms are caused by exposure to penicillin through her boyfriend's semen after a first-time sexual encounter. But when House learns the young man is on a different antibiotic — one to which she's not allergic — he rethinks his position. House hypothesizes that a tick somehow managed its way onto Melinda by way of her boyfriend. Her symptoms fit perfectly, but no one believes him — and as he starts to search Melinda for the tick, her heart begins to fail. Cuddy and Foreman believe House is wasting precious time, but Wilson becomes House's silent collaborator in as he continues to search for the seemingly invisible pest.

As House puzzles out what's causing Melinda's increasingly dire symptoms, he tries to provoke Wilson into taking some action with regard to his dissolving marriage.

**Zebra of the Week:** Tick paralysis.
**Epiphany!:** All symptoms point to tick paralysis, but House nails it when he real-

izes Melinda's boyfriend may have gone through tall grasses to get into her house. He finally finds the tick after looking in a very unlikely place.

**Iconic Moment in *House* History:** House searches for the tick while he and Foreman race against time in a stopped elevator. He looks everywhere, but finally finds it by examining her vaginal area — just as the door to the elevator opens on Melinda's father, who tries to take a swing at House, calling him a pervert — before he sees that House is right.

**A Fine Bromance:** As House and Wilson continue to live together, House plays an increasingly intense series of pranks to provoke Wilson into seeing a lawyer and finalize his divorce plans. House wants Wilson to fight back against his pranks — prank him back. *Do* something! But he just seems to take it like the martyr he can be. Eventually Wilson pays House back by sawing his cane (almost) in two. It's a potentially dangerous prank against the disabled House, although he seems to appreciate it.

**House Is a Jerk:** House erases a message for Wilson about a condo for sale and never tells Wilson about it.

**Casting Call:** Michelle Trachtenberg played Nurse Chloe Payne in NBC's *Mercy* (2009–2010), but fans may also recognize her as Dawn Summers on *Buffy the Vampire Slayer* (2000–2003).

**Title Tale:** There is only so much a mother can do to keep her child safe. House grows frustrated with the passive-aggressive Wilson playing it safe.


## * 2.17 "All In"

**Writer:** David Foster **Director:** Fred Gerber
**Patient of the Week:** Ian (Carter Page)


What more can be said about House in a gorgeous tux and silver-tipped cane? However, all the pretty trappings do not conceal House's anguish as he tries to save the life of Cuddy's six-year-old patient. Ian may have the same unidentified condition that killed Esther, House's patient from years earlier. House has been haunted for 12 years by his failure to cure her.

House believes the elderly Esther was killed by Erdheim-Chester disease. But as the team rules it out in Ian's case, he begins to question his original assumption. While House continues treating the worsening Ian behind Cuddy's back, Wilson keeps her occupied at a Texas hold 'em poker benefit in the hospital lobby. Once Cuddy discovers that House has not only been treating her patient, but is once again trying to "cure Esther," she bars House and the team from the case.

**Zebra of the Week:** House has been right all along — it's Erdheim-Chester. It's also called polyostotic sclerosing histiocytosis, a rare disease characterized by abnormally multiplying histiocytes (a type of white blood cell).

**Epiphany!:** Brooding on his balcony as dawn approaches, no closer to an answer, Wilson interrupts House to tell him he's won the poker tournament, holding "pocket aces." House realizes they may have tested too early in Ian's case to detect Erdheim-Chester, and perhaps the "aces" have been hiding the whole time, causing him to make the leap back to his original (hidden) diagnosis.

**Iconic Moment in *House* History:** Frustrated with the lack of answers, House walks away from the team, needing a moment to compose himself. He goes to sit with the dying little boy. As he sits on Ian's bed, he lays his cane across the boy's still body, seeking inspiration.

**A Fine Bromance:** House alternately plays mentor and antagonist to Wilson during the poker tournament. He makes veiled reference to Wilson's failed marriages with irritating comments about the size of mammalian sexual organs. But he also coaches him on poker strategy against Cuddy using colorfully coded messages.

**Shipper Alert!:** Cuddy looks in on House as he sits with Ian. She looks as if she wants to reach out and help him. She looks helpless observing the anguish on House's face. **Shipper Alert #2:** House gasps audibly when he turns from the whiteboard to see the stunningly attired Cameron. He is speechless. **Shipper Alert #3:** Before House excuses himself from the game to treat Ian, Cuddy notes that House should have spent more time looking at his cards than gazing at her breasts.

**Musical Notes:** At the end of the episode House plays Oscar Peterson's "Hymn to Freedom" on a grand piano left from the poker gala.

**Judgmental Fellow Alert:** Everyone accuses House of going to extremes as he obsesses over an old case. Wilson insists House's medical genius is actually just luck and his diagnosis of Ian, correct as it is, is merely a guess.

**Props Department:** Kudos to the costumers for the gorgeous formal attire. We also see a reappearance of House's black silver-tipped cane, which goes perfectly with the tux.

**Casting Call:** MacKenzie Astin (Ian's father) was a series regular on the 1980s CBS comedy *The Facts of Life* playing Andy Moffet (1985–1988). He is the son of Patty Duke and John Astin and brother of Sean (*Lord of the Rings*).

**Title Tale:** "All In" is a poker term used in the Texas hold 'em poker game being played at the hospital benefit. House is certainly "all in" when it comes to finding the cause of Ian's symptoms. In the end, House goes "all in" gambling that he's right with the last remaining piece of tissue for them to test.

**Why It's a Classic:** Neither House's team, nor we as viewers, have seen House quite so openly emotional about a patient to this point in the series. The blend of quick, witty dialogue, the fluff of the poker game, the deadly seriousness of the medical case, along with House's obsession illustrate why *House* is such a brilliant series.

### House's Windmill — Death: A Closer Look at "All In"

In a sense, death can be viewed as House's archenemy, something with which he does battle relentlessly — sometimes to a point beyond which other doctors would turn in their scalpels and wave their white coats in surrender. It's part of what makes House heroic, especially because he often does it with little regard for his own comfort or career (or life), but House's medical relentlessness also is part of what makes him a medical outsider.

House doesn't always win; death is a powerful adversary, and despite House's sometimes-heroic efforts, it defeats him and patients die. But sometimes he won't even stop there, continuing to pursue the illness beyond death. He needs to know the cause: what went wrong and why. It's not (just) morbid curiosity with him. Figuring out the "why" even after death has won allows House to add one more case, one more bit of knowledge, one more weapon, should that disease ever come round again. It's not something that his colleagues always (or even most of the time) understand. It's why he continued in "Occam's Razor" (1.03) to search for the mistaken colchicine pills long after the patient was cured, why he needed to know the source of the girl's infection in the third-season episode "House Training" (3.20) even after it was too late to save her. It's why, even 12 years later, House still can't let go of Esther succumbing to a rampantly aggressive disease — one that killed within hours, a disease that House could not defeat in time to save the patient, a cause of death he could never confirm. And it's what drives him in "All In" to push himself to the brink to save a young patient presenting with the same symptoms.

Of course you might say that House's obsession with Esther's case is part of his "Rubik's complex" (as Wilson termed it in "DNR," 1.09). "Some doctors have a Messiah complex; you have a Rubik's complex — you have to solve the puzzle."

Is it a simple case of an unsolved puzzle — like a word in a "super-challenge" crossword puzzle you've never been able to figure out, still bugging

## 2.18 "Sleeping Dogs Lie"

**Writer:** Sarah Hess **Director:** Greg Yaitanes
**Patient of the Week:** Hannah (Jayma Mays)

Hannah cannot sleep although she's taken a bottle full of sleeping pills. When her liver fails, her partner, Max, offers a piece of her own as a live donor. Although it's not a cure, it will buy the team some time to diagnose what's really wrong. But when Cameron discovers that Hannah plans on breaking up with Max, she insists that Max be told before she risks her life. House considers the information medically irrelevant and demands that no one tell her. The transplant eventually takes place, and in the end, Max discloses to Cameron that she knew of Hannah's feelings — and is exploiting her liver donation as security that Hannah will never leave her.

In the meantime, Foreman has stolen Cameron's idea for a journal article. Now published while Cameron's paper still sits unsigned on House's desk, the article drives a wedge between the two fellows. Cameron whines to House, Cuddy, and Foreman, none of whom have much sympathy. Foreman coldly tells her they aren't really friends, only colleagues, and has no remorse about stealing her idea.

There is a mild suggestion that perhaps House snubbed Cameron's paper intentionally to harden her to the cold facts of academic competition. But no one really comes off sympathetically in this episode, including the patient and her girlfriend.

**Zebra of the Week:** Bubonic plague!
**Epiphany!:** House realizes the patient's dog was bred in the Southwest, where it's possible to pick up this rare infection.
**Clinic Duty:** A Chinese-American teenage girl visits the clinic with the ailment "SAC" (Stupid American Child). She brings her non-English speaking mother into the clinic hoping for birth control pills, but really wants them for herself.

**A Fine Bromance:** Wilson, an early riser, is still camped out on House's sofa. House, who has difficulty sleeping and tends to be a night owl, is getting even less sleep than usual.

**House Is a Jerk:** Not nice of House to leave Cameron's paper sitting in his inbox for weeks. On the other hand, is he trying to teach her a lesson in assertiveness?

**Housian Ethics:** Foreman steals Cameron's idea for an article. **Housian Ethics #2:** When Cameron learns that Hannah is about to break up with her girlfriend, she believes that they cannot go ahead with the transplant without full disclosure to Max. House believes saving Hannah's life trumps the disclosure and prohibits anyone from telling Max the truth.

**Judgmental Fellow Alert:** Cameron believes Hannah is exploiting Max's love simply to get a piece of her liver. To punish Hannah, she purposely makes a painful procedure even more so. But, no one, not even House, is very sympathetic towards Hannah.

**Lost in Translation:** House speaks Mandarin for the first time in our presence. He doesn't speak it again until "Epic Fail" (6.03) in season six. Is any language beyond him?

**Casting Call:** Jayma Mays (Hannah) stars as Emma Pillsbury in the critically acclaimed Fox series *Glee*.

**Title Tale:** The source of Hannah's illness is a dog, and she cannot sleep. She also is lying to her girlfriend. House is also losing sleep because Wilson's still staying with him.

## 2.19 "House vs. God"

**Writer:** Doris Egan **Director:** John Showalter
**Patient of the Week:** Boyd (Thomas Dekker)

House, a self-professed atheist, treats Boyd, a faith healer who collapses at a healing service. Needless to say, House is skeptical about Boyd's "powers." Boyd believes God talks and works through him, and when he lays his hands on Grace, one of Wilson's terminal cancer patients, she suddenly feels better — and her latest scan reveals that her tumor is shrinking. The cause of Boyd's illness and Grace's "cure" is much more of this world than the next. But during the differential diagnosis, Chase raises the question as to whether a spark of the divine may be somehow involved.

Wilson wheedles his way into House's weekly poker game, easily reading his tells, hence eliminating House's big advantage over his card buddies. House is not pleased at all, but soon ends the game when he makes a shocking discovery about Wilson.

**Zebra of the Week:** Boyd has sexually contracted herpes from his all-too-human behavior. The virus, contracted from Boyd, also temporarily shrinks Grace's tumor.

**Epiphany!:** House and Wilson discuss the possible reasons for Grace's improved condition when House recalls reading an early 20th century Italian paper on viruses that attack tumor cells.

**Iconic Moment in *House* History:** House's weekly poker game.

**A Fine Bromance:** Wilson is great at reading House's poker tells — no wonder House has never invited him before. They argue heatedly in the street about the wisdom of Wilson's affair with a patient. But when House gets an emergency call from the hospital and they leave together, the argument is forgotten.

**Housian Ethics:** Is it ethical for House to argue with Boyd about his belief system? **Housian Ethics #2:** House discovers that Wilson is sleeping with Grace, his cancer patient. It's a huge ethical breach for a doctor, one that can cause Wilson to lose his license, and House lectures him on the risk he's taking if he continues.

**Classic Rant:** House rants about people who believe in God, miracles, and faith healers like Boyd.

**Did You Know?:** When House plays poker he seems to never drink alcohol. The first time to notice this is in "All In" (2.17).

**Musical Notes:** House plays a bluesy rendition of "What a Friend We Have in Jesus."

**Casting Call:** Thomas Dekker (Boyd) played John Connor in the Fox series *Terminator: The Sarah Connor Chronicles* (2008–2009) and Zach on NBC's *Heroes* from 2006 to 2007. Boyd's father is played by William Katt, who was the Greatest American Hero in the 1980s series of the same name on ABC.

**Title Tale:** The whiteboard says it all. Chase keeps score on the whiteboard, and as the differential diagnosis continues, House and God trade the lead.


## * 2.20 "Euphoria, Part 1"

**Writer:** Matt Lewis **Director:** Deran Sarafian
**Patient of the Week:** Joe (Scott Michael Campbell)

House is famous for refusing to become involved with patients. But what happens when the patient is someone already close to him? The clock is ticking as Joe, a pot-growing cop shot in the line of duty, comes down with a deadly infectious disease, characterized first by giddiness and euphoria.

After he investigates Joe's apartment, Foreman begins to exhibit the same symptoms. Guilt-ridden and worried, House becomes more cautious than usual, unwilling to risk anyone else on the team by sending them back to the apartment for further clues. But Foreman takes matters into his own hands, intentionally exposing Cameron to the unknown infectious agent, making her a stakeholder in the diagnosis — and sending her back to the apartment. House believes they've found the possible infectious source — a can of guano Joe has been using to fertilize his plants. But he is wrong, and when the cop dies at the end of the episode, there are still no answers — as Foreman continues to worsen. Cliffhanger!

**Zebra of the Week:** The cop dies at the end of part one. We still do not have a cause.

**Iconic Moment in *House* History:** Wilson accuses the usually-reckless House of being *too* cautious with his diagnostic process. Because it's Foreman, Wilson points out, House isn't taking the usual risks with the patient's life. House is furious at the suggestion, demanding to know how Wilson would feel if it was one of *his* fellows.

**House Is a Jerk:** House takes a bagful of parking tickets to Joe's police partner, hoping to get them fixed.

**Judgmental Fellow:** Foreman has no sympathy for the pot-growing cop, even as he treats him.

**Housian Ethics:** House violates Foreman's patient rights by doing a brain biopsy without his consent. **Housian Ethics #2:** Foreman stabs Cameron in the thigh with a potentially tainted needle, for the sole purpose of investing her in his illness.

**Casting Call:** Scott Michael Campbell starred with Hugh Laurie in the remake of *Flight of the Phoenix*. During the filming of the movie, shot in Namibia, Laurie made his now-famous *House* audition tape in a hotel bathroom with Campbell's help. House's signature scruffy, unshaven look was sealed during that audition tape as the normally clean-shaven Laurie was then playing the part of a marooned airplane crash victim.

**Title Tale:** The first symptom of this deadly infection? Euphoria. But no one seems especially happy.

## * 2.21 "Euphoria, Part 2"

**Writers:** Russel Friend, Garrett Lerner, David Shore **Director:** Deran Sarafian
**Patient of the Week:** Foreman

Foreman's condition continues to deteriorate after Joe dies. House believes the easiest way to diagnose Foreman would be to autopsy the dead cop, but Cuddy isn't willing to risk exposing the entire hospital to the mystery bug.

House attempts to expose his pet rat Steve McQueen to everything Foreman may have touched. But the rat doesn't exhibit symptoms. Foreman wants House to do a dangerous deep-brain biopsy, but he resists, knowing it could leave him brain damaged. But Foreman enlists Cameron's aid — naming her his medical proxy.

With time running out, Cameron produces her medical proxy and orders the brain biopsy, but House wants to go back one more time to the apartment. Just as he locates the infection source, Cameron begins the biopsy.

**Zebra of the Week:** The waterborne parasite Naegleria has contaminated the water Joe has been using on his marijuana plants.

**Epiphany!:** After locating a sick bird on the roof, House notices a water supply line into the shed. He realizes the water is sprayed on the plants using a timer — something previous trips to the apartment missed.

**Iconic Moment in _House_ History:** House explains the risks of the deep-brain biopsy that Foreman is demanding, reminding him that it could leave him disabled. House wants to pursue another route, but it requires that Foreman take medicine that will mean the return of the severe pain caused by the illness. House understands Foreman's fear of pain. Speaking from years of experience, House explains why Foreman should not let pain drive his decisions. "Pain makes you make bad decisions," he advises. "Fear of pain is almost as big a motivator." Applied to House, these words reverberate throughout the seasons to come.

**Clinic Duty:** In one of the best clinic scenes ever, a mother brings her toddler daughter to the clinic, sure she has epilepsy. Examining her, House suggests she's only trying to "ya-ya the sisterhood." Or "find Nemo." She has the misnamed "gratification disorder." (She's masturbating.)

**Housian Ethics:** Cuddy refuses to allow an autopsy of Joe's corpse, concerned about the danger from his unknown infection. She will not back down, even to save Forman's life. **Housian Ethics #2:** When Foreman appoints Cameron as his medical proxy rather than his own father, he quotes Cameron's article (the one he stole). She explains in the paper that families are asked to make impossible decisions after a 10-minute briefing — decisions that doctors agonize over, "even after years of medical training." He believes Cameron's medical experience and her natural compassion make her a more logical proxy.

**Pop Culture References:** House makes reference to Jack Bauer (from the Fox series _24_) when Cuddy insists Joe's body is a biohazard and cannot be autopsied at Princeton-Plainsboro.

**Casting Call:** Actor/director Charles S. Dutton plays Rodney Foreman, Eric's father. Dutton has won two Emmy Awards for his guest-starring roles on *The Practice* (1997) on ABC and *Without a Trace* (2002) on CBS. He has also won a directing Emmy for HBO's *The Corner* (2000) and a Directors Guild Award for Showtime's *Sleeper Cell* (2006).

**Why It's a Classic:** "Euphoria" (parts 1 and 2) presents a close examination of House and his team under unique circumstances.

## 2.22 "Forever"

**Writer:** Liz Friedman **Director:** Daniel Sackheim

**Patient of the Week:** Kara (Hillary Tuck)

Kara nearly drowns her baby in the bathtub while having a seizure. Is she physically ill or a psychotic would-be murderer? Chase cares for the baby in the Neonatal Intensive Care Unit (NICU), having requested a break from House's team. When House prevents Kara from suffocating the baby while both are being treated in the hospital, they are certain the cause is psychosis. But it's too late to save either mother or baby when the infant dies in the NICU.

Meanwhile, Foreman has returned from his brush with death, but he has changed — at least for now. House is upset at the new, happy-to-just-be-alive Foreman. He wants his old, combative neurologist back.

And a new several-season long character arc begins for Cuddy when she asks Wilson out to dinner, piquing House's insatiable curiosity.

**Zebra of the Week:** Mother and infant both have celiac disease, an autoimmune disorder of the intestine that prevents the body's absorption of essential nutrients. It's triggered by the consumption of gluten, which is used to bind the medicine given the baby, leading to his death. Kara also has a complication of the disease: malt lymphoma.

**Epiphany!:** After Kara's baby dies, House realizes the baby's meds were bound with wheat gluten, deadly to those with Celiac disease.

**Iconic Moment in *House* History:** House has an honest, compassionate conversation with Kara after the final diagnosis. He tries to reassure her that her son's death is not her fault. Although House may be right, she argues that she no longer wants to live, refusing treatment for the malt lymphoma. House accepts her answer and allows her to die in peace. **Iconic Moment #2:** After the baby dies, Chase does the autopsy, but prays over him, the former seminarian emerging through this very poignant moment.

**A Fine Bromance:** Wilson insists that his dinner with Cuddy is a date. House insists she must have another agenda. He can't believe Cuddy has a romantic interest in Wilson. "You're too nice for her; she's not needy enough for you!" House contends. On the other hand, House can think of several reasons for Wilson's interest: "She's smart, she's funny, she has a zesty bod."

**House Is a Jerk:** He's pretty cruel to Chase after Kara's baby dies. He's also awfully intrusive with Cuddy's private life.

**Housian Ethics:** After Wilson and Cuddy have dinner, Wilson sneaks a sample of Cuddy's saliva left on a spoon to test for cancer markers — without her consent.

**Shipper Alert!:** House seems very concerned about his boss' health, especially because she's asked Wilson to dinner. Does she suspect cancer or is this a date? House's detective work (we won't call it stalking) reveals that Cuddy is looking for a sperm donor! Cuddy is certain her secret will soon be the subject of hospital gossip, but House unexpectedly keeps her secret, even from Wilson.

**Casting Call:** Hillary Tuck (Kara) has performed a variety of guest roles on TV and was a series regular as Amy on the Disney Channel series *Honey I Shrunk the Kids* (1997–2000).

**Title Tale:** Foreman returns from his illness still affected by the brain biopsy. He tells House he's changed and grateful for every day. House replies, "Almost dying changes everything forever — for about two months."


### * 2.23 "Who's Your Daddy?"

**Writers:** Lawrence Kaplow, John Mankiewicz **Director:** Martha Mitchell
**Patient of the Week:** Leona (Aasha Davis)

Dylan Crandall, a friend of House's from his college days, seeks his help when his newly discovered teenage "daughter" suffers serious hallucinations. Leona is a Katrina victim and granddaughter of New Orleans jazz legend Jesse Baker (and hero of House's). Crandall has written a biography of the jazz musician, who supposedly tanked his career while suffering alcoholism and drug abuse.

Leona is suffering cardiogenic shock in addition to the hallucinations. Eventually she also suffers reverse peristalsis, and waste oozes from her mouth. House eventually diagnoses an excess buildup of iron in Leona's blood, but the treatment damages her lungs. Not until Leona admits she lied about where she stayed in the aftermath of Katrina is House able to understand the cause of her symptoms. He attempts to prove that Leona is not really Crandall's daughter, but Crandall refuses to give a DNA sample.

Meanwhile, Cuddy continues to pursue motherhood. She asks House to give her needed fertility injections and review files of potential sperm donors.

House works on the case in much more pain than usual. He has had a sleepless night, pacing his apartment until he can no longer stand it. Finding a metal box, out of reach at the top of the bookcase, he locates a supply of morphine. But he avoids using the powerful drug until the case is solved.

**Zebra of the Week:** Zygomycosis, a fungal infection caused in the mold-rich environment of post-Katrina New Orleans.

**Epiphany!:** Although Foreman has diagnosed a fungal infection, broad spectrum anti-fungals are not working. House harangues Leona into admitting where she stayed in post-Katrina New Orleans so they can identify the specific fungal infection.

**Iconic Moment in *House* History:** There are several in this episode, but House going down the morphine path at the episode's end leads directly into themes explored in the season finale.

**Clinic Duty:** A young, inexperienced mother brings in her toddler who seems to have an angry red rash. The cure? A warm soapy washcloth. The cause? A brand new red sofa used by the toddler to rest and watch TV.

**A Fine Bromance:** Wilson goads House about his friendship with Crandall, but then eventually tells House it's comforting to know his friend will be there to protect him. (He's being sarcastic, of course.)

**House Is a Jerk:** House brings one of Cuddy's anonymous sperm donor candidates into the office to see what she might be getting into. The donor, a medical student, is a high-grade idiot. Point proven. House uses fear tactics to make his points more than usual.

**Housian Ethics:** House promises Crandall he won't take a DNA sample for a paternity test. He does it anyway, but never tells Crandall the results — which prove he's not the father. **Housian Ethics #2:** House nearly breaks Leona's finger trying to trigger a hallucination while she's hooked up to a CAT scanner.

**Shipper Alert!:** House gives Cuddy her first two injections. The first time is one of most sensual straight-on medical scenes in the show's history, as House gently rubs a cotton swab on Cuddy's derriere. There is an intimacy and warmth between the two of them that suggests a long-standing mutual trust. In the second injection scene, House admonishes Cuddy that selecting a sperm donor requires more than simple genetic matching from anonymous files. "Pick someone you trust," he suggests to her. "Oh? Like you?" Cuddy responds sarcastically. "Someone you like," he responds, shyly averting his eyes and walking away. When she goes up to his office at the end of the episode, you just know she wants to ask him to be her donor . . . or something. But she chickens out.

**Gross-out Warning:** Leona's reverse peristalsis causes her bowels to empty backwards and into her mouth. Ick!

**Musical Notes:** Lots of House listening to New Orleans–style piano. House also figures out one part of the medical mystery by listening to an old Baker recording. Noting that Baker's hearing must have been off, House has a new clue.

**Casting Call:** Aasha Davis (Leona) played Waverly in NBC's *Friday Night Lights* (2007). D. B. Sweeney plays Leona's wannabe father Dylan Crandall. He is known for roles in several notable films and television productions, including John Sayles' *Eight Men Out* (1988) as Shoeless Joe Jackson, and the acclaimed CBS miniseries *Lonesome Dove* as Dish Boggett (1989).

**Title Tale:** Two for one: is Crandall Leona's dad? Who will be the father of Cuddy's baby?

**Why It's a Classic:** There is a lot going on here that impacts future story lines. Cuddy's motherhood quest and the uptick in House's pain and drug use are both themes explored in seasons to come. We also get a rare glimpse of House's backstory.


## * 2.24 "No Reason"

**Writer:** David Shore **Director:** David Shore

**Patients of the Week:** Vince (Chris Tallman), Moriarty (Elias Koteas)

"No Reason" is a surrealistic glimpse into House's subconscious after he is near-fatally shot. The episode's 45 minutes take place as a series of intertwining hallucinations within the few minutes from the shooting until House is raced to the emergency room.

The shooter (called "Moriarty" in the original script) shares a room with House in the Intensive Care Unit (ICU). Moriarty mocks House for wasting his life as a misanthrope, devoid of emotion and love. It's a bitter indictment from the shooter — made all the more harsh when you realize it is House's own self-assessment.

In the hallucination, Cuddy administers ketamine (a veterinary anesthetic that works also to "reboot" the brain's pain centers) while House is being treated for his gunshot wounds. Done without his permission, in a weird replay of Stacy's actions in "Three Stories" (1.21), House fears that the procedure will rob him of his gifted intellect, rendering his life meaningless.

Interwoven throughout, House's team treats a man with a swollen tongue. His symptoms grow more dire as other body parts swell and explode. But it is through this nightmarish case that House reasons his way back to consciousness and out of the hallucination just as he is being rushed to the ER.

**Iconic Moment in *House* History:** House "chooses life" as he sits in a car with Moriarty's wife as she's about to commit suicide. She goes ahead, but House fights his way out of the urge to join her as he wrestles his way out of the interwoven hallucinations.

**House Is a Jerk:** House mocks the patient with the swollen tongue to the team — just before the shooter enters the office.

**Shipper Alert!:** In his hallucination, House demonstrates a robotic surgical machine on Cameron. She lies on the operating table with House at the controls from afar. In an extremely sensual scene, House moves the robotic pincers to caress and begin to undress the slightly unnerved, but aroused Allison Cameron. It's as close as House and Cameron have gotten to having sex with each other.

**Gross-out Warning:** The patient with the swollen tongue now has swollen testicles. While using the men's room, they explode. Ick!

**Casting Call:** Elias Koteas (Moriarty) is a film actor, notably in several David Cronenberg films, including *Crash* (1996) in which he played Vaughan. He was also Monsieur Gateau in *The Curious Case of Benjamin Button* (2008).

**Why It's a Classic:** The season-two finale provides another exploration into House's subconscious. For a character so closely guarded, these peeks into his mindscape are fascinating for what they tell us. The story structure with its multilayered hallucinations let us into House's mind, his fears — and perhaps what he's really seeking in life.

---

### Ketamine: A Closer Look at "No Reason"

Ketamine is primarily a veterinary anesthetic drug, but is used in humans to treat several conditions. In "No Reason" (2.24), House lies unconscious on his office floor, bleeding from wounds to his abdomen and neck after being shot point-blank in his office. He hallucinates that Cuddy has, without his consent, arranged to have ketamine administered to him during surgery instead of using more conventional anesthetic.

Cuddy tells him that ketamine has been used in a German experimental protocol to treat some types of chronic pain. The procedure has had some success, although it is not currently under clinical investigation in the United States. Patients are given 600 to 900 milligrams of the drug, which puts them into a dissociative coma; when they awaken from the coma, their pain is gone. As Cuddy explains, the procedure "reboots" the brain.

When the third season begins with "Meaning" (3.01), three months after the shooting, House is no longer in pain, and has spent time doing physical therapy, which has strengthened the remaining muscle in his leg, allowing him to run and giving him greater mobility. In real life, this is unrealistic, but in the show, House is able to run eight miles and turn on a dime. The original injury, of course, is not repaired, but the absence of pain allows him to work on gaining strength and enables him to give up narcotic pain relievers.

In the actual German ketamine trials, when the procedure works, patients are able to go back to the same activities they had to give up years earlier. Even those who were tied to morphine pumps due to their chronic pain have been able to remove them. Unfortunately, the ketamine treatment doesn't always work permanently in every case, and this is true for House, whose pain returns within a few months.

# SEASON 3
## Finding Meaning

There is cohesion to season three that is absent from the first two seasons. The show found its true focus as a character drama structured around a medical procedural with a season-long arc to the overall story. On the other hand, the third season also sometimes stretched believability, challenging viewers' ability to suspend disbelief to the extent necessary.

Season three picks up more than two months after House is shot by a still-at-large former patient (or the husband of a patient — it's never made clear). During the hiatus, between seasons two and three, House has surgery to repair wounds to the neck and abdomen — and has undergone an experimental pain treatment with the veterinary anesthetic ketamine. By the season three premiere, House is running the eight miles to work from his home. It's completely unrealistic, of course, given the extent of damage to House's leg, but this bit of dramatic license provides an effective starting point for the story.

It only takes a couple of episodes for House's pain to return. His search for meaning is supplanted by the need to defend himself against a vindictive cop. Detective Michael Tritter views House as a menace: a drug-addicted physician who risks his patients' lives with every decision. Although the Tritter story line raises some interesting questions about House, and there are some excellent episodes within it, it seems to go on about two episodes too long, dragging the story out, and at the end leaving House essentially unchanged. Or is he?

Although House seems untouched by his brush with the law and the near-loss of his medical license, his post-Tritter actions subtly suggest some effect. House seeks alternative ways to deal with his pain, and takes baby steps towards more socialization.

By season's end, Foreman has had enough of House's methods and resigns from the team. His fear of "becoming" House in order to save lives hits home when Foreman's arrogance loses one patient, and he saves another using dubious methods that even House might not use. In the end Cameron and Chase join him in leaving the team.

*House* "classics" are starred.

## * 3.01 "Meaning"

**Writers:** Russel Friend, Garrett Lerner, Lawrence Kaplow, David Shore
**Director:** Deran Sarafian
**Patient of the Week:** Richard (Edward Edwards)

House comes back from his summer of healing feeling exuberant and ready to find some meaning in his life. He treats Richard, a quadriplegic who cannot talk due to past brain cancer. Richard presents with no apparent medical puzzle, and House claims that he merely wants to help him live a more comfortable life. Taking the case simply to "do something for the pain," leaves Wilson, Cuddy, and the team skeptical of House's motives.

When he concludes that a treatable underlying condition may be causing Richard's paralysis, House believes he can cure and restore him, whole, to his family. House's colleagues accuse him of creating a puzzle for his own amusement where none exists. But House is right (duh!), as Cuddy discovers when she uses House's diagnosis to cure Richard. She and Wilson conspire to deny him this first post-shooting victory in order to teach him a little "humility" — that he can't always be right.

As House says to Foreman (prophetically) in "Forever" (2.22), "Almost dying changes everything forever — for about two months!" The pain in House's leg makes a surprise comeback appearance, and House's fear drives him to steal Wilson's prescription blanks after he refuses to write a new Vicodin prescription for House.

**Zebra of the Week:** Addison's disease.
**Epiphany!:** After House becomes overheated while running and takes a dip in the university fountain, he realizes Richard has a bum thermostat in his brain. He has hypothalamic dysregulation caused by brain scarring, which led to Addison's disease.
**Iconic Moment in *House* History:** House is running and happy as the season opens. The ecstatic expression on his face as he pauses to check his elevated heart rate is priceless.
**Manipulative Wilson:** Wilson and Cuddy fear that, now off Vicodin, House will become even more reckless with his patients. To teach him some humility, they conspire to keep the news of Richard's recovery from him.
**A Fine Bromance:** House confesses to Wilson he's not sure how he should feel when Richard's family thanks him. Wilson reminds House that his "feeling" muscle has atrophied, and he just needs to keep working at it.
**House Is a Jerk:** House believes that a yoga aficionado in treatment for leg paralysis is faking. He holds a lighter to her feet proving she can move her legs.

House makes his point, but rather cruelly.

**Shipper Alert!:** House asks Cameron out for a drink. She says no, and House smiles in response, believing that now that he's "healed" she's no longer interested. **Shipper Alert! #2:** House breathlessly runs to Cuddy's apartment in the middle of the night excited after an epiphany. She opens the window dressed only in a summer nightgown and they argue about the case.

**Props Department:** The cane doesn't make an appearance in this episode.

**Casting Call:** Richard's wife is played by Kathleen Quinlan who received Golden Globe and Oscar nominations for her supporting role opposite Tom Hanks in the critically acclaimed *Apollo 13* (1995).

**Title Tale:** House is looking for meaning and tries valiantly to define the term for himself, questioning Wilson and even the patient's wife about it.

**Why It's a Classic:** We see House as he might have been before the leg injury.

---

### Setting Up the Downfall: A Closer Look at "Meaning"

There is a scene at the beginning of the season three *House* premiere, "Meaning," revealing a healed Gregory House. Graceful and quick, he runs through a park, free of pain and the shackles of disability. It is but a brief glimpse, and by the end of the episode, we know that for House it will be (as Wilson will say by episode two) only a taste of what is not meant to be. By midway through the season, House will have crashed and burned, reaching the depths of despair.

Throughout "Meaning," House struggles to find his sense of self in his new reality, having gone through two life-changing events: being near fatally shot and attempting a radical therapy to rid himself of pain (and painkillers). Convinced after his fevered hallucinations in the season two finale, "No Reason" (2.24), that he lacks humanity, House takes the case of Richard, a brain-damaged quadriplegic cancer patient for the sole purpose of helping him with pain. He's nearly daring himself that he can find "meaning" in normal "doctor stuff." But he can't quite figure out how to react when the patient's family thanks him for a kind word and a compassionate gesture.

In House's mind, he's done nothing; he hasn't cured the patient or done anything significant. Confused, House believes he should "feel" something, and he doesn't. He confesses to Wilson: "I wasn't even sure what I was supposed to feel." Wilson tells House, rightly, that he doesn't *have* to do or feel anything different, but should appreciate it for what it is. He need not change anything; it's a matter of perspective — of perception. House simply has to learn to appreciate what he already does for people.

Wilson has the right idea, supporting House as he feels his way through this, awkwardly searching for who he is and what he is. Unfortunately, this Wilson disappears fairly quickly (by the episode's end, at the latest).

House even seeks answers about "caring" from the patient's wife, asking her why she doesn't put her husband in a nursing home. What does she get out of her self-sacrifice? It's as if House is trying to understand this level of devotion and compassion for its own sake. She's "sacrificing (herself) and gets nothing in return." Why would she do that? Does it make her happy? Fulfilled? No, she explains. But not doing it would leave her even emptier.

In House's "No Reason" hallucination, Moriarty tells him that he sacrifices himself for "no reason." Now House wonders how Richard's wife can derive something from what he sees as a miserable life. Can he apply this to his own life? Does House need to do what he does best to keep himself from being even more miserable?

While House wends his way through this uncharted emotional territory in "Meaning," everyone suspects that he has an agenda, that he's playing with the patient for his amusement, creating a puzzle for himself where there is none. That's not quite what's going on. House is seldom satisfied with just fixing the immediate problem and returning the patient to his or her "normal" when he believes something better can be gained. When he hears Richard grunt (which House translates as speech), House considers the possibility that his paralysis might actually be curable. But everyone attacks House's motives. Cameron mocks him; Cuddy accuses; Wilson lectures and scolds, accusing him of fabricating a mystery for his amusement.

Playing up his image as a jerk, House retorts that he's built up Richard's family with too much false hope and can't let them down. It's a safe fall-back position for him. But in his encounters with Richard and his wife, there is nothing in House's demeanor, body language, or remarks that suggest anything other than sincere belief that the paralyzed, wheelchair-bound patient has something curable. House envisions a chance for the quality of life of both patient and family *will* be improved. There is an idealism in House's approach to medicine that comes out in moments like this.

At the same time, House begins to fear that the ketamine treatment is failing. Skateboarding in the park, House feels a sudden pain in his thigh.

Clearly unnerved by this sudden pain, House confides his fears to Wilson, asking him to write a prescription for pain medicine. Dismissing House's soreness as "middle-aged aches and pains," Wilson suggests that House is scamming him. But if House is concerned enough to tell Wilson, it has to be extremely unnerving to him. House has been riding high on his newly pain-free life, suddenly able to do (physically) what he's been unable to do for years. The return of the pain is probably his deepest fear. As House leaves his office, Wilson finally acknowledges the extent of House's fear, reassuring him that the procedure worked and that it will just take some time to feel good again (in all ways).

But that time is never going to come, and you can feel it in the episode's second running scene. The joy and light of the House's first run in the park is absent. Starkly shot and darkly atmospheric, it is devoid of the first scene's promise and hopefulness. The gracefulness of the first running scene is replaced by desperation. Now, House is running away — from his fear, his demons, and the inevitable return of the pain.

But House has an epiphany about his patient during that run, the answer dawning on him as he wades (shoes and all) in a university fountain. Soaking wet and as excited as a 10-year-old with a new video game, House taps at Cuddy's window, waking her. Breathing heavily, hot, exhausted and talking a mile a minute he runs (not walks) Cuddy through his scientific reasoning. "I can make him walk, I can make him talk!" House implores Cuddy. ("I can help him — I can make his life better — I can make his family's life better" is what he's really saying.) This is the "fulfillment" that House gets; this is the joy and satisfaction he derives from the diagnosis. Yes, the final piece of the puzzle falls neatly into place, but it's meaningless to House unless it means something to the patient — unless he can send the patient home better off than when he came into his service. This is ultimate job satisfaction for House. It's exactly what Wilson had been speaking of earlier: this *is* "meaning," but it's uniquely House's.

Unfortunately, Cuddy shuts him down, believing that House has to learn when "enough is enough." House's self-esteem is completely tied up in his ability to make inspired connections between disparate facts that no one else can. Taking that away from him, which is what Cuddy does in this episode, strips House of the very thing that makes his medical value unique. If they can't let House be House, then who is he? From where do they expect him to derive meaning? With Wilson, Cuddy, and Cameron all accusing House of playing at some sort of game with a traumatized patient, and in light of House's own fear of the ketamine's cognitive side effects, his confidence begins to unravel.

Worn down by a combination of his own confusion and the barrage from his closest colleagues, House is convinced that his motives and judgment are wrong. He broods in his office the next morning, depressed that he's failed not only the patient, but his own impossible test. "Cuddy was right; I was only in it for the puzzle," he confesses bitterly to Wilson, defeated, his voice tinged with self-loathing. "She was right to shoot me down."

Wilson has often stated that House's success is all about luck, and this plays out in the final scene, as Cuddy herself uses House's diagnosis to successfully treat Richard. House is right, but Wilson insists they not tell him, in order to rein him in. The short-term result is to leave House feeling both isolated and desperate. And it sets him on a path that will lead to nearly tragic consequences by Christmas ("Merry Little Christmas," 3.10).

## * 3.02 "Cane and Able"

**Writers:** Russel Friend, Garrett Lerner **Director:** Daniel Sackheim
**Patient of the Week:** Clancy (Skyler Gisondo)

House's fears about the pain returning are valid as the team treats a Clancy, a young boy found bleeding from his rectum. Clancy believes he's been abducted by aliens and insists he has an implant in his neck left from his abduction. His embarrassed parents think he's imagining it, but Chase feels the parents may be judging their son too harshly. When Clancy begins imagining the aliens in the hospital, the team wonders if it's all connected.

While on clinic duty, Cameron unintentionally encounters Richard (from the last episode, "Meaning"), who is now nicely recovering from Addison's disease. She is stunned, believing, as House does, that Richard had been discharged undiagnosed. When she angrily confronts Cuddy about it, Cameron wonders if House's diminishing self-confidence and increasing pain are caused by what he believes to be a missed diagnosis. Eventually, Cuddy confesses to House about it.

**Zebra of the Week:** Chimerism. When conceived, Clancy had a twin who died in the very early stages of development, but some of the cells never died off, becoming invaders, interfering with Clancy's eyes, heart, and brain.

**Epiphany!:** Cuddy stops House as he's about to give up on the case. As he teases her about her motherhood dreams and her need to use in vitro fertilization, the lightbulb goes off. House realizes that in vitro fertilization often results in twins.

**Iconic Moment in *House* History:** After Wilson goads him, House tries to push himself on a treadmill in the deserted physical therapy room. Desperate, he tries to deny the pain its final victory. **Iconic Moment #2:** As the episode ends with John Mayer's song "Gravity" in the background, House sadly finds his cane in his golf bag. House is right back where he began.

**Manipulative Wilson:** Cuddy and Wilson continue to keep Richard's cure a secret from House, until Cuddy confesses to him. Wilson explains to House his fear that a high-flying, now healed House might fly too high and melt his wings.

**Judgmental Fellow Alert:** Foreman and Wilson continually remind House he's been "wrong a lot" lately.

**Shipper Alert!:** Cameron is protective of House throughout the episode, insisting Cuddy and Wilson inform House about Richard, "or I will!" **Shipper Alert #2:** There is a memorable scene in House's office when Cuddy tries to cut through his defenses and see how he's really doing. Her concern, as House deflects the question, is evident.

**Did You Know?:** There's a reason this episode may remind you of the 1990s hit series *The X-Files*. The episode's director is Daniel Sackheim, who also served as a producer/director on that show.

**Pop Culture References:** There are references to *Star Wars* and *X-Files* scattered throughout the episode. When Clancy goes missing, House suggests they search for him on Tatooine, Luke Skywalker's home planet. There's also a reference to Hugh Laurie's old series *Blackadder* when Cameron insists that Cuddy and Wilson "better come up with a 'cunning plan.'"

**Casting Call:** Child actor Skyler Gisondo (Clancy) is a regular on *The Bill Engvall Show* (2007–present).

**Title Tale:** Cane and Able is a biblical reference to Adam and Eve's sons, Cain and Abel, referring to Clancy and his unseen (chimeric) brother. And of course, House goes back to using his *cane*, and thinks he's no longer *able* to diagnose, which was one of his biggest fears about the ketamine treatment.

**Why It's a Classic:** "Cane and Able" presents an interesting *X-Files*-ish case and an exploration of House's mindset as he crashes back to his "normal."

## 3.03 "Informed Consent"

**Writer:** David Foster **Director:** Laura Innes
**Patient of the Week:** Ezra Powell (Joel Grey)

Renowned cancer researcher, Dr. Ezra Powell presents symptoms pointing to both the heart and lungs. He has difficulty breathing and is in great distress. After a series of tests and still no diagnosis, Powell requests that House euthanize him. To keep him both alive and in the hospital for further tests, House feigns injecting Powell with a lethal dose of morphine, but has instead only put him deeply to sleep.

At first, Cameron is indecisive, unwilling to participate in the deception, but also unwilling to euthanize Powell. The team finally diagnoses him with an untreatable, fatal illness. When Powell dies suddenly and prematurely, Cuddy incorrectly suspects that House ended his life.

And . . . House has a stalker, a 17-year-old blond named Ali. Her father comes into the clinic with a rhinovirus — and Ali leaves with a crush.

**Zebra of the Week:** Amyloidosis, type AA (which is fatal).
**Epiphany!:** House notes Ali's red thong peeking out the top of her jeans as he brushes her off, and makes an associative leap to the dye "Congo red," used in diagnosing amyloidosis. The team stains a sample of Powell's tissue and it turns positive.
**Clinic Duty:** House is flattered when Ali, the daughter of a clinic patient develops a crush on him. But she stalks him, phoning incessantly and finally sending him a calendar with her 18th birthday circled in red.
**Judgmental Fellow Alert:** House orders Cameron to obtain a skin sample for biopsy. After reading about Powell's experiments on babies, she rather mercilessly slices a piece from his arm with a scalpel — no anesthetic. Ouch!
**Iconic Moment in *House* History:** House finds Cameron in the chapel after he guesses that she has euthanized Ezra. Placing a comforting hand on her shoulder, House tells her that he's proud of her.
**Housian Ethics:** The entire team hotly debates the issue of euthanasia, with each member of the team, including House, weighing in on this important public policy issue. House himself is reluctant to euthanize Powell without knowing for certain that he's terminal. But could it also be that House is unwilling to kill Powell without first having the answer to the puzzle? **Housian Ethics #2:** Powell's cancer research in the 1960s included irradiating babies with no informed consent of the parents. Although his cancer research arguably saved millions of lives, Cameron (and by implication House) questions the ethics of this research.
**Housian Ethics #3:** Of course House totally ignores Powell's wish to die rather

than subject himself to more tests: very unethical.

**Shipper Alert!:** House refers to his teenage stalker as Cameron's "protégé."

**Gross-out Warning:** In the teaser, Powell's rats nibble at his face after he collapses. It's a sort of poetic justice for the experimental animals. Ick.

**Casting Call:** Noted Broadway and film actor Joel Grey (*Cabaret*) guests as Ezra. House's stalker, played by *Gossip Girl*'s Leighton Meester, stars with Hugh Laurie in *The Oranges* (2011).

**Title Tale:** The team runs tests and diagnoses Powell without his consent. The title may also refer to House's stalker who has not yet reached "the age of consent." Powell conducted his cancer research on babies without the informed consent of parents.


## * 3.04 "Lines in the Sand"

**Writer:** David Hoselton **Director:** Newton Thomas Sigel
**Patient of the Week:** Adam (Braeden Lemasters)

House diagnoses Adam, an autistic boy who cannot stop screaming and coughing. His resistance and unresponsiveness make him a particularly difficult patient. House wonders how it's possible for Adam's parents to be fulfilled by the all-consuming task of raising their needy son — never to see him improve. What is the meaning they derive from it? But when House makes an astonishing connection with the Adam, he is rewarded with a gift that both stuns and moves him.

In the meantime, Cuddy has finally replaced the carpeting in House's office, still bloodstained after House's shooting. Surprising her, he insists she return the old carpet to its proper place. In an episode-long temper tantrum over the carpet, House refuses to work in his office, holding differential diagnosis sessions all over the hospital — from a conference room to Wilson's office to the chapel. His bizarre behavior prompts Wilson to pose a question: Does House have Asperger syndrome, a mild form of autism?

House's teenage stalker continues to harass him, but he eventually rebuffs her.


**Zebra of the Week:** Raccoon roundworms. Adam has been eating them along with the sand in his sandbox. **Zebra #2:** Ali's crush on House is caused by breathing in spores after an earthquake during a family vacation to Fresno.

**Epiphany!:** As House plays with a Slinky in Adam's room, his eyes fall on Adam's drawings of squiggly lines — worms. House realizes that this is what Adam sees — and has been seeing all along, trying to communicate it best he could.

**Iconic Moment in *House* History:** The autistic Adam, who is unable to make eye contact, makes a rare connection with House, giving him a valuable gift: his handheld game system. Wilson notes that the experience is a "10 on the happiness scale" for the parents (and possibly House as well). **Iconic Moment #2:** House rebuffs stalker Ali by reenacting an iconic scene from *Casablanca*: "We'll always have Fresno." **Iconic Moment #3:** House persuades Adam to undergo anesthesia, inhaling the anesthetic himself and demonstrating to the frightened boy that it's not going to hurt him.

**Clinic Duty:** Ali continues to harass the very flattered House.

**Shipper Alert!:** Still a bit stoned after inhaling the anesthetic, House compliments Cameron, telling her she has "pretty hair." At the episode's end, she joins House as he stands vigil watching the carpet installers returning his blood-stained carpet. **Shipper Alert #2:** After Cuddy chases away his stalker, House tells her he's feeling a little "frisky." Cuddy zings him back. "Let's go," quips the mommy wannabe. "I'm ovulating!"

**Classic Rant:** House rants about "circle queens," and how those in the mainstream try to remake or stomp on anyone who doesn't fit in physically or socially.

**Pop Culture References:** House channels *Casablanca*'s Rick Blaine to dismiss his lovesick stalker.

**Casting Call:** Child actor Braeden Lemasters (Adam) is a regular on TNT's series *Men of a Certain Age* (2009–present).

**Title Tale:** There are lots of "lines in the sand" in "Lines in the Sand." Adam's worms come from the sand. There's the line at which we find House and Cuddy locked toe-to-toe in battle over carpets. And then there's the line of propriety across which House is unwilling to cross with an all-too-willing teenage girl.

**Why It's a Classic:** So many memorable scenes — poignant and funny — make this a must-see. How can you not put an episode with a scene right out of *Casablanca* among the "classics"?

---

### The Happiness Scale: A Closer Look at "Lines in the Sand"

In "Need to Know" (2.11), Wilson accuses House of wanting to be miserable. Sending away Stacy, the love of his life, House returns to his melancholic, pained status quo. Wilson believes House wants to be miserable — that he feels it somehow makes him special.

But it's not that House likes to be miserable. Until season six ("Broken"

6.01, 6.02), when he finally gets some help in understanding the root of his misery, House has no idea how to emerge from the terrible hole in which he's been trapped.

Yes, he's snatched tastes of happiness here and there: a mindless foosball game, monster trucks, riding his bike, music (his true solace), and of course his medical puzzles. But happiness is probably something that has eluded House much of his life (maybe with the exception of when he was with Stacy).

When House recovers the use of his leg at the beginning of season three he is as happy as we've seen him to this point in the series. He's running, happily sweating, enjoying the lightness of foot that's been missing for years. He searches for meaning, but it's elusive.

It's not that House can't feel. It's more that he has trouble connecting to his feelings. He feels — deeply — if we judge by what we observe of him, and not what we hear him say. House is annoyed by Wilson's "happiness scale" ("Meaning" 3.01), as if you can assign a value to the things that satisfy and give meaning to life, which brings us to "Lines in the Sand" (3.04).

House comes to work at the episode's start to learn that Cuddy has finally replaced the bloodstained carpet in his office. She has removed the last physical evidence from the room that House was nearly mortally wounded; at the same time she has erased the cruel reminder that House has tried to make a change in his life and failed.

House is obviously upset by Cuddy's decision to replace the carpeting and he spends much energy (including several temper tantrums) in an effort to get the old carpet restored to its rightful place. The bewildered team, Cuddy, and Wilson all believe that House is trying some sort of power play to exert his willfulness. But balancing this obnoxious behavior is the fragility that frames and gives context to House's actions, his situation, and his connection to his young patient, the autistic Adam.

By this episode, House is living on a precipice. He is back to square one with his pain; his unresolved issues regarding the shooting could not be more suppressed. He envies his severely autistic patient — who doesn't have to conform to the norms of society — in a way that none of his colleagues can understand in ordinary terms. At the same time, and in a self-loathing frame of mind, he is flattered by the pursuit of an underage young woman, Ali, the daughter of a clinic patient, who seems to like him for himself.

But what's really going on with the carpet? Does House want to have a nearby reminder that (as much as one might wish it) you cannot change reality? Is it a reminder to avoid attempting positive change because it leads only back to more disappointment? Or is the carpet a reminder that the changes brought by the ketamine were real — and tangible — and might be achieved again?

In the season's later episodes, we learn that House has continued to try finding ways to recapture the physical changes (and to a degree the emotional changes) that the ketamine brought about — especially in "Insensitive" (3.14), "Half Wit" (3.15), and, to a lesser degree, "Fetal Position" (3.17).

As House diagnoses Adam, he observes that the parents live an unrewarding and unfulfilled life. As with his patient's wife in "Meaning" (3.01), they don't "like" what they're doing, but not to do it would make them miserable. So, they trudge onward. The best they can hope for (in House's view) is a return to the status quo — a difficult and unrewarded life.

But with Adam, House accomplishes a minor miracle. He calms him easily, while Wilson and the team struggle to settle the terrified child about to undergo a scary procedure. House is completely unaware that he has done something "special" or praiseworthy. He dismisses it quickly, brushing it off as nothing. As House tells his psychiatrist in "Broken" (6.01, 6.02), "success is fleeting; failures last forever."

But it's not "nothing" to Adam. And after House cures him, Adam gives him three gifts. The first is his beloved electronic game, something totally unexpected that stuns House speechless. He says nothing, but at the end of the episode as he watches his old carpet being put back, House is still clutching the gift in his hand. Who knows how many hours he's been standing there holding the game — and watching the installers?

The second gift is Adam's eye contact. A boy who cannot make this sort of connection easily (or at all) seeks House's eyes and makes contact. But the third gift flows from the second. The parents are changed by their interaction with House and House's interaction with their Adam.

"Now that . . . that's a 10," remarks Wilson to House referring to his happiness scale. Is Wilson talking about the parents or House — or both? Adam isn't cured; he isn't fixed. He's still autistic, but this little step is profound for Adam — and his parents. And it rates a "10."

Is this, in fact, what Wilson's point has been all along? That happiness, fulfillment, whatever, isn't an all-or-nothing proposition? To the young autistic boy, House has made a difference. He has taken away the boy's pain and returned him to his "normal." House's interaction with Adam has caused the boy (for a brief moment) to come out of himself and interact with another human being. And for his parents (if not for House), it is an extraordinary moment, something life changing.

It is a point addressed again with House as he undergoes treatment at Mayfield Psychiatric Hospital at the beginning of season six. House cannot always fix everything. Some things are unfixable. And for House it's a difficult pill to swallow — and one of the keys to his misery.

## 3.05 "Fools for Love"

**Writer:** Peter Blake **Director:** David Platt
**Patients of the Week:** Tracy (Jurnee Smollett), Jeremy (Ricky Ullman)

The team treats a young couple, Tracy and Jeremy, after Tracy collapses with severe stomach pain during a robbery. Shortly thereafter, when Jeremy also develops stomach pain triggered by stress, House believes the cause must be either infectious or environmental. But when Tracy falls into delirium, hallucinating that Jeremy's father is breaking his arm, Tracy then reveals a bit of family history, which leads House to the answer.

He is less successful in solving the puzzle of why new pediatric nurse Wendy is hanging out near his office. First thinking that Wilson has a new girlfriend, House eventually learns that Wendy is Foreman's new love.

And in a move that will cause him grief for weeks to come, House offends the wrong patient in the clinic, a vindictive detective who sees House's relationship with Vicodin as a menace to society. In Detective Tritter, House has found his own personal Javert (the policeman who doggedly pursues Jean Valjean throughout Victor Hugo's novel *Les Misérables*). House sees Tritter as a bully to be ignored, but Cuddy wants House to apologize to him, something he assiduously avoids.

On his way home from work, Tritter lies in wait, stopping House as he speeds down the streets of Princeton at 40 miles per hour in a 25 miles per hour zone. With probable cause, Tritter searches House, finds his Vicodin supply, and throws him in jail.

**Zebra of the Week:** Hereditary angioedema: a rare genetic disorder.
**Epiphany!:** House wonders how Tracy and Jeremy both can have the same illness. After the team rules out infection and environmental causes, the only remaining explanation is genetic. That also means they must be related: they are

half-siblings.

**Iconic Moment in _House_ History:** Tritter arrests House for possession of narcotics without a prescription.

**A Fine Bromance:** House believes Wendy is involved with Wilson, which he vehemently denies. Wilson foreshadows his fourth season relationship with Amber when he observes that House's biggest fear is for him to have a "good relationship" and thus shut House out of his life.

**House Is a Jerk:** House leaves a thermometer stuck up Tritter's butt before leaving for the day.

**Housian Ethics:** Foreman doesn't want to destroy the young couple's happiness by telling them they are half brother and sister. But House insists, telling Foreman it's not for him to decide; their future children are at risk, and they need to know.

**Casting Call:** Detective Michael Tritter is played by veteran film and television actor David Morse, who has played a whole range of memorable characters, from the innocent young intern Boomer on NBC's _St. Elsewhere_ in the 1980s to his Emmy-winning performance as George Washington in HBO's miniseries _John Adams_ (2008). His role on _House_ earned him an Emmy nomination for Best Guest Actor in a Drama.

**Title Tale:** There are fools for love, and just plain fools in this episode. This week's patients are certainly "fools for love," as are Foreman and his new girl-friend Wendy. Then there are the fools in this play. House has absolutely no sense of the forthcoming danger looming with Tritter. Tritter is a fool who goes overboard in charging a physician with a limp — someone who clearly needs pain medication.

## 3.06 "Que Será Será"
**Writer:** Thomas L. Moran **Director:** Deran Sarafian
**Patient of the Week:** George (Pruitt Taylor Vince)

The 600-pound George is brought to Princeton-Plainsboro in a coma, and Cuddy asks the team to diagnose him while House is nowhere to be seen. The obvious course would point the diagnosis towards George's extreme weight. However, nothing is ever obvious on _House_.

House finally shows up and George emerges from his coma as the team continues the diagnosis, focusing the differential on his weight. Vehemently opposing this approach, George refuses to cooperate with any test that might prove the theory. Demanding to be discharged and go back to his (solitary) life, legally, House can't prevent him from leaving. But Cameron, who strongly sympathizes with George, slips him a "Mickey," as he leaves, causing him to collapse (and take a glass wall with him). Although House continues to push for a diet-related diagnosis, he eventually notices something odd about George's fingers.

House has spent the night in jail. He has been without his pills and his cane all night — until Wilson arrives with money for his bail ($15,000) and a couple of Vicodin, which House swallows down like a starving man.

With House bailed out, Tritter hangs around the hospital to get something on his quarry. When he returns to his apartment, House finds it trashed and Tritter awaiting his return. According to Tritter, a search has turned up at least 600 pills — enough to suspect that House is trafficking. Cuddy and Wilson advise House to consult an attorney.

**Zebra of the Week:** Inoperable small cell lung cancer that has metastasized to the lymph nodes. It is an ironic diagnosis for non-smoker George, who will soon die.

**Epiphany!:** House notices George's misshapen fingers when tussling with him over a diagnostic test; it's a rare symptom of this disease.

**Clinic Duty:** A man comes in with pain in his arm from sleeping on it. House's solution? Amputate!

**A Fine Bromance:** Tritter shows Wilson what appears to be his forged signature on several Vicodin prescriptions for House. Wilson lies, stating that they aren't forgeries and that House needs the pills.

**Judgmental Fellow Alert:** Chase's bias against overweight people again emerges (see "Heavy," 1.16). Here, he disappears mid-case, unwilling to continue helping George, who he believes is responsible for his own illness. Chase never reappears.

**Housian Ethics:** Cameron lies about George's weight so they can put him in the MRI, although he outweighs the maximum limit by 150 pounds. If it breaks, it could put the machine out of use for weeks, denying it to other patients in need. She also slips George chloral hydrate to knock him out, preventing him from checking out against medical advice.

**Shipper Alert!:** Don't you just love the way Cuddy can enter House's personal space without asking? Concerned about the police investigation, she visits him as he rests in his Eames chair. Sitting on the attached ottoman, Cuddy nudges away his legs to make room when she comes to advise him about getting a lawyer.

**Musical Notes:** Returning to his trashed apartment at the end of the case, House plays the blues on his electric guitar.

**Casting Call:** Pruitt Taylor Vince (George) played Mose Manuel on the HBO series *Deadwood* from 2005 to 2006. He was also memorable as a psychopathic

killer in the *X-Files* episode "Unruhe" (1996).

**Title Tale:** "Que Será, Será" is a Doris Day hit from the 1950s, meaning "What will be, will be." It very much describes George's attitude towards life, and House's uncertain future.

## * 3.07 "Son of Coma Guy"

**Writer:** Doris Egan **Director:** Daniel Attias

**Patients of the Week:** Kyle Wozniak (Zeb Newman), Gabriel Wozniak (John Larroquette)

House temporarily wakes Gabriel Wozniak from a 10-year vegetative state in order to diagnose Gabriel's son Kyle who is in a coma after suffering seizures. House's cocktail of drugs will only be effective for about a day. Surprisingly, instead of wanting to be at his son's bedside or provide House with the information needed to make the diagnosis, Gabe wants to go to Atlantic City for a hoagie sandwich.

With House at the wheel and Wilson in the backseat of his own car, Gabe refuses to provide any information that might be crucial to saving Kyle. Instead, he demands that for every question House asks, Gabe gets to ask one in return. Wilson has some pointed questions of his own for House, and, in the end, as important truths about Gabe emerge, so do a few of House's. House eventually realizes that Kyle has a genetic condition, but by now he has deteriorated to the point where he needs a heart transplant.

Knowing he is doomed to life as a vegetable once the drugs wear off, Gabe resolves to donate his heart — sacrificing his life to save his son's. House agrees to help Gabe commit suicide.

**Zebra of the Week:** Ragged red fiber disease, a genetic condition passed on by Kyle's mother.

**Epiphany!:** House connects Gabe's diverse anecdotes about his wife's annoying family to ascertain Kyle's illness.

**Iconic Moment in *House* History:** House explains why he became a doctor. It's a revelation surprising even to Wilson. **Iconic Moment #2:** House's grave conversation with Gabe about the best way to commit suicide with minimal damage to the heart.

**A Fine Bromance:** House and Wilson on a road trip is always "bromantic," no matter what else happens. When House sends Wilson away so he won't be a party to Gabe's suicide, Wilson provides him with an embarrassing alibi.

**Housian Ethics:** Waking someone temporarily from a vegetative state with a highly suspect cocktail of substances stretches the bounds of medical ethics. But this episode's biggest ethical question concerns Gabe's suicide and House's complicity.

**Did You Know?:** In the season one episode "Cursed" (1.13), the adolescent patient Gabe is concerned because his Ouija board told him "Gabe" is going to die. Chase reassures him, saying that there is another "Gabe" in the hospital who is "very old, very sick." Continuity, or happy coincidence?

**Casting Call:** Gabe is played by John Larroquette, who won four Supporting Actor Emmy Awards for his role as Dan Fielding on the classic CBS comedy series *Night Court*.

**Title Tale:** Actually, "Son of Vegetative State Guy" might have been a more accurate title.

**Why It's a Classic:** Besides the important reveal about why House became a doctor, the episode also explores several other critical *House* themes: the conditional nature of love, what it means to "do the right thing," and the shades of gray present in medical ethics. The mesmerizing chemistry between Laurie and Larroquette makes this episode especially memorable.

### 3.08 "Whac-A-Mole"

**Writer:** Pamela Davis **Director:** Daniel Sackheim
**Patient of the Week:** Jack (Patrick Fugit)

Eighteen-year-old Jack is a busboy — and guardian to his two young siblings. He collapses after vomiting at work, and while being diagnosed, he exhibits infection after infection. As soon as one is treated, another pops up. A bone marrow transplant from one of his siblings may cure him, but he refuses to put his brother at risk. Is his motive altruistic or will being too ill to care for his siblings be his way to rid himself of them?

On the Tritter front, Wilson finds his car has been impounded as part of an "ongoing police investigation," and his prescription-writing privileges have been revoked. The inability to prescribe means that Wilson is essentially out of business. House grows anxious as his Vicodin supply dwindles and he begins to have problems with his shoulder.

**Zebra of the Week:** The genetic condition chronic granulomatous disease makes Jack susceptible to serial infections.

**Epiphany!:** Cuddy notes that stress can trigger physical symptoms (pointing out that stress may be the source of House's shoulder pain). House realizes that Jack's illness has been triggered by the stress of raising two young children on his own after his parents died.

**Iconic Moment in *House* History:** When House sees a physical therapist for his shoulder, she insists that House use the cane on the "correct" side for once (the left hand for a right leg injury). House's "wrong" use of his cane has been a source of much discussion the online fan since the beginning of the series. The moment is surely a nod to this long-running debate!

**A Fine Bromance:** After the DEA revokes Wilson's prescription-writing privileges, House agrees (in theory) to let his fellows write for him. But at a critical moment in the diagnosis, House refuses to let Cameron go. Wilson blows up at House, finally blaming him for all the havoc being caused by Tritter — something House patently rejects.

**Judgmental Fellow Alert:** After Foreman assumes Jack's motives are selfless in refusing to put his brother through the risk of a live organ donation, he is proven wrong when House reveals Jack's true motives. Foreman is disappointed in Jack and tries to persuade him to change his mind; House's perspective is different. He sees Jack as being honest with himself: that they are all much better off being raised by real adults.

**Shipper Alert!:** House offers to father Cuddy's child if she writes him a prescription for Vicodin. **Shipper Alert #2:** Cameron refuses to write a prescription for House, handing him a bottle of her over-the-counter PMS (pre-menstrual syndrome) medicine. She tells him, "It does wonders for me!"

**Housian Ethics:** With new infections cropping up one after the other, House treats Jack with an aerosol cocktail of infectious agents to see how they affect him. As he tells Jack, the protocol is not FDA-approved.

**Pop Culture References:** When Jack's foot begins to itch, House places on the whiteboard a sealed envelope with only "the game is an (itchy) foot" scrawled on it. "The game's afoot," is a classic line from the Sherlock Holmes stories (and Shakespeare's *Henry V*).

**Casting Call:** Guest star Patrick Fugit played the lead in Cameron Crowe's autobiographical Oscar Award–winning film *Almost Famous* (2000). (It won best screenplay.) Alan Rosenberg plays Wilson's lawyer. Rosenberg has made somewhat of a career playing attorneys, and his most notable legal role is perhaps Eli Levinson, a regular character first on ABC's *Civil Wars* and then on NBC's *L.A. Law*.

**Title Tale:** Whac-A-Mole is a popular arcade game. When you "whack" a mole popping up from beneath the game's surface, it retreats and another pops up.


## 3.09 "Finding Judas"

**Writer:** Sarah Hess **Director:** Deran Sarafian
**Patient of the Week:** Alice (Alyssa Shafer)

Virtually cut off from his Vicodin supply, House tries to diagnose Alice, a little girl caught between her feuding divorced parents. When the parents lose sight of Alice's best interests, the court appoints Cuddy as her guardian.

As Tritter keeps up the pressure on everyone at Princeton-Plainsboro, Cuddy now carefully administers House's pills one at a time. Such a dramatic reduction in his dosage does nothing for House's mood, much less, his pain. He blames Alice's worsening condition on Cuddy's tendency for caution, having prevented House from pursuing a more aggressive treatment plan.

When Alice spikes a fever, Cuddy is caught between her responsibilities to the patient and her belief in House. And when she goes along with House's diagnosis of necrotizing fasciitis, the results are nearly tragic. House's solution is to amputate two of Alice's limbs, but at the last minute, Chase has another idea, which will save her from a life-altering surgery. Nearly out of his mind with uncontrolled pain, House has no time for Chase's ideas and slugs him in the jaw for blocking his way out of the hospital.

On the Tritter front, the DA freezes Cameron and Foreman's bank accounts, while the detective sets up Chase as a stooge. After learning that House has physically attacked Chase, Wilson agrees to cooperate with Tritter — to preempt the fellow from acting against his boss.

**Zebra of the Week:** Congenital erthropoietic porphyria, a serious disease that causes extreme sensitivity to light exposure.

**Epiphany!:** It's Chase's: the diagnosis occurs to him as he plays with a laser pointer. He realizes that Alice's symptoms have worsened every time she has been exposed to intense light while in the hospital.

**Iconic Moment in *House* History:** House hits Chase, knocking him to the ground. It's a pivot point for the story line, leading directly to Wilson making the deal with Tritter on House's behalf. This episode is a rarity in that House is completely wrong about the diagnosis — and his fellows get it right.

**House Is a Jerk:** House tells Cuddy it was fortunate that she never got pregnant because she would "be a terrible mom." Bad House!

**Housian Ethics:** Should House really be practicing medicine at this point?

**Casting Call:** Paula Cale (Alice's mother) was a series regular as Joanie Hansen on the 1999–2002 NBC series *Providence*.

**Title Tale:** Tritter seeks his "Judas" throughout the episode, and many fans believed Chase would reprise his role from season one by betraying his boss. But surprisingly, after Wilson sees the damage House has done, he decides to ask for his 30 pieces of silver to avoid complete disaster — and save House from certain conviction.


## * 3.10 "Merry Little Christmas"

**Writer:** Liz Friedman **Director:** Tony To
**Patient of the Week:** Abigail (Kacie Borrowman)

Wilson makes a deal with the devil: Tritter will have the charges dropped if House agrees to drug rehab. Unsurprisingly, he refuses. To force the issue, Wilson and Cuddy conspire to cut off House's Vicodin supply entirely.

House takes the case of Abigail, a teenager with (presumed) cartilage-hair hypoplasia dwarfism who comes to the clinic with severe respiratory issues. But as he begins the diagnosis, Cuddy tosses him from the case, suspending him until he reconsiders Tritter's deal. The team tries to diagnose Abigail without House's help, first considering an autoimmune condition, and then cancer, while House suffers narcotics withdrawal, continuing to refuse the deal.

At a loss with Abigail's symptoms, first Cuddy and then Cameron visit House at home trying to appeal to his better nature to look into the case, even as Cuddy continues to refuse Vicodin. Cameron is horrified that House has now started cutting himself to redirect the pain from his leg, but has better success than Cuddy in convincing him to help. He eventually relents; the puzzle is too irresistible even without his demand being met. His diagnosis of Stills disease — something neither Cuddy nor Wilson has considered — seems to fit the symptoms. Although, the diagnosis ultimately proves incorrect, House's ability to see the connection to Stills demonstrates his skill as a superior diagnostician.

Returning to the hospital, a physical wreck at this point, House steals a bottle of oxycodone from Wilson's dead patient. Feeling better after downing a few of them, he perceives the correct diagnosis.

House returns home after solving the medical mystery, the clock still ticking down on the three-day time frame of the deal. He finishes off the 30 oxy pills in the bottle, chasing them with a tumbler of whiskey. Wilson finds House semiconscious on the floor and leaves him there. Reviving himself the next morning, House decides to take the deal, but it's too late.

**Zebra of the Week:** Langerhans cell histiocytosis. It's a small tumor that once removed will eradicate her symptoms. She is not, after all, a dwarf; taking growth hormones will allow her to grow to her normal stature.

**Epiphany!:** House has a conversation with a young hospital patient about faulty syllogisms and her stuffed dog (or is it a bear?). He realizes that his patient might not actually be a dwarf, but may simply lack growth hormones.

**Iconic Moment in *House* History:** House reaches rock bottom. It is Christmas Eve and House has returned home facing a bleak future. He calls his mother. Knowing that she is attending a family Christmas party, he speaks into her answering machine — haltingly, wistfully, heartbreakingly, leaving a voice mail message that seems to be as much "goodbye" as it is "Merry Christmas."

**A Fine Bromance:** Wilson finally realizes that House's gift isn't just "luck," and that there's true genius at work. Expressing to Tritter that he cannot deprive the world of House's brilliance, he tries to retract his testimony. But it's too late. Worried about House returning home alone on Christmas Eve, Wilson asks if he wants some company. House emphatically declines the invitation.

**House Is a Jerk:** He is needlessly cruel to the just-widowed wife of Wilson's patient.

**Shipper Alert!:** Cameron is angry with Wilson for making the deal with Tritter. She thinks he's done it to help himself. **Shipper Alert #2:** While House is home and in withdrawal, Cameron gently dresses his self-inflicted wounds while urging him to take the deal. **Shipper Alert #3:** House really seems to click with Abigail's mom, who can match his sarcasm snark for snark.

**Housian Ethics:** Is it ethical to force House into cold-turkey withdrawal?

**Gross-out Warning:** House lying in his own vomit is not a pleasant sight.

**Classic Rant:** Abigail refuses to take the prescribed growth hormones. Her mother, a true hypoplasic dwarf, aggressively supports her decision to remain "special." House acknowledges that being a freak, like they — and he — are, makes them stronger. But why put a child unnecessarily through the hardships of being so different when there's another option?

**Casting Call:** Abigail's mother Maddy is played by Meredith Eaton, who played Bethany Horowitz on *Boston Legal* from 2006 to 2008.

**Title Tale:** The episode takes place in the days before Christmas, with the obvious symbolism of House as Jesus being forsaken by his friends and unfairly persecuted, with Wilson cast as Judas. Of course there is the additional connection that House is treating a small-of-stature person.

**Why It's a Classic:** The penultimate episode of the Tritter story arc has House crash landing after he's been emotionally battered all season. It casts in high relief both House's self-destructiveness and his genius.

### 3.11 "Words and Deeds"

**Writer:** Leonard Dick **Director:** Daniel Sackheim

**Patient of the Week:** Derrick (Tory Kittles)

The team treats Derrick, a firefighter who collapses while fighting a blaze. But as House's preliminary hearing nears, and facing the inevitability of what lies ahead, he checks himself into the hospital's drug rehab program, leaving Derrick to the fellows.

The team diagnoses Derrick first with male menopause, and then with "broken heart syndrome" when his heart goes haywire in the presence of his firefighting partner, Amy. Derrick's in love with her, but there's a complication: he tells Cameron that she's engaged to his brother. Not wanting to stand in the way of his brother's happiness, Derrick agrees to undergo electro convulsive therapy (ECT), which the team believes is the only solution to prevent further heart issues. But they are wrong.

House, who only takes the rehab seriously enough to prove himself to Tritter, co-opts an aide on the unit once he realizes nothing he does will satisfy the detective. At his hearing, Cuddy stuns House by lying to the judge about the stolen oxycodone, telling her that it was a placebo. House's case is dismissed; Cuddy now "owns his ass."

**Zebra of the Week:** Spinal meningioma, a spinal tumor creating false memories, and ultimately the broken heart syndrome.

**Epiphany!:** When House's middle-aged female judge raises her voice at him, he notices the high pitch her voice makes, reminding him that Derrick's voice does the same thing. House realizes that something is affecting Derrick's brain, causing the menopausal symptoms and the broken heart syndrome.

**Iconic Moment in *House* History:** House apologizes to Tritter, explaining that his behavior is driven by a life in pain, with "good days merely intolerable" and bad ones that "suck the soul right out of you."

**A Fine Bromance:** Wilson brings House a tie on the eve of his hearing and House apologizes for blaming him for his troubles. "You were only trying to help me, protect me," House admits. After telling Wilson the entire rehab thing was a scam, and he's been on Vicodin all along, Wilson wonders if the apology was genuine. House tells him to think what he wants. Their "Good night Wilson," "Good night, House" at the end of the episode tells each that all is back to normal between them.

**Judgmental Fellow Alert:** Cameron, angry with House for stealing the oxycodone, pointedly declines to attend his trial.

**Housian Ethics:** Cuddy commits perjury to protect House.

**Shipper Alert!:** House teases Cuddy about conjugal visits when he is cited for contempt and has to spend a night in jail. She is not amused. **Shipper Alert #2:** Cameron hugs House after she learns he's apologized to Wilson for stealing his dead patient's oxycodone pills in "Merry Little Christmas" (3.10).

**Pop Culture References:** *Harry Potter*: House nicknames the burly aide in the rehab unit Voldemort.

**Casting Call:** Kadeem Hardison plays House's attorney. He is probably best known for playing Dwayne Wayne on NBC's popular comedy *A Different World* (1987–1993).

**Title Tale:** *House, M.D.* has always been about the difference between words and deeds. House's deeds are usually nobler than his words; this time his deed, scamming the rehab system, is a lie. It's unclear when during the episode House begins getting his Vicodin fix again (before or after Tritter's visit to House in rehab, when he tells House, "even your actions lie"). The title also reflects Cuddy's perjury.

## * 3.12 "One Day, One Room"

**Writer:** David Shore **Director:** Juan J. Campanella
**Patient of the Week:** Eve (Katheryn Winnick)

After getting out him of legal trouble last episode, Cuddy insists House spend several days working in the clinic. One of those episodes fans either loved or hated, it eschews the usual series formula and focuses on House's encounter with Eve, a young rape victim.

Diagnosing Eve with chlamydia, House discovers she's been raped. He feels ill-equipped to help her and asks Cuddy to reassign the case. But Eve refuses to talk to anyone else, including a psychiatrist. Although House isn't interested in treating Eve — or talking to her — he is intrigued as to why she has chosen *him*. And when he learns she is pregnant as a result of the rape, he tries to convince her to abort the fetus.

While House struggles to deal with Eve, Cameron treats a homeless man who doesn't want to die alone.

**Zebra of the Week:** The biggest mystery is why Eve insists on talking only to House.

**Iconic Moment in *House* History:** Eve reveals that she sees in House a kindred spirit. "There's something about you; like you're hurt, too," she observes. Finally, his question answered, House reveals to Eve that he is an abuse survivor.

**Clinic Duty:** House sees a whole lot of STDs in the clinic, and an obsessively fastidious guy with athlete's foot in his nose from clipping his nasal hairs too closely.

**A Fine Bromance:** Wilson finds House hiding from clinic duty in a jogging park: the last place Cuddy would look for him, he sadly acknowledges. When Wilson asks him why a jogging park when he can't even walk, House confesses, "I sit; I watch; I imagine."

**Judgmental Fellow Alert:** The persnickety clinic patient arrogantly disses House for his sloppy appearance. Hey, at least House doesn't have fungus in his nose.

**Housian Ethics:** House convinces Eve to abort her pregnancy and "talk about" the rape. But is it the "right" thing to do? In the end, House is not so sure. "It makes us feel good about ourselves," he reflects. But "maybe all we've done is make a girl cry." **Housian Ethics #2:** House and Eve debate the morality of abortion and divine retribution.

**Shipper Alert!:** Cuddy finds House lying on a picnic table in the park, avoiding clinic duty. He asks her if she's planning to kiss him. She convinces him to go back and do his job, but tries to make it more interesting, offering $10 for every patient he can diagnose without touching. But he owes her $10 for every patient he has to touch.

**Gross-out Warning:** A man with a cockroach embedded in his ear runs screaming through the clinic. The cockroach is never seen, but ick anyway.

**Casting Call:** Katheryn Winnick appears in the 2009 movie *Cold Souls* with Paul Giamatti.

**Title Tale:** Eve notes that our lives are comprised of a series of rooms, and those with whom we spend time in those rooms. In his day in the one room with Eve, House is able to confess something he's probably never talked about before, not even with Wilson.

**Why It's a Classic:** The revelation about House's history.


### 3.13 "Needle in a Haystack"

**Writer:** David Foster **Director:** Peter O'Fallon

**Patient of the Week:** Stevie (Jake Richardson)

House and the team treat Stevie, a Romany (Gypsy) teen suffering from internal bleeding. He suffers a bleed in one organ, only for it to be replaced by a new bleed somewhere else. House immediately suggests they need a "plumber" to fix Stevie leaky pipes, and he's ultimately proven right. Something is poking holes in Stevie's organs. Meanwhile, House has his handicapped parking spot moved farther from the hospital entrance to make room for a new wheelchair-bound researcher. He protests, making a bet with Cuddy: if House spends an entire week in a wheelchair, she will return his spot.

**Zebra of the Week:** An inadvertently swallowed toothpick wreaks havoc as it courses through Stevie's internal organs.

**Iconic Moment in *House* History:** House does wheelchair wheelies like a pro, and manages to navigate the chair down an entire flight of stairs. This leaves fans to wonder if House acquired his pro wheelchair skills while recovering from his leg surgery long before we met him.

**Clinic Duty:** A mother brings her child into the clinic with a "sore throat," but she's really there to have the doctor scare the kid into going to school.

**House Is a Jerk:** He's a jerk throughout the episode (even more than usual) as he plays up his disability for all it's worth. He also uses Romany cultural epithets, trying to distract Stevie's family to enable the team to run needed tests without his family's knowledge.

**Judgmental Fellow Alert:** Foreman notes Stevie's interest in anatomy and suggests he abandon his family's traditions to pursue college — and perhaps even medical school. Foreman can't understand why Stevie rebuffs the suggestion.

**Housian Ethics:** House raises the issue of handicap accessibility and the Americans with Disabilities Act. Technically, the researcher has rights to the closer space, since she is able to walk a shorter distance than House can. But she has a wheelchair, and House has to manage with a cane. Who should have the right to the closer space?

**Pop Culture References:** Wilson refers to *Ironsides*, the old Raymond Burr television series when he sees House in his wheelchair.

**Casting Call:** Jake Richardson (Stevie) has appeared in several acclaimed series since his role on House, including ABC's *Boston Legal* and HBO's *In Treatment*.

**Title Tale:** Needle = toothpick; haystack = Stevie's body.

## 3.14 "Insensitive"

**Writer:** Matthew Lewis **Director:** Deran Sarafian

**Patient of the Week:** Hannah (Mika Boorem)

The teenage Hannah comes to House through the ER, injured after a car accident on a snowy night. She's examined while her mother, much more severely injured, is elsewhere in the hospital. House notices that she cannot feel any pain (although she tries hard to hide it). Intrigued, he concludes that she has Congenital Insensitivity to Pain and Anhidrosis (CIPA), which prevents her from feeling pain. Testing Hannah to rule out internal injuries, House seems more interested in her lack of pain.

Along with the other tests, House insists they perform a spinal nerve biopsy, a seemingly odd procedure. Hannah soon spikes a high fever and suffers psychotic episodes. When Hannah's legs become paralyzed, a nerve biopsy does seem necessary, but the team argues that taking a tissue from a peripheral nerve is safer than House's insistence on a spinal nerve. Turns out that House has been researching nerve transplantation and has designs on tissue from Hannah's insensate nerves. Wilson eventually discovers House's plans, calling him on his ethics and his objectivity.

It's Valentine's Day at Princeton-Plainsboro, and Cuddy has a blind date. The always-curious-about-Cuddy House crashes her date — twice — on the pretext of needing her advice. Foreman's girlfriend, Wendy, is surprised when he gives her an unusual Valentine's Day gift: a ticket to a specialized training program in another city! Bye-bye, Wendy.

Chase and Cameron also feel the Valentine spirit, deciding to start a sex-with-no-commitment relationship.

**Zebra of the Week:** A 25-foot tapeworm, feasting on Hannah's B12!

**Epiphany!:** While mooching Wilson's late-night snack, House realizes that although Hannah received B12 when she arrived at the ER, her symptoms point to a B12 deficiency. Something's mooching Hannah's B12!

**Iconic Moment in *House* History:** Wilson reminds House that transplanting nerve cells into his leg would mean a shorter life-span and require a lifetime on immunosuppressant drugs. House argues that his life would be "shorter, but normal." It's the first direct admission from House that he would sacrifice a great deal for a more "normal" life.

**A Fine Bromance:** The case solved, Wilson encourages House to ask Hannah directly for the nerve tissue he so desperately wants. Probably considering his earlier ethical lapse, House demurs.

**House Is a Jerk:** Breaking in on Cuddy's date, House tries to find reason to mock her new friend. Discovering that he's in auto repair, House misunderstands that he's a mechanic. His initial amusement is short-lived when Cuddy's date tells him that he owns "Eastern Lube," a large and lucrative company.

**Housian Ethics:** Wilson accuses House of insisting on a spinal nerve biopsy in lieu of the safer peripheral biopsy, to harvest the spinal nerves for himself. House realizes Wilson is right, and instructs his staff to do what they think is safest for the patient, recusing himself from the decision.

**Shipper Alert!:** House is too interested in Cuddy's blind date to be simply a casual bystander. When he visits her, mid-date to ask her opinion about the case for the second time, she asks him point-blank, "Do you like me, House?" He has no answer. **Shipper Alert #2:** Chase and Cameron initiate a "friends with bene-fits" sex arrangement that avoids the baggage of a real relationship: a sort of anti–Valentine's Day valentine to each other.

**Gross-out Warning:** House pulls a 25-foot tapeworm from Hannah's belly to the surprise and fascination of all in the OR. Ick.

**Casting Call:** Mika Boorem (Hannah) had a recurring role on *Dawson's Creek* from 2002 to 2003.

**Title Tale:** Lots of insensitivity going on for a Valentine's Day episode. Hannah is insensitive to pain; House is insensitive to the needs of his patient — and, apparently, to Cuddy's sexual and social needs. Foreman is insensitive to Wendy. On the other hand, this is *House*!

## * 3.15 "Half Wit"

**Writer:** Lawrence Kaplow **Director:** Katie Jacobs

**Patient of the Week:** Patrick (Dave Matthews)

Patrick is a musical savant, whose genius appeared only after the left side of his brain was damaged when he was involved in a car accident at 10 years old. His hands painfully contort as he is about to perform at a classical piano concert. Patrick's musical abilities fascinate House as much as his illness as the team continues the diagnosis. They identify a bleed in Patrick's brain, eventually suggesting an autoimmune condition.

House notes that the musically gifted Patrick has the cognitive ability of a very young boy. He cannot button his own shirt; he has no insight into his gift; he cannot even state whether it makes him happy. House proposes a radical surgery that could restore Patrick's ability to reason, but only at the cost of his musical gift. Is it a fair trade?

Meanwhile, House lets everyone believe he has terminal brain cancer after the team discovers he has enrolled in a clinical trial at a Boston hospital. Against his wishes, they insist on re-evaluating all his records in the hope that it's not cancer. Eventually the team discovers House doesn't actually have cancer, and has faked tests and brain scans to qualify for the trial, which involves placing an implant into the pleasure center of the brain. The fellows are angry to learn of House's scam, believing he is trying to find a new "high." Are they right? Or is it another desperate attempt to address his pain? Or is it as Wilson believes: that House is depressed and isolated?

**Zebra of the Week:** Takayasu's arteritis, an autoimmune condition. Also, the damaged part of Patrick's brain causes seizures and interferes with his cognitive growth.

**Iconic Moment in *House* History:** After Wilson advises that House be more social, House sees his team in a bar having a drink and laughing. Considering whether to join them, he finally puts his hand on the doorknob. The scene cuts before we know whether he actually goes in.

**A Fine Bromance:** When he learns House doesn't have cancer after all, Wilson assumes House is trying to treat depression and suggests something simpler. He should try, instead, to be more social: "Like having pizza with a friend," Wilson offers, gesturing towards himself.

**Judgmental Fellow Alert:** House confesses he falsified records to get qualify for the clinical trial so "they could implant a cool drug right into pleasure center of my brain." Without digging deeper, Cameron and Foreman assume it is just another way for House to get high.

**Housian Ethics:** House lies his way into a clinical trial by falsifying his records. Chase and Cameron break into House's apartment for clues about his secret.

**Shipper Alert!:** Cameron kisses House to show she cares, but she has an ulterior motive. She wants to swipe a blood sample. **Shipper Alert #2:** House visits Cuddy late at night to discuss Patrick's case. She embraces him, wishing him luck in Boston, and House's hand moves to her derriere. Asking if she can do anything for him, he takes a step to follow her to the bedroom. She stops him, wise-cracking: "Call the Make-A-Wish Foundation."

**Did You Know?:** Legendary rocker Dave Matthews, a guitarist, required a double for the piano scenes (Matthews is not a pianist); Greg House's piano playing is genuinely Hugh Laurie's.

**Pop Culture References:** House gives the team access to his falsified files, telling them he's used the alias "Luke N. Laura," the legendary super-couple from his favorite soap opera, *General Hospital*.

**Musical Notes:** There are many. House and Patrick play duets on the piano. House starts playing Joe Purdy's "I Don't Like Mondays," which Patrick effortlessly picks up and plays with him. Then House hesitantly plays the opening from a piece he composed in junior high but was never able to complete. Patrick takes the piece and completes it — and House is quite moved.

**Props Department:** House now uses reading glasses.

**Casting Call:** Dave Matthews (Patrick) is, fittingly, a world-famous musician. Veteran character actor Kurtwood Smith (Patrick's father) is well known for playing the father of Eric Forman (no, not that one — this is Forman without the "e") in the Fox series *That '70s Show* (1998–2006).

**Title Tale:** It's not a slur! Patrick is literally a "half wit." Half his brain is damaged and destructive to the other half.

**Why It's a Classic:** Dave Matthews, lots of music, and some real insight into House's state of mind create a nearly perfect episode.


## 3.16 "Top Secret"

**Writer:** Thomas Moran **Director:** Deran Sarafian
**Patient of the Week:** John Kelly (Marc Blucas)

House dreams that his leg is shot off in a war zone. It spooks him when one of the soldiers in the dream turns up as a patient complaining of Gulf War syndrome. Perplexed that he can't figure where he's seen Iraq War veteran John Kelly before (because you "can't dream someone you've never met"), House goes to great lengths to research everything about him, while the team tries to explains his condition. Initially complaining of joint pain and fatigue, John soon exhibits a whole host of symptoms, including vaginosis in his mouth, paralysis, loss of hearing, and tumors that seem to appear and disappear.

House processes John's symptoms through a series of vivid dreams. As he tells Wilson, paraphrasing 20th century psychiatrist Carl Jung, dreams are a way of figuring out what we can't process awake.

Meanwhile, House suffers from urinary retention and can't find relief, eventually resorting to drastic measures. Wilson wonders if it's the result of long-term Vicodin use, a theory House rejects — at least when talking to Wilson.

**Zebra of the Week:** "A bloody tissue issue," hereditary hemorrhagic telangiectasia is a genetic disorder causing problems in John's capillaries. It probably first presented with a bloody nose when he was a kid.

**Epiphany!:** House figures it out in a dream: a confluence of his subconscious thoughts about his urinary problem, Cuddy, John, and a bloody nose.

**Iconic Moment in *House* History:** Cuddy tells House to stop fantasizing about her and staring at her like some lovesick school boy. Yeah, we know how much good that will do.

**Clinic Duty:** While suffering from urinary retention, House treats an obsessive-compulsive young woman carrying a large water bottle. The full bottle seems to taunt him.

**Judgmental Fellow Alert:** Wilson blames House's urinary problems on Vicodin abuse, and initially refuses him medication for it.

**Housian Ethics:** The team debates the existence of Gulf War syndrome. House invades John's privacy by examining his personal and financial records to determine why he's appearing in his dreams. Chase and Cameron have sex in the sleep lab while they're supposed to be monitoring the patient.

**Shipper Alert!:** Cameron and Chase continue to have sex everywhere and House catches the two of them in foreplay in the janitorial closet. Chase thinks Cameron wants House to know about the affair to make him jealous. **Shipper Alert #2:** Cuddy is the key to the patient mystery. She appears in and out of House's dreams, which confuses him. It is suddenly clear when House finally recognizes John from years earlier, having seen him making out with Cuddy at a hospital benefit. Cuddy is flattered that House is so intensely focused on her.

**Gross-out Warning:** It's a tie between John, who develops with a case of bacterial vaginosis — in his mouth — and House. In a dream, after House catheterizes himself to relieve his urinary retention issue, the full urine collection bag bursts, which is a little more graphic than most viewers may appreciate.

**Pop Culture References:** Wilson knows way too much about the Village People.

*House* **Canon:** We now know that House and Cuddy had sex years earlier.

**Casting Call:** Marc Blucas (John Kelly) played Riley Finn on *Buffy the Vampire Slayer*.

**Title Tale:** The patient doesn't disclose a childhood chronic bloody nose problem, a clue to his illness. Cuddy keeps secret how she knows the patient.


## 3.17 "Fetal Position"

**Writers:** Russel Friend, Garrett Lerner **Director:** Matt Shakman

**Patient of the Week:** Emma (Anne Elizabeth Ramsay)

House treats a pregnant photographer, Emma, who has a stroke with her baby's due date four months away. He diagnoses maternal mirror syndrome; there is something wrong with the baby that is manifesting in Emma. House's solution is easy: abort the fetus. But Emma refuses, insisting that House diagnose what's wrong with the fetus and fix it.

Cuddy sides with Emma, closely identifying with the middle-aged woman whose biological clock is ticking in overdrive. House believes that Cuddy has lost her objectivity and is risking both Emma's and her unborn child's life. But this time, Cuddy is right, and after "becoming" House, she diagnoses the baby. House proposes a fetal surgery to repair a problem in the baby's lungs. But when Emma crashes during surgery, Cuddy again intervenes, saving mother and child.

Meanwhile, House tries to plan a vacation, considering places someone in his physical condition cannot possibly visit with ease: the Galápagos Islands, the Johnston Straight, and the Andes Mountains. He imagines, he desires, he watches the Discovery Channel. But to actually do it would require bigger steps towards change than he is emotionally able, or willing, to make, even after Cuddy buys him a first-class ticket.


**Zebra of the Week:** Congenital cystic adenomatoid malformation (CCAM) in the fetus' lungs.

**Epiphany!:** It's Cuddy's epiphany. She knows the baby's problem must be in the lungs since they've looked everywhere else. But the baby's lungs aren't yet developed enough to see an issue. Cuddy loads Emma up on steroids, which is dangerous, but will speed the development of the baby's lungs.

**Iconic Moment in *House* History:** During the fetal surgery, the baby's tiny finger seems to reach up and grasp House's hand briefly. House is stunned, briefly caught up in a moment of true awe.

**Shipper Alert!:** Cameron wonders why, after catching her and Chase in the janitor's closet last episode, House has not yet reacted.

**Housian Ethics:** Should Cuddy have agreed to abort the fetus when House proposed it?

**Did You Know?:** During a real fetal surgery in 1999, the fetus seemed to grasp the surgeon's finger, as Emma's baby did with House.

**Pop Culture References:** Emma is photographing All American Rejects' rocker Tyson Ritter for an ad campaign in the teaser.

**Musical Notes:** Lucinda Williams' "Are You Alright?" is an appropriate backdrop for the final scene as House tears Cuddy's airline ticket in half, unable to bring himself to attempt something as risky for him as a vacation. Instead, he takes the phone off the hook and watches a documentary on the Galápagos Islands.

**Props Department:** Trying to be as House-like as possible, Cuddy moves into his office to play with his ball and other trinkets on his desk.

**Casting Call:** Anne Ramsay (Emma) was a series regular on NBC's *Mad About You*, playing Helen Hunt's sister Lisa Stemple (1992–1999). She's also had recurring roles on *Dexter*, *Six Feet Under*, *The L Word*, and *Dharma & Greg*. Tyson Ritter from the pop-rock band All-American Rejects appears in the teaser as himself.

**Title Tale:** The patient pair includes a fetus. House's inability to take a vacation suggests he's curled himself in a fetal position, self-protected and afraid to get out into the world.

### 3.18 "Airborne"

**Writer:** David Hoselton **Director:** Elodie Keene

**Patients of the Week:** Peng (Jamison Yang), Fran (Jenny O'Hara)

As House and Cuddy are on their way home from a medical conference in Singapore, an epidemic seems to breaks out on their flight, after one of the passengers starts vomiting. As more people get sick on the plane, including Cuddy, they fear it's a meningitis outbreak. House enlists three passengers to serve as surrogate fellows as he diagnoses on a makeshift whiteboard. House instructs: one must agree with everything he says (and fake an Australian accent), one must disagree with everything he says, and one must be morally outraged at everything he says.

Back at Princeton-Plainsboro, the team helps Wilson diagnose a middle-aged woman who collapses while about to have sex with a female hooker. The two cases are contrasted with each other: one in the relative comfort and with all the high-tech gadgetry of a medical hospital, and one in the improvised MASH-type unit of a plane.

Wilson is drawn to Fran's hooker companion, who is both beautiful and very nice.

**Zebra of the Week:** On the flight, House diagnoses mass hysteria. After Peng falls ill, so does everyone else. But what's wrong with Peng? He has the bends from flying too soon after scuba diving. Back at the hospital, Fran has pesticide (methyl bromide) poisoning.

**Epiphany!:** House tests for mass hysteria by suggesting to the passengers a false symptom for meningitis. The hysteria is confirmed when the passengers develop the false symptom. **Epiphany! #2:** Chase uncovers Fran's methyl bromide poisoning when he notices that her cat is dead. Discovering a pipe leading from her neighbor's home to hers, he realizes that methyl bromide traveled from the neighboring house during termite fumigation.

**House Is a Jerk:** House is a complete ass to Cuddy on the flight home. He cashes in *her* first-class ticket for an economy seat, giving up *his* first-class seat to her only when a passenger in his cabin falls very ill — so that House won't be bothered to have to treat him.

**Shipper Alert!:** After being such a jerk to Cuddy when she falls ill, House does a very close, caring examination. **Shipper Alert #2:** Chase and Cameron go at it in Fran's House, but when Chase tells Cameron he wants more than a "friends with benefits" arrangement, Cameron drops him, coldly telling him he's ruined a good thing.

**Gross-out Warning:** Lots of vomiting on that plane as many passengers become sick. Ick!

**Lost in Translation:** Cuddy is surprised when House doesn't understand enough Korean to diagnose Peng.

**Props Department:** House has a new $900 vintners cane, which is confiscated as a potential weapon before he gets on the plane.

**World-Famous Doctor Moment:** House is in Singapore to deliver an address, which is intended to bolster the hospital's standing; House reminds us he's an infectious diseases expert.

**Casting Call:** Jenny O'Hara has had a distinguished career onstage, playing opposite such luminaries as Sir Alec Guinness early in her career, and then appearing in numerous films and television series, including *The King of Queens* (1998–2007) and *Big Love* (2006–present).

**House Doing "Doctor Stuff":** House performs a precarious lumbar puncture on Peng at 35,000 feet — with improvised equipment. The risk of paralyzing the patient is not lost on House, whose care and skill are evident. It also lays to rest an argument in the fandom after season two's "Deception" (2.09) about whether

House is still skilled enough at procedures to perform a lumbar puncture.

**Title Tale:** House diagnoses and treats while "airborne." Fran's illness is an airborne chemical toxin.

### 3.19 "Act Your Age"

**Writer:** Sarah Hess **Director:** Daniel Sackheim

**Patients of the Week:** Lucy (Bailee Madison), Jasper (Slade Pearce)

House treats Lucy, a little girl exhibiting signs of premature aging, including problems with her heart, lungs, and kidneys. When the team finds a discarded bloodstained shirt, they first suspect the widowed father of abuse. But the blood is endometrial (menstrual), seemingly impossible from six-year-old Lucy. When her brother begins to show signs of premature puberty, the team focuses on the likelihood of an environmental cause.

House gives Wilson theater tickets, not knowing he's going to invite Cuddy. When Wilson asks her to the play, House is concerned that Cuddy may be destined to become the fourth "ex–Mrs. Wilson."

Chase and Cameron try to deal with their breakup. Chase is still smitten, but Cameron is angry at him for ruining their little arrangement.

**Zebra of the Week:** An over-the-counter "male-enhancement" cream, laden with testosterone, leeched from daddy's skin to the kiddies whenever they hugged.

**Epiphany!:** When Lucy's brother develops the same symptoms — and House discovers that dad is dating their *much* younger day-care teacher — he realizes the dad has been using the cream to keep up with his girlfriend.

**Iconic Moment in *House* History:** Chase buys flowers for Cameron, a sweet gesture, with no expectation for either reciprocity or sex. It's the next salvo in Chase's gentle courtship, which lasts the remainder of the season.

**A Fine Bromance:** After Wilson takes Cuddy to the play, House buys flowers for Wilson in Cuddy's name. It's an elaborate prank to get Wilson to admit he wants to have sex with her.

**House Is a Jerk:** House asks Dad's girlfriend rather indelicately whether she's had an upper lip wax job.

**Judgmental Fellow Alert:** The team suspects the dad of child sexual abuse before they have all the facts.

**Shipper Alert!:** House and Cuddy share some serious conversation about the difficulties of relationships. House invites her to a play at the end of the conversation. **Shipper Alert #2:** Chase continues to pursue Cameron although she has broken up with him, deciding that he has the right to tell her he likes her every Tuesday.

**Casting Call:** House's slacker clinic patient is Joel Moore, who plays Norm Spellman in *Avatar* (2009).

**Title Tale:** The two very young patients are certainly not acting their age; neither is their father by dating a much younger woman. And House and Wilson are acting like two teenage boys about Cuddy.


## * 3.20 "House Training"

**Writer:** Doris Egan **Director:** Paul McCrane

**Patient of the Week:** Lupe (Monique Gabriela Curnen)

The impoverished and out-of-work Lupe collapses on the street while helping to run a Three-card Monte scam. Foreman diagnoses a transient ischemic attack after Lupe reports she suddenly became indecisive before the attack. As her organ systems fail one-by-one, Foreman believes she has cancer. He presses to do a full-body radiation treatment, which House approves. After the procedure, the team discovers she's in septic shock. There is nothing they can do for her; the radiation treatment has trashed her immune system, leaving her unable to fight off the infection. They've essentially killed her.

On a lighter note, Wilson's second ex-wife Bonnie, now a real-estate agent, drops in, asking Wilson to take in their aged dog. But the jealous House is more interested in finding how Bonnie and Wilson's relationship worked (or didn't) as Wilson continues to pursue Cuddy (sort of), taking her to an art exhibit.

Foreman's parents visit. He has difficulty dealing with the impact of his mother's Alzheimer's disease, knowing she only intermittently recognizes him.


**Zebra of the Week:** A simple staph infection caused by an abrasion from a bra hook.

**Epiphany!:** A blood pressure cuff causes excruciating pain. "Too much pain," as Cameron says. Lupe is in septic shock from the uncontrolled infection.

**Iconic Moment in *House* History:** After Lupe dies, House explains to Foreman why they missed a diagnosis that more mainstream doctors would have caught. "We'll save more people than they will," he says, but they also run the risk missing the obvious.

**A Fine Bromance:** As House awaits Lupe's inevitable death, Wilson is supportive, bringing his friend coffee and sitting with him on his deathwatch. While House autopsies his now-dead patient, Wilson secures consent from her grandparents.

**House Is a Jerk:** House allows Bonnie to believe that he's interested in buying a new condo from her. He's really only looking for dirt on Wilson's second marriage.

**Judgmental Fellow Alert:** Foreman lectures Lupe on how she's wasted her life. He's also angry with House for planning a biopsy on Lupe to identify the infection source as she's dying. Foreman insists he wait until she's dead before violating her body, believing House is simply satisfying a ghoulish need to know everything about everything.

**Housian Ethics:** The episode calls into question the nature of House's high-risk, high-stakes medical practice.

**Shipper Alert!:** House becomes obsessed over Wilson's possible interest in Cuddy. **Shipper Alert #2:** Chase continues his gentle courtship of Cameron despite her resistance.

**Pop Culture References:** Wilson takes Cuddy to what is supposed to be a David Hockney exhibit. Hockney is an influential English painter, photographer, printmaker, and stage designer, who was a key contributor to the pop art movement of the '60s.

**Plot Hole:** Bonnie says that Hector is 17 years old and was named for House. Does that mean Bonnie and Wilson were married at least 17 years earlier? Information about Wilson's first wife revealed during season six seems to contradict this bit of House canon.

**Casting Call:** Monique Gabriela Curnen (Lupe) co-starred in 2008's *The Dark Knight* as corrupt detective Anna Ramirez.

**Title Tale:** Bonnie tries to persuade Wilson to take her bad-tempered and house-training resistant dog. The episode title also refers to one of the potential risks of training under House — missing an occasional easy diagnosis.

**Why It's a Classic:** One of the season's more thought-provoking episodes, it explores House's zebra-hunting diagnostic practice, and what can go wrong when the team encounters a "horse." The episode is only marred by Foreman's overlong monologue as Lupe lies dying.


### 3.21 "Family"

**Writer:** Liz Friedman **Director:** David Straiton

**Patients of the Week:** Nick (Jascha Washington), Matty (Dabier Snell)

House treats Matty, a boy with upper respiratory symptoms as he prepares to donate his bone marrow to his brother Nick, Wilson's leukemia patient. The team needs to isolate the infection, working against the clock while Nick awaits the transplant in a clean room. Foreman takes a special interest in the family as Lupe's death still haunts him. He wants to take a cautious route to diagnose Matty, opposing House's more aggressive approach. When House wants to perform surgery to fix Matty's damaged mitral valve, Foreman insists it's too risky, convincing the parents — over House and Wilson's objections — to find a different donor rather than risk Matty's life.

As House predicts, after the transplant, Nick gets graft versus host disease: he is dying. After Matty has finally been diagnosed and treated, Foreman performs a questionable bone marrow extraction procedure on him without the parents' consent or House's permission, subjecting Matty to excruciating pain in a last-ditch effort to save his brother's life. It works, but the experience has soured Foreman on House's damn-the-consequences medicine, and he resigns, telling House that "to be a doctor like you, I have to be like you as a human being."

House has agreed to look after Bonnie's dog, Hector, who is making his life even more miserable than usual. The little dog eats through House's expensive shoes, his bedside copy of *Kim*, and his cane. House tries getting rid of the annoying animal without success. (Ever hear the old folk song "The Cat Came Back"?)

**Zebra of the Week:** Matty has the fungal infection histoplasmosis from chickens. The family's house sits atop of an old chicken farm.

**Epiphany!:** Wilson, surprised that the suburban family has an old water pump in their yard, suggests the team find out why. It leads directly to the diagnosis.

**Iconic Moment in *House* History:** House tells Foreman he did the right thing by torturing Matty because it saved his brother's life. It's what they sometimes must do in House's practice. But Foreman perfectly summarizes the dilemma faced by House. "You may save more lives, but I'll be okay with killing less."

**A Fine Bromance:** House apologizes to Wilson for calling him a coward in dealing with the parents.

**House Is a Jerk:** House insists that Wilson replace his chewed-through cane.

**Housian Ethics:** Wilson refuses to exert pressure on the parents, leaving a difficult medical decision completely in their hands, which conventional wisdom and medical ethics would suggest is the correct approach. But House argues that allowing the parents to decide could lead to Nick's death. Who's right — and who's doing the right thing? **Housian Ethics #2:** With both boys dying, House proposes using Nick, whose life is already forfeit due to the graft versus host disease, as a petri dish to diagnose Matty. The parents refuse.

**Shipper Alert!:** Cameron is getting really annoyed with Chase's ongoing courtship.

**Props Department:** Hector chews through House's cane, causing him to fall; he replaces it with a new "bitchin'" cane, decorated with flames.

**Casting Call:** Adina Porter (the boys' mother) appears as Lettie Mae Thornton in HBO's hit series *True Blood* (2008–present).

**House Canon:** Chase discusses patient deaths with Foreman, recalling the mistake he made a year earlier, which led indirectly to a patient death ("The Mistake," 2.08).

**Title Tale:** The episode is about keeping one family whole. Hector begins to become House's little family, before he has to give him back to Bonnie.


## 3.22 "Resignation"
**Writer:** Pamela Davis **Director:** Martha Mitchell
**Patient of the Week:** Addie (Lyndsy Fonseca)

House and the team treat Addie, a college student who is coughing blood. A series of infections leads House to believe that she suffers from complement H deficiency, a fatal genetic condition. But her indifferent reaction upon receiving this dire news leads him to reconsider.

Word gets out that Foreman has resigned and Chase wonders why, believing that both House and Foreman are "ashamed" of whatever it is. House seems uncharacteristically chatty and in a good mood. Turns out that Wilson has been slipping antidepressants into House's coffee. Wilson is uncharacteristically sleepy.

**Zebra of the Week:** Addie unsuccessfully tried to commit suicide using kitchen cleanser. Her body's incomplete healing from this trauma enabled bacteria to course through her bloodstream.

**Epiphany!:** House realizes Addie lacks any curiosity about her diagnosis.

**Iconic Moment in *House* History:** Wilson is on uppers. House deduces that Wilson has been taking antidepressants. He tests his theory by giving Wilson amphetamines, which cause the silliest and funniest behavior we've ever seen from the boy wonder oncologist.

**Clinic Duty:** House treats a pretty vegan's boyfriend. He's been cheating . . . with a hamburger. House later meets her for peppermint tea after work. Maybe Wilson has a point by putting House on antidepressants!

**A Fine Bromance:** House is intensely curious about why Wilson is constantly yawning. Is it a vasovagal heart issue — or is the yawning a side effect of antidepressants? House needs to know.

**House Is a Jerk:** House just keeps describing Addie's fatal illness although both she and her parents insist that he get out of the room.

**Housian Ethics:** House promises not to tell Addie's parents she's suicidal. But Addie's inability to understand her own motives resonates strongly with House, and he believes she may try it again. So he feels compelled to inform Addie's parents, despite her wishes and U.S. privacy laws. **Housian Ethics #2:** Should Wilson really be slipping antidepressants into House's coffee? On the other hand, House strikes back by putting speed in Wilson's. . . .

**Shipper Alert!:** Cuddy tries, unsuccessfully, to get Foreman to understand House as a much better person than he lets on. "There are worse things to turn into [than House]," she explains after House saves Addie's life.

**Gross-out Warning:** Addie's brain becomes exposed during an MRI. Ick!

**Casting Call:** Lyndsy Fonesca who plays Addie has had recurring roles on *Desperate Housewives* as Dylan and *How I Met Your Mother* as the daughter.

**Title Tale:** The episode deals with Foreman's resignation — and Addie's resignation with life.


### 3.23 "The Jerk"
**Writer:** Leonard Dick **Director:** Daniel Sackheim
**Patient of the Week:** Nate (Nick Lane)

House treats Nate, a 16-year-old chess prodigy who beats an opponent to a pulp after winning a match. In addition to unexplained rage attacks, Nate suffers severe headaches. The kid has been an obnoxious brat for years, and now with these symptoms, House wonders if there's a physical reason behind the bad attitude.

In the meantime, Foreman scores an interview for a new job, only to find someone has canceled it. He accuses House, but before we know the real answer, everyone in House's orbit comes under suspicion of undermining the interview. Chase ultimately realizes that in fact House is the saboteur.

**Zebra of the Week:** Hemochromotosis — a build-up of too much iron in the body. Unfortunately for Nate's mother, the disease is not responsible for his personality problems.

**Epiphany!:** House notices the way Nate holds the chess pieces while they play a game, observing his misshapen and contorted fingers.

**Iconic Moment in *House* History:** The ongoing chess match between House and young Nate.

**Clinic Duty:** House treats a man with extensive sunburn all over his torso, except for several unburned white circles. Much to the amusement of the patient's young son, House realizes the boy placed coins on his sunbathing father's tummy.

**House Is a Jerk:** Sabotaging Foreman's interview is a pretty underhanded thing for House to do — even if he did it to keep him around.

**Housian Ethics:** How ethical is it for House to sabotage Foreman's opportunity for success away from Princeton-Plainsboro Teaching Hospital?

**Gross-out Warning:** Nate pees on the floor in a rage, but the urine stream turns to blood. Ick!

**Did You Know?:** During the shooting of the episode, everyone became a chess fanatic, spurred especially by Omar Epps, who is a ranked player. On the season three *House* DVD set, Hugh Laurie recalls playing many games against his long-time friend and comedy partner Stephen Fry back in the day. Each chess move used during the episode was thought out and planned by an on-set chess master.

**Casting Call:** Nick Lane (Nate) appears in the 2010 horror film *The Gauntlet*.

**Title Tale:** Nate is a jerk, pure and simple. The title also refers to Princeton-Plainsboro's resident jerk, Dr. Gregory House.

### 3.24 "Human Error"

**Writers:** Thomas L. Moran, Lawrence Kaplow **Director:** Katie Jacobs

**Patient of the Week:** Marina (Mercedes Renard)

A Cuban couple, Esteban and Marina, risk their lives to travel in a small boat from Havana to New Jersey to see the famous Gregory House. He diagnoses Marina, trying to distinguish symptoms caused by the trip from those caused by her illness. When her heart stops, House places her on heart-lung bypass. But as the days pass with still no answer and no cure, Cuddy asks House to take Marina off bypass and allow her husband to say goodbye. As House prepares Esteban for Marina's death, he turns off the life-support machinery, but Marina doesn't die. She wakes as if by a miracle, throwing the atheist House for somewhat of a loop, as both Marina and Esteban thank God. House eventually discovers there is a completely mortal reason for Marina's condition.

Foreman says his goodbyes, and Wilson tries to convince House to say what he feels so Foreman doesn't quit. Wilson reminds him that Foreman is leaving because he doesn't want to be what *he thinks* House is. House not only lets Foreman go, but fires Chase and accepts Cameron's resignation to boot, leaving him completely without a team.

After this stunning turn, season three ends quietly as House shares cigars and whiskey with the patient's husband and then buys himself a new guitar. House seems to have made peace with everyone leaving. Perhaps he feels he was drawing too close to them anyway.

**Zebra of the Week:** An extra "ductus" (a flap in the heart) caused Marina's problem.

**Iconic Moment in *House* History:** Esteban, a mechanic by trade, asks House a pivotal question: How can you "fix her without seeing her?" It's an astute observation, and one that gets to the heart of an ongoing theme: can House properly diagnose his patients with minimal contact? **Iconic Moment #2:** In the chapel, Esteban weeps on House's shoulder, mourning the imminent death of his wife.

**A Fine Bromance:** Wilson is very protective of House, both defending him and worrying about his state of mind as everyone abandons his ship. He finally convinces House to ask Foreman to stay, but when he does, Foreman reiterates how much he disdains everything House stands for. House then reminds Wilson about the futility of words.

**House Is a Jerk:** He fires Chase for no apparent reason, although you may speculate it's simply because, unlike Foreman, he's quite ready to leave House's nest.

**Shipper Alert!:** Chase and Cameron finally get back together, starting a new story line that will lead them through the next two seasons. **Shipper Alert #2:** Late at night, Cuddy visits House in his office, telling him gently to take Marina off the bypass machine and let her die. "What if I find something on the autopsy I might have been able to fix?" he asks. He may be reflecting on Lupe ("House Training," 3.20) and her unnecessary death. Cuddy has a more romantic explanation: House can't bring himself to kill the couple's hopes. By early season four ("The Right Stuff," 4.02), there's evidence that Cuddy may be right. House does have a difficult time trampling on people's dreams.

**Musical Notes:** House gets a new guitar: a Gibson Jumbo Hummingbird acoustic. Hugh Laurie, as House, closes out the season enjoying the new instrument.

**World-Famous Doctor Moment:** The couple travel all the way from Cuba to see the famous Dr. House.

**Casting Call:** The actors playing Esteban and Marina are Cuban-Americans, cast to ensure accuracy in the distinctive Cuban accent.

***House* Canon:** According to Wilson, House hasn't moved in 15 years. Sharp-eyed viewers are aware, however, that House has had two or three residences since "Pilot." His first season apartment ("Socratic Method," 1.06) was clearly on an upper floor.

**Title Tale:** Is House making an error by letting his team go? Is Foreman making a mistake by leaving the nest before he's ready? Only time — and the next season — will tell.

> "I would guess that there's a certain element of wanting to save others because he can't save himself."
>
> **— Jennifer Morrison, March 2009 interview**

# SEASON 4

## A Shake-up at Princeton-Plainsboro Teaching Hospital

It takes courage for the producers of a hit (and critically acclaimed) television series to shake things up while the show is still in its prime. "If it ain't broke, don't fix it" is the conventional wisdom usually bandied about when discussing major changes to a show, its cast, or characters. So, when David Shore and company decided to rework *House, M.D.* for its fourth season, fans (and critics) held their collective breath to see what would transpire.

Season four is an anomaly, but as House often says, anomalies can be good things. Shortened from the ordered 24 episodes down to 16 when a three month Writers Guild of America (WGA) strike began in November 2007, the season was dominated by the first story arc of the season: House's *Surivor*-style audition to hire a new staff.

Had the season been its planned length, the hiring story arc would have only taken up a third of the season. While some welcomed the changes, many fans were angry about replacing House's original fellows with new faces. They were justifiably concerned that Chase, Cameron, and Foreman would be placed so far out on the sidelines they would become invisible.

Although Foreman makes his way back onto House's team, Chase and Cameron are, indeed, put on the bench for much of season four — and most of season five. Now out of the Diagnostics Department, Cameron runs the emergency room and Chase is on the surgical staff. Although Chase's new gig seems plausible — a critical care specialist might easily have had surgical training — Cameron's new job seems a bit out of left field, unless her main function in the ER is administrative. She's had a lot of administrative experience keeping House's house in order, so perhaps it's not that far a stretch.

During much of early season four, the episodes sometimes seemed rushed, with the focus on the fellowship audition. With so many new characters, staple elements of the series — including the clinic — were sacrificed far too often. Most episodes also lacked the important quiet reflective moments: House alone pondering a problem; at his piano, playing some melancholy tune; or deep in conversation with a patient. Those moments keep House sympathetic, even when he's at his most unlikable. And for many episodes, he was not.

> "We have to service the story — the medical mystery. The people circling House and circling the medical mystery are going to get screen time. We're bending our brains in knots trying to figure out how to get the other people into each episode. We're still struggling. And it's something on our minds."
>
> **— Executive producer/writer Russel Friend on the larger cast in season four,**
> **May 2008 interview**

Because of the strike, what would have been transitional episodes dominated the season, taking up half the episode run. But viewed as a whole, and in retrospect, without the long, strike-related gaps between episodes, the season did a nice job exploring themes of illusion, perception, and reality.

House's first-episode delusion that he could be effective without talented doctors challenging every theory was put to rest by the end the premiere "Alone" (4.01). From an older man's dream that he could become a doctor without actually going to medical school ("The Right Stuff," 4.02) to a young woman's belief that her dead mother was still with her ("Guardian Angels," 4.04) to House's near-death experience in "Wilson's Heart" (4.16), the season explored the interface between fantasies, dreams, and the harsh truth of reality.

Episode titles with an asterisk are *House* classics.


## 4.01 "Alone"

**Writers:** Peter Blake, David Shore **Director:** Deran Sarafian
**Patient of the Week:** Liz (Liliya Toneva)

House tries to diagnose this week's patient on his own, trying to prove he doesn't need a team. Cuddy and Wilson disagree, and Wilson kidnaps House's new guitar to force him to hire a new group of fellows. House enlists the janitor and others to fill the roles of the now departed Chase, Cameron, and Foreman.

Crushed beyond recognition after a building implodes, the patient exhibits symptom after symptom, each of which point to a lifestyle that is as unrecognizable to her family as her face is. After House digs into her background, the patient seems nothing like the loving, sweet young woman her fiancé and mother have known. As House treats each condition, "curing her," she develops a new symptom. House realizes late in the diagnosis that they have been using the wrong person's medical history. Might House have solved the case quicker with a team of inquisitive fellows challenging his every thought?

**Zebra of the Week:** A tragic case of mistaken identity.

**Epiphany!:** House discovers that his injured patient is an alcoholic, depressed, and has had a recent abortion. None of this jibes with what either the patient's mother or fiancé knows of her. When the patient proves allergic to a drug with which she had been recently treated with no problem, House realizes the patient is literally not who they thought she was.

**Iconic Moment in *House* History:** House finally agrees to hire new fellows, and he goes about it as only he can. Assembling a group of 40 candidates in a lecture hall, he will pare the group down to three in an eight-week take-no-prisoners competition. As he says, "Wear a cup."

**Manipulative Wilson:** Wilson kidnaps House's brand new $12,000 Flying V guitar and won't give it back until he agrees to hire new fellows.

**A Fine Bromance:** The guitar kidnapping side-plot is one of the funniest in the series' history. Wilson first sends House threatening notes made of newspaper lettering, and finally a broken piece from the guitar with a dire warning. Wilson warns House what will happen if he continues to avoid hiring fellows. "You ever tighten a guitar string really, really slowly?" he asks diabolically.

**House Is a Jerk:** Rather than admit he needs a team, House tries wrangling ideas from random hospital employees.

**Metaphorically Speaking:** House uses janitorial jargon to explain the medicine to his newest recruit: the hospital janitor.

**Musical Notes:** House plays Eddie Van Halen riffs on the Flying V while doing his best to avoid patients.

**Casting Call:** Kay Lenz (the distraught mother) received two Best Supporting Actress Emmy nominations for her role in the NBC series *Reasonable Doubts* (1991–1993).

**Title Tale:** House is "alone" and wants to stay that way. The patient is also alone, unable to communicate who she really is.


## * 4.02 "The Right Stuff"

**Writers:** Doris Egan, Leonard Dick **Director:** Deran Sarafian
**Patient of the Week:** Greta (Essence Atkins)

House tries to diagnose Greta, a young Air Force captain and astronaut candidate who "hears with her eyes." Trying to keep her secret from NASA, she approaches House hoping he will treat her "off the books." As he diagnoses Greta, House begins to weed through his fellowship candidates. Meanwhile, he believes he's seeing Cameron, Chase, and Foreman at the hospital, although they've supposedly been gone for months.

**Zebra of the Week:** Von Hippel-Lindau disease, a rare genetic condition that causes cysts and tumors. In this case a pheochromacytoma (an adrenaline producing tumor) causes Greta's neurologic symptoms.

**Epiphany!:** No House epiphany this week. Chase appears for real in the operating room gallery while House and the candidates perform a procedure on Greta, and he suggests the diagnosis.

**Iconic Moment in *House* History:** Fellowship candidate Lawrence Kutner nearly fries Greta, setting her on fire while trying to restart her heart in an oxygen-rich hyperbaric chamber.

**Manipulative Wilson:** As House "sees" his former fellows around the hospital, he begins to wonder if he's losing his mind. Wilson suggests they are visions brought on by House's feelings of grief and guilt. But it's all a mind game to get House to admit he feels bad about the loss of his old team.

**House Is a Jerk:** House summarily fires a whole row of candidate wannabes before they even begin, then commands another group to wash his car. He also berates one candidate for his Mormon beliefs.

**Housian Ethics:** Should House treat Greta off the books, even if it's to protect her? **Housian Ethics #2:** Hoping for a position on House's team, a brilliant older fellowship candidate poses as a doctor, appealing to House's willingness to cross ethical lines. But this is a step over House's ethical boundary. Letting the man down gently, House keeps him on for now, offering only a chance at to be (at most) an assistant.

**Shipper Alert!:** Cameron sees House as more idealistic than he sees himself. She sends Greta to him, knowing he will be willing to keep her secret, and unable to "kill her dream." **Shipper Alert #2:** Cameron and Chase are still together, though Wilson leads House to believe they've gotten married and are living in Arizona.

**Pop Culture References:** The fellowship competition begins with a differential diagnosis on Buddy Ebsen (*The Beverly Hillbillies*), who was the originally cast Tin Man in *The Wizard of Oz*. House makes a reference to Kitty Carlisle, a regular on the long-lived panel game show *To Tell the Truth*.

**House Doing "Doctor Stuff":** House uses his very sensitive musician's ear to detect subtle masses in Greta's chest using only a stethoscope. It's a procedure called auscultatory percussion.

**Casting Call:** "Harold" of the *Harold & Kumar* movie series guest starred in "Love Hurts" (1.20); "Kumar" (Kal Penn) now joins the cast as a fellowship candidate. Essence Atkins (Greta) was featured in the 2009 movie *Dance Flick*.

**Title Tale:** The episode title is taken from Tom Wolfe's novel *The Right Stuff* (or the subsequent movie) about the early days of NASA's astronaut program. And as House's fellowship audition begins, the question is: who has the right stuff to be on House's elite team?

**Why It's a Classic:** The opening salvo of House's survivor fellowship game is effectively balanced by watching him do what he does best — practice insightful medicine. We also get a significant glimpse into what Cameron sees in House: a closeted romantic who cannot kill others' dreams.

> "[Cameron is] safe sending this woman to him because first he's going to like the challenge of everything being a secret, but she also knows that at the end of the day, he's not going to be able take this woman's dream away from her."
>
> — **Jennifer Morrison on "The Right Stuff," April 2009 interview**

## 4.03 "97 Seconds"

**Writers:** Russel Friend, Garrett Lerner **Director:** David Platt
**Patient of the Week:** Stark (Brian Klugman)

House treats Stark, a man with spinal muscular atrophy (SMA) while continuing to audition fellowship candidates. He splits the candidates into two teams, pitting the men against the women. Their intense competition and ambition get in the way of an easy diagnosis, indirectly leading to the patient's death.

Meanwhile, a patient pulls a knife while House prepares to examine him in the clinic. Instead of attacking House, he inserts the knife into a live electrical outlet, stopping his heart. House wonders why anyone would do that. The patient, who has recently been involved in a terrible car accident, explains that he had experienced the best moment of his life while "dead" before the paramedics resuscitated him. House's curiosity gets the best of him, and he tries to replicate the patient's experience to prove there *is* nothing after death.

Across town, Foreman finally has his own Diagnostics Department, where he plans to be a "nicer" version of House. But House's influence is powerful. Foreman defies protocol and his boss to save a patient's life — and he is fired.

**Zebra of the Week:** Strongyloides (threadworms), a parasite contracted while Stark was vacationing in the Far East. Candidate "13" has the correct diagnosis, but she fails to notice whether Stark actually takes the ivermectin pills needed to treat the worms. When House finally realizes the error, it's too late.

**Epiphany!:** House eventually realizes Stark's dog may have eaten the pills.

**Iconic Moment in *House* History:** House sticks a knife in an outlet, nearly dying to prove to the clinic patient that there is no afterlife. But Wilson wonders why House is so willing to carelessly risk his life.

**A Fine Bromance:** Wilson worries about House's state of mind after his stunt with the knife. He sits at his bedside waiting for him to wake, and lectures him about his seeming ambivalence towards living.

**House Is a Jerk:** House tries to shatter Stark's belief in a better world to come when he coldly avers that there is no "better place" to which he'll go after death.

**Housian Ethics:** What is House thinking by pitting all those young, reckless, competitive doctors against each other, believing he could control them? It causes the patient's death and House is partially culpable.

**Gross-out Warning:** Amber and her team use xenodiagnosis on Stark, releasing a bottle of tiny bugs onto his arm to bite and poop. This will help the team identify any bloodborne parasites. Ick.

**Did You Know?:** One of the episode's writers, Garrett Lerner, has a young son with SMA. The episode brought some much needed attention to the rare disease.

**Pop Culture References:** House refers to magician David Blaine.

**Casting Call:** Brian Klugman (Stark) wrote the screenplay for the 2010 movie *Tron Legacy*, which stars . . . Olivia Wilde!

**Title Tale:** The clinic patient was "dead for 97 seconds," a transitory state between life and death. There are other transitory states in House's world. House is in transition between his old fellows and a new team. Foreman tries to transition into a new life away from him.


## 4.04 "Guardian Angels"

**Writer:** David Hoselton **Director:** Deran Sarafian
**Patient of the Week:** Irene (Azura Skye)


Irene is a funeral home cosmetician who sees — and talks to — dead people. She also has seizures and a failing liver. Irene's treatment is complicated by the delusion that her mother (by her side the entire episode offering warm milk) is still alive.

House continues his fellowship audition. Candidate Henry, whom House has dubbed "Ridiculous Old Fraud" because he is not really a doctor, serves as

House's surrogate. He thinks eerily like House, but in the end poor old Henry gets the axe. What does House need with someone on his team who thinks just like him?

Fired from Mercy in "97 Seconds" (4.03), Foreman tries to get a job at another hospital, but finds he's been blackballed for being too much like House. Cuddy offers him his old job — with a twist. He is to be her eyes and ears on House's team.

**Zebra of the Week:** Ergot poisoning from moldy rye bread.

**House Is a Jerk:** House is particularly obnoxious to Jeffrey Cole, an African-American candidate who is also a Mormon. He insults Joseph Smith, the founder of the Mormon Church, which provokes the usually quiet, gentle Cole to take a slug at his boss. Surprisingly, Cole's act doesn't get him fired.

**Pop Culture References:** "Guardian Angels" riffs on the 1970s television series *Charlie's Angels* with House as Charlie and Henry as Bosley.

**Casting Call:** Azura Skye had a recurring role on *CSI: Miami* from 2003 to 2005.

**Title Tale:** The patient's mother, ever hovering at her daughter's side, encouraging her to drink "warm milk" is an obvious angel. Cameron serves as Cole's guardian angel, goading him into slugging House to earn his respect. Cuddy, too, is a guardian angel, rescuing Foreman and giving him a role as "House-Lite."

## 4.05 "Mirror Mirror"

**Writer:** David Foster **Director:** David Platt
**Patient of the Week:** Robert Elliot (Frank Whaley)

Mugged on a dark street before collapsing, this week's patient has no identification, neither memory nor sense of himself. He copes by mimicking — or "mirroring" — the people around him to fill in the memories he doesn't possess.

His condition enables him to identify most strongly with the dominant personality in a group. He almost seems to be able to read minds, which intrigues (and unnerves) the team. Each fellowship candidate, as well as Foreman, House, and Wilson learn something about themselves through their encounters with Robert.

As the candidate audition continues, House and Chase conspire to rig a bet on who will next get the axe. As the whole hospital watches in anticipation, House decides to fire no one, causing the house . . . er, House win — meaning Chase and House split the substantial take.

**Zebra of the Week:** Giovannini's mirror syndrome. It is triggered by the bacterial infection *Eperythrozoon* contracted from pig dung. Robert is a farm implement salesman.

**Epiphany!:** Kutner reveals that the patient had an original, not mirrored, thought while submerged in water. "We need to splash him again," House says, and he visits the patient to confirm.

**Iconic Moment in *House* History:** With only a couple of the patient's personal items and dressed in his clothing, House has a notable one-on-one encounter with him. Leaving his cane behind, he tries to be Robert's own reflection in the mirror. Using his skill as an acute observer, House gently coaxes the patient into recognizing himself.

**Clinic Duty:** To retaliate for Cuddy undermining his authority by hiring Foreman back on his team, House incites everyone in the clinic without health insurance to demand their rights. "Michael Moore was right!" he yells, referring to the maverick documentary maker.

**A Fine Bromance:** Wilson gloats when Robert identifies him as dominant in the House-Wilson relationship.

**Shipper Alert!:** Cuddy and House enter the patient's room to gain insight into their own dynamic. Who is the dominant? Cuddy believes it's ambiguous. But House is certain it's him.

**Casting Call:** Frank Whaley (Robert Elliot) has made several films with Oliver Stone, beginning with *Born on the Fourth of July* (1989); he also had a small but memorable role as Brett in Quentin Tarantino's *Pulp Fiction* (1994).

**Title Tale:** There are many mirrors in "Mirror Mirror." Robert has "mirror syndrome," reflecting the fellows and their personalities back at them; House is a mirror for Robert — allowing him finally to see himself. There are also several inverted mirrors: Foreman is oddly happy to be back on the team; House is smiling and dancing; and Chase and House form a (gambling) confederation.


## 4.06 "Whatever It Takes"

**Writers:** Thomas L. Moran, Peter Blake **Director:** Juan J. Campanella
**Patient of the Week:** Casey (Amy Dudgeon)

House is secretly (of course) recruited by CIA physician Samira Terzi to diagnose an agent's mysterious illness, leaving Foreman in charge of the fellowship candidates as they attempt to diagnose a race car driver who collapses after a race. Foreman thinks the cause is dehydration, but fellow candidate Brennan comes up with a wild theory that Casey has polio — something virtually non-existent in the U.S. He wants to cure her with massive doses of vitamin C. And it works.

Of course it does: Brennan poisoned Casey to make it appear that she has polio. Needless to say, this week Brennan gets the axe.

Over at the CIA, House pits his brilliance against a doctor from the Mayo Clinic to tend to the dying CIA agent. Has he been poisoned, as Terzi believes? The CIA handcuffs the doctors by sharing only minimal (and inaccurate) information about the spy: he has been stationed in Bolivia and eats a lot of "chestnuts."

An episode with a lot of promise, it suffers for its portrayal of House. House should never be stupid. Unfortunately, House is not only stupid here, he's buffoonish. Well-deserved reputation aside, House simply looks ridiculous next to the Mayo Clinic doctor for much of the episode.

**Zebra of the Week:** Selenium poisoning from overconsumption of Brazil nuts; the race car driver is not sick, she's just a victim of Brennan's manipulation.

**Epiphany!:** Speaking with the spy House realizes that he couldn't have been in Bolivia, but was actually stationed in Brazil. Knowing that Brazilians call Brazil nuts "chestnuts," House concludes that the spy has selenium poisoning from overconsumption of the nuts.

**Iconic Moment in *House* History:** To his disbelief, House is flown to the CIA in his own black helicopter.

**A Fine Bromance:** House gleefully calls Wilson from the CIA. At first impressed, Wilson quickly becomes unnerved at the prospect of the agency doing a background check on House — and maybe his friends.

**House Is a Jerk:** Whatever filters House may nominally possess are absent through most of the episode as he makes lewd comments to his CIA contact and insults the physician from the Mayo clinic.

**Housian Ethics:** Brennan believes House will condone his polio experiment, but it is a step too far, even for House.

**Shipper Alert!:** House offers Dr. Terzi, the CIA doctor, a position on his staff. At the end of the episode, she takes him up on his offer and House is at a complete loss that she actually did it.

**Pop Culture References:** The CIA doctor tells House that the X-Files Department is located in the basement.

**Lost in Translation:** House is familiar with the Brazilian name for Brazil nuts, *castenas dupara* (chestnuts from Para), and knows the subtle differences between the Carnivale seasons in Bolivia and Brazil.

**World-Famous Doctor Moment:** House is brought in by the CIA to treat an agent because of his reputation.

**Casting Call:** Amy Dudgeon played an assistant DA in *Street Kings*, which also starred Hugh Laurie. Michael Michele (Dr. Samira Terzi — the CIA doctor) played Dr. Cleo Finch from 1999–2002 on NBC's long-running medical series *ER*.

**Title Tale:** "Whatever It Takes" is a perfect title for this episode. House's reputation is based on his genius for putting together the puzzle, and doing "whatever it takes" to save the life of a patient. He will bend, even break, rules; ignore established medical ethical standards; lie and steal. But only as it will benefit the patient, which fired fellow-candidate Brennan doesn't realize. He misunderstands that House advocates "whatever it takes" regardless of illegality or ethics even when not in the service of the patient, but for some other goal — noble or not. Of course the CIA does "whatever it takes" to get its job done, too.

## * 4.07 "Ugly"

**Writer:** Sean Whitesell **Director:** David Straiton
**Patient of the Week:** Kenny (Khelo Thomas)

Teenager Kenny has been brought to Princeton-Plainsboro for surgery to repair a severe facial deformity. His surgery is funded by a group of filmmakers, who will record Kenny through the process for a forthcoming documentary. But the teen suffers a heart attack as the surgery is about to begin, putting the complex procedure on hold until they can diagnose the cause.

Enter House and company to figure out why. But House doesn't want the film crew following his team through *their* process believing that the cameras will inhibit the free flow of debate and prompt the team to perform for the camera rather than do their best for Kenny.

Adding to the mix, Dr. Terzi from last week's episode has now become part of the fellowship pool, much to the chagrin of the candidates, who have no desire for the additional competition. House is smitten with her and eventually realizes his judgment is affected when he become overly solicitous about her ideas on the case.

Fellowship candidate Taub, a former plastic surgeon, is at particular odds with House during the case as he advocates pushing ahead with Kenny's plastic surgery before House thinks he's ready.

The episode uses an interesting storytelling technique by viewing part of the action through the black and white lens of the filmmakers' camera.

**Zebra of the Week:** Lyme disease, masked by Kenny's deformity.
**Epiphany!:** Fellowship candidate "13" notes a change on the imaging scan as Chase is about to start the facial surgery, revealing a skin discoloration not

present earlier. It points to Lyme disease, which had already been ruled out.

**Iconic Moment in *House* History:** House and Cuddy view the finished version of the documentary, which paints House as a cheerful, caring, Patch Adams–type doctor. He is mortified that the filmmakers have so completely misrepresented him.

**A Fine Bromance:** Wilson is highly amused at House's crush on the nubile Dr. Terzi. Also, when the filmmakers interview Wilson about House on camera, he refers to him — straight-faced — as a Wiccan.

**House Is a Jerk:** Taub undermines House's credibility with the patient. Seeking dirt on the irritating fellowship candidate, House inquires with Taub's former plastic surgery practice partners. Gloating, he publicly confronts Taub about cheating on his wife.

**Shipper Alert!:** Cuddy is pleased and happy after watching the finished and edited documentary, smiling as she sees Kenny thank House for saving his life. **Shipper Alert #2:** In an unguarded moment, Cameron tells the film crew she "loves Dr. House." Flustered, she tries to awkwardly explain what she "really" means, but isn't very convincing as she digs herself in deeper. **Shipper Alert #3:** Chase, who has the patience of a saint, listens to Cameron trying to practice her "explanation" in the mirror.

**Classic Rant:** Lecturing Kenny about wanting to be "normal," House argues that plastic surgery will only make him physically different. It won't repair the internal scars caused by years of isolation and being "different."

**Pop Culture References:** On camera House disingenuously says the film *Patch Adams* inspired him to become a doctor. The sarcasm is lost in the final cut, which leads to House's assertion that he can no longer trust documentarians, including iconoclastic documentary filmmaker Michael Moore.

**Casting Call:** Khelo Thomas (Kenny) was featured in the Disney feature *Holes* (2003), playing Hector.

**Title Tale:** The camera detects the details we never see: every flaw, every mole, and every bit of ugliness. We may not like what like what we see, but no amount of plastic surgery can change whom we are inside. Those scars cannot be erased by the artful use of a scalpel.

**Why It's a Classic:** The combination of unusual filming techniques and a good story nicely interweaving the patient plot and the other threads make this a must-see — as is watching House act like an adolescent boy in front of his new fellowship candidate.

## Learning to Be a Doctor from a Doctor Like House

In "Ugly" (4.07), Cameron describes herself as a "doctor who learned how to be a doctor from House." Cameron's words are a fabulous definition of what House does as a teacher and mentor. It's not easy training under House. It's rigorous, he's harsh, and his doctors seldom get a pat on the head or slap on the back. But they do learn — and from a gifted master physician. But at times, you can't help wondering if his fellows appreciate what they're learning.

House employs the Socratic method of teaching, which he says is the "best way to teach anybody about anything except juggling chain saws" ("The Socratic Method," 1.06). He challenges and asks questions, fostering debate, and encouraging argument all in the name of solving the medical case. His fellows usually don't realize they're being taught so much as mocked.

"Autopsy" (2.02) provides a great example of House's teaching method with his fellows. Trying to locate a heart abnormality in a young cancer patient, House records her heart sounds. Playing the sounds on his iPod for the fellows, they listen for something that sounds wrong. Replaying the three types of rhythms (aorta, mitral valve, and bicuspid), at first they hear nothing untoward. But House presses them, insisting that if they'd only listen properly, the abnormality will be obvious. They continue listening until Cameron finally hears it. He never tells them the answer, but makes them reason (or in this case, hear) their own way through the problem. None of them will ever listen to heart sounds quite the same way again.

Of course House mocks them, encouraging them to be competitive with each other and be persistent researchers, never giving up until the answer is reached. He refuses to compliment, cajole, or mentor them in any conventional manner, prompting Wilson to ask House if he wouldn't be better off being kinder. House replies that being kinder and gentler may make them feel better about themselves, but won't make them better doctors.

House is usually way ahead of his team, and, if the situation isn't urgent, he will leave them to sort out the diagnosis and catch up. As he says to Chase in "Autopsy" when they've finally caught up, "Welcome to the end of the thought process."

What does it really mean: to be a doctor who learned to be a doctor from House? House trains his fellows to be independent thinkers who trust their own judgment and are willing to defend and stand up for what they believe is correct and right. He doesn't want them to feel intimidated by any threat coming from him or anyone else. If they believe they are right, they should act on it and not defer to him. In "Damned If You Do" (1.05), House reprimands Cameron for not trusting her own judgment. "Your unwillingness to stick by your diagnosis almost killed this woman," he criticizes.

If House's fellows believe he is wrong or out of line, he respects them more if they challenge him — or even go over his head — rather than give him their blind allegiance. When one of his team goes behind his back to stop him from performing a too-risky procedure, House may get annoyed, but seldom punishes.

In "Skin Deep" (2.14), Cameron goes to Cuddy when she thinks House should have called social services on the teenage patient's father for suspected sexual abuse. Cameron fears House's reaction, but although angry, he understands that they all have to do what they believe is the "right thing." He may not be happy, but House respects her nerve in going against him. In "Frozen" (4.11), after House finally hires his new team of fellows, he creates an elaborate game to show them that they must stand up to him and challenge what he does if they think it's unreasonable.

House also teaches the fellows to always "do the right thing, consequences be damned," as Wilson nicely puts it in season six ("Known Unknowns," 6.07). It's an important lesson, but one that carries some risk, because sometimes doing the "right" thing conflicts with medical guidelines, standards, and ethics, and even the law. It presents a tricky terrain for any physician willing to venture on that path.

House's doctors have to be creative and think outside the box. House is a "lateral thinker," which means he casts aside assumptions and tries to look at a problem with a fresh perspective each time, through oblique angles, but informed by his vast medical and historical memory.

When one of the team members out-diagnoses him, he appears to appreciate it, rather than feel threatened, and although there are no pats on the head or "attaboys," when House responds to an educated guess with "Niiice . . ." it is a gesture of deep admiration. Most of the time, House's fellows don't recognize that they're being taught; often viewers don't either.

Is House a good teacher? Under House's tutelage, Chase learns to be nearly as creative a thinker as House, as he looks at the facts and tests, trying to find the oblique angles that lie beyond "the box." Cameron has learned House's methods so well that she feels that they are in her head, making it impossible for her to supervise him when she's temporarily put in charge of the hospital in "Big Baby" (5.13). She understands why House makes seemingly insane requests, and she can't say no to him.

All of his fellows learn to think outside the box, color outside the lines, and look for subtle clues that would never be found in a patient medical history or lab test. Even Foreman, as much as he detests his methods, understands the value of what House has taught them all.

In "97 Seconds" (4.03), in a new job away from House and Princeton-Plainsboro, Foreman can't help but hear House's voice in his head when he realizes his patient will die if he follows guidelines and protocols. Foreman has learned the value of doing the right thing, despite the consequences. But when he tries it outside House's (and Princeton-Plainsboro's) protection, it doesn't work out very well. Although Foreman cures his patient, he is fired by his new dean, and blackballed for being too influenced by his mentor.

Of the new fellows, Kutner is a great House disciple, curious and unconventional in his approach to medicine. But when he comes to House with a new patient in "You Don't Want to Know" (4.08), he is still a candidate for a fellowship position and does not know if he will be selected for House's new team.

House believes the patient, a magician, is a fake, but Kutner persists. Allowing him to perform tests, House informs Kutner that there are potentially game-ending consequences for the young doctor if he's wrong. If the magician isn't really sick, House warns, Kutner will be out of the running for a fellowship. Kutner takes the threat seriously and reconsiders briefly before House berates him for putting his own interests above the patient's.

Taub is a more paint-by-the-numbers doctor, and eventually House challenges him to begin thinking more creatively or risk losing his job ("Here Kitty," 5.19).

Although House's primary teaching activity is to train fellows, we experience his lecture-hall style as well in the first season episode "Three Stories" (1.22), and at the beginning of season four during the fellowship audition. House's classroom lecturing style provides an interesting view into his teaching method beyond what we observe within the realm of his whiteboard. In both situations, he drives his students to cast aside conventional wisdom and assumptions; criticizing the students who offer up "usual suspect" diagnoses, calling them useless and clueless. It's something he takes personally as conventional wisdom cost him the full use of his right leg and left him in pain.

In the lecture hall, he shows students how to make medical decisions under pressure, something that he and his team do every day. He badgers them into thinking on their feet. "It's hard to think under these conditions," says a frazzled student in "Three Stories." House responds with a reality check. "You think it's going to be easier when you've got a real patient really dying?" When they're really practicing medicine with real, dying patients, they will, indeed, be reacting under similar fast-paced conditions.

## 4.08 "You Don't Want to Know"

**Writer:** Sara Hess **Director:** Lesli Linka Glatter

**Patient of the Week:** Flynn (Steve Valentine)

Fellowship candidates Kutner and Cole attend Flynn's magic show. The magician recreates Harry Houdini's stunt, trying to escape — handcuffed and submerged upside down — in an enclosed water tank. Flynn suffers a heart attack during the stunt and Kutner and Cole bring him to Princeton-Plainsboro for treatment. House believes that Flynn is simply a second-rate magician whose trick went bad; the heart attack was faked. But, as Flynn's symptoms worsen, House is eventually convinced.

The team believes Flynn may have gotten tainted blood at the hospital and House agrees to test it on himself, certain that they're wrong. But when he suffers a reaction, House insists his fever and chills have nothing to with medical mystery at hand. Not buying it, the team dopes him and uses the opportunity to grab biopsy samples to test House's organs.

The five remaining fellow wannabes now have a new challenge: steal Cuddy's thong underwear. Cole undermines the challenge by conspiring with her for their mutual benefit, and gets him the axe. But is it fair that House fires him for successfully winning the challenge albeit not in the manner House envisioned?

**Zebra of the Week:** After more than three seasons, it's finally lupus!

**Epiphany!:** As Wilson and House discuss blood types and transfusion, House suddenly realizes that Flynn may have gotten the wrong type of blood when he was transfused while being treated. A transfusion reaction and lupus explain the symptoms.

**A Fine Bromance:** When House offers to test the potentially tainted blood on himself, Wilson worries that House has once again risked his life, not caring whether he lives or dies. When he learns that House is blood type O-negative,

Wilson remarks that being a "universal recipient" is perfectly in keeping with House's perpetual self-centeredness. He takes from everybody.

**House Is a Jerk:** It's amazing that House can make the thong challenge without being slapped — or being slapped with a sexual harassment lawsuit. **House Is a Jerk #2:** House is also intensely curious about whether fellowship candidate "13" has Parkinson's, and he switches her usual decaffeinated coffee for the high octane stuff to observe her reaction when she becomes jittery from it. It's not Parkinson's disease; her mother died of the genetic disease Huntington's chorea.

**Housian Ethics:** Spiking House's tea with narcotics is not very ethical — nor wise, considering that House already takes opioids for pain.

**Shipper Alert!:** Wilson tells House that in some countries the thong challenge would be "considered courtship."

**Casting Call:** Steve Valentine (Flynn) was a regular on NBC's *Crossing Jordan*, playing Dr. Nigel Townsend and writing one episode during the series' 2001–2007 run.

**Title Tale:** The magician believes that knowing how a trick is done ruins the magic; House believes the opposite, he thinks it's much "cooler to know." Candidate "13" doesn't want to know whether she carries the genetic marker for Huntington's. Not knowing frees her to take risks (like working for House). House, who *has* to know everything, tests her himself. But when she still doesn't want to know the answer, he discards the results envelope without opening it.


## 4.09 "Games"

**Writer:** Eli Attie **Director:** Deran Sarafian
**Patient of the Week:** Jimmy Quidd (Jeremy Renner)

House begins his final fellowship selection round by diagnosing and treating Jimmy Quidd, a 38-year-old, punk-rocking heroin addict. Quidd has a whole host of symptoms that may — or may not — be attributable to his drug addiction. Throughout the diagnostic process, House observes the way in which each of the remaining four fellow candidates diagnose and relate to Quidd. He judges their characters and analytical skills one final time to assess how they would fit into his unique department. He wants to keep them all, but clearly cannot.

The key to the patient lies in his past. Somewhere along the line, Jimmy Quidd, folk singer — a young man who loves children, who, as House says "has a heart, perhaps a soul" — changed. And discovering the real Jimmy Quidd beneath his punk persona and drugs leads House to the answer.

**Zebra of the Week:** Measles, which Quidd's drug-abused immune system could not handle, and he acquired via his interactions with children.

**Epiphany!:** House connects Quidd's work with abandoned children — which may have exposed him to measles — with his drug use. He puts it all together using the incorrect diagnoses and assumptions of his fellowship candidates.

**Iconic Moment in *House* History:** House has his new team: Lawrence Kutner, Chris Taub, and "13" (also known as Remy Hadley).

**A Fine Bromance:** Wilson learns that a patient he had diagnosed as terminal is actually cancer free. But the patient is oddly unhappy with the news. It seems that his "terminal" condition gave license to live as if tomorrow was his last day on earth. He sold his house and planned to travel. And, now, thanks to Wilson's good news, he's out some money for a sold house he still needs. Feeling guilty, Wilson wants to compensate him. But House urges the man to sue instead of taking Wilson's token ($5,000) offering, knowing he can't win. In his own way, House is trying to protect Wilson and to teach him that he cannot be responsible for other people's happiness.

**House Is a Jerk:** He fires "13" and Kutner mid-episode simply to stir competition among the team.

**Judgmental Fellow Alert:** Foreman and fellowship candidate Amber believe Jimmy Quidd's symptoms are exclusively due to drug use. They're only partially right.

**Housian Ethics:** Amber plays the "game" a little too well but doesn't know when to end it. Insisting that being right trumps everything, she doesn't quite fit House's team, where learning to be wrong is just as important as saving lives. She is regrettably fired by episode's end.

**Musical Notes:** House plays a blues riff on the piano in the lecture hall — an improvisation by Hugh Laurie. Laurie also wrote and recorded the "folky" guitar melody attributed to Jimmy Quidd, which House plays as background during the final team selection scene.

**Casting Call:** Jeremy Renner (Jimmy Quidd) starred in the critically acclaimed 2009 film *The Hurt Locker*, earning him an Academy Award nomination for Best Actor in a Drama.

**Title Tale:** This is the conclusion of the arguably overlong hiring game. The title also refers to the power game between Cuddy and House. Through expert gamesmanship, House gets what he wanted all along — to hire three new fellows. Cuddy expresses relief that the "games are finally over," to which House retorts suggestively, "How long have you known me?"

In a very bold move (and in the fan community, a very controversial one) at the end of season three, David Shore scuttled House's original team of fellows, all of whom had come to the end of their three-year fellowship gigs with House. Insisting throughout the season four premiere that he can get along just fine without a new team, House realizes he can't. Not really, and not without losing some of the edge that helps form his brilliance. As he says to the lecture hall full of fellowship wannabes at the end of "Alone": "Wear a cup."

And so House embarks on hiring a new staff. As with the old one, House needs people with highly specialized talents — not the least of which is putting up with House's antics, however reluctantly.

Chiding House that he will ultimately hire only people he can't stand, Wilson believes that House wants to protect himself from getting too close to his fellows. Of course, House would vigorously beg to differ with that sentimental assessment, and suggest instead that he wants fellows who would make "interesting" playthings to study and manipulate for his personal amusement ("Ugly," 4.07).

After a far-too-long tryout of eight episodes, House has his new team assembled: two guys and a girl. Sound familiar? He selects: Chris Taub, a plastic surgeon; Lawrence Kutner, a specialist in sports medicine; and Remy Hadley ("13"), an internist. Their specialties are less important than those of the original team and seldom come up or are called upon — although, as a plastic surgeon, Taub's skills do get called into action occasionally. As with the original team, House sees beyond their medical training to find their real value to him. But who are the ones who got away?

**"Ridiculous Old Fraud" Henry** (fired in "Guardian Angels," 4.04): We learn in "The Right Stuff" (4.02) that Henry isn't really a doctor. An admissions counselor at Columbia University Medical School for years, Henry has audited practically every class offered by the prestigious medical school. He applies for a fellowship with House because of House's reputation for bending the rules, and wrongly believes that House won't really care if he has an actual medical degree. But even House won't allow someone to practice medicine on his staff without a license. House appreciates Henry's encyclopedic book (if not practical) knowledge. But ultimately, House has to draw a professional line; he can't really hire him as a medical fellow. And although House could theoretically hire him as a research assistant, Henry's way of processing information is too like House's. Like Henry himself says, House "doesn't need someone around who thinks exactly like him."

**"Grumpy" Dr. Brennan** (fired in "Whatever It Takes," 4.06): Brennan mistakenly believes that House will approve of his enterprising attitude when he exploits a sick patient as a pretext to advance his own research ambitions. "Isn't that why you hired us? To do whatever it takes?" he asks House in the end, completely misunderstanding one of House's most important ethical principles. House has been known to do anything, say anything, and even risk his career (and his life) to test a new theory, but with few exceptions, he does it to serve the patient — and not personal need. House neither wants nor needs some self-serving, glory-seeking (albeit very creative) doctor on his staff, and Dr. Grumpy is quickly disappeared — and reported to the authorities!

**Jeffrey "Big Love" Cole** (fired after conspiring with Cuddy to win in "You Don't Want to Know," 4.08): In "Guardian Angels," Jeffrey Cole strikes House after he insults the founder of Mormonism, Joseph Smith. Rather than getting him fired, the act earns House's respect. However, several episodes later, Cole does get fired for doing the unthinkable: conspiring with the enemy. "Bring me the thong of Lisa Cuddy," House challenges his team. The point of the game is to do something risky without getting caught. "You told us to do whatever it takes to win," Cole explains to House, bewildered why after winning the game, he's been summarily fired. But he misunderstood the actual challenge. Breaking the rules is acceptable — but only Cuddy's. Breaking the "House" rules will never do. Giving her "powers she didn't already have" is a high crime, with the highest penalty to be paid.

. . . And of course **"Cutthroat Bitch" Amber Volakis** (fired in "Games," 4.09): She plays the game better than anyone, according to House. Brilliant, creative, manipulative, and ruthless, it is a match made in heaven. When House tells Cuddy in "Games" that Amber "cares" more than she lets on, he observes something in her that most others missed. House fires her anyway, but she doesn't go away for long. She turns up late in season four after she becomes romantically involved with Wilson.

## 4.10 "It's a Wonderful Lie"
**Writer:** Pamela Davis **Director:** Matt Shakman
**Patient of the Week:** Maggie (Janel Moloney)

Maggie's genetic defect predisposes her to breast cancer. Long ago she'd undergone a prophylactic radical mastectomy (without reconstructive surgery) as insurance against the disease. When she presents with symptoms suggesting breast cancer, the team understandably dismisses it. But we learn that not only does "*everybody* lie," every *body* can lie as well. Despite her mastectomy, some breast tissue remained in an unlikely place.

**Zebra of the Week:** Breast cancer — under Maggie's knee!

**Epiphany!:** As House and Wilson argue about the incongruity of dreidels on Christmas trees, House realizes that breast tissue, hence breast cancer, can materialize in incongruous places.

**Iconic Moment in *House* History:** House attends his clinic patient's Christmas pageant — she rides a donkey, playing the Virgin Mary. He is amused at the irony.

**Clinic Duty:** House treats a hooker wearing a St. Nicholas medal (the patron saint of children, seamen, and prostitutes). Why would a hooker wear a religious medal? He finds out when he attends her "donkey show."

**A Fine Bromance:** At the hospital Christmas party a tipsy Wilson wears a reindeer hat that House calls "a moose on a Jew."

**House Is a Jerk:** A trifecta this week. House tells the team that "13" has Huntington's chorea. As well, he proposes a "Secret Santa Game" — but writes his own name on all the slips of paper to cause conflict among his new fellows. He is also obnoxious to the patient's daughter, asking her overly direct questions about her mother's sex life.

**Gross-out Warning:** To prove his theory about breast cancer, House gives Maggie a drug to induce swelling and milk production in any breast tissue. House extracts milk from a swelling beneath Maggie's knee with a syringe — and shoots at her daughter's mouth. Ick.

**Pop Culture References:** The title is a direct reference to the James Stewart Christmas classic film *It's a Wonderful Life*. A point of trivia: On Hugh Laurie's comedy sketch show in the U.K. in the mid-'90s, he and his comedy partner Stephen Fry did a brilliant parody of *It's a Wonderful Life*, but with Fox owner Rupert Murdoch in the Jimmy Stewart role. The sketch skewered the Newscorp executive, with Laurie little aware at the time he would one day be working for Murdoch's mega-media company.

**Props Department:** House receives a watch from Kutner in the Secret Santa game, something House continues to wear over the seasons. He also receives a book from Taub: a "Second Edition Conan Doyle" — another Holmes reference.

**Casting Call:** Janel Moloney (Maggie) was a series regular on *The West Wing* (1999–2006) playing Donna Moss. She received two Supporting Actress nominations from the Screen Actors Guild for her performance in the acclaimed series.

**Title Tale:** Maggie and her daughter have vowed never to lie to each other. In theory, it's a completely open relationship, but is it? (Of course not — this is *House*!) When it appears that Maggie needs a bone marrow transplant, she refuses to allow the team to test the daughter. House deduces that Maggie's daughter is adopted, and in a classic House-patient conversation, the mom explains that she promised to never reveal the girl's biological mother to her, thereby living a significant lie of omission.

---

### Truth Begins in Lies: A Closer Look at "It's a Wonderful Lie"

House has an intense love-hate relationship with the truth. We know from season two's "Daddy's Boy" (2.04) that House's father never let anyone lie, and never lied to young Greg. "Great for Boy Scouts and witnesses, but terrible for a father," he reflects to Cameron, brooding in the dark of his office after his parents' visit. Being truthful to the point of hurtfulness is "child abuse," he remarks to Wilson in "It's a Wonderful Lie" (4.10). It's a throwaway line, but one that has greater resonance if you know House's history.

When House utters that first "everybody lies" in the pilot episode, it's an accusation. But later in the same episode tells Foreman, "Truth begins in lies." At the time, it confuses Foreman, the new kid on the block. But it's more than a clever "House-ism."

House gets to the truth of each case through examining the lies: lies people tell; secrets kept and symptoms that lie all the time; symptoms that hide or are masked by other symptoms. Even "things" like cancer cells or other diseases "lie."

In "It's a Wonderful Lie," House articulates a taxonomy of lies to the patient's daughter, Jane, telling her there are all sorts of lies people tell all the time without a second thought. There are lies of commission; lies of omission (what you don't know won't hurt you); white lies (to avoid hurting someone); and rationalizations (lies to yourself). But when Jane claims that Mom never, ever lies, House doesn't believe her. And he's right. Because Mom has kept a very large secret from her daughter — she is adopted. But she has promised the biological mother never to disclose the truth to Jane — and she has kept her promise for years.

Failing to understand why the patient insists on complete truth with her daughter, House extols the virtues of an occasional lie. When you care about someone, he suggests to Wilson, "You lie to them. You pretend that their constant ponderous musings are interesting." (Never mind that House's comments are directed specifically towards Wilson.)

Late in the episode, Jane confronts her mother, who has kept telling her daughter that everything will be fine. Everything is not fine, Jane reminds her. And then in the coldest terms possible she breaks her mother's small bubble of hope. "You're dying. Nobody can help you. It's not going to be okay." It's intended to shock her mother out of her self-deception. As they stand stunned in their patient's room, neither House nor "13" can believe the coldness of this truth told by the young Jane, who does not know how to lie (or even sugarcoat the truth) to her mother.

House views this as a sort of once-in-a-lifetime occurrence. "Pure truth," he calls it — a hard truth told out of caring and for good; not used as a weapon, to beat down, break or control, as we might imagine his own father did, but to help her, wake her, and call her to action.

House lies all the time, despite the way he tries to yield the truth like a battle axe, and to no one more than himself. He lies to those closest to him to maintain a stark emotional distance. He lies that he doesn't care; that people don't matter to him; that his leg doesn't matter — that nothing matters. But by the end of season five, the cascade of self-delusion — that nothing matters — crumbles and nearly destroys House.

## * 4.11 "Frozen"

**Writer:** Liz Friedman **Director:** David Straiton
**Patient of the Week:** Cate Milton (Mira Sorvino)

House treats psychiatrist Cate Milton, who is stranded in Antarctica with a research team. He has limited resources to diagnose her from thousands of miles away. She courageously runs her own tests, including a biopsy as House examines and consults with her via webcam — both from his office and in his apartment. House strongly connects to her, and his uncharacteristic solicitousness almost leads him to miss the diagnosis.

The episode is noteworthy for allowing House's colleagues to experience a different, less guarded and more caring side of him. He stuns Foreman when he vetoes a simple test for an autoimmune disease as too dangerous in Cate's compromised condition.

**Zebra of the Week:** A fat embolus in Cate's toe caused by an undetected fracture in her perpetually freezing foot.

**Epiphany!:** House realizes that in his concern for Cate's comfort, he lets her keep her socks on during his long-distance exam. If he had observed her foot earlier as he'd planned, he would have immediately seen that her toe was broken.

**Iconic Moment in *House* History:** House allows others to witness what only his patients get see: a passionate, even compassionate doctor. Ironically, Foreman who constantly seethes about House's perceived lack of humanity witnesses House imploring Cate's colleague to run a dangerous test. "I won't let you do anything to hurt her. Please," he pleads. "This is her only chance."

**A Fine Bromance:** Wilson teases House about his feelings for Cate — and House suspects Wilson is dating someone. It's Amber.

**House Is a Jerk:** House tries to coerce Cameron into restoring the hospital's free cable TV policy. He assigns his fellows to harass her until she gives in. But the exercise has a point: to force the team to refuse to do his bidding. "I need someone to stand up to me, to challenge me," he tells them finally.

**Patients Know Best:** Cate's a psychiatrist, and after House shows her his living room via webcam, she observes that House may have some issues. But she disarms any possible defensiveness by admitting "I never said you need fixing."

**Gross-out Warning:** In the teaser, a vane from a windmill slashes the femoral artery of Cate's mechanic, spurting blood all over the snow. Later, Cate stabs herself in the chest to inflate her lung. And the mechanic has to drink her urine as a diagnostic test. Triple ick.

**Did You Know?:** There were rumors floating around at the time that Cate would make a return appearance as a potential love interest for House. This has (so far) never materialized.

**Props Department:** More makeup than a prop, but we do see House's scar again. Cate asserts that House would rather reveal his soul to her than his scar. But when he examines her a second time, he wears only boxer briefs. His scar is clearly visible, although neither Cate nor House mention it.

**Casting Call:** Mira Sorvino (Cate) is probably best known for her Oscar-winning performance in Woody Allen's *Mighty Aphrodite* (1995).

**Title Tale:** Cate's toe is frozen and she is marooned in the frozen land of

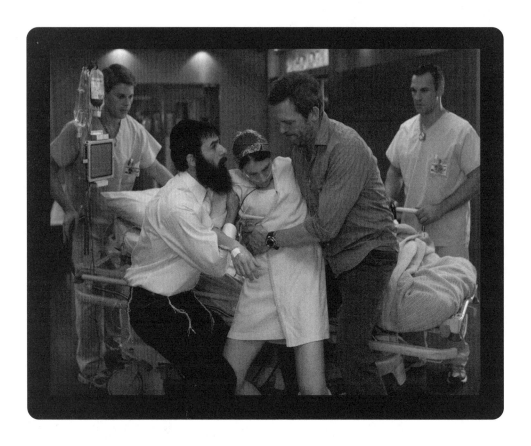

Antarctica. House seems to thaw a bit while treating Cate, dropping his guard in front of his colleagues.

**Why It's a Classic:** Cate Milton is a great patient who has considerable long-distance chemistry with House.

### 4.12 "Don't Ever Change"

**Writers:** Doris Egan, Leonard Dick **Director:** Deran Sarafian
**Patient of the Week:** Roz (Laura Silverman)

A former record producer and heroin addict, Roz has become a *"ba'alat t'shuva"* — a Jew who has "returned" to traditional Judaism, in this case Hasidism. After collapsing at her wedding and bleeding from her vagina, she comes under House's care to determine the cause. House insists that no one would make such a radical lifestyle change on her own, and it is a symptom. As the team treats Roz, Taub, a secular Jew, becomes intrigued by her lifestyle.

House interferes with Wilson's new relationship. Certain that Amber is dating his best friend to wheedle her way back onto his team, House confronts her, insisting that she leave Wilson alone. He is shocked that Wilson would be interested in someone so different than his usual fare. But he eventually realizes that Wilson is enjoying the benefits of having such an assertive and manipulative girlfriend.

**Zebra of the Week:** Floating kidney: the structure that holds up Roz's kidney is defective.

**Epiphany!:** House fumes about things not being "where we want them to be just because we want them to be there," making the associative leap to Roz's problem. Her kidney isn't where it should be, causing bizarre swings in her blood pressure, among other symptoms.

**Iconic Moment in *House* History:** House realizes that Wilson is actually dating a female version of himself!

**Judgmental Fellow Alert:** Taub, a secular Jew, is dismissive of the religious couple's lifestyle, assuming they're "a little nuts." House is always suspicious of religion and religious people.

**Did You Know?:** Chase makes an oblique reference to consulting "twin rabbis." Series creator David Shore has twin brothers who are Orthodox Jewish rabbis with the organization Aish HaTorah.

**Lost in Translation:** House translates the prayer *"Eishet Chayil"* ("A Woman of Valor") from its Hebrew and wishes Wilson *"Shabbat Shalom."* He also speaks Latin when he's with Amber and Wilson: *"Quod erat demonstrandum"* (better known as "QED" meaning "which was to be demonstrated."

**Musical Notes:** Beautifully authentic Jewish wedding music underscores the teaser.

**Casting Call:** Laura Silverman (Roz) is a series regular on her sister's offbeat comedy series *The Sarah Silverman Show* on Comedy Central.

**Title Tale:** The episode asks whether it's possible to "change." House believes that people cannot alter their intrinsic nature. Roz has changed her life; Wilson is trying to change his by becoming involved with a different sort of woman.

### People Don't Change: A Closer Look at "Don't Ever Change"

One of House's mantras is that people cannot change; they lack the ability to alter their intrinsic nature. The theme of "change" plays throughout the aptly named "Don't Ever Change" (4.12), asking the question: can someone change by reaching beyond oneself to something better?

Can Wilson change his unsuccessful relationship pattern? Can Taub find an affinity for a religious life he seems to detest? Can Amber be other than a "cutthroat bitch"? And what of the patient, Roz Viner, who seems to have found a way to make a fundamental change away from a destructive life in the fast lane to something simpler, and hopefully more authentic?

House contends we are who we are. Certain aspects of our personalities and natures come to the fore at various times and in differing situations, but fundamentally changing who you are may not be possible. When House allows a more compassionate, thoughtful part of his nature to show, as he does in the previous episode, "Frozen" (4.11), it is not that he is different — or that he's somehow changed (or inconsistently written). Those things have always been part of his nature, and brought into relief by circumstance.

The episode explores the idea of "change" in several ways through the main and side plots, one of which focuses on the unique relationship between House and his best friend Wilson. Thrice-divorced Wilson tends to become involved only with needy women (in House's view, anyway). Under Wilson's attention, they become less needy (as House explained in season two's "House vs. God," 2.19). Wilson gets bored, goes elsewhere, divorces, feels guilty, and goes on to save another needy woman as the pattern repeats.

But this time, Wilson becomes involved with a wholly other type of woman — strong, intelligent, and resourceful: Amber Volakis, also known as "Cutthroat Bitch," one of House's former fellowship candidates. It looks like Wilson is trying to change his pattern.

Hugh Laurie has often commented on the difference between the central characters in films and television. In film, the central character changes while the peripheral characters remain static. In television, Laurie says, the central character must remain unchanged while everything around him changes. So, guest characters can change, Wilson can change, and certainly Amber can veer from her evil ways to something kinder and gentler, but not House.

Much can be revealed, but he can't change. When you start with such a flawed character, one whose very existence would seem to call out for change, where do you go? It's never been said that House doesn't want to change, doesn't crave change. So it's this character's struggle with living, with wanting to somehow gain some grain of normalcy in his life (or at least crawl out of the hole in which he dwells) that makes the series so compelling and watchable. We root for him, even knowing that to be successful would be the death knell for the series. He takes a step forward and then three backwards. He hits rock bottom and somehow "chooses life," bouncing back only to fail again.

Certainly, the creators and writers of *House, M.D.* have no qualms about shaking up the world of its central character. They've confronted him with the return of a former lover — the same woman who so badly betrayed him.

He's been shot and has undergone radical pain therapy to eradicate the seemingly intractable pain in his right leg, only to have the treatment fail miserably. They've sent in bullies to torment him (and arrest him) and made him endure narcotics withdrawal four times. He's confessed to being an abuse survivor (but only to a stranger) and has had his team quit on him (okay, so Chase was fired).

But "not changing" doesn't mean "not wanting to change." It's that journey, and what it's revealed about House, that is so compelling. It's what makes his tale romantic and heroic.

When we meet House, he's a recluse, refusing to emerge and treat patients, and perfectly willing to let his elite team of fellows sit and do crossword puzzles. He has to be manipulated or tricked into seeing even an interesting patient. He's come a long, long way from that moment, but for every step or two forward, there's a step or three back. Change is incredibly difficult, and House's struggle with pain, with connection, even his own personality requires huge effort.

## 4.13 "No More Mr. Nice Guy"

**Writers:** David Hoselton, David Shore **Director:** Deran Sarafian
**Patient of the Week:** Jeff (Paul Rae)

Can indiscriminate niceness be a symptom? The cynical House believes it can when Jeff, who never gets angry, collapses on the picket line during a nurses' strike. At first, the team is certain that House is simply trying to prove Jeff's happiness is a pathology. But after Jeff worsens, they consider neurosyphilis, which can cause personality changes. This leads the team to wonder if House's personality, too, could be due to the same sexually transmitted disease. So they endeavor to find out.

House and Amber squabble over Wilson's time and affection. And Cuddy demands that House conduct performance reviews on his team — which he then pawns off on Foreman.

**Zebra of the Week:** Encephalitis caused by the parasitic disease, Chagas. It has swollen Jeff's brain, causing his personality changes. House is right; Jeff's niceness is only a symptom!

**Epiphany!:** After Amber informs the team that House has set them up and does not have syphilis, Kutner wonders if Jeff might have Chagas disease, contracted when he was in the Peace Corps years earlier.

**Iconic Moment in *House* History:** With Wilson focusing his attention on Amber, House needs a new friend. He goes bowling with Chase.

**Manipulative Wilson:** Wilson thoroughly enjoys the conflict between Amber and House as they battle for his affections. When Cuddy enforces a "custody agreement" among the three of them, both Amber and House violate it. Wilson watches with amusement as they are punished for their infractions.

**A Fine Bromance:** The entire episode is a bit "bromantic" with House being very possessive of Wilson. He gets Wilson drunk at a bar, ensuring he gets home late from their boys' night out.

**House Is a Jerk:** He manipulates the team into thinking he has syphilis. There is no purpose to this prank other than to screw with them. He hits a 10 on the jerk-o-meter.

**Shipper Alert!:** Ordered to give his team performance reviews, House also delivers an uninvited performance review of his boss, the dean herself. "You want to have someone jump you and tell you 'I love you'; you run away from what you need; you have no idea of what you want." What clues do we take away from House's review?

**Did You Know?:** The episode is set during a nurses' strike, which parallels the writers' strike that had just ended after three long months. This episode is the first written after the strike.

**Casting Call:** Paul Rae (Jeff) has guest starred in numerous television series, including *Californication* on Showtime, *The West Wing* on NBC, and *Fringe* on Fox.

**Title Tale:** Once cured, Jeff is no longer the "nice guy" he was when he came into the hospital ER. And House is never a nice guy.


### 4.14 "Living the Dream"
**Writers:** Sara Hess, Liz Friedman **Director:** David Straiton
**Patient of the Week:** Evan (Jason Lewis)

House kidnaps Evan, his favorite soap opera actor, believing he has noticed a symptom while watching the actor on-screen. Evan thinks House is insane, and even for viewers accustomed to House's out-of-the-box antics, this act seems a bit over-the-top. While House tries to diagnose the reluctant soap star, an accreditation inspector visits Princeton-Plainsboro, adding to the chaos. Amber and Wilson argue over mattresses and the direction of their relationship while House gives Wilson relationship advice.

**Zebra of the Week:** A severe allergic reaction to quinine.

**Epiphany!:** House shops in a bedding store with Wilson, and as he lies down on a mattress with floral cover, he realizes Evan has an allergy.

**Iconic Moment in *House* History:** House wants to treat Evan, now in a coma, with steroids, certain his symptoms are caused by an allergic reaction to flowers. Foreman believes Evan has infection — and that the steroids could kill him. Cuddy, aware of the omnipresent hospital inspector, is unwilling to cut House the usual amount of slack. But House has no time to argue as Evan rapidly deteriorates. Putting himself on the line, he tells her to leave. "You wait three minutes, then you call security. By the time they get here and lock me up, I'll be done. He gets to live and your ass gets to be covered." It's a classic case of House risking his job for the patient.

**A Fine Bromance (and Amber):** Wilson and Amber want to buy a mattress. Amber insists Wilson buy one *he* wants. When Wilson predictably buys a mattress to please Amber, she is angry. Wilson and House go mattress shopping together and Wilson buys what he really wants — a waterbed. House is sad.

**House Is a Jerk:** House threatens to sabotage the inspection if Cuddy doesn't buy him a new television for his office.

**Housian Ethics:** Is there anything ethical about kidnapping someone to perform medical tests, even if you're certain his life is in danger?

**Shipper Alert!:** At the end of the case, House phones Cuddy, waking her up late at night to tell her he was wrong about the floral allergy, and she should have stopped him (the allergy is to quinine). Their banter is laden with sexual tension.

**Classic Rant:** House rants to the depressed Evan about suicide, airplanes, and living: "Life is an airplane, sometimes you just have to jump off," House tells him metaphorically.

**Casting Call:** Jason Lewis (Evan) was a regular in *Sex and the City*'s final season (2005–2006), playing Smith Jerrod. He reprised his role in 2008 and 2010 in both *Sex and the City* movies.

**Title Tale:** "Living the Dream" refers (among other things) to taking hope beyond fantasy and making that leap out of House's metaphorical airplane. For the patient it means stepping beyond the confines of acting in a soap opera, despite the fact that it's "complicated." House talks a good game, but is he able to practice what he preaches?

## * 4.15 "House's Head"

**Writers:** Peter Blake, David Foster, Russel Friend, Garrett Lerner
**Story by:** Doris Egan **Director:** Greg Yaitanes

> "House wakes up in a coffee shop and doesn't know how he got there. He knows that something bad has happened: he's seen a fatal symptom in somebody. But can't access his brain."
>
> — **Russel Friend on Doris Egan's story idea for "House's Head," May 2008**

House tries to make sense of fractured bits and pieces of his memory after a serious head injury leaves him with retrograde amnesia. Finding himself in a strip club, dazed and bleeding, he has no idea how or when he got there. He leaves and wanders aimlessly into the street where he sees the aftermath of a horrific bus accident.

As he is treated in the Princeton-Plainsboro Emergency Room, House insists he noticed a serious symptom in one of the passengers. Concerned that the passenger will die if he can't remember, House drives himself to divine the answer while fighting the effects of his own injuries.

His colleagues want to know why it's so important to solve the mystery. House can't explain — he only understands it's something he must do, whatever the risk.

**Zebra of the Week:** The only mystery is the name of the person House is trying to recollect — Amber.

**Epiphany!:** Tormented and taunted by a dark-haired woman wearing an unusual necklace, House knows she is the key to what he's forgotten. Finally, long after the audience has figured it out, House realizes she's wearing an amber necklace. The victim is Amber!

**Iconic Moment in *House* History:** The entire episode, from start to finish, is iconic for the series. It's impossible to isolate any one scene.

**A Fine Bromance:** While under hypnosis House recalls seeing Amber while he was drinking in a bar. Wilson immediately wants to know why Amber is appearing in House's subconscious.

**Shipper Alert!:** House fantasizes about Cuddy: she is a stripper dressed in a school uniform. They engage in a very suggestive and sensual differential diagnosis.

**Pop Culture References:** House tries doing time in a make-shift isolation chamber to heighten his senses and spark his memory, referring to the movie

*Altered States.*

**Casting Call:** Ivana Milicevic is House's mysterious woman with the amber necklace. She appeared in the James Bond film *Casino Royale* (2006) as Valenka.

**Title Tale:** The episode's entire mystery is locked up in House's head.

### A Truth Just Beyond His Grasp:
### A Closer Look at "House's Head"

Reality merges with fantasy, visions, dreams, and hallucinations as House tries to make sense of his fractured memory in hopes of discovering just what he saw during a horrific bus crash. House is certain that if he cannot put the pieces together, someone will die. As he frantically searches for clues, House uses every weapon in his arsenal from medical hypnosis to sensory deprivation and Alzheimer's drugs to stimulate memories. Along the way, he is haunted by the presence of a mystery woman. Part seductress, part spiritual guide, she teases House's memory, always just beyond his grasp. Even when the symbolism of her amber necklace becomes obvious to viewers, it still eludes House. Is his mind trying to suppress the fact that Amber is the injured passenger he's trying to remember?

Cuddy, too, appears to House as both seductress and guide in one of his fantasies. As he sits at the back of the bus, it slowly morphs into the strip club seen in the teaser. As Cuddy pole dances, she and House debate the victim's symptoms. The differential is nearly as seductive and sensual as the strip routine itself, the thrust and parry of their discussion mirroring Cuddy's bump and grind. But House's subconscious knows that Cuddy's dance is too distracting. And she is taking him away from what he must do.

Another thwarted seductive scene occurs in House's apartment as he dreams. Cuddy, asleep in the living room, becomes the dark-haired mystery woman. She takes his hand, sensually caressing her face. Suddenly noticing that she's wearing a red scarf, House tells her, "I need to tie this on you."

As he ties the sash around her thigh, one wonders if this is sensual game playing. "I'm cold," she tells him, beckoning. "Just stay with me," he replies gently. But the fantasy becomes macabre as blood drenches the scarf. House, startled from his dream, knows this must be a significant signpost.

Jungian psychology tells us that dreams are the answers to questions we don't even know how to ask. But what is the elusive question? When House's memories come flooding back, we are only left with more questions.

And how does the bus driver figure into the mix? He certainly keeps popping in and out of House's subconscious. Is he a diversion, created by House's mind to keep him distanced from a truth too painful at this moment? The bus driver provides House with a conventional medical mystery: What are the symptoms? What are the possibilities? What treatment do we try next? As his mind focuses on the driver, House is unable to tap into the clues he needs to solve the real mystery.

"I know what's really bugging your subconscious," the mystery woman reveals, trying to lead him past his own emotional barricades. But insistent as he is about getting to the truth, his subconscious won't allow him access.

Finally, pushing himself to the limit, self-administering a dangerous drug, understanding it could kill him, House drags colleagues and fellows back onto the bus. And suddenly we are there with him. In a breathtaking and heartbreaking scene, House's memory comes flooding back, and we experience it along with him as the bus crashes and overturns before crashing again. House's cane flies from his grasp as he watches Amber slide helplessly away from him, her leg impaled on a pole.

Barely conscious, House finally reaches Amber and we understand the significance of the red scarf. It is no longer a sensual object as House ties it on Amber's leg — it's a tourniquet.

House has his answer, or at least a part of it, but at what cost? His heart stopped, House is resuscitated by Cuddy in another sensual image — the kiss of life she imparts to him — and Wilson who violently pounds on his chest. We are left with the "who," but not the "why."

## * 4.16 "Wilson's Heart"

**Writers:** Peter Blake, David Foster, Russel Friend, Garrett Lerner
**Director:** Katie Jacobs

"Dreams are informed by what has happened to you during the day, or things that had an impact on you."

— **Garret Lerner on House's dreams during "House's Head" and "Wilson's Heart,"**
**May 2008 interview**

Recalling at the end of "House's Head" that Amber may be dying, House, accompanied by Wilson, identifies her at another hospital where bus crash victims had been taken. She is unconscious as Wilson and the amnesia-stricken

House bring her back to Princeton-Plainsboro. Amber's heart stops en route and rather than try to revive her immediately, Wilson convinces House to lower her body temperature and place her on heart bypass to keep her alive while he continues to retrieve pieces of his memory.

Unable to rest, not certain whether he has betrayed his best friend, House's mind continues in overdrive. Each time he tries to sleep, Amber invades his subconscious, seductive and frustrating. Did they have an affair? Is this the terrible truth House's mind won't allow him to recall?

If only it were that simple. House is living on a knife's edge as the physical and emotional toll mounts. Exhausted and "barely coherent" (as he tells Wilson), House is too emotionally invested on several levels in the case, as he tries to diagnose Amber.

**Zebra of the Week:** Amantadine poisoning. Amber takes Amantadine for the flu, but when her kidneys are damaged during the crash, Amber's body loses the ability to filter the drug and it becomes toxic to her.

**Epiphany!:** While undergoing a deep brain stimulation procedure to recover his memories, House realizes that Amber has the flu. He recalls seeing her take the pills — but also realizes the nature of her injuries would have rendered the pills poisonous.

**Iconic Moment in *House* History:** As the second half of "House's Head," this episode is a singular iconic moment for the series. Especially noteworthy is a scene towards the end of the episode in which House floats between life and death. He meets Amber, who is already dead. It's comforting to House to be on this side of living: he is not in pain; Wilson doesn't hate him for his indirect role in Amber's death. But Amber, quoting "the philosopher Jagger," reminds House that "you can't always get what you want."

**A Fine Bromance:** Wilson asks House to make an incredible sacrifice: to undergo a dangerous brain procedure that may give him the key to Amber's illness, but may also cost House his life. House agrees to do it.

**Shipper Alert!:** As House lies unconscious after further traumatizing his brain during the deep brain stimulation, Cuddy sits endlessly at his bedside, holding his hand and simply being there for him.

**Housian Ethics:** Is is ethical for Wilson to ask House to risk his life to save Amber's?

**Title Tale:** What is in Wilson's heart? Undoubtedly, there is love there for both House and Amber, but who does he love more?

## To the Limit: A Closer Look at "Wilson's Heart"

Life, living life, is sometimes brutal. It's fraught with tragedy and pain, things we cannot control, and things we maybe could have, but have let careen out of control. A solitary figure sits in a bar trying to escape from the pain and loneliness that enshrouds his life; a bartender takes his keys after one too many, and a young woman dies as a result. It's no one's fault, but everyone carries some responsibility. "Am I dead?" the comatose House asks Amber as they sit bathed in white light at the end of "Wilson's Heart." "I should be . . . lonely, misanthropic drug addicts should die on buses." And so House trudges on to face himself — and Wilson as season four ends. Wilson lectures House in "Games" (4.09): "Dying is easy; living, that's hard."

As in "House's Head," dreams are fantasy infused with fragmented reality, and they emerge as parts of a whole, providing only vague clues. In one fantasy, House dreams that Amber pours him sherry and seduces him. Passive, but completely into the moment, House suddenly awakens sparked by a new clue: "electricity."

But he also wonders why Amber poured him sherry. What is House's subconscious trying to help him recall? He still doesn't know, but the fantasy helps him realize that electrical stimulation of his brain might help recover his broken memory. Wilson and Cuddy veto this dangerous and possibly fatal procedure, but we know House will not rest until he discovers the missing pieces.

The "sherry" leads House to Sharrie's Bar, where he was drunk the night before — with Amber! Wilson is crushed, and House is upset and clueless about why they would have been together.

The team wants to aggressively treat Amber, but Wilson insists they proceed cautiously and take the "safe" route, which House and his team rarely do. But House complies with Wilson's wishes, backing off where he would normally charge ahead, his legendary objectivity in tatters.

With Amber barely holding on, and House still unable to recall events that may lead to diagnosis, Wilson asks him to undergo the same brain procedure he and Cuddy vetoed earlier as too risky for House's compromised medical condition. "You want me to risk my life to save Amber's?" House asks, making certain that he and Wilson both understand just what he is asking.

It is an act of pure selflessness, pure friendship, pure love — something of which most would never suspect House capable. But it is the essence of House — stripped of all defenses, of all bullshit.

The procedure works, and House's memories come flooding back; House is drinking alone, but too drunk to drive. He calls Wilson, setting off a chain of events ending with Amber's death. A tragic set of random occurrences — if any one is missing, Amber lives — results in the loss of her life and Wilson's love, irrevocably. Flu medicine is now nothing but poison; Amber's kidneys, injured in the crash are unable to process it, killing her.

And the tragedy is made clear. House understands that this is something he cannot fix. No words, no apology, no action can reverse time. The raw emotion of the moment is made exquisitely powerful by twin close-ups: one of House, weeping over what he set in motion, and the other of Wilson at the moment he knows Amber is going to die. The truth finally emerges, and House suffers a seizure serious enough to cause further trauma to his brain.

As Wilson says his tearful goodbye to Amber, House is left in a coma, once again hovering between life and death. Back on the bus now bathed in white light, he sits with the dead Amber as he wrestles with how he can face life (and Wilson). "I want to stay here with you," he says to Amber.

This is a place where it doesn't hurt and there are no betrayals. It is safe and free of despair and misery. But it is not his time. "You can't always get what you want," Amber tells him, sending him back to the land of the living to face what lies ahead.

House struggles through the fog back to consciousness, finding Cuddy, teary-eyed at his side, grateful he's alive and aware. On to season five.

# SEASON 5
## Upheaval and the Ultimate Escape

Although there were a few wrong steps here and there, season five may have been the most cohesive of the entire series to date. With no artificially inserted House nemesis (à la Vogler in season one, and Tritter in season three), no survivor games, and a narrative that threaded a direct line from the fourth season finale right through the final season five episodes and into season six, the series presented a strong and compelling story. Some fans resented the prominence of the "13" and Foreman story line, dubbing it "Foreteen," vehemently protesting the focus on it. Throughout season five, the weekly medical mystery took a backseat to the higher drama surrounding all the main characters: Cuddy's attempt to adopt a baby, Wilson's continued grief over Amber's death, Chase and Cameron's rocky path to marriage, Kutner's departure, and House's season-long downward spiral.

House has dwelled upon a precipice since we met him in the first season. An essentially unstable character, teeter-tottering on the edge, House has danced with self-destruction that has occasionally bordered on suicidal. In an interview with Elvis Mitchell in the early days of season two, Hugh Laurie acknowledged this, wondering how long it would be before the audience finally cried: "For heaven's sake, just jump already!"

Well, he finally jumps, albeit metaphorically. Unlike Kutner's abrupt and shocking exit ("Simple Explanation," 5.20), which no one foresaw, House's demise has many clues, many cues. Loss piled upon loss until finally he simply snaps, crushed beneath the weight of too much misery, punctuated by the loss of the only thing he could rely upon: belief in himself and his own mental acuity.

Should his colleagues see it coming? Are there neon signs and marquees pointing to House's inevitable crash? Yes and no. Yes, they might see it coming from miles off, but House's own personality — in denial nearly until the end — prevents anyone from really helping him.

Amber's death, House's father's death, the (albeit temporary) loss of Wilson's friendship, and his intensifying feelings for Lisa Cuddy all contribute to House's season five crash. But his slow descent into madness really begins in "Painless" (5.12), the exact midpoint of the season when House's chronic physical pain and his ever-increasing internalized anguish really begin to take their toll.

The extent to which everything is weighing on House is expressed explicitly in "The Social Contract" (5.17). The patient is someone who has lost all of his social filters and has become an exaggerated version of House. He mourns what it has cost him and asks House to perform a dangerous operation that could bring his life back to normal — or could kill him, a risk the patient is willing to take.

House pleads with Chase to take the case, but Chase is unwilling to get involved unless House can explain why he cares so much, given that there's no medical reason for the operation. House reluctantly explains. "When he leaves here, he's going to lose his family. He's gonna alienate the people he works with. And if he ever finds a friend who's willing to put up with his crap, he'll be lucky. Until he drives them away too." Chase understands how much of an admission this is, and House's haunted expression as he essentially bares his own soul seems to stun Chase with its rawness.

By "Locked In" (5.19) we learn that House has been to see a psychiatrist. This, too, is a stunning development for a man who has placed no value in therapy since we've met him. Yet, here it is. So, what drives him to consult a therapist? Is House beginning to doubt himself? His worldview? His attitude? Does he think he's losing his mind? His skill? His gift? Is it that House is desperate to try anything at this point to help him change? Is he already experiencing visual hallucinations in some form? Is there something scaring him with regard to his Vicodin use that's causing him to try other things — anything? Or is he beginning to wonder why he has to negate everything, deflect everything and refuse to deal with himself? Maybe all of the above.

Classic episodes are indicated by an asterisk.


## 5.01 "Dying Changes Everything"
**Writer:** Eli Attie **Director:** Deran Sarafian
**Patient of the Week:** Lou (Christine Woods)

Picking up two months after the fatal bus crash, House diagnoses the executive assistant to a high-powered feminist. Wilson has also returned from a two-month leave after Amber's death in "Wilson's Heart" (4.16), but he's only come back to pack up and say goodbye.

The news hits House hard, and even as he tries manipulating Wilson into staying, House insists that he cannot apologize to Wilson for his part in Amber's death (even if an apology might cause Wilson to reconsider). "It would be meaningless," he keeps saying — as if taking Wilson out for a couple of beers will bring back his dead girlfriend, a sentiment restated under different circumstances in the season six premiere, "Broken" (6.01, 6.02).

**Zebra of the Week:** "Pretty" leprosy.

**Epiphany!:** House notices that after treatment, the patient looks her actual age, and not 10 years younger as she had looked earlier. Her other symptoms and her high-powered lifestyle suggest "pretty" leprosy.

**Iconic Moment in *House* History:** Wilson walks out of his relationship with House, denying they were ever friends — leaving House speechless and numb in his wake.

**A Fine Bromance:** House mourns Wilson's decision to leave as much as he had feared Wilson's return to the hospital.

**House Is a Jerk:** House is in particularly nasty form for much of the episode. He outs "13's" Huntington's to deflect from his own issues, and abandons his case to blackmail Wilson into staying.

**Gross-out Warning:** The patient has a very graphic rectal bleed. She also hallucinates ants crawling all over her skin, which we see from her point of view. Ick.

**Casting Call:** Christine Woods (Lou) was a regular on the ABC science-fiction series *FlashForward*, playing Special Agent Janis Hawk from 2009 to 2010.

**World-Famous Doctor:** The patient's boss brought her to Princeton-Plainsboro to be seen by the renowned diagnostician.

**House Doing "Doctor Stuff":** House performs an ultrasound on the patient after his team fails to observe her ectopic pregnancy. House finds the implantation in the intestine — a rare presentation.

**Title Tale:** The title is a riff on an oft-repeated House axiom: almost dying changes nothing. But dying, it seems, changes everything — an unexpected death tilts House's world askew. Amber's death has irrevocably altered the dynamic between Wilson and him and forms the starting point for a season-long journey of upheaval for House.


## 5.02 "Not Cancer"

**Writers:** David Shore, Lawrence Kaplow **Director:** David Straiton
**Patient of the Week:** Apple (Felicia Day)

After several transplant recipients die suddenly, the team tries to save the life of Apple, another transplant recipient of the same donor. House thinks cancer was transferred by donor organs, but everyone else disagrees.

As House continues to grieve the loss of Wilson, he hires Lucas Douglas, an eccentric private investigator to help him investigate patients — and keep tabs on Wilson. As House grows less and less able to hide his grief over Wilson, it seeps into differential diagnosis sessions and encounters with the patient. Even Lucas feels House's pain over losing Wilson's friendship.

**Zebra of the Week:** Defective stem cells transplanted during eye surgery.

**Iconic Moment in *House* History:** House sits on the floor alone in Wilson's empty office trying to solve the case — and consider the loss of his best friend.

**House Is a Jerk:** House is a particular ass to Apple's nurses, pressing the call button incessantly on Apple's bed to bring the nurses running just to prove he can.

**Patients Know Best:** Apple discloses to House that she gave up architecture after her corneal transplant, because although she was told she would see a more beautiful world, she didn't. She tells House that she perceives a similarity between them. And it's something for which he has no ready retort.

**Casting Call:** Felicia Day (Apple) appeared in the recurring role of Vi on *Buffy the Vampire Slayer* (2003). She has also gained a reputation as one of the foremost creators of original digital material, particularly for *The Guild*, which she writes, produces, and stars in. Michael Weston debuts as House's quirky PI, Lucas Douglas. Weston played Jake on the HBO series *Six Feet Under*. He is the son of actor John Rubinstein (who guest stars on *House* in season two's "The Mistake") and grandson of legendary pianist Arthur Rubinstein.

**Title Tale:** What is cancer, but not cancer? That is the question. House spends the episode looking for something that mimics cancer in the transplant patients.

### 5.03 "Adverse Events"

**Writers:** Carol Green, Dustin Paddock **Director:** Andrew Bernstein
**Patient of the Week:** Brandon (Breckin Meyer)

Brandon is a mediocre painter who has sold only one painting in three years. He exhibits agnosia, a recognition disorder, making him paint distorted images. House realizes what the problem is fairly quickly: he's been enrolled in multiple clinical trials, leading House and the team to think it's all due to drug interaction. House also has Lucas investigate the team to uncover all sorts of inside information on them.

**Zebra of the Week:** Bezoar — a hairball formed by ingesting an experimental antacid. The bezoar trapped several other experimental drugs, which were then released into Brandon's system, causing his problems.

**Epiphany!:** It's not until Taub discovers the agnosia only seems to occur in the months that Brandon is taking all three experimental drugs that House can put it all together.

**Iconic Moment in *House* History:** Lucas shows Cuddy an old photograph of House as a cheerleader for his college lacrosse team.

**A Fine Bromance:** House and his PI, Lucas Douglas, are getting quite chummy, and Lucas seems to have taken up residence in House's apartment.

**House Is a Jerk:** House uses Lucas to dig up dirt on Taub and "13," sharing the info with everyone just to see how they'll react.

**Housian Ethics:** House should not have invaded his subordinates' privacy.

**Shipper Alert!:** The more socially adept Lucas provides a bit of competition for House in his glacially slow pursuit of Cuddy, betting House that he will beat him to Cuddy.

**Gross-out Warning:** Brandon's face swells up like a balloon after they detox him from all the experimental drugs he's taking.

**Props Department:** House has a new piano! This time, it's a Yamaha.

**Musical Notes:** House and Lucas jam at the end of the episode playing the blues, with House on guitar and Lucas at House's piano.

**Casting Call:** Breckin Meyer (Brandon) is perhaps best known for the Emmy Award–winning animated series *Robot Chicken*, for which he and Seth Green provide the voices. Meyer has also written many of the series' episodes.

**Title Tale:** A play on the medical term "adverse effects," which are reported by clinical researchers when conducting drug studies. Less obviously, what are the adverse events of House hiring Lucas? Will he put the moves on Cuddy? Only time will tell.

## * 5.04 "Birthmarks"

**Writers:** Doris Egan, David Foster **Director:** David Platt
**Patient of the Week:** Nicole (Samantha Quan)

> "We know from our earlier episodes that House has had a troubled relationship with his father. Being forced to deal with that troubled relationship and what that means or doesn't mean to House personally — I thought was an interesting thing to think about."
>
> **— David Foster, October 2008 interview**

A young woman searching in China for her birth parents collapses after lifting a statue of Buddha. As the team begins the diagnosis, they learn that House's father has died — and that he refuses to attend the funeral.

Cuddy drugs House, and, against his will, Wilson drags him to the funeral where House's mother wants him to deliver a eulogy. It's a pivotal episode as Wilson returns, and we learn the House-Wilson "origin story" as House tries to lead the team through the diagnosis via cell phone. House and Wilson eventually make it to the funeral and House finds proof of something he's suspected since he was 12 years old: that John House is not his biological father.

**Zebra of the Week:** Literally scarred by her parents, Nicole was an unwanted daughter in 1980s China. Intending to kill her, the father placed pins into the fontanelle (soft spot) on her head, and then abandoned her to an orphanage. When she tries moving the Buddha, which contains a strong magnet, the pins move, causing her symptoms.

**Epiphany!:** Fitting for his return to House's side, the epiphany is Wilson's. He recalls the Chinese political situation — the one child policy — at the time of Nicole's birth. Putting two and two together leads House right to the diagnosis.

**Iconic Moment in *House* History:** House's delight at Wilson's return as he wakes up in the car after being drugged is a series highlight. **Iconic Moment #2:** House's powerful eulogy about fathers and sons starts as a tirade and ends poignantly as he realizes how much he is, in some significant ways, like the father who raised him.

**Manipulative Wilson:** Drugging House and taking him to the funeral is Wilson's idea. As a favor to House's mom, he is determined to get House there, drop him off, and leave.

**A Fine Bromance:** Wilson explains to a police officer how he and House met at a medical conference years earlier. Wilson got into a brawl and House, a stranger at the time, bailed him out of jail.

> "It's an iconic moment that reflects back on their 'superhero origin story.'"
>
> — Doris Egan, October 2008 interview

**House Is a Jerk:** He whacks Wilson with his cane, causing his car keys to fall into a deep gutter, annoying Wilson and further delaying their arrival at the funeral.

**Housian Ethics:** You might wonder if it is ethical for Cuddy to drug House and Wilson kidnap him to get him the funeral.

**Shipper Alert!:** Cuddy gives House an injection in a "large muscle" — his tush.

**Gross-out Warning:** After House tearily ends his eulogy, he leans in to the casket and snips a piece of his father's ear. This is no sentimental reminder of dad, but will be used for a DNA test that proves John House is not Greg's biological father.

**Classic Rant:** House's eulogy begins as a rant on powerful men like his father and their powerless underlings.

**Metaphorically Speaking:** Metaphorus interputus. House's metaphor about steamrollers and the pancreas misleads the team when he is forced to hang up the phone after he and Wilson are stopped by the police for speeding.

**Pop Culture References:** Coincidence or homage? The 2009 remake of Sherlock Holmes virtually lifts a pivotal scene between House and Wilson during which House provokes Wilson into admitting he's missed their friendship. In *Sherlock Holmes*, Holmes goads Watson, using House's exact words and intonation, to "Admit it! Admit it! Admit" that he is attracted by the adventure Holmes offers after Watson threatens to quit.

**Casting Call:** Diane Baker and R. Lee Ermey reprise their roles as House's parents. Ermey doesn't have a speaking role, since John House is dead.

***House* Canon:** In addition to establishing a time for John House's death, and the fact that he's not Greg's biological father, we are also able to fix a time on House and Wilson's first encounter as just after Wilson finishes medical school. We also establish that the first of Wilson's three marriages ended around this time.

**Title Tale:** Our parents all leave their marks in one way or another. Nicole's biological parents left their permanent mark in her brain, affecting the rest of her life. House's mother had an affair shortly after his parents married. The man who raised House, although not his biological father, also left his mark, raising his son to be his diametric opposite in some ways — and like him in others. House has a birthmark on his scalp similar to that on the head of his presumed biological father.

> "The tragedy of this episode and many people's relationships with their parents is that the parent dies before there ever was any closure, if closure was ever possible. But I think, certainly that one of the reasons that Wilson wants House to go to the funeral, in addition to doing it for his mom, is that he believes that House will regret it for the rest of his life if he doesn't at least get some sort of symbolic closure by going to the funeral and talking about his father."
>
> **— Doris Egan, October 2008 interview**

## 5.05 "Lucky 13"

**Writers:** Liz Friedman, Sara Hess **Director:** Greg Yaitanes
**Patient of the Week:** Spencer (Angela Gots)

After a very graphic sexual romp with "13," a young woman (Spencer) goes into seizures and "13" brings her to House for diagnosis. Actually, she has been seeking a consult with House for some time. Although "13" thinks she's not actually sick and wants her immediately discharged, House disagrees and thinks that her four previous doctors missed something. He is also concerned about "13's" apparent downward spiral after he discovers her coming into work hungover. Wilson has returned to Princeton-Plainsboro and House tries to assure himself that things are back to normal between them.

**Zebra of the Week:** Sjogren's syndrome, an autoimmune disease in which the white blood cells attack moisture-producing glands, causing serious complications elsewhere in the body.

**Epiphany!:** House asks "13" if Spencer has wept. Apparently, she lacks tears, and the lack of moisture there and elsewhere created a nice home for opportunistic infections.

**Iconic Moment in *House* History:** House describes "13's" self-destructiveness to her and how it will end if she keeps it up; it is almost as if he is talking about himself.

**A Fine Bromance:** Wilson is back! House welcomes him with a practical joke. But Wilson one-ups him by staging his own elaborate prank to make House believe he is dating a hooker — and has started using heroin during his absence.

**House Is a Jerk:** House fires "13" when she comes into work hungover. The team pleads her case, but House will hear nothing of it. His act is justified because it does have a purpose — a much needed wake-up call for the young, reckless doctor.

**Judgmental Fellow Alert:** "13" wants to boot Spencer from the hospital as a hypochondriac.

**Shipper Alert!:** While investigating her apartment with House, Foreman uncovers "13's" Huntington's test results, which reveal that her disease is an aggressive type. He gives the letter to her, rather than let House get his hands on it. **Shipper Alert #2:** Cuddy goes crib shopping with Wilson after she learns that she has been approved to adopt a baby. House's speechless reaction, as if he's been sucker punched, baffles Cuddy and Wilson.

**World-Famous Doctor:** Spencer has been seeking a consult with the renowned diagnostician for months.

**Casting Call:** In 2008, Angela Gots appeared in several episodes of Showtime's

*The L Word* as Cammie/Shaun.

**Title Tale:** The title refers to the very unlucky "13."


## 5.06 "Joy"

**Writer:** David Hoselton **Director:** Deran Sarafian

**Patients of the Week:** Jerry Harmon (Salvator Xuereb), Samantha Harmon (Joanna Koulis), Becca (Vanessa Zima)

Jerry Harmon is a work-at-home product tester. While testing coffee, he suddenly loses awareness of time. The team determines that his blackouts are actually sleepwalking. Taub and "13" follow Harmon as he sleepwalks, learning that he uses cocaine, although he isn't even aware he's using the drug. As he gets sicker, his daughter begins to experience similar symptoms.

Meanwhile, Cuddy prepares to adopt a baby from a young woman, Becca. When she discovers a rash on Becca's arm, she brings the pregnant young woman into the hospital to figure out the cause. House has not accepted the fact that Cuddy plans to adopt soon, and pulls out the stops to show her the true hardships of parenthood: broken lamps, stained blouses, and incessant neediness.

At first, House doesn't think Cuddy will go through with it (wishful thinking), taking bets on how quickly she'll back out. But Cuddy is in this for the long haul. When Becca gives birth, House finally recognizes Cuddy's seriousness — and her happiness — with her new role as he observes adoptive mom and newborn in the delivery room. But Becca is also taken with the new daughter. She changes her mind and decides to keep the baby, devastating Cuddy.

**Zebra of the Week:** A genetic condition called familial Mediterranean fever. A rare symptom of this condition, anhedonia (literally the inability to experience pleasure), afflicts the patient and his daughter.

**Epiphany!:** House realizes father and daughter are both anhedonic, and wonders whether they are of Middle Eastern descent.

**Iconic Moment in *House* History:** House visits Cuddy after she loses the baby. In a mutually vulnerable moment, they share a passionate kiss.

**A Fine Bromance:** House wonders why Wilson isn't harassing him for being annoying to Cuddy. He tells House it's probably good practice for her. If she can't put up with his "insanity," there is no hope for her as a mother.

**House Is a Jerk:** House is chronically annoying to Cuddy.

**Housian Ethics:** House assigns Taub and "13" to score cocaine from Harmon's dealer to test for other toxins. The street-smart "13" seems to know a lot about the street drug!

**Shipper Alert!:** The kiss between House and Cuddy ignites some powerful feelings in both of them, which both are too emotionally inhibited to act upon.

**Casting Call:** Salvator Xuereb (Jerry Harmon) has had a long career in independent films, including Oliver Stone and Quentin Tarantino's *Natural Born Killers* (1994).

**Title Tale:** Cuddy wants to name her new baby "Joy," and the Harmons are incapable of feeling joy. Unlike the Harmons, House's misery isn't directly driven by illness, but circumstance. And although House has little joy in his life, he can, unlike his patient, find comfort in music, beauty in art, and satisfaction in his work. But he finds little joy in the prospect of Cuddy's impending motherhood.

### 5.07 "The Itch"

**Writer:** Peter Blake **Director:** Greg Yaitanes
**Patient of the Week:** Stewart (Todd Louiso)

While doing community outreach, Cameron refers the agoraphobic Stewart to House after he suffers a seizure. Stewart refuses to go to the hospital for treatment and the team sets up shop in his apartment. But performing tests and procedures in the small, unsanitary apartment is a challenge. Cameron thwarts two attempts to move an anesthetized Stewart to the hospital, but eventually House figures out that he's been poisoned.

Meanwhile, House has a mysterious mosquito bite on his hand that won't seem to leave him alone — and the mosquito that bit him still roams free in his apartment. Drastic measures are needed, but Wilson dismisses the mosquito and insists that House's "itch" is really a metaphor for his feelings about Cuddy. He's been "bitten" ever since their kiss in "Joy" (5.06), and Wilson tries valiantly to play matchmaker.

**Zebra of the Week:** Many years after being shot, lead bullet fragments left in Stewart's hip bone are beginning to deteriorate, causing the metal the enter his bloodstream.

**Epiphany!:** When House realizes Stewart is having severe stomach pain even on morphine, he guesses it's lead poisoning; knowing that Stewart was shot by a mugger, he guesses the source of the lead.

**Iconic Moment in *House* History:** House dreams of combating his pesky mosquito with a propane-fueled insect-killing contraption. Chasing the mosquito around his apartment, he pays little regard to the fact he's allowing propane to escape from the tank, and lights his stove. As realization dawns, House's apartment explodes. Fortunately, it's just a dream.

**A Fine Bromance:** House visits Wilson, unable to sleep after his crazy mosquito-killing dream. Wilson assures him that the mosquito is simply a symbol for his feelings towards Cuddy. He kicks House out of the apartment, telling him to head for where he belongs: Cuddy's arms.

**House Is a Jerk:** He brings strangers into the agoraphobic man's home to scare him into a seizure, which is needed for the diagnosis.

**Housian Ethics:** Unable to safely operate on Stewart in his home, the team conspires to put him under anesthesia at home, transport him back to Princeton-Plainsboro, do the surgery, and have him back before he wakes up. However, once at the hospital, Cameron insists on waking him to tell him the truth. Stewart panics, pulls out his central line, and ruins any chance of doing the procedure in the sterile conditions of the hospital. The team has a second chance to get him to the hospital when he goes into cardiac arrest. House gets permission from Stewart's medical proxy to rush him to the hospital, but Cameron uses paddles to start his heart, giving him no reason to leave the apartment.

**Shipper Alert!:** House follows Wilson's advice and visits Cuddy at home at the end of the episode. Resolved to go there "whole" and without his cane, he makes it all the way up to her doorstep. While peering into her window, he loses his nerve. **Shipper Alert #2:** Cameron and Chase have relationship issues when, after months together, Cameron's dead husband continues to get in the way.

**Classic Rant:** House rants about people isolating themselves. "Don't believe your own rationalizations. Don't lock yourself up and pretend you're happy," House admonishes Stewart before realizing that his words apply equally well to himself with regard to Cuddy. Cameron also takes House's words to heart, resolving to open herself to deeper a commitment with Chase.

**Props Department:** When House goes to visit Cuddy, he deliberately leaves the cane at home, trying to present himself as normal as possible.

**Casting Call:** You may recognize character actor Todd Louiso (Stewart) from his roles in *High Fidelity* (2000), *Thank You For Smoking* (2005), and *School for Scoundrels* (2006).

**Title Tale:** House is plagued by a real (or metaphorical) mosquito. He "itches" for Cuddy, but is afraid to scratch.

## 5.08 "Emancipation"

**Writers:** Pamela Davis, Leonard Dick **Director:** James Hayman
**Patient of the Week:** Sophia (Emily Rios)

Sophia is an emancipated minor who collapses while at her factory job, coughing blood. First thinking drug abuse and then infection, the team finally determines that she has leukemia and needs a bone marrow transplant. Knowing the best donors would be her parents, Sophia nonetheless refuses to contact them, claiming that her father raped her while her mother did nothing to stop it. When she deliberately chooses death over contacting her parents, House knows there must be some other secret in Sophia's background — something worse than rape.

In the meantime, Foreman wants to strike out on his own and do clinical trials. He asks House's permission, which is curtly refused. So Foreman tries to prove he can do both House's job and take on additional cases without sacrificing anything. Taking the case of a young boy, with some help from Chase and Cameron, Foreman diagnoses the case. Going back to House, Foreman *tells* him he plans on going ahead with the clinical trials; House puts up no fight this time.

**Zebra of the Week:** Sophia has leukemia, but the real mystery is why she refuses to allow House to contact her parents to donate needed bone marrow for the transplant.

**Epiphany!:** When Sophia decides to die rather than contact her parents, House realizes she's lying about being raped. And to get to the answer he has to confront Sophia.

**Iconic Moment in *House* History:** House confronts Sophia to find out what's happened to her that's "worse than rape." She eventually confesses that her brother drowned while she was supposed be watching him. She ran away soon thereafter, consumed by guilt, and hasn't been in contact with her parents since. House is stunned and gently persuades Sophia that not to contact them, given her situation, would only make matters worse — she would be killing her parents' only living child. It's a wonderful moment that illuminates a side of House few ever see — and the effectivenss of his real bedside manner.

**A Fine Bromance:** Wilson's refusal to give advice about Cuddy oddly annoys and frustrates House.

**Shipper Alert!:** House continues to think about his relationship with Cuddy, seeking advice from Wilson, who suddenly seems unwilling to help.

**Casting Call:** Emily Rios starred as Magdelena in the critically acclaimed independent film *Quinceañera* (2006).

**Title Tale:** Foreman wants emancipation from House, but it's not until House schemes to set Foreman free that he finally gets it. Sophia is an emancipated minor, but still not free of the terrible burden she bears over her brother's death.

## 5.09 "Last Resort"
**Writers:** Matthew Lewis, Eli Attie **Director:** Katie Jacobs
**Patient of the Week:** Jason (Zeljko Ivanek)

Jason is desperate. He's gone to 16 other doctors and no one can figure what's wrong. He can't breathe, he's exhausted, gets skin rashes, has heart palpitations, and can't sleep. He's had enough, and takes House, "13," and several others hostage in Cuddy's office until someone can diagnose him. He wants "the best doctor," and coincidentally he's locked himself in with House. Eventually getting drawn into the case, House thinks he can handle the volatile Jason.

The SWAT team arrives and Jason begins to release some of the hostages in exchange for medical supplies. Jason insists that anything House administers to him is also given to one of the hostages. Thirteen volunteers, continuing the self-destructive spiral she begins in "Lucky 13" (5.09). Eventually leaving Cuddy's office, they set up shop in the MRI room, where House gets Jason to give up his gun so it won't interfere with the MRI. But House is so caught up in Jason's diagnosis that he returns the weapon, allowing Jason to maintain his position and House can continue his diagnosis. But "13" gets sicker and sicker with each new treatment given to Jason and her.

House makes one final diagnosis, but Jason still insists that self-destructive "13" try it first, knowing it will likely kill her. Despite House's pleading, Jason won't let her go in the last moments, sending House out when he agrees to let go a final hostage. Ultimately, he shows mercy to "13" before injecting himself.

**Zebra of the Week:** Melioidosis (*Burkholderia pseudomallei*), a bacterial infection.
**Epiphany!:** Meliodosis explains all of Jason's symptoms, but the bacteria is confined to tropical regions. Jason has insisted he's never been to the tropics. But when they review his travel history, he admits having been to Florida, which is tropical enough.
**Iconic Moment in *House* History:** When he has the opportunity to end the hostage crisis, House returns Jason's gun. It demonstrates the degree to which House's obsession with the answer can affect his judgment. **Iconic Moment #2:** After a self-destructive arc lasting several episodes, "13" concludes that she wants to deal with her disease; she does not want to die.
**House Is a Jerk:** House gives back Jason's gun — continuing to endanger two lives other than his own.

**Shipper Alert!:** In the aftermath of the crisis, House and Cuddy discuss whether she would have reacted differently to the situation had House not been one of the hostages. Does Cuddy urge more caution to the SWAT team commander because House is inside? Nothing overt in the episode suggests that, but it's possible. **Shipper Alert #2:** Foreman tries to convince "13" to enroll in a Huntington's clinical study to begin to do something about her disease. She refuses, not being motivated to help herself. But by the end of the episode, she agrees to enroll in Foreman's study.

**Pop Culture References:** House asks Jason if he's ever seen *Dog Day Afternoon*, the 1975 Al Pacino film about a hostage situation, reminding him how badly that ended.

**Casting Call:** Zeljko Ivanek (Jason) won an Emmy Award for his supporting performance in the television series *Damages*.

**Title Tale:** House is, in essence, a medical court of last resort, and for the desperate Jason, that certainly is true. And taking a room full of hostages is a desperate, "last resort" measure.


## * 5.10 "Let Them Eat Cake"

**Writers:** Garrett Lerner, Russel Friend **Director:** Deran Sarafian

**Patient of the Week:** Emmy (Samantha Shelton)

House treats a weight loss guru who collapses while filming a fitness video. As they diagnose her, the team realizes she has had gastric bypass surgery. Her own weight loss was due not to exercise and diet, but due to surgery. After ruling out nerve and muscle issues, the team thinks lymphoma, but it's not, and the eventual diagnosis is very, very ironic.

The hostage crisis in "Last Resort" (5.09) leaves Cuddy's office damaged and in need of extensive remodeling. She decides to share House's office while she's homeless, and they exchange a series of pranks designed to annoy each other. But do they really mind being in such close quarters? Foreman's clinical work on the Huntingon's study is in full swing, and "13" has enrolled in it, but she is seemingly repulsed by the presence of Janice, another study patient in a more advanced stage of the disease.

Kutner has been running an Internet medical consultation service using House's name and reputation. But DeeDee, one of his patients, is unhappy regarding Kutner's advice on her breast implants. Her hair is now falling out! As Kutner involves Taub and Chase, especially after DeeDee shows up at the hospital. They insist on a large slice of Kutner's pie in exchange for not ratting him out to House. But DeeDee gets sicker, with uncontrollable singing and eventual death.

**Zebra of the Week:** Hereditary coproporphyria causes a lack of a vital enzyme to the liver. The ironic cure for the health guru is a diet high in carbohydrates.

**Epiphany!:** Emmy feels better after she eats a piece of chocolate cake. House realizes something in the cake has treated her condition — the carbs.

**Iconic Moment in *House* History:** House confronts Kutner and Taub in the morgue after DeeDee dies, yelling at them both for their stupidity and Kutner's chutzpa in using his name for his medical site. He has an epiphany and leaps onto the table where DeeDee lies ready for embalming. As he tries to revive her, she suddenly rises. She is alive! And House is delighted with his successful scheme to get back at Kutner, in which he has involved both Chase and Cameron. House had already known about the website and although Kutner's shocked reaction is sweet payback, House wants more: a large cut of the profits.

**Judgmental Fellow Alert:** Taub thinks our patient Emmy is a cheat, having lost a lot of weight through gastric bypass surgery, while making a fortune advocating diet and exercise to her overweight followers.

**Housian Ethics:** How ethical is it for Kutner to set up a medical hotline under House's name, using his reputation?

**Shipper Alert!:** Wilson suggests to Cuddy that she only wants to share House's office (rather than use an empty office elsewhere) to be close to House. He gives similar advice to House. Cuddy is stunned when she returns to her remodeled office to find that someone has substituted her newly ordered desk with her old medical school desk, restored and delivered from her mother's home. She realizes only House could have even known about the desk. But as she approaches his office to thank him, Cuddy observes him in intimate conversation with DeeDee. She backs off, certain that she's misread House's intentions.

**Musical Notes:** DeeDee cannot stop singing Harry Nilsson's "Coconut," which also underscores the episode's final scene as Cuddy approaches House's office.

**Props Department:** The story of House, Cuddy, and the desk is a story still to be told. But there must be some significance that this particular desk holds for them.

**World-Famous Doctor:** Kutner's Internet site uses House's name and reputation to sell its services.

**Casting Call:** Singer/actress Samantha Shelton plays Emmy. She had a supporting role in the 2009 film *Inglorious Basterds*. Lori Petty is introduced in "Let Them Eat Cake" as a Huntington's patient enrolled in Foreman's clinical study. Petty is best known for her role in *A League of Their Own*.

**Title Tale:** Cake is the cure for Emmy's illness.

**Why It's a Classic:** The case is not particularly memorable; the pranks between House and Cuddy are silly. (Although House's gift of the desk reveals his seldom observed romantic streak.) But the side story about the Kutner's fraudulent medical website is one of the funniest in the series.


### 5.11 "Joy to the World"

**Writer:** Peter Blake **Director:** David Straiton
**Patient of the Week:** Natalie (B. K. Cannon)

An overweight teen, Natalie, collapses after becoming dizzy while singing in her school's Christmas concert. The team discovers that her liver is failing and that her classmates have been victimizing her. They wonder whether they are connected, and if her classmates have done something to make her sick. Although the students have given her potentially toxic psychedelic mushrooms, they are not the cause.

The doctors consider alcohol, painkillers (which they find in her locker), and TB contracted in a soup kitchen where she volunteers. But none of these provide the answer either.

As Natalie gets sicker and sicker, she confesses that she had been pregnant after becoming secretly involved with a boy at school. Apparently, Natalie delivered alone and prematurely, abandoning it when she thought the baby was dead. There is nothing more House can do for the young woman, and as Natalie is in her final hours, Cuddy searches the building where Natalie says she abandoned the baby's corpse. There, she finds the infant girl alive, but ill, and in the care of a drug-addicted couple. Rescuing the child, Cuddy brings her to Natalie as she dies. With neither Natalie's parents nor the father's parents willing to adopt the child, Cuddy takes it, applying for foster parent status.

It is Christmas at Princeton-Plainsboro and Kutner discovers a gift for House in the office, something House tosses in the garbage to keep the team wondering who has given it to him. Opening it, they see it's a valuable book, and ask Wilson about it, who realizes it's the gift he gave House the year before — but which he never opened. The team has been pranked.

Foreman continues his work on the Huntington's clinical trial. When "13" notices that Janice, the patient with advanced Huntington's has quit the trial because of a bad reaction, Foreman asks his supervisor about what he can do. He learns, however, that working on double-blind clinical research trials means being completely detached from the patients. "Patients are numbers," the supervisor tells him, revealing she hired him because he works with House and detachment would have certainly been part of his training with the famously detached diagnostician.

**Zebra of the Week:** Eclampsia, an often-fatal complication of pregnancy, can be contracted up to a month after delivery.

**Epiphany!:** After House treats a pregnant woman in the clinic, Cuddy suddenly realizes Natalie's symptoms add up to eclampsia — she must have recently given birth.

**Iconic Moment in *House* History:** Cuddy finally has her baby. Her quest for motherhood, begun at the end of season two, is now realized. **Iconic Moment #2:** We learn that the affable, cuddly Kutner was once a bully as events in the episode compel him to apologize to one of his victims.

**Clinic Duty:** House treats a pregnant woman who insists she can't be pregnant because she and her boyfriend practice abstinence. House lies to the couple that their baby is a virgin birth, created by parthenogenesis. House also treats a woman who doesn't quite know how to use her inhaler. It's everything House can do to keep from laughing as she demonstrates, puffing it on herself as she would perfume.

**A Fine Bromance:** Wilson bets that House is incapable of being nice enough to earn a gift from a patient. But House plays nice, giving a grand Christmas gift to a clinic patient (see "Clinic Duty" entry), earning him a gift — and winning the bet.

**House Is a Jerk:** House never opened Wilson's Christmas gift from a year earlier, and now uses it to play mind games with his staff. He also lies to his gullible clinic patient that she has experienced Immaculate Conception so he can win the bet made with Wilson.

**Shipper Alert!:** House looks in on Cuddy as she watches over the baby in the hospital. He lingers a while, wishes her a quiet Merry Christmas, and leaves.

**Shipper Alert #2:** Foreman and "13" draw closer as she continues treatment in the Huntington's trial.

**Pop Culture References:** The "secret" gift to House is a copy of Dr. Joseph Bell's *On Surgery*. Bell was Sir Arthur Conan Doyle's mentor. Conan Doyle wrote the Sherlock Holmes stories. Wilson tells Kutner an elaborate lie about how House got the book, explaining about a patient named Irene Adler and House's obsession with her. Adler is often considered "the one who got away" in the Holmes stories.

**Casting Call:** Sherilyn Fenn, who plays Natalie's mother, may be best known for her role as Audrey Horne on David Lynch's cult classic television series *Twin Peaks* from 1990 to 1991.

**Title Tale:** "Joy to the World" is season five's Christmas episode. It brings "joy" to

Cuddy's world as she finally gets her baby. It also brings joy to the young, naive clinic couple who now believe their baby is the result of a Christmas miracle.

## 5.12 "Painless"
**Writers:** Thomas L. Moran, Eli Attie **Director:** Andrew Bernstein
**Patient of the Week:** Jeff (Martin Henderson)

Jeff, a young family man, suffers from intractable chronic pain, despite treatment with narcotics. After three years with no diagnosis and a bleak future, Jeff "just wants it to be over," attempting suicide before his wife brings him to the Princeton-Plainsboro Emergency Room. Treating him in the ER, Cameron refers Jeff to House, believing that treating someone in even more pain than he is would be a beneficial lesson.

At first, the team thinks Jeff's pain is mental, since no doctor has been able to diagnose a cause. But House orders a pain profile and sends the team to search his home for an environmental cause.

Jeff attempts to kill himself twice more while in the hospital. Eventually his wife appeals to House, asking him to stabilize and then discharge her husband so he can go home and finally end his life. Jeff's case comes while House is experiencing intensified leg pain. House agrees to the wife's request, unsure whether he, himself, wouldn't consider suicide under the same circumstances.

Elsewhere around the hospital, Cuddy tries to balance being both dean of medicine and a new mother, with limited success, while House deals with a serious plumbing problem in his apartment. And Kutner wonders why Taub is so unsympathetic to Jeff, asking him whether he, or someone close to him, has ever attempted or committed suicide. Although "13" seems to be doing well on the clinical trial, Foreman discovers by the end of the episode that she is actually on the placebo.

**Zebra of the Week:** Epilepsy.
**Epiphany!:** House observes his plumber scratching his crotch. He realizes that epilepsy may have rewired Jeff's pain neurons. Testing would not have detected this if it originated too deeply in the brain, like the area controlling testicular muscles. House confirms that Jeff's pain started near the scrotum.
**Iconic Moment in *House* History:** House's battle with his leaky pipes is amusing. He discovers the problem as he hears water dripping. Seeing a spot on his ceiling, House gingerly probes the area with his cane — but not gingerly enough. Water pours from above, drenching him as he stands there stunned.
**Patients Know Best:** Jeff reminds House of his likely future, noticing that House

is having a particularly "bad day." House responds by swallowing a pill, but Jeff suggests that there will come a time when the pills no longer help.

**Housian Ethics:** Is House right to discharge Jeff, knowing that he's certainly going to kill himself the first chance he gets?

**Shipper Alert!:** Wilson brings Cuddy a large stuffed duck for the new baby.

**Pop Culture References:** The episode's title "Painless" refers to the theme song from the film and hit 1970s–1980s television series *M\*A\*S\*H*, "Suicide Is Painless." Although it's not quite as pervasive a *House* theme as "pain," suicide has been tackled several times during the show's run.

**Musical Notes:** House reminds the plumber not to touch his piano — twice.

**Casting Call:** New Zealander Martin Henderson (Jeff) played to rave reviews opposite Juliette Lewis in London's West End in *Fool for Love* (2006).

**Title Tale:** House's own pain is a major series trope, and he seems to have hit another bad patch now.


## 5.13 "Big Baby"

**Writers:** David Foster, Lawrence Kaplow **Director:** Deran Sarafian

**Patient of the Week:** Sarah (Erika Flores)

Sarah is an infinitely patient special education teacher. She collapses at work after coughing blood. Although the team initially believes she has potentially fatal bleeding issues, House eventually concludes it's in her brain. The team disputes him, thinking the chronically cynical House wants to prove her patience is a symptom, not part of her personality.

Cuddy, trying to deal with new motherhood, puts Cameron in charge of the hospital and — more importantly — House. House immediately tries to test Cameron's resolve, but Cameron believes she's up to playing House's game. When House wants to do a risky brain procedure, however, he is able to persuade Cameron to assist him with it.

Cuddy is having problems adjusting to motherhood, as she fails to "instabond" with her daughter. Wilson is sympathetic, but House wonders if she should simply give up on it and return the baby, who would be too young to be traumatized by the experience.

Now that Foreman has discovered that "13" is on the placebo in the drug trial, he is tempted to subvert the study and put her on "the real stuff." He seeks everyone's advice, including House's. House does a rational cost-benefit for Foreman, adding, however, if you love someone, "you do stupid things." Foreman switches her to the "real stuff" at the episode's end.

**Zebra of the Week:** Patent ductus arteriosis. The ductus is open during fetal development, but normally closes at birth. Sarah's has remained opened. It causes her neurological symptoms as well as low blood pressure when she's under stress.

**Epiphany!:** Sarah is annoyed when she hears Cuddy's baby screaming in the background while she sits in on a procedure via speakerphone. Although Sarah is annoyed and under stress, her blood pressure lowers: the opposite of what's expected. House wonders why until Cuddy's baby spits up on him. Cuddy is amused, which sends House into a rant about human development. He realizes Sarah's problem is developmental.

**Iconic Moment in *House* History:** Cameron quits as Cuddy's replacement. She says as a doctor trained by House, he's always in her head. She will always understand the merits of his arguments — even when she shouldn't.

**House Is a Jerk:** House suggests the answer to Cuddy's "failure to bond" problem is to give the baby back.

**Housian Ethics:** Foreman breaks his study protocol to help "13."

**Shipper Alert!:** Cuddy visits the hospital, missing her "other" baby: Princeton-Plainsboro. She stops in at House's office with the baby. Placing her in House's hands, Cuddy hopes they'll bond. They actually do — until the baby spits up on him. Cuddy thinks it's cute. She's right.

**Casting Call:** As a teenage actress, Erika Flores (Sarah) played Colleen Cooper on the CBS show *Dr. Quinn, Medicine Woman* (1993–1995).

**Title Tale:** The episode revolves around Cuddy's bonding issues, House's potential for being a big, bratty baby, and Sarah's medical problem.


## 5.14 "The Greater Good"
**Writer:** Sarah Hess **Director:** Leslie Linka Glatter
**Patient of the Week:** Dana (Judith Scott)

Dana is a former cancer researcher, retired after being treated for uterine cancer. She suddenly collapses at her cooking class, her lips turning blue, and she's rushed to Princeton-Plainsboro. She presents with spontaneous pneumothorax. As the team considers a series of lung issues, Dana starts to bleed internally and blood seeps through her skin and from her nose and eyes.

As the team diagnoses her, each of the fellows, and Wilson, an admirer of Dana's research, cannot understand why she would retire from such important work, giving it up for cooking. They begin to examine their own happiness from her perspective. Taub asks his wife to reconsider a decision never to have kids; Wilson wonders about moving past Amber.

Cuddy, blaming House for her premature return from motherhood leave, executes a series of mean-spirited pranks to exact revenge. But no matter what she does, House refuses to engage her, content to let Cuddy "punch [herself] out," if it means that things will go back to normal between them.

With "13" now on the real Huntington's medicine, she begins to exhibit adverse effects. Her vision declines and she eventually goes blind.

**Zebra of the Week:** Ectopic endometriosis. When the surgeons cut through Dana's uterine wall during her previous cancer surgery, endometrial cells leaked into her bloodstream causing menstrual bleeding from multiple sites in her body.

**Epiphany!:** When Cuddy apologizes for the pranks, House sarcastically wonders if she has premenstrual syndrome (PMS). House gets a brainstorm and makes the connection with Dana's symptoms.

**Iconic Moment in *House* History:** House appeals to "13" not to let her anger at Foreman cause her to "torch his career" by going to the pharmaceutical company running the clinical trial and confess to subverting it.

**A Fine Bromance:** Wilson wonders why House hasn't schemed to pay Cuddy back for her pranks.

**Shipper Alert!:** After the pranks are over, House reverts from accepting to snarky. Cuddy wonders if he's just slipping back into the role he feels he must play with her.

**Did You Know?:** This is the milestone 100th episode of *House*.

**Pop Culture References:** "Shocks without shock, an itch that won't stop," remarks House, describing Dana's syptoms. Paging Dr. Seuss!

**Casting Call:** Judith Scott appeared in the 2006–2007 season of Showtime's *Dexter* as Lieutenant Esme Pasquale.

**Title Tale:** Dana is doing "what she wants to do, and not what she's expected to do," now valuing happiness in her life over serving the "greater good" of research. By tampering with the clinical study, Foreman sacrifices the greater good of the clinical trial for his self interest in saving "13's" life. However, by saving her life, Foreman potentially sacrifices his relationship with "13," as Stacy did when she saved House's life at the time of the infarction. Both were willing to risk their relationships and their personal happiness by serving the greater good of saving the life of a loved one.

## * 5.15 "Unfaithful"

**Writer:** David Hoselton **Director:** Greg Yaitanes
**Patient of the Week:** Daniel (Jimmi Simpson)

Daniel is a disillusioned priest. Accused of child molestation four years earlier, he has been transferred from parish to parish and when we meet him, he is a wreck of a man. Opening the door on a cold snowy night, he is greeted by the vision of a bleeding Jesus. Seriously freaked out, he goes to the Princeton-Plainsboro Teaching Hospital Emergency Room. House takes the case only as a diversion, while demanding that Foreman and "13" either break up or resign, having decided that their relationship is affecting the department.

Finding nothing wrong with Daniel except the easily dismissed hallucinations, the team is ready to discharge him as an alcoholic. Except for one teensy tiny problem. Daniel's toe, completely necrotized, falls off, turning Daniel into a real case. The team diagnoses AIDS, but Daniel insists that he has always been celibate — the child molestation charges are false.

Cuddy prepares to welcome her baby, Rachel, into her religious heritage with a *simchat bat* (literally, rejoicing the daughter) ceremony. Cuddy's ambivalence about inviting House to the ceremony is only matched by his ambivalence about going. Ultimately she tells him she doesn't want him there, and he agrees that he doesn't want to be there. They are both lying.

**Zebra of the Week:** The genetic condition Wiskott-Aldrich syndrome, like AIDS, suppresses the immune system.

**Epiphany!:** When an angry rash appears on Daniel's chest, House revisits symptoms on the whiteboard. Wilson interrupts to change his mind about the *simchat bat*. "Overlook her hypocrisy," Wilson counsels. Instead, House rethinks the diagnostic process, overlooking the symptom that brought Daniel to House in the first place — something House would never do. But by eliminating the religious vision as an alcoholic hallucination, the constellation of symptoms finally makes sense.

**Iconic Moment in *House* History:** Daniel considers the convergence of coincidences that has saved his life. House argues that every coincidence can be rationally explained. "That's a lot of coincidences," Daniel argues, quoting Einstein: "Coincidences are God's way of remaining anonymous" — words that leave House reflective and quiet.

**A Fine Bromance:** Wilson urges House to attend the ceremony, but House continues to insist that the Cuddy is being hypocritical. He has no intention of feeding her hypocrisy.

**Judgmental Fellow Alert:** The team, especially Taub, assumes the worst of Daniel, dismissing his insistence that the molestation accusation is false.

**Patients Know Best:** Daniel points out House's hypocrisy, telling him that his uncaring attitude is a pretense. "You say you don't care about people, but yet here you are, saving lives." He accuses House of wanting his cynical worldview to be proven wrong: "You want to believe," he insists.

**Housian Ethics:** Believing that Daniel has AIDS, Taub finds Daniel's alleged molestation victim and tells him that he should get tested. Taub has violated Daniel's privacy — and confidentiality.

**Shipper Alert!:** Wilson and Cameron know Cuddy wants House at the *simchat bat*, recognizing how the two feel about each other despite anything they might say. Even the patient, Daniel, observes that House has a "thing" for his boss.

**Did You Know?:** "Cuddy's Serenade," played by House at the episode's end, was composed by series star Hugh Laurie.

**Musical Notes:** The episode's final montage qualifies as an "iconic moment" as well as musical moment. As Rachel's naming ceremony goes on, House sits alone in his apartment at the piano. He plays an evocative composition, filled with Judaic celebratory musical themes and lullabies, which segue eventually into the Rolling Stones song "You Can't Always Get What You Want" (practically a *House* anthem). The piece perfectly underscores both House and Cuddy's emotions.

**Casting Call:** Jimmi Simpson may look familiar if you watch *Late Night with David Letterman* on CBS. He appeared intermittently through 2009 as Lyle the Intern.

**Title Tale:** The episode is about the nature of faith, God, and religious practice.

**Why It's a Classic:** Exploring familiar House themes of religion, belief, and hypocrisy, "Unfaithful" also does a fine job of elaborating on House and Cuddy's interesting relationship.

---

### Coincidence vs. Divine Intervention: A Closer Look at "Unfaithful"

Albert Einstein once said, "Coincidence is God's way of remaining anonymous." What is it that brings a disillusioned priest with a rare, but hidden (and incurable) medical condition to the attention of a master diagnostician on a cold winter night? Who is to say whether it's coincidence or an anonymous God opening small doors of oblique opportunity that brings Daniel into House's den? Are his visions of Jesus a simple whiskey-soaked hallucination, or the hidden miracle of coincidence? By the end of "Unfaithful" (5.16), neither the atheist priest nor the atheist doctor is completely certain anymore.

Amused by the notion of a disillusioned priest, House decides to meet the man face-to-face, his "ridicule muscle" at the ready. But the priest's bitter words — and his rant against the pain and suffering inflicted by a cruel God who has forsaken the world (and him personally) — strike a resonant chord in House. Daniel's words could just have easily come out of House's mouth, and have in one way or another over the course of the years we've known him. But when House is only able to diagnose Daniel correctly after eliminating the one symptom that brought him to the hospital, Daniel's faith is restored. House knows he has arrived at the answer through science and reason. But Daniel wonders at the convergence of circumstance that has saved his life. House argues that everything can be rationally explained and can be interpreted as mere coincidence. Ah, but Daniel counters, quoting Einstein on God and coincidence: "That's a lot of coincidences." It is something that leaves House uncharacteristically quiet and thoughtful.

Two episodes closely following "Unfaithful" continue to explore this theme.

In "Here Kitty" (5.18) House treats Morgan, who insists she's dying because a psychic cat sleeps next to her. House spends most of the episode trying to diagnose the rational/scientific reason for the cat's strange and prophetic behavior. And of course he's successful: there is a perfectly rational — and mortal — explanation. House figures it out just in time to rescue Morgan from a dangerous — and unnecessary — brain surgery as the cat chooses just the right moment to leap onto House's computer keyboard. To House, it's coincidence. But, like Daniel in "Unfaithful," Morgan wonders if there might have been divine intervention by an anonymous God.

In "Locked In" (5.19) House encounters Lee, who is lying immobile on a gurney in a New York emergency room. Involved in a bicycle accident, Lee seems all but dead. His ER doctor has diagnosed a fatal brain stem injury and is already assessing his organs for donation. But chance has placed House in the same ER suite at Middletown General Hospital, having been in a motorcycle accident.

House believes Lee has "locked-in syndrome," and is not brain-dead. The ER doctor accuses him of "wishful thinking," but House is able take over Lee's case, transport him back to Princeton, and set to work on saving Lee's life. In "Locked In" we view House mostly through Lee's eyes, which conventional wisdom would suggest is frightening point of view.

Lee insists that God has sent House to him, which plays out in Lee's mindscape. House is with Lee in every fearful moment. In Lee's "quiet place," whether it is with the cool MRI glasses or in Lee's dreams, House is there as guide and guardian. He is there to see Lee through his ordeal — whether relaxing on a sandy beach as he watches his children build sand castles, or discussing philosophy cynic to skeptic. To Lee, House has been sent to rescue him from certain death, listening to him when (literally) no one could — or would.

Coincidence or divine intervention? It depends on your point of view and your belief system.

## 5.16: "The Softer Side"

**Writer:** Liz Friedman **Director:** Deran Sarafian
**Patient of the Week:** Jackson (Dominic Scott Kay)

The team treats Jackson, a boy born with both male and female DNA (genetic mosaicism) and genitalia. At his birth, the parents made the medical decision to perform surgery and raise Jackson as a boy. While playing basketball, Jackson collapses with severe stomach pain. The team tries to determine what's wrong, and if it's connected to either physical or psychological issues related to his gender. House immediately rules out a "blind uterus," a female vestige from Jackson's original surgery. But surprisingly, when the parents insist on doing an MRI to test for it, House agrees.

Wilson, Cuddy, and the entire team wonder why House is being so agreeable — not only with Jackson's parents, but in general. Wilson and Foreman speculate that House is experimenting with heroin, especially after his breathing suddenly stops while resting in his office. But it's not heroin; it's methadone. And when Wilson and Cuddy find out they are furious, insisting he immediately stop using it. Given a choice between methadone or his job, House chooses methadone. He has to: it completely eliminates his leg pain.

Meanwhile, "13" and Foreman launch a charade that they've broken up to appease House, who has insisted they break up or quit.

**Zebra of the Week:** Dehydration, an easy explanation, missed after House agrees to the parents' request to perform an MRI to look for a "blind uterus."
**Epiphany!:** House realizes all of Jackson's symptoms can be traced to his decision to perform the MRI — and simple dehydration.

**Iconic Moment in *House* History:** Returning home after quitting Princeton-Plainsboro over the methadone issue, House embarks on a new life. He shaves, dresses for "success," and heads to an interview at another hospital. **Iconic Moment #2:** Concerned about his too-nice-for-House behavior, Wilson and Cuddy go to confront House in his office and find that he has stopped breathing. Foreman, noting that House's heart is still beating, believes all he has to do is send a pain signal to the brain to revive him. Twisting House's nipple is painful enough and the shock causes House to wake up gasping for air.

**Clinic Duty:** House is nice in the clinic after Cuddy sends him the most idiotic patients she can to test if he's really had a personality change. One of the patients has a pain everywhere he touches: his leg, his arm. It turns out the pain is actually in his finger — it's broken. But House doesn't mock him. Something must be terribly wrong!

**A Fine Bromance:** Wilson takes House out for a burger — and a drug lecture.

**Judgmental Fellow Alert:** Wilson jumps to the conclusion that House is on heroin because he's happy (which must mean he's "high"). Both he and Cuddy insist he quit methadone (which has been used as a legitimate drug in chronic pain management) or lose his job. House angrily asserts that Wilson always assumes the worst of him, offering him a bourbon (a respiratory depressant) after he's just been in respiratory distress to prove he's on heroin. House downs the shot and walks away in a huff.

**Housian Ethics:** Do Wilson and Cuddy have the right to decide House's legitimate pain management needs for him? Cuddy makes him choose between being pain free and keeping his job. When House chooses to quit, she asks him accusingly if he's really choosing methadone over his job. But House corrects her. "I'm choosing lack of pain over this job." He's not using drugs to "get high"; he uses them to manage severe pain.

**Shipper Alert!:** Wilson assumes House's good mood is because he and Cuddy have had sex. **Shipper Alert #2:** In the end, Cuddy comes to House to administer the methadone, finally agreeing to it. But House has changed his mind, believing that the drug, while making his physical pain go away, has dulled his edge to the point that he missed an easy diagnosis. Cuddy begs him to reconsider. But he tells her, "This is the only 'me' you get." **Shipper Alert #3:** Foreman asks "13" if she misses sex with women.

**Props Department:** No longer feeling any pain, House walks away from the clinic twirling his cane à la Charlie Chaplin.

**Casting Call:** Child actor Dominic Scott Kay played Will Scott, son to Orlando Bloom's and Keira Knightley's characters, in *Pirates of the Caribbean: At World's End* (2007).

**Title Tale:** We see House's "softer side," while Jackson's parents have always fretted about his "softer side."

## * 5.17 "The Social Contract"

**Writer:** Doris Egan **Director:** Andrew Bernstein
**Patient of the Week:** Nick (Jay Karnes)

Nick is a book editor who suddenly finds that he lacks any social filters. He cannot help himself from berating everyone from his prize author to his wife — even his daughter. House and the team try to determine what's causing Nick's symptoms, which worsen markedly as the team continues to diagnose him. Nick is obnoxious to everyone: he leers, makes a sexist remark, and calls both his wife and daughter stupid.

Meanwhile, House is curious when Wilson tries to keep a secret after turning down House's invitation to a monster truck rally. But nothing can prevent House from learning the truth and when he discovers that Wilson has found his schizophrenic brother Danny, missing for at least 13 years, House offers to accompany him when he visits his brother for the first time in years.

**Zebra of the Week:** Doege-Potter syndrome. Nick has a benign tumor on his lung that secretes human growth hormone. But an infection picked up from the family dog has caused damage near Nick's brainstem, resulting in his personality changes, something only dangerous brain surgery can reverse.

**Epiphany!:** House believes Wilson has overreacted to Danny's disappearance ever since, realizing that Nick's problem is also an overreaction — his body's autoimmune response to the various treatments given to him during his stay at Princeton-Plainsboro.

**Iconic Moment in *House* History:** With brain damage from the infection, an elective surgery to reverse the damage is extremely dangerous and could easily kill Nick. He appeals to House, willing to take the risk — insisting that he can't continue to live as a jerk. House asks Chase to perform the surgery, but Chase demands to know why House cares, especially now that the case is solved and Nick is ready to be discharged. House passionately argues that Nick will suffer without the surgery: without the ability to filter his thoughts, his family and friends will abandon him. House is clearly talking about himself.

**A Fine Bromance:** House approaches the question of Wilson's brother Daniel with quiet compassion, friendship, and sympathy that we rarely witness in him — that is, after House has invaded Wilson's privacy to learn all he can about Wilson's secret. From the small gesture of getting Wilson a cup of coffee to his assurance that Daniel's condition is not Wilson's fault, House is being a good friend — in his own way.

**House Is a Jerk:** House is a jerk to Taub, trying to find out if he really has a racquetball date with Wilson.

**Shipper Alert!:** House pages Cuddy to the MRI room, where Nick is making leering comments to "13." But when Cuddy enters, Nick focuses on her attributes instead. Cuddy leaves in a huff, realizing that House set her up. But House wonders if she isn't a bit flattered, knowing that Nick would prefer the more mature and curvy Cuddy to "13."

**Casting Call:** Jay Karnes played Detective Holland Wagenbach on the FX Network series *The Shield* (2002–2008).

**Title Tale:** "Does it bother you that we have no social contract?" House asks Wilson regarding the unique nature of their relationship. While exploring the necessity of the social niceties and collaborative lies we sometimes need in order to survive in society, the story provides a framework for examining House and Wilson's personalities and their deep friendship — and their own somewhat perverse "social contract."

**Why It's a Classic:** The story of Wilson's brother is picked up from season one.


### 5.18 "Here Kitty"

**Writer:** Peter Blake **Director:** Juan J. Campanella
**Patient of the Week:** Morgan (Judy Greer)

Morgan, a nurse at a nursing home, fakes a seizure to see House, bringing with her a cat she says has been predicting imminent deaths at the home. She has no symptoms, but claims that the cat slept near her the night before and she's afraid she will be the next to die. Cuddy and Taub believe she's a Munchausen's sufferer and should be discharged, but House wants to exploit the situation to debunk Morgan and her cat. But Morgan is actually sick, and she believes the cat proves she's going to die. Eventually, House discovers the rational reason for the cat's prophet-like behavior, and saves Morgan from unnecessary brain surgery in the process.

Taub is having financial woes and is getting tired of being a House underling. When a supposed old high school friend turns up in the clinic, Taub sees a way out for himself after learning his friend is the CEO of a surgical device company.

**Zebra of the Week:** A corticotrophin-producing tumor in Morgan's appendix.
**Epiphany!:** The cat had briefly disappeared, but when it reappears late at night in House's office, it jumps onto his laptop computer. He realizes that it's not

death the cat's seeking, it's the warmth emanating from warming blankets and feverish dying people, both of which are commonly present in nursing homes.

**Iconic Moment in *House* History:** House holds the cat, cigar in his mouth, and does dead-on imitation of Auric Goldfinger: "No, Mr. Bond, I expect you to die." One problem: Goldfinger didn't have a cat. Another Bond archenemy Ernst Blofeld had a cat. House has mixed his Bond metaphors.

**Clinic Duty:** A very bored Dr. House constructs an elaborate motor speedway for his Matchbox car in a clinic exam room.

**House Is a Jerk:** House learns Kutner is afraid of cats. He hides the cat in the fellow's backpack, which freaks him out when he tries to pick it up. He also exploits Kutner's superstitious nature by rigging the office with ladders, salt, and other "old wives' superstition" paraphernalia. House also blows cigar smoke into the patient's face, trying to elicit a symptom while diagnosing her.

**Classic Rant:** House lectures Morgan about superstition and belief in cats that usher dying people "to the other side." But she counters that something made the cat climb on House's computer just in time to save her from brain surgery. Coincidence? Or God working in mysterious ways?

**Did You Know?:** Debbie the cat is based on a real cat named Oscar, who also seemed to predict the deaths of nursing home patients in Rhode Island.

**Pop Culture References:** House's Goldfinger imitation conflates two James Bond villains: Ernst Blofeld and Auric Goldfinger.

**Casting Call:** Judy Greer (Morgan) had a recurring role on the television series *Arrested Development*. She played George Bluth Sr.'s partner-in-crime Kitty Sanchez from 2003 to 2005.

**Title Tale:** The title obviously refers to Debbie the cat, but also to Taub being beckoned into a financial scam by his old chum.


### * 5.19 "Locked In"

**Writers:** David Foster, Russel Friend, Garrett Lerner **Director:** Daniel Attias
**Patient of the Week:** Lee (Mos Def)

House encounters Lee while being treated in an emergency room after crashing his motorcycle in New York. The ER doctor has diagnosed severe brain stem injury and is ready to declare Lee organ-donor material. House intervenes, noting subtle activity on Lee's monitor, disagreeing with the ER doctor, and arguing that Lee is "locked in" and cannot move; he can only blink. There is something interfering with his brain.

House takes over the case at the request of Lee's wife and brings him back to Princeton-Plainsboro to find the cause of his condition. But diagnosis is nearly impossible with Lee only able to respond to "yes and no" questions.

The team, especially Wilson, wonders why House was in New York. He deflects, refusing to give a straight answer. But ultimately Wilson discovers that House had been to see a psychiatrist. The question is "why?"

The episode allows us to see House (and the rest of the team) through the patient's eyes. It's a unique perspective as the camera also takes us into Lee's mind allowing us to understand House as Lee sees him: as an agent of God sent to save his life.

**Zebra of the Week:** Leptospirosis infection contracted from rat urine through a paper cut.

**Epiphany!:** Kutner notices a rash on "13's" wrist after she came into contact with Lee's urine while tending to his catheter. Knowing that Lee has worked in a dirty basement, Kutner realizes that there must have been rats.

**Iconic Moment in *House* History:** After Wilson discovers that House is seeing a psychiatrist, House immediately erases the phone number from his cell phone. He's not going back, he tells Wilson, stepping into the elevator on his way home. "Whining on somebody's couch. That's an excellent use of my time," he retorts when Wilson congratulates him on finally doing something about his misery. But Wilson offers a dire warning, foreshadowing the conclusion of season five and most of season six. "You'll be alone." The doors close as House's vision goes blurry. Is House "locked in" as well?

**A Fine Bromance:** Wilson goes to House-like extremes to unwrap the mystery behind House's trip to New York.

**House Is a Jerk:** House is down on Taub, calling him useless and unnecessary. He demands that Taub produce some sort of creative solution to Lee's diagnostic dilemma or be fired. Although Taub comes up with a novel — and critical — idea to communicate with Lee, House refuses to credit him even for this. It is only when Taub proves that he's willing to steal credit from Kutner that House believes he really wants his job.

**Shipper Alert!:** Cuddy is very concerned seeing the banged-up House walking alongside Lee's gurney. Lee notes that Cuddy is "into" House. **Shipper Alert #2:** Cameron tends to House's wounds, knowing that he would never do it himself.

**Metaphorically Speaking:** House describes the liver as a cruise ship taking on water.

**Casting Call:** Lee is played by actor-rapper Mos Def who received an Emmy nomination for *Something the Lord Made* (2004).

**Title Tale:** Lee and House are "locked in" in different ways.

**Why It's a Classic:** House viewed through the patient's eyes offers a unique perspective.

## * 5.20 "Simple Explanation"

**Writer:** Leonard Dick **Director:** Greg Yaitanes
**Patients of the Week:** Charlotte (Colleen Camp), Eddie (Meat Loaf)

Eddie has terminal cancer and as his wife and their friends say their goodbyes to him on his deathbed, Charlotte is suddenly stricken by respiratory distress. But the medical mystery is almost irrelevant in this episode as an early scene reveals that House's fellow Lawrence Kutner has committed suicide. The team tries to diagnose Charlotte while dealing with their grief over Kutner's death, trying to make sense of his senseless act.

Although "13" believes they should pass on the case, House wonders how many cases it will take before "it's okay that Kutner's dead." As each of Kutner's colleagues react to his death and try to move on, House tries not to react and is unable to move on. He attempts to find meaning in the meaningless and a reason for something that has none.

**Zebra of the Week:** Eddie has cardiac blastomycosis brought on by a fungus infection. His condition is treatable. Charlotte's has leishmaniasis, an infection contracted during a trip to Rio. But it's too late by the time the team diagnoses it; she dies.

**Epiphany!:** Cameron notices nodules on Eddie's fingers; House realizes that Charlotte must have been on a secret trip to the tropics.

**Iconic Moment in *House* History:** Foreman and "13" discover Kutner's body in his apartment.

**Clinic Duty:** House treats a very young beauty pageant contestant who has been downing mommy's alcohol-containing mouthwash and swallowing it (just like mommy does).

**A Fine Bromance:** When Wilson sees House obviously distraught over the suicide, Wilson suggests that they get plastered in a bar. But watching House wander around Kutner's apartment looking for clues, almost wraith-like, Wilson believes that it's not Kutner's death upsetting House: it's that House missed any sign of it. "You're terrified of losing your gift, about losing yourself." Wilson is worried what House might do in that event. (And his fears are justified in this bit of foreshadowing.)

**House Is a Jerk:** House insults Kutner's grieving parents, telling them that they probably never understood their son.

**Housian Ethics:** Eddie wants to "die" on the table so that he can donate his liver to Charlotte.

**Shipper Alert!:** Cuddy tries to console House, telling him it's understandable that he's upset — something he completely denies. House knows that she's worried about him, believing that the case is the only thing holding him together.

**Casting Call:** Eddie is played by Meat Loaf, an iconic rocker, who starred as another "Eddie" in the cult classic film *The Rocky Horror Picture Show* (1975).

**Title Tale:** There are some things for which simple explanations exist, but then there are other things that defy explanation, like suicide.

**Why It's a Classic:** A powerfully told story. No further explanation necessary.


## 5.21 "Saviors"

**Writers:** Thomas L. Moran, Eli Attie **Director:** Matthew Penn
**Patient of the Week:** Doug (Tim Rock)

Cameron brings House the case of a radical environmentalist who is suddenly unable to walk as the police try to arrest him at a protest. Doug has sacrificed his family life and his relationship with his wife for his cause. He rationalizes that his passion for the environment is for his son — and all future generations. But his medical problem originates in a marital problem — an ironic ailment.

In order to work on the case with House's team, Cameron has forced Chase to postpone their planned vacation, something about which Chase is not too happy. He believes Cameron is still conflicted in her feelings about House, and she is reluctant to move their relationship forward. But the explanation is simpler as the House and the entire team continue to grapple with Kutner's death.


**Zebra of the Week:** A sporotrichosis infection contracted from the thorns of a commercial bouquet of roses.

**Epiphany!:** House concludes that all marriages suck, including Doug's. He wonders if his patient might have violated his own ethics by buying his wife a bouquet of environmentally unfriendly commercial flowers after a quarrel.

**Iconic Moment in *House* History:** At the end of the episode, case solved, House sits at his piano. He looks up from the keys. . . to find *the dead* Amber staring at him.

**Clinic Duty:** House treats a domineering woman with a rash.

**A Fine Bromance:** Wilson mysteriously starts eating a healthy diet — much to House's dismay. But it's with good reason: he's trying to provide House with a puzzle to solve, wanting House to "get back to normal" in the aftermath of Kutner's death.

**Shipper Alert!:** Cameron stalls taking a vacation with Chase because she knows he is about to propose. In the aftermath of Kutner's suicide, she thinks Chase is being impulsive. Finally, Cameron tells Chase the truth — and he proposes. She accepts. **Shipper Alert #2:** Chase asks Cuddy if Cameron's still in love with House. Then he asks if she's in love with him. This sends Cuddy to visit House in the clinic, wondering what's up between him and Cameron.

**Musical Moments:** House tries to lose himself at the end of the episode, playing "Georgia on My Mind" on the piano. It works until he looks up to see the ghost of Amber.

**Casting Call:** Tim Rock is a Chicago-based stage actor, a product of the Steppenwolf Theatre, the renowned repertory company founded by Gary Sinise that has been the theatrical home to numerous acclaimed actors over the last 30 years, including John Malkovich, John Mahoney, William Petersen, and Joan Allen.

**Title Tale:** Doug considers himself a "savior" of the environment, willing to risk it all for his cause; Wilson is House's savior, leaving the cookie crumbs of an elaborate mystery for House to follow, solve — and put things back to "normal."

## * 5.22 "House Divided"

**Writers:** Liz Friedman, Matthew Lewis **Director:** Greg Yaitanes
**Patient of the Week:** Seth (Ryan Lane)

House and the team treat wrestler Seth, a deaf teenager who collapses at a high school meet. As he tries to diagnose Seth's condition, House is trailed by the hallucinated Amber. House believes her presence is due to insomnia, and he obtains a prescription for sleeping pills from Wilson. Planning on going home to sleep, House become intrigued when he discovers that through his hallucination he has access to the remote and inaccessible regions of his brain, and he tosses the sleeping pills in the garbage.

Although Amber goads him into inserting a cochlear implant in Seth's ear without consent, she also provides House with the clues to diagnose and cure the deaf teen — to a point.

Meanwhile, learning that Cameron has asked Wilson to plan Chase's bachelor party, House takes over and plans an elaborate and wild affair, complete with strippers, a flaming fountain of alcohol, and loud music. Wilson wants no part of the festivities, but he has no choice: the party is at his apartment!

But the party comes to an abrupt end when Chase suffers a severe allergic reaction. House blames Amber and decides he must rid himself of the hallucination before he does any real damage. Going back to his apartment, House removes himself from the case — and finally gets that prescription for sleeping pills.

**Zebra of the Week:** Sarcoidosis, an inflammatory disease with the potential to affect several organ systems. It results from a failure of the body's immune system and normal inflammatory response to attack and destroy invading harmful agents.

**Epiphany!:** Foreman notices tobacco stains on Seth's teeth. Chewing tobacco hid the sarcoidosis symptoms — until Seth only recently stopped chewing to "cut weight" for wrestling.

**Iconic Moment in *House* History:** Chase's bachelor party is a wild and crazy affair with House as the convivial MC. But he soon disappears, preferring the solitude of Wilson's bathtub and a bottle to the party atmosphere **Iconic Moment #2:** House prepares for the party by practicing the flaming booze trick in the morgue. He sets a corpse on fire, demonstrating Hugh Laurie's agility and gift for physical comedy.

**A Fine Bromance:** Why is House hallucinating Wilson's dead girlfriend? Also, Wilson, so resistant to the very notion of House's party, seems to have great time — and somehow loses his trousers in the midst of it.

**Housian Ethics:** House should not have performed the cochlear implant surgery on Seth without consent.

**Shipper Alert!:** Cameron tells the guys to take care of Chase when he's "kidnapped" for the party. **Shipper Alert #2:** Foreman and the bisexual "13" check out female strippers at House's request. They take turns admiring the scenery.

**Shipper Alert #3:** At the end of the episode, House asks Cuddy for sleeping pills, finally confessing that he hasn't slept since Kutner's suicide. She is obviously worried, but not surprised, knowing that House internalizes everything.

**Casting Call:** *House*'s producers cast a deaf actor, Ryan Lane, in the pivotal role of Seth.

**Title Tale:** Abraham Lincoln once said, "A house divided against itself cannot stand." He was speaking of the United States, but the saying equally applies to House, who increasingly edges towards emotional collapse.

**Why It's a Classic:** The haunting of Dr. Gregory House by the ghost of Amber is by turns amusing and chilling, and sets the stage for the season's dramatic conclusion.

## * 5.23 "Under My Skin"

**Writers:** Lawrence Kaplow, Pamela Davis **Director:** David Straiton
**Patient of the Week:** Penelope (Jamie Tisdale)

House and his team try to treat a prima ballerina who collapses during a rehearsal. As her skin sloughs off due to an extremely rare antibiotic reaction, she is in danger of losing her career and her life all due to a lifestyle choice. She has an STD contracted during an affair — and passed on to her current boyfriend. House tries to diagnose her, still plagued by his Amber hallucination, which does not disappear even after a good night's sleep. By the end of the episode, House wonders if his descent into madness has been caused by his own lifestyle choices.

**Zebra of the Week:** Gonnorhea.

**Epiphany!:** House notes guilt in Penelope's boyfriend, leading him to think sexually transmitted disease. He is correct only in the diagnosis, not its source. The STD does not originate in Penelope's boyfriend but in Penelope herself. It's an important distinction for House: he has reached the correct conclusion through a guess, and not by reasoning. The realization is earth-shattering to House, who now knows that he's still thinking irrationally.

**Iconic Moment in *House* History:** House has an especially chilling vision into his own torutured psyche when his Amber hallucination picks up a letter opener and slices her arm wrist to elbow and taunts him about how little he has to look forward to in life.

**A Fine Bromance:** House finally confesses to Wilson that he's been hallucinating. Although at first, he lies, saying that he's seeing visions of the dead Kutner, House lets slip that his hallucination is female — Amber. Wilson wonders why House would be hallucinating about his dead girlfriend. It raises several questions, doesn't it?

**Shipper Alert!:** After a long night helping House detox from Vicodin, Cuddy observes that House wants to kiss her, to which he replies, "I always want to kiss you." Passion ensues . . . or does it?

**Casting Call:** Jamie Tisdale plays Nicole Reilly in the 2010 film *The Obama Effect*, which stars (and is written and directed by) *House* alumnus Charles S. Dutton (Foreman's father).

**Title Tale:** Our ballerina patient has lost much of her skin due to a medication reaction; Amber is under House's skin and he can't seem to get rid of her. House tries to get beneath the skin of what's ailing his psyche.

**Why It's a Classic:** House makes a fateful decision to rid himself of his hallucinations.

### On the Edge of Reality:
### A Closer Look at "Under My Skin"

We think of our skin as being a tough outer layer, protecting us from things that would harm us. But in reality, skin is paper thin, nearly transparent: a fragile covering without which we would be exposed, raw, and bleeding.

With Amber haunting his every waking moment, House is filled with self-doubt and remorse in the aftermath of Chase's bachelor party. He blames himself for forgetting that Chase is allergic to strawberries, which sent him into anaphylactic shock in "House Divided" (5.22). House doesn't trust himself to do much of anything but sit in front of the television.

But they have a new case and Cuddy has threatened to fire House if he doesn't come into work. Trying to diagnose their ballerina patient is almost impossible with Amber's constant hovering, an unnerving and intrusive presence increasingly in the foreground of his mind. House tries to ignore her, refusing to listen to her diagnostic ideas. But she's persuasive — and not always wrong.

Unable to decide when he should listen to his "Amber voice," House finally confides to Wilson that he's hallucinating — but doesn't say who he's seeing. Confessing that he cannot trust his own instincts, he asks Wilson to monitor his work, making sure he's making sane decisions. Trying to diagnose himself, House considers sleep apnea, infection, multiple sclerosis, trauma, schizophrenia . . . and, reluctantly, Vicodin use. Drug use/overuse is the simplest explanation, and may in fact be much higher on his internal list, but it's the last thing he wants to know. But Amber knows better. "It's a nicer diagnosis — doesn't make it a better one," she taunts.

House eliminates everything from his list except schizophrenia and Vicodin use. Holding an Exacto knife to her wrist, during one differential, Amber relentlessly torments House about his future: "Severe mental illness and drugs are the only things left," she mocks. "Mental illness means you can no longer practice medicine. Vicodin means detox, which means pain for the rest of your life, which means you can no longer practice medicine . . ." These words — House's own subconscious laying out in stark relief that he has no future — are House's worst nightmares come true.

House watches in horror as Amber slits her arm elbow to wrist, the blood pouring freely. Is this House's suicidal inner voice telling him that he's crossed a line between living in misery and dying in it — something that House notes in "Simple Explanation" (5.20) distinguishes him from Kutner?

By now realizing that the only possible remaining diagnoses are Vicodin and schizophrenia, House clings to the possibility he's suffering from schizophrenia, continuing to ignore the more likely diagnosis of opioid abuse.

Wilson reminds House that he won't be able to practice medicine on antipsychotics, and would require regular Electroconvulsive Therapy (ECT, shock treatments). House is okay with this until Wilson hits him with the one potential ECT side effect worse (for House) than death: "You live but you destroy your rational mind, the only thing you care about."

Still insistent that schizophrenia is causing his symptoms, House administers himself insulin, starting a chemical form of shock therapy, only (according to Wilson) slightly less dangerous than ECT. Finding him on the floor of his office in convulsions, Wilson is upset at House's recklessness. But it seems to have worked, and Amber is gone! Elated and in a good mood at being back to normal — and able to diagnose the case — House celebrates alone in a restaurant.

But when he turns to the bandstand, she is there. "Enjoy yourself; it's later than you think," she croons, performing the 1949 Guy Lombardo hit, smiling at him evilly. "Enjoy yourself, while you're still in the pink." She laughs at him cruelly, in a subversion of the song's upbeat message.

Terrified and traumatized, and at the very end of his emotional rope, House calls Wilson, deeply shaken, his voice trembling. He's defeated and ready to try rehab. But as he packs for this new journey, House realizes that he's too good at playing the system for conventional methods to work. So he turns to the only person he believes can help him through it: Cuddy.

Unaware he's been hallucinating, Cuddy is not receptive to his intrusion as she prepares to leave for the day. But he is ready to bare his soul. And, of course, because she loves him — perhaps more than the baby she's leaving with a sitter — she goes home with him to help him through detox.

As House goes though his dark night, his dancer patient learns the infection has spread and she risks losing her feet and fingers — who she is. Just like House, who is in grave danger of losing himself and his mind.

With Cuddy's help, House is astoundingly clear-headed by morning. He is detoxed and, although suffering some aftereffects, seems to be doing quite well — almost too well. And Amber is nowhere to be seen.

Having shared the intensity of the night, House's feelings for Cuddy are finally revealed honestly and without the filters, sentries, and castle walls normally between them. They confess their mutual affection and one thing leads to another. Or does it?

### * 5.24 "Both Sides Now"
**Writer:** Doris Egan **Director:** Greg Yaitanes
**Patient of the Week:** Scott (Ashton Holmes)

Dr. Gregory House wakes up in bed after making love to Dr. Lisa Cuddy. She is gone, but not the memory, as House finds her lipstick sitting on his bathroom sink. He smiles, noting the lipstick smear on his face, the happy recollection of their ardent lovemaking. He pockets the lipstick, noting its color, with a clear attachment to it. It's a talisman and a symbol of what lies ahead for the clean and sober House.

Singing as he enters his office the next day, still holding onto Cuddy's lipstick, House is in a spectacular mood. Not just for having sex, but for having won Cuddy. "Zing, zing, zing went my heart strings . . ." The sappy lyrics of James Hanley's 1934 tune tells us that House in love, much as in season two when his night with Stacy in "Need to Know" (2.11) inspires him to sing a sappily romantic aria from the Romberg operetta *The Student Prince*.

> "Someone can be saved through the love of a good woman. Usually the idea is that her strength and her mothering and her understanding, which is like unto no one else's, will pull a man back from the edge, and he will become a better person. It's a romantic idea, and in real life, most of us would say you can't really change people that way."
>
> **— Doris Egan on House's fantasy about Cuddy, May 2009 interview**

This week's patient, Scott, has undergone surgery on his corpus callosum that stopped his seizures, but destroyed communication between the left (rational) and right (aesthetic) parts of his brain. In his case, his left brain doesn't like what his right brain is doing. And miscommunication between the two has led to something called alien hand syndrome, causing his left hand to do what it wants, when it wants, consequences be damned.

The left brain does the math, analyzes the parts. It's the logician: rational, analytical. It is the most obvious part of House's personality. The right brain is intuitive, holistic, random, and subjective. And without it, House would never be able to synthesize or imagine. House calls the right brain the brain irrelevant. He dismisses it because it's his most fragile part: his creativity, his romanticism, his love of music and art. It reveals him, therefore it must be suppressed. But you can only suppress it for so long until it comes back to bite — hard.

**Zebra of the Week:** Propylene glycol toxicity is causing Scott's left hand to rebel against him. It seems to know that the chemical is in Scott's high-powered antipersperant.

**Epiphany!:** The epiphany about the medical case is Taub's when he realizes Scott's deodorant is causing all of his problems. But the real epiphany of the episode for House, and for the viewers, is that House's detox and intimate encounter with Cuddy were all in his battered mind. House comes to this devastating revelation during an argument with Cuddy about what really happened "the night before."

**Iconic Moment in *House* History:** It is impossible to choose just one scene from this pivotal episode, so here are two: the scene in which House finally realizes that his romance with Cuddy is all in his mind — a delusion. The second is the final scene of season five as House walks those final steps to Mayfield Psychiatric Hospital, where he hopes to heal his troubled mind.

**A Fine Bromance:** Wilson is stunned but pleased when House tells him that he spent the night with Cuddy.

**Shipper Alert!:** Chase and Cameron finally get married.

**House Is a Jerk:** He shouts from the hospital mezzanine that he "slept with Lisa Cuddy." She is, needless to say, furious.

**Casting Call:** Ashton Holmes played Private First Class Sidney Phillips in the HBO series *The Pacific* (2010)

**Title Tale:** To paraphrase Joni Mitchell's 1969 folk classic "Both Sides Now": It's life's (and love's) illusions I recall; I really don't know life (or love) at all. It's an apt sentiment for both this week's patient and for House, who at this point has no concept of reality as the curtain goes down on season five.

**Why It's a Classic:** House's world crashes down around him, resetting the entire series.

> "We basically take the weirdness of the universe and make it make sense to us. There's always a story you tell when you hear about something to make your own life make sense of it."
>
> — Doris Egan, May 2009 interview

### It's a Nice Story: A Closer Look at "Both Sides Now"

"Both Sides Now" plays with the concept of self-perception. Who we are? What makes us . . . us? How much of it is wishful thinking, a slightly deluded perception of who we might be; and how much is the reality? Our emotional well-being relies on us being able to tell the difference between the two.

No longer able to distinguish reality from illusion, House confabulates a fantasy that does not render him isolated and alone, his life falling apart. What line is crossed in House's mind that causes it to snap? Has he reached the same level of despair that Kutner had weeks before: that moment where the line between living and dying in misery blurs? House's mind makes a choice, and he could just as easily have committed suicide, as Kutner did in "Simple Explanation" (5.20). But, instead, his mind chooses the comfort of Cuddy's healing sensuality; the warmth of her body, and the belief that he could be happy.

It is not as he imagined: a late night visit to Cuddy's office to confess his hallucinations; a teary plea for help that moves Cuddy to hire a baby sitter for Rachel and go home with him to sit vigil as he detoxes from years of Vicodin use: part guard, part guardian. No early morning conversation. No lovemaking.

The revelation that it is all a delusional fantasy is as heartbreaking as it gets. Cuddy never goes home with him, instead stalking angrily from the room after he mocks her angrily about motherhood and her new baby. He never confesses that he's hallucinating; she never turns back into the room to comfort him.

Instead he goes home alone. His support systems gone, House sinks further, his mind creating the fantasy that he is both loved and redeemable.

House's night of detox and romance with Cuddy is a nice story, filled with the promise of love and redemption, hope and happiness. But unfortunately for House, none of it is real. "This is the story you made up about who you are. It's a nice story," House hears Amber say in his ear.

The final scene between House and Cuddy nearly parallels his imagined night of detox as Cuddy forgets her anger, replacing it with concern, support, and love as House begins to realize that he is no longer simply suffering hallucinations, but full-blown delusions.

"Are you okay?" she inquires, worried as House, who is visibly shaken, nearly collapses into the wall. But House barely hears her as his mind tries to sort reality from illusion. House's halting "No, I'm not okay," finally realizing the cruel trick played on him by his own mind, has been months coming.

In the midst of all this sadness, Chase and Cameron move ahead with their wedding, marrying in a beautiful ceremony intercut with House's journey towards his own uncertain future. It is poignantly ironic that House, understanding Cameron's fears and advising her to take a chance on happiness, saves her relationship with Chase, as his own possibility for happiness evaporates like a mirage in the desert. The beautiful and haunting melody of the Rolling Stones' "As Tears Go By" gives the illusion of a love song. But the lyrics are starkly evocative of where House's life now stands as he travels the long road to the Mayfield Psychiatric Hospital: "I want to hear the children sing/All I hear is the sound/Of rain falling on the ground/I sit and watch as tears go by."

## From the Writer's Mouth . . .

The day after "Both Sides Now" (5.24) aired, I interviewed writer Doris Egan for my *Blogcritics* House feature "Welcome to the End of the Thought Process." This is her take on the episode.

Already beginning to break with reality, suffering hallucinations, "House's brain handed him this gorgeous rationalization all glittery and shiny." Egan explained that throughout the episode, House's right brain, "which is associated with insight taking in all the details that the left brain isn't even paying attention to and making connections that the left brain can't make" is trying to signal House as he deals with Mr. Schwartz, an annoying and elderly clinic patient whom House believes has simple indigestion. With House's brain not working properly, he isn't able to make the sorts of connections he usually does but, Egan said, "gradually he starts picking up on things." Once he does realize how much he has missed, it all begins to unravel completely.

"House realizes that what happened with Cuddy probably never happened. And it's probably to him the biggest shock of his life — that he cannot trust his own intellect," noted Egan. One of House's most important gifts is his insight. Although House mocks the value of the right brain, Foreman rightly reminds him that House owes much of his diagnostic gift to his right brain. "And now," Egan explained, "it's actively working against him."

Cameron and Chase's glitchy wedding plans also weave through the episode and pick up on the self-deception theme. Cameron insists on keeping a vial of her husband's frozen sperm as insurance against an eventual divorce. But is that why she wants to keep the sperm, even if means losing Chase? Egan explained, "Cameron's self-deception was pretty obvious. Believing that she wanted to hang onto the sperm as an insurance policy fit her image of herself as a reasonable person. Hanging onto the only thing left of your husband because you simply can't bear to let go is far less reasonable, though perhaps more understandable." But in the end, Chase understands Cameron's emotional stake in the frozen sample. Perhaps it's a more comforting story for him as well: more romantic and less practical — it has nothing to do with him.

Egan noted, "This is entirely my own take, but I also think Chase's initial feelings about Cameron wanting to keep the sperm were colored by his internal narration. We've seen Chase grow into a confident doctor and a confident person at ease with himself and his relationships. He graduated from 'House school'; he wooed and won the woman of his choice. But internally, he still has some old storytelling about himself that he hasn't entirely shaken off. Chase fears he's Cameron's second choice. He knows she had a thing for House; he knows she was married before; where does he come into this? The guy who's available because the other two aren't? And now she chooses to keep the sperm of a dead guy, over choosing marriage with him? What does that say?"

### Kutner's Death and House's Crash

By the time of Kutner's suicide, House is already questioning something in his life — enough to seek out professional help (something that shows him as both vulnerable and desperate). House never sees Kutner's death coming — and it eats away at him for the rest of the season. But why is it eating away at him? Is it just the puzzle of it (as Wilson ultimately suggests after thinking there is something more to it)?

Cuddy knows that House has taken the death much harder than he is willing to let on. The man who saves everyone can't save his own employee — never saw it coming. Taub nails it when he says about the patient (but also about House), "You can't feel that much guilt without love [read 'caring']." House feels guilty that he perceived nothing wrong that might have saved Kutner. It is the second death in the course of a year he could not prevent.

Kutner's death continues to plague House as his confidence flags in "Saviors" (5.21). And by the end of the episode we, and House, know that something is terribly, terribly wrong as House's mind conjures a vision of the dead Amber, whose sole intention is to taunt and terrorize him.

The three episodes that follow, and conclude season five, are an exquisitely wrought filigree of a tragedy in the making: a perfect storm of loss and self-doubt in a man who cannot express the deepest emotions he feels.

Confessing that he hadn't slept a full night since Kutner's death stuns House's colleagues — more for the fact he's actually revealed it than anything else. And over the final two episodes, "Under My Skin" and "Both Sides Now," House's troubled subconscious paints him an alternate reality — one that eventually shatters when confronted with the harsh glare of reality in "Both Sides Now."

House's hallucination is a nicer, more comforting story — an escape and a safe place for the character to hide from anguish built up over not one season, but several. It's a dream in which he can leave behind the painkillers and win the girl of his dreams. But then reality hits. Hard. Fact counters House's distorted reality and his entire world implodes.

If House has had nothing else, he has always had his rational mind, his keen focus on reality. The foundation of his whole being is ripped away. House's terrified expression and tormented eyes suggest a depth of despair that must only hint at the turmoil boiling within. We didn't see it coming. But, in House's case, it was almost inevitable.

# SEASON 6

## People Don't Change . . . Or Do They?

House's fear of pain (physical and emotional) has fueled many of his life decisions since we met him six years ago. But he is now thrust into a reality where his past pain control methods will cause him greater misery. If one thing scares House more than increasing pain, it is the return of his season five hallucinations. And finally, House is sick of the sadness and the misery that has ruled his life. "I want to be happy," he resolves. And like a hero on a quest for something intangible and perhaps indefinable, he sets out on a season-long journey . . . to change his story.

He is guided by the invisible (to us) hand of Dr. Nolan, whose influence is clear only in retrospect. It's not completely evident that House continues to see him until late in the season, when we learn that he has been having regular sessions all year. There are hints here and there, but viewing the season as a whole, you can perceive Nolan's influence and guidance as House navigates the rocky shoals of his post-Mayfield life.

> "We had talked about whether House was still seeing Nolan and came to the conclusion he was. We didn't necessarily think way back at the beginning of the season that we must have an episode where we see them together again, but we were always open to the idea of getting Andre Braugher back."
>
> — **Doris Egan, May 2010 interview**

What does that mean for Dr. People-Don't-Change? For House, at least, it means that he's going to have to try, no matter what he believes. And try, he does. He cooks, he dances, he makes love. He goes out drinking with his fellows, and even does karaoke!

With blinders firmly in place, neither of House's best friends seem to offer much support: to both Wilson and Cuddy, little about House has changed —

and any odd behavior on House's part leads Wilson to think he's back on Vicodin. But House's evolving attitude is evident in nearly every episode. There are subtle and not-so-subtle kindnesses he does for patients and for colleagues even when he's at his most unlikeable. Although, anonymous and highly disguised benevolent gestures have always been a part of the character, they seem more in evidence this season. They are identified in the guide under the heading "House Isn't a Jerk."

Season six has a transitional feel to it in several ways. Familiar techniques and trappings are absent as House feels his way through life without the numbing effects of narcotics. House is a voyager traveling long-uncharted waters and we are, perhaps, meant to feel as much at sea as he is. Gone is House's beautifully detailed apartment as he moves in with his best friend, Wilson. Gone is the baby grand (and until episode 6.10, so are House's guitars). Gone is the whiteboard. Gone is the motorcycle (until the season finale).

Gone also is the spark between House and Cuddy after "Epic Fail" (6.02) — in fact Cuddy is missing from House's universe for much of season six. But in retrospect, perhaps Cuddy's seeming absence from House's life — as well as her chilly attitude — suggest her effort to distance herself from this man about whom she cares so deeply.

Even House's friendship with Wilson is askew. For five seasons, theirs is a relationship of equals, and the only voluntary association in House's life, but season six finds Wilson as much House's guardian as his comrade. The power in their relationship is no longer quite equal — nor voluntary, as Wilson becomes responsible for House's well being.

Heading into the season's final episodes, House is no happier than when it begins. Wanting to believe in the possibility of healing and happiness, House is all the more bitter when, having done all the right things, he still seems stuck. Only now, everyone else seems to be moving on, leaving him behind. But, as he learns, redemption — or at least the hope of redemption — may be something attainable, even for him.

Season six featured not only some of the series' best episodes, but some of the more significant as well. Unlocking doors to House's psyche, heart, and mind, as well as providing insight into the rest of the series' regulars, season six highlights include: "Broken," "The Tyrant," "Wilson," "Known Unknowns," "Moving the Chains," "The Choice," "Baggage," and of course the stunning season finale, "Help Me."

Classic *House* episodes are marked with an asterisk.

## "Broken" 6.01/6.02

**Writers:** Garrett Lerner, Russel Friend, David Foster, Peter Blake
**Director:** Katie Jacobs
**Patient of the Week:** Dr. Gregory House

"Broken" opens on House in the throes of detox, and within the first five seconds, we know this is not a typical episode. There is no teaser, nor familiar "Teardrop" opening theme, nor anatomical drawings, nor boat on the river. Opening credits drift aimlessly across the screen to an ironically upbeat carnivalesque melody as we watch House go through narcotics withdrawal.

Neither as pretty nor as fast as his imagination paints in "Under My Skin," (5.23), narcotics withdrawal takes days of agony. It's painful to watch him from outside his small cell, pounding on the glass until his fist bleeds. "Help me!" he screams. Finally, with Vicodin cleared from his system, the hallucinations are at last gone. Still in pain but "dealing," House, at Mayfield voluntarily, is ready to pack up and go, demanding his immediate discharge.

But that is not to be in this two-hour season premiere as we follow House through a two-month stay at Mayfield Psychiatric Hospital. Running the gamut from outright (and destructive) hostility to the ultimate acceptance of much needed psychiatric care, House begins the slow process of finding peace with himself. It is a season–long process.

> "With the character of House already at such a low point, it would have been difficult to start from there and have the same show. Instead, executive producer [and episode director] Katie Jacobs decided to take the risk of doing a two-hour episode and 'follow House through that experience.'"
>
> — **Executive producer/writer Russel Friend on "Broken," September 2009 interview**

**Zebra of the Week:** Although it's not really a zebra, House is formally diagnosed with narcissism and depression.
**Epiphany!:** It is not until House's recklessness nearly leads to a patient's death that he really — and finally — realizes he needs psychiatric help.
**Iconic Moment in *House* History:** The entire episode is iconic. It's impossible to isolate one moment — or even five.
**A Fine Bromance:** House tries to engage Wilson in a scheme to get out of Mayfield. Wilson refuses, hanging up the phone on him.
**House Is a Jerk:** House cuts a wide swath, cruelly mocking his fellow patients for their various emotional problems.
**House *Isn't* a Jerk:** Although misguided and nearly ending in tragedy, House

kidnaps fellow patient Steve, taking him for a moment of real delight.

**Judgmental Fellow Alert:** House presumes his psychiatrist is having an affair after seeing him with with a younger woman.

**Housian Ethics:** House is upset with himself for failing to intervene when he believes that another patient is being treated cruelly by one of the doctors.

**Shipper Alert!:** House strongly connects with Lydia, the sister-in-law of a another patient.

**Casting Call:** Andre Braugher (Nolan) has received numerous accolades and awards for his television work, including starring roles in the FX Network television movie *Thief* (2006) and ABC's *Gideon's Crossing* (2000–2001), and his role on NBC's *Homicide: Life on the Street* from 1993 to 1998. Lin-Manuel Miranda (Alvie) is a Tony Award–winning composer/lyricist and Tony-nominated actor for his hit Broadway show *In the Heights* (2008). Franka Potente (Lydia) is an award-winning German actress, best known in the United States for her role as Marie in *The Bourne Supremacy* (2004).

**Title Tale:** Mayfield is a hospital for broken people. House admits to a fellow patient that he is "broken" and finally wants to heal.

## A New Journey Begins:
## A Closer Look at "Broken"

There are many ways of being "broken": a broken mind, a broken body, a broken spirit. Dr. Gregory House's body has been broken for years. Never healed, his leg a constant and ever-painful reminder of what he was and can never again be, he hasn't learned to move on from that defining moment.

By the end of season five, House's spirit is likewise broken — bombarded with loss upon loss, the wound deepening with every new hurt. Like a misshapen bone that needs breaking before it can be set, it is sometimes necessary to reach a point of such brokenness that healing can commence. But the process is both difficult and painful.

When House first considers rehab in "Under My Skin," he tells Wilson that it will ultimately fail because he's too manipulative, and it's too easy for him to "game" the system. What he needs, he says, is someone with the skill to save him from himself. House meets his match at Mayfield when he is assigned to the hospital's director, Dr. Darryl Nolan, someone as tough and stubborn as House himself.

Although Nolan agrees that House is free to leave whenever he wants, it will be without his medical license. Reinstatement requires a recommendation letter, and Nolan rightly believes there's something beyond detox that House needs. Nolan thinks that House knows that too — or why admit himself to a psychiatric hospital and not a drug rehab program?

House tries to make Nolan regret his decision — declaring war on Mayfield, including his patients. House has a field day, coldly and clinically diagnosing their issues during group therapy. He sticks daggers into their most sensitive wounds with surgical precision — an obnoxious playground bully.

Although House is often blunt to the point of nastiness, it's not really like him to cut a swath quite this wide and deep. But House sees himself as a prisoner held against his will; he's fighting the system with the only weapon under his control.

The only one he can't taunt into misery is his roommate, a manic and chronically upbeat Puerto Rican rapper, Alvie. House's relationship with Alvie grows from irritation to annoyance to an eventual genuine fondness. Alvie shares House's rebelliousness and provides him a willing conspirator for his schemes, to the point of voluntarily getting himself punched out.

But despite his best efforts, House finds that he is unable to even get a rise from Nolan. Refusing to be baited, he understands that House's behavior is a symptom. House is a patient, and during his long career Nolan has undoubtedly encountered others with similar issues.

The episode pulls one of the series' signature left turns, throwing the story in another direction, when a young man named Steve arrives on the unit. Calling himself "Freedom Master," he lives with the delusion that he is a superhero.

Steve believes that he is a visitor from another planet sent to right life's wrongs. In reality, his wife is dead, and "Freedom Master" is his way of dealing with the horror of her death. House overhears Steve's psychiatrist, Dr. Medina, break brutally through Steve's delusion as they play cards in the day room. Challenging "Freedom Master" to move a 500-pound piano, Medina's only intention is to break through the delusion in the starkest way possible. He blurts the unvarnished and terrible truth that no superhero can redeem the evil that killed his wife. Instead of breaking through Steve's delusion, however, Medina sends him reeling. Only two orderlies and a syringe of Haldol can subdue him.

Horrified by Medina's seemingly gratuitous cruelty, House resists the impulse to react. But, when Steve fails to appear at a ward gathering, House goes to Steve's room, finding him nearly catatonic. Frantically trying to will

Steve from his bed with no success, House then wheels on Medina, confronting him for the pointlessness of his actions.

Why would Medina's truths upset House so much? He is all for telling the unvarnished truth "in the harshest manner possible" ("No Reason," 2.24), isn't he? Hasn't Medina only done what House does all the time? Nolan is also curious about House's reaction. Perhaps House is angered by the sheer gratuitousness of Medina's actions. House would argue that he employs bluntness for good reason, Medina is simply being cruel. Or is House being protective of Steve for some unknown reason that he alone understands?

Whatever his motivations, he takes a keen interest in the broken down young man. Hijacking a car, House takes Steve to an amusement park skydiving ride. It carries them both soaring above the crowd superhero style. It's a sweet moment of pure joy for Steve — and perhaps for House as well. But House's big adventure lands Steve happily back inside his "Freedom Master" delusion. Elated, he tries to fly for real, leaping from a parking garage wall — and falling several stories to the pavement. Helpless to react before Steve jumps, House can only watch in horror as the young man plunges to disaster.

Much later, bloodstained and numb, waiting for word about Steve outside the hospital Emergency Room, House finally acknowledges that something is terribly wrong. "I need help," he pleads to Nolan, barely able to get out the words. He is finally "broken" enough to begin the process of healing.

This is the turning point in the episode — perhaps the entire series.

Nolan's advice seems deceptively simple: apologize to Steve. But how can two words set things right? "Apologies are powerful things," House observes cynically to Nolan. "Get someone to jump off a building, say two words, then go on with your life." Nothing is ever that simple, especially not to House, and here we begin to understand the root of his misery. Tragic mistakes cannot be undone, and in a just world, he believes, you shouldn't get off with an easy (or not-so-easy) "I'm sorry" — no matter how sincere.

House screws up, kills a patient, indirectly contributes to a tragic death — and he believes that he deserves to suffer for it. It's only fair. An occasional series trope, it will be revisited again as season six draws to a close.

In "Dying Changes Everything" (5.01), House finds it impossible to apologize to Wilson about Amber's death, telling Cuddy it would be hypocritical and meaningless. "Only actions change things," he insists. How many times in six seasons has House expressed those sentiments? Nolan has unlocked a crucial door to understanding his patient.

Although House is now more receptive to the power of the words "I'm sorry," the words fail to emerge from his mouth when he tries. Instead, he stands frozen and impotent beside Steve's broken body. Falling back on the only meaningful concept in his worldview, House tries to "fix" Steve's situation and undo the damage he has wrought. But that's no good either, and House is devastated by his failure.

Further beaten down, House is finally ready to try anything. After confessing that he wants to "be happy," Nolan wants to start him on antidepressants in addition to group and one-on-one psychotherapy. Although deeply concerned that the pills will take away his edge, House is out of options and ready to try them.

It's probably been years since House has been able to connect romantically with anyone except Stacy. He has never been able to reach that point with either Cuddy (except in fantasy) or Cameron. But allowing himself to be less guarded in the relative safety of Mayfield's closed environment, House is ready to try this as well.

During his stay at Mayfield, House connects with Lydia, the sister-in-law of Annie, a patient who has been mute for 10 years. He hears Lydia playing piano and is immediately drawn to her. Their relationship builds slowly from flirtation to something more. He has ideas about how she might be able to reach Annie; she brings classical duets to share with him.

She kisses him casually goodbye at a hospital social event, and it deeply affects him. Although it may be innocent (as Nolan suggests), House has probably spent hours considering its meaning. But House hesitates taking a more significant step and risking his heart. "There are two ways this could end," he explains to Lydia. "We stop and someone gets hurt, or we don't and someone gets hurt."

Yet in spite of his doubts, when he sees Lydia alone and sobbing late one night, House instinctively comforts her. Comfort leads to passionate, but gentle lovemaking — something that affects House so deeply, he weeps. In a September 2009 interview, Garnett Lerner noted, "It was something Hugh Laurie came up with on the set that day. He felt he wanted to try it. He felt it was the appropriate thing. And then when we saw it on the monitor, it was incredibly moving."

Even when confined to a psychiatric hospital, House is fundamentally a healer. And using his keen observational powers, this time as a force for good, he realizes that he holds the key to helping both Steve and Annie. With one small gesture involving a blue wooden music box, Steve is responsive for the first time since his fall; the silent Annie is no longer silent. Soon Silent Girl is ready to leave the safety of Mayfield and begin her re-entry back into society — but in Arizona. Her departure also means Lydia's as well.

Losing Lydia is devastating to House, but instead of keeping the hurt bottled up and finding solace in drugs, he seeks out Nolan. It's a breakthrough, and Nolan realizes that House is ready to move on and away from in-patient psychiatric care.

Though perhaps no longer broken, House is still fragile, and finally on the road to recovery. Can he break through the misery and find happiness? Only time (and the rest of season six) will tell.

## Diagnosing Dr. House: A Conversation with a Clinical Psychologist

Dr. Robert Spector is a respected clinical psychologist in the Chicago suburbs. His practice is in child and family psychology. He is a *House, M.D.* fan, fascinated by the character and the issues raised by the series.

After watching the sixth season premiere "Broken," Dr. Spector shared his thoughts about House (the character) and his mental health. He explained the types of depression that might be applicable to Greg House, considering Nolan's diagnosis in the episode. Spector suggested, based on what he can surmise of the character in the five years of the series, House has what is called "dysthymia," an "enduring depression," characterized by a generally pessimistic and negative view of life. House is a functional, but depressed person, and his depression is low level — a sort of "life sucks" attitude.

Spector noted that in real life, antidepressants like the SSRIS House is prescribed are not as effective as therapy for dysthymia, but dysthymic people often do have major depressive episodes for which SSRIS may be more useful. Nolan's goal of course, explained Spector, is to get House healthy enough to be discharged from his in-patient treatment status. So the immediate treatment with antidepressants combined with therapy is appropriate.

"House probably also has an attachment disorder," Spector explained. Common in neglected and abused children, it occurs when infants fail to make an empathic connection with their parents. "If children fail to make that connection, they learn to mistrust people. The world isn't a safe place for them, and you lose your ability to develop deep connections with people."

It's not that House is incapable of relationships, noted Spector, but he's so fragile as a person it would be difficult. He'll dabble in relationships when they are not — or cannot — be enduring. Those are safer for him.

He also sees in House a *mensch* (Yiddish for "a good person") who's disgusted with being a *mensch*. Spector believes that's what people who see past the subterfuge find, and what draws them in. But House also a very nasty side to him. "He builds himself up by bringing others down, fueled by insecurity." Like Cuddy says, House knows where to point that sharp stick. "He uses words like a dagger," noted Spector.

This is why the character of House can be so toxic to those around him. "He is so cut off from people, he can cause pain without even realizing it. He feels so threatened by people, House is constantly pushing people away — and preying on them. And the more vulnerable he's feeling, the worse his behavior can be."

Spector also commented on the relationship between Nolan and House during episode 6.01. He described Nolan's actions as "counter-transference": "Nolan identifies too strongly with House's isolation and loneliness." Spector suggested that maybe Nolan is trying to show House an appropriate response to attachment and loss by bringing House to his father's deathbed. But it's an incredibly fine line for a therapist to bring a patient into their private world. "It's a slippery slope Nolan is on to expose his own vulnerability" — especially to someone like House, who is perceptive enough to absorb it and use it against him.

## 6.03 "Epic Fail"

**Writers:** Liz Friedman, Sara Hess **Director:** Greg Yaitanes
**Patient of the Week:** Vince Pearson (Rick D. Wasserman)

Returning to Princeton-Plainsboro after two months at Mayfield, House shocks Cuddy and Foreman by resigning. Not wanting to be tempted by old environments and pressures, he intends to switch to research as soon as his medical license is restored. Foreman is more than anxious to pick up the director's mantle, and although the Diagnostics Department has been mothballed since the end of season five, he convinces Cuddy to let him take a stab at filling House's considerable whiteboard.

The team treats a Vince, a young whiz-kid virtual reality game designer whose hands burn like they're on fire after testing out a cool new game. As his condition worsens, he begins to lose confidence in the diagnostics team, posting his symptoms on the Internet — inviting more creative minds to solve the medical mystery. Foreman's not too happy about this, especially when the rest of the team — including girlfriend "13" — begins to question his authority. Eventually, Foreman solves the puzzle, but not before "13" discovers the correct diagnosis in a pile of submitted Internet diagnoses.

With Foreman's trial run successful, Cuddy offers him the department directorship. But Taub isn't interested in becoming a Foreman follower. And Foreman says he can't date "13" and be her boss at the same time. "Thirteen" isn't exactly thrilled with her boyfriend, and breaks it off; Foreman loses her on both counts. In the end, he is a department of one.

House begins adjusting to life without Vicodin — and without the distraction of medical mysteries. Nolan believes that House isn't quite ready to live alone, so House moves in with Wilson, still residing in Amber's old apartment. With no distractions, House fears a return of the pain and a return to his old ways. Nolan advises House to get a hobby, and suggests he join Wilson's cooking class. House has a surprising flair for it, applying chemical principles to his methods and creating gourmet delights. Although the new hobby proves to be a good diversion, it only works temporarily; the pain soon begins to creep back into House's leg. It seems there is just one method House can use to cope: go back to his old job as a medical zebra hunter.

**Zebra of the Week:** Fabry disease, a genetic condition that prevents the breakdown of lipids in the body.

**Epiphany!:** "Thirteen" decides to take another look at the stack of Internet diagnoses and encounters one faxed diagnosis that fits perfectly. At the same time, Foreman realizes that Vince's fingers don't prune up in a cooling bath used when he spikes a fever — something that would also point to Fabry.

**Iconic Moment in *House* History:** House visits his apartment for the first time after being discharged from Mayfield, desperately seeking Vicodin to relieve his increasing pain. He is obviously afraid of slipping back into narcotics use, and until the end of the episode we're not sure if he's headed back to that "very dark place." What we don't know at that point is that House is the one who posts Vince's correct diagnosis on the Internet. Despite an earlier warning from Nolan to stay away from diagnostics, he can't help himself. House sees it as a "slip," but Nolan rethinks his recommendation.

**A Fine Bromance:** House cooks with chemistry to save Wilson's (meat) balls with a little vinegar.

**Housian Ethics:** Foreman fires "13" because of their relationship. It's a sexual harassment lawsuit waiting to happen. (Talk about using power inappropriately!)

**Judgmental Fellow Alert:** So begins an entire season of Wilson's mistrust. Noting House's suddenly better controlled pain, Wilson suspects that House has gone back to Vicodin, and immediately hatches an elaborate scheme to catch him. Always anticipating that Wilson will think the worst of him, House counters effectively.

**Shipper Alert!:** Cuddy visits while House is busy cooking with a classmate. Cuddy wants to make sure he's okay, but House's cooking partner immediately observes the sexual tension between them. "Either kiss him or leave," she scolds.

**Shipper Alert #2:** Foreman and "13" frolic in bed while she seductively tells him about her old roommate at Sarah Lawrence College. On the other hand, Foreman, you're an idiot! Did you really think she'd remain your girlfriend after you fired her? And we thought House was delusional.

**Lost in Translation:** House once again demonstrates his linguistic proficiency, conversing in Mandarin with his cooking partner.

**Title Tale:** Oh, so many fails: Foreman fails at playing House. Hardly House "2.0," as he claims to the patient, he's really still "House lite." Taub quits; Foreman fires "13." House has failed to distance himself from diagnostics, although he doesn't fail staying off the Vicodin. And Wilson fails to give House any benefit of the doubt.

## * 6.04 "The Tyrant"

**Writer:** Peter Blake **Director:** David Straiton

**Patient of the Week:** President Dibala (James Earl Jones)

Foreman is still in charge of the department, and with Taub and "13" gone, Cuddy recruits Chase and Cameron to help him treat a visiting African president. But President Dibala is a dictator with genocidal tendencies; he has already murdered thousands of a minority tribe in his country and promises to continue what is "necessary" for the good of his government. Dibala collapses in the backseat of his limo on the eve of a UN address.

Still without his medical license, House returns to diagnostics, where he can do little more than offer an opinion. Foreman protests his presence, but Cuddy says they'd be foolish to not to listen to anything he has to say. House seems fine with this new arrangement; he can play mad scientist with no real responsibility for the patient. As the team treats Dibala, Cameron and Chase both consider the moral question of how much — or even whether — to treat him. If Dibala dies, the genocide in his country will likely stop, and if he lives, nearly half his population will be murdered.

In the end, Chase makes a fateful decision to falsify Dibala's records, intentionally leading the diagnosis astray. Based on Chase's false records, they treat Dibala for a nonexistent condition, killing him in the process. When Foreman learns what Chase has done, he burns the evidence — protecting the department and Chase, but implicating himself in the murder.

House continues living with Wilson, but there's a problem with their downstairs neighbor Murphy. He's annoyed by the sound of House's cane, which he can hear through the ceiling. An amputee, he lost his arm during the Vietnam War. He also possesses a giant chip on his shoulder, possibly caused by a 35-year-old case of phantom limb syndrome.

**Zebra of the Week:** The team erroneously treats Dibala for scleroderma, a chronic autoimmune disease that affects the connective tissue. Dibala really dies of blastomycosis, a fungal infection.

**Iconic Moment in *House* History:** Foreman discovers that Chase has falsified Dibala's test results, causing his death. **Iconic Moment #2:** House thinks he can cure Murphy's phantom pain using mirrors. Of course he has to bind and gag him to do it, but when it works, House is both surprised and delighted. Curing a patient's pain has always been particularly important to House. Something he cannot have for himself, it seems to give him a measure of satisfaction when is able to help a patient improve their quality of life. Murphy is grateful and in tears — and much happier with his upstairs neighbors.

**A Fine Bromance:** It's not very bromantic, but at the neighbor's insistence, Wilson evicts House. It's the first of two times he does this in the early season six episodes, notable especially since House still should not be living alone.

**House Is a Jerk:** House accuses Murphy of lying about how he lost his limb based on circumstantial evidence. House is wrong — and unjust.

**House *Isn't* a Jerk:** Curing the phantom pain is a nice, yet very Housian, gesture.

**Judgmental Fellow Alert:** Wilson continues to assume the worst about House, blaming him for Murphy's ill will.

**Housian Ethics:** Is it morally just to assassinate a mass killer to prevent the genocide of thousands? And in so doing, has Chase performed a courageous act — or is he simply a murderer?

**Casting Call:** The great James Earl Jones (Darth Vader in the original *Star Wars* films) guest stars as President Dibala.

**Title Tale:** The episode revolves around a genocidal dictator, who, of course is the main tyrant in this tale. While in the hospital, he bullies Cameron and several others. Wilson's neighbor is a lightweight tyrant, possessing a belligerent attitude that shocks even House.

**Why It's a Classic:** The events in this episode propel the next story arc, which addresses Dibala's assassination and its effect (especially) on Chase and Cameron. "The Tyrant" also raises some serious questions about the morality of murdering a mass murderer — and of doctors playing God. It's also interesting to observe House trying very hard to be a good friend to Wilson and avoid making waves with the misanthropic Murphy. But House kills the beast inside this petty tyrant by curing him. House not only eliminates the amputee's pain, his act is transformative. Having been House's avowed enemy during most of the episode, the neighbor thanks him for helping him as no one had been able to for decades.

## 6.05 "Instant Karma"

**Writer:** Thomas Moran **Director:** Greg Yaitanes
**Patient of the Week:** Jack Randall (Tanner James Maguire)

Roy is Midas with an MBA: everything he touches in turns to gold — except when it comes to his family. He has suffered terrible personal losses: the death of his wife and now the serious illness of his son Jack. How can he be so lucky in one area of life, and so unlucky in everything that really matters? Is it karma?

Desperate to help his son, Roy seeks out Dr. Gregory House; money's no object. No one else has been able to diagnose Jack, and House is Roy's last chance to save him. There's one hitch: House hasn't yet recovered his medical license. He can't perform any medical procedures or have patient contact. Although Cuddy brings House in on a non-official consult, Foreman remains technically in charge of the case.

When House diagnoses a fatal disease, Roy is certain that it's karmic payback for his mega-success in business: he is only getting what he deserves. Only by destroying his fortune — bankrupting himself — will he be able to save his son's life.

House knows this is nonsense. "People don't get what they deserve; they get what they get, and nobody can do anything about it," he tells Roy.

As the team diagnoses Jack, Foreman and Chase prepare to present President Dibala's case at the hospital's weekly Morbidity and Mortality Conference (a conference designed to comprehend the circumstances of an unusual patient death, educating the staff and medical students alike). Given the circumstances of Dibala's death, presenting this case is the last thing Foreman and Chase need. The test results falsified by Chase do not match up with Dibala's other blood work, and anyone looking too closely may suspect foul play — unless there's a logical reason for the differing results.

"Thirteen's" vacation plans for Thailand are aborted when someone sabotages her plane reservation. Who would do that?

As for House, being finally back in the diagnostic game (if not in charge) must feel good after more than two months away. But he isn't entirely sure he wants his department back. The combination of "power and puzzles," is seductive, but House worries that the pressure will lead him back to that dangerous territory he's trying to leave behind. Ultimately, House may have no choice; leadership of the Diagnostics Department may simply be his destiny.

**Zebra of the Week:** Jack has antiphospholipid syndrome, a manageable autoimmune disease that causes clotting issues.

**Epiphany!:** House and Wilson argue about the size of House's heart, which leads him away from his initial — and fatal — diagnosis.

**Iconic Moment in *House* History:** House confesses to Cuddy that he is worried about returning to run the Diagnostics Department. He argues that Foreman likes "power" while he loves "puzzles" — a perfect balance. But Cuddy reminds House that he likes both. Not disputing the observation, House notes that it is a dangerous combination for him.

**A Fine Bromance:** Wilson puts in his pitch for "13" to stay on House's team. She is the only one who resists being sucked into his "crazy House vortex" — and that's why House needs her.

**House Is a Jerk:** House insists that he has no heart to Wilson, disclosing that he's made a stock market killing using the information that Roy's company is about to go belly up.

**House *Isn't* a Jerk:** House is the saboteur of "13's" Thailand plans. Wilson believes that House has done it to save her relationship with Foreman, playing a Housian version of cupid. He insists that House is "not as big a jerk" as everyone thinks he is, a charge the House flatly denies.

**Housian Ethics:** Chase and Foreman try to concoct a plan to cover up Dibala's assassination before they present the case. But everything they consider only makes the case seem more suspicious. Observing Chase's anxiety and the unusually tense departmental dynamics, it doesn't take House long to figure out that something's up. Quietly and anonymously, House provides Chase with information that will explain Dibala's test results, likely saving the careers of both Foreman and Chase. What is House's motivation? Is it right to cover up the murder? Is he simply protecting his turf — or does he understand Chase's actions as just? House coldly explains that he is acting only in self-interest. But House's motivations are rarely that simple.

**World-Famous Doctor Moment:** Millionaire Roy doesn't want "good" for his son; he wants "the best." And that would be Dr. Gregory House.

**Casting Call:** Lee Tergesen (Roy) portrayed Tobias Beecher in HBO's acclaimed series *Oz* (1997–2003).

**Title Tale:** "There's got to be some sort of balance," argues Roy, irrationally bankrupting himself, thinking his act will save his son. Much of this episode is devoted to restoring balance: to the diagnostics department, to the mess made of the Dibala affair, to Jack and his family, to House after a terrifying and tumultuous three months, and to the relationships in his universe. House becomes the fulcrum in the restoration of his universe to its correct balance, which ultimately means that he is back in charge of diagnostics. But, at what cost? Hopefully, with his tenuous support system and Dr. Nolan's help, he will cope.

## * 6.06 "Brave Heart"

**Writer:** Lawrence Kaplow **Director:** Matt Shakman
**Patient of the Week:** Donny Compson (Jon Seda)

The team treats a policeman with an apparent death wish. Trying to leap a tall building in single bound, Donny crashes to the ground with broken limbs and no other symptoms. But he insists he is dying and will, in fact, die before his 40th birthday like his father, grandfather, and great grandfather before him.

When the team finds nothing wrong, Foreman, on House's advice, discharges Donny, who then appears to die only hours later. House and Foreman prepare to autopsy his body. As they make the first slice into his chest, the corpse screams out, seriously freaking out both doctors. Oops! Now with more to go on, House and company try to diagnose what's killing their patient — and what may have killed his forebears. And it seems like old times as Chase and Cameron are called in to pinch-hit for the missing Taub and "13."

House moves from the sofa to a spare bedroom, which Wilson has outfitted as a shrine to his dear departed soul mate. Lined with Amber mementos and photos, the room spooks House to begin with, and when he starts hearing voices, he is completely unnerved. Is he beginning to lose it again (and this time off Vicodin)?

House visits the hospital audiologist to rule out a hearing problem, but she does little to allay his fears. Of course, it doesn't help when she reminds him that if he's hearing sounds he shouldn't, "it's psychosis." He's concerned enough to further delay his return to medicine. But House finally learns the truth; Wilson is having bedtime conversations with Amber.

Chase's torment over his deed in "The Tyrant" (6.04) intensifies; he's now seeing gruesome visions of Dibala every time he ventures near the icu. He is unable to tell Cameron the truth, severely straining his marriage. Ultimately seeking the counsel of a priest in the confessional, Chase desires absolution — something the priest cannot (or will not) grant.

**Zebra of the Week:** The self-destructive Donny has a self-destruct button: an aneurysm in his brain stem that can explode at any moment. It is the congenital defect that killed both his father and grandfather.

**Epiphany!:** After House makes a tiny (read: glacial) move towards Cuddy, she assures him that their relationship is just fine as it is. "You push my buttons; I push yours." The word "button" triggers the idea that Donny possesses an inherited "self-destruct" button.

**Iconic Moment in *House* History:** Following Wilson's lead, House takes a self-conscious, yet deliberate, step and tries to remember the better times of his childhood, conversing with his now-deceased father.

**A Fine Bromance:** Wilson catches House "picking lint" from his navel early one morning, raising the question of why House is still sleeping on the couch after five weeks, and not the empty bedroom. Wilson agrees to ready the room, sarcastically pointing out the need to first transition from his "dead girlfriend's shrine to [House's] 'morning glory.'"

**House Is a Jerk:** Cuddy forces House to fulfill a medical recertification requirement of 120 hours of patient rounds along with the medical students. Believing it's simply a power play, House makes life miserable for everyone involved.

**House *Isn't* a Jerk:** House persuades Donny to connect with the young son he had never known.

**Housian Ethics:** The burden of murdering Dibala continues to weigh on Chase. Asking a priest if it is not better to kill a man responsible for the deaths of thousands, he is told that it is not his place — as a doctor — to play God.

**Shipper Alert!:** When Cuddy badgers House about his attitude toward requalifying for his medical license, one of the medical students notes that they're not arguing — it's "foreplay." **Shipper Alert #2:** Talking to Amber gives Wilson comfort. He tells her about his day and his renewed concern for House's mental health. **Shipper Alert #3:** Cuddy visits House in his office, having signed off on his recertification. House wants confirmation that things are okay between them. He tells her in a particularly Housian way that he "likes" her — she makes him "feel funny."

**Gross-out Warning:** Donny wakes "from the dead" after House and Foreman begin their autopsy — and after they've sliced open his chest with an electric saw. Ick.

**Casting Call:** Jon Seda starred as Sergeant John Basilone in HBO's miniseries *The Pacific* (2010).

**Title Tale:** Donny is a brave cop, reckless because he knows he is going to die. But he uses bravery as an excuse as well — he thinks he is being noble in preventing his son from getting to know him, knowing that his son soon will be fatherless. But after House calls him on it, Donny takes a brave and tentative step towards a relationship with the boy. And then there's Chase, who has the courage of his convictions in murdering Dibala, but whose bravery is crumbling in the aftermath. House, too, must muster his own "brave heart" as he tries to find his footing back in medicine. He's getting back on the "zebra," taking de facto command of the department (albeit without a medical license), but afraid that he's not yet emotionally ready. The spooked House must also muster his courage in tracking down the mysterious voices he hears. House also takes a hesitant step towards Cuddy and an equally brave step in coming to terms with his father.

**Why It's a Classic:** "Brave Heart" is one of those old-school, multilayered *House* episodes, which offer much more than initially meets the eye. An emotionally complex story, the medical case is seamlessly interwoven with the character drama.

## * 6.07 "Known Unknowns"

**Writer:** Doris Egan **Director:** Greg Yaitanes
**Patient of the week:** Jordan (Anna Attanasio)

The team treats Jordan, a teenage girl who collapses after a supposedly wild night of partying with a rock band. Jordan's appendages are severely swollen after her night out, and the baffled team learns that the girl is lying about her exploits. Chase, Cameron, and Foreman try to wend their way through the girl's tangle of lies to arrive at a truth that will save her life. It turns out that her wild night is a fantasy; she had really been stalking the creator of her favorite science-fiction television series.

As the team works the case, Wilson, House, and Cuddy travel to a medical conference. After taking a hesitant step towards Cuddy in "Brave Heart," House seems resolved to pursue things further while at the conference. He finds the perfect opportunity at an '80s party, where he demonstrates his grace, charm, and the ability to talk seriously and unguardedly. He even offers to babysit Cuddy's daughter, whom she has brought with her to the conference. But House's plans are thwarted after discovering Private Investigator Lucas (from season five) has arrived — and that he and Cuddy are involved.

Wilson is scheduled to present a potentially career-killing paper on euthanasia, hoping to introduce the taboo subject into the medical community for a much-needed debate. Wilson plans to relate his personal experiences as an oncologist who sometimes enables terminal patients to die rather than suffer needlessly. House thinks he's insane and he tries to protect Wilson from himself by drugging him. Stealing the speech while Wilson's unconscious, House delivers the paper under an assumed name. This puts the issue on the table for discussion without risking Wilson's career.

Chase's assassination of Dibala continues to tear him apart, driving him further and further away from Cameron, who can't explain his extreme edginess and distance. Chase is afraid to tell Cameron the truth, given her usual moral stance. But silence also has its consequences. Cameron knows something's wrong and assumes (not unreasonably) that Chase is having an affair, despite his denials. The secrets and lies may be toxic to the new marriage.

**Zebra of the Week:** Jordan has vibrio vulnificus, a rare bacterial infection contracted from eating undercooked seafood. It's normally not life-threatening, but can be fatal in people with hemochromatosis, which they confirm in Jordan.

**Epiphany!:** While arguing with Wilson about stealing his euthanasia speech, House points out that of 10,000 oncologists who do it, only Wilson would feel guilty enough to give a speech about it. This triggers House's connection between something Jordan eats and a very rare presentation of vibrio, only possible if the patient also has hemochromatosis.

**Iconic Moment in *House* History:** After rescuing Cuddy from a lounge lizard at the party, House and Cuddy dance to an upbeat rhythm. Suddenly the music slows down and shyly, they continue, now "slow dancing." After all the sparring they have done over the years, it is the first *quiet*, genuinely romantic moment we've seen between them. **Iconic Moment #2:** Wilson arrives at his conference session in time to witness House give the paper. He is furious, even as House speaks directly to Wilson from the heart.

**A Fine Bromance:** Yes, what House does is manipulative and underhanded, but he does it to save Wilson's career. Eventually, Wilson understands that House is being a very good friend.

**House Is a Jerk:** House uses Wilson's (very overpriced) hotel room minibar unrepentantly and with singular abandon.

**House *Isn't* a Jerk:** It takes awhile for Wilson to realize it, but House's scheme to steal the speech has only the most benevolent of intentions. It's what any good friend would do (especially if he's House). When Lucas crassly and casually brings up the taboo subject of House's delusions as they are all having breakfast together, House accepts this tirade calmly. He might easily have ripped into both Lucas — and Cuddy for having disclosed the confidential information — but instead plays the adult.

**Judgmental Fellow Alert:** House deems Jordan's parents neglectful, leaving their teenager essentially on her own while they pursue their business.

**Shipper Alert!:** As they dance at the '80s party, House and Cuddy discuss their brief encounter years earlier while students at the University of Michigan. House stuns Cuddy when he tells her that after a one-night stand, he'd planned on pursuing something more serious with her before learning he'd been expelled. **Shipper Alert #2:** Cuddy has been keeping her relationship with Lucas a secret, believing that House is still too emotionally fragile to handle the news.

**Shipper Alert #3**: Chase finally tells Cameron the truth about Dibala's death.

**Housian Ethics:** Wilson points out that he has learned from House that it's sometimes necessary to do what is right without regard to consequences. Apparently Chase has also internalized this same lesson. On the other hand, House points out, it hasn't worked out all that well for him.

**Did You Know?:** This isn't the first time we've seen actor Hugh Laurie dress for the late 18th century. As the intellectually challenged and frivolous Prince

George (the Prince of Wales), Laurie co-starred with Rowan Atkinson in the BBC television series *Blackadder the Third* (1987). Laurie also had roles in two other *Blackadder* series.

**Pop Culture References:** The cake at the '80s party is a giant Rubik's cube — the quintessential '80s fad. And as we all know, House has a ginormous Rubik's complex — an insatiable urge to solve the puzzle ("DNR," 1.09).

**Props Department:** The '80s outfits at the party are great. But House's 1780s costume is splendid with muted brocades and laces, a powdered wig, and era-appropriate walking stick.

**Casting Call:** Anna Attanasio is the daughter of *House* executive producers Katie Jacobs and Paul Attanasio.

***House* Canon:** The episode suggests that House and Cuddy were in medical school at the same time. House is several years older than Cuddy, so the logic of this timeline is suspect. However, it would explain how he remembers her medical school desk (which he restores to her as a gift in "Let Them Eat Cake," 5.10). Perhaps she was an undergrad while he was in medical school. We also learn that the University of Michigan was the first medical school from which House was expelled. He was also expelled from Johns Hopkins ("Distractions," 2.12).

**Title Tale:** "There are known unknowns. That is to say, things that we now know we don't know," said Donald Rumsfeld in 2002 about Iraq. Taking steps into the unknown requires leaps of faith most of us try to avoid. It takes courage and belief that what you are doing is right, consequences be damned. Forays into the unknown are risky, whether you're going to war, giving a controversial speech, taking a bold step with your heart, or attempting a potentially life-altering move. "Known Unknowns" explores what it means to take such a leap — for House, Chase, Wilson, and even Cuddy.

**Why It's a Classic:** Road trip episodes are always memorable. This one is no exception, with its serious exploration of House's influence and ethical code, the House and Cuddy backstory, and a compellingly twisted examination of House and Wilson's relationship.


## 6.08 "Teamwork"

**Writer:** Eli Attie **Director:** David Straiton

**Patient of the Week:** Hank Hardwick (Troy Garity)

His medical license finally restored, House reclaims his rightful place as department head. He begins his tenure by treating Hank, a male porn star with sensitivity to light and a sudden bleeding problem. A nice boy "from the 'burbs," he was raised by an over-protective mother who wouldn't let a cough go by without a visit to the doctor. He is happily married to another porn star and they are both matter-of-fact about their unusual line of work. It's just a job, they claim. But apparently not — the team discovers Hank's liver is filled with strongyloides worms (apparently an occupational hazard for porn actors). Although the team treats the infection, Hank's condition continues to worsen.

Reacting to Chase's confession about Dibala's death, Cameron believes they can deal with it as long as they leave Princeton-Plainsboro (and presumably House's sphere of influence). Grateful, Chase is ready to do whatever she asks, although his heart remains in diagnostics. With "13" and Taub now pursuing other career paths, House tries to lure all four doctors back into the fold, involving them in the case any way he can. He argues that their reasons for leaving have nothing to do with the work — or him. But Cameron has had enough. Although she seems to forgive Chase, she cannot forgive House for the toxic, morally bankrupt environment she believes he has created, which has poisoned her husband's mind to point where he doesn't know "right from wrong."

**Zebra of the Week:** Hank has extraintestinal Crohn's disease. "Thirteen" explains that he's a victim of the "hygiene theory" — a too-clean childhood that leads to an increased likelihood of an autoimmune disease.

**Epiphany!:** After going down a risky diagnostic path, Foreman, Chase, and Cameron are about to zap Hank's blood and kill his immune system. Taub and "13," unable to resist the medical mystery, call House, suggesting that curing his threadworm problem has caused his new symptoms. They stop the procedure just in time. Has this been House's plan all along? Is this just part of a game to lure back Taub and "13"?

**Iconic Moment in *House* History:** After more than five seasons, Cameron leaves the House universe behind to start a new life in Chicago. During her emotional farewell to House, she accuses him of ruining Chase, warning that he'll poison everyone else as well. "I was in love with you," she acknowledges, disappointed that she no longer perceives the same man under whom she had studied. Paralleling their goodbye in "Love Hurts" (1.20), House cannot take her proffered hand. Stunned and silent, he can only gaze at her.

**A Fine Bromance:** Wilson insists that House must be more hurt than he lets on that Cuddy is dating Lucas, one of the few people that House calls "friend" (something House learns in "Known Unknowns," 6.07). Wilson sees this as the reason House insists on hiring back the four fellows who have resigned. "You feel abandoned by Cuddy," he argues; the fellows "are comfortable." Ever protective of House, Wilson confronts Cuddy, wondering what she sees in Lucas — and letting her know that she's hurting House.

**House Is a Jerk:** House is a bigger jerk than usual, playing puppet master in the most destructive way possible: he picks at Chase and Cameron's already rupturing marriage, completely indifferent to the damage he wreaks. House is so unlikeable in "Teamwork" that it's difficult to have any sympathy for him, no matter what his motives.

**Judgmental Fellow Alert:** Oh, snap! Cameron calls House and Chase irredeemable and lost, unable to tell right from wrong and bereft of shame. She believes House has poisoned Chase, and wants nothing more to do with either of them. She also blasts the porn star patient and his wife for their unconventional lifestyle.

**Housian Ethics:** Chase considers the morality of murdering Dibala: "It might have been the worst thing I've done; it might have been the best," he tells Cameron.

**Shipper Alert!:** House cannot look Cuddy in the eye when they speak, suggesting he's not quite as calm as he says he is about her new relationship. **Shipper Alert #2:** Cameron tearily tells House she had once been in love with him, and gently kisses him farewell. House begins to follow her, perhaps wanting to explain. But he pauses, letting her go.

**Gross-out Warning:** A scan reveals that Hank's liver is completely filled with worms. After treating the parasitic infection, the team learns that the worms are actually protecting his health. New prescription: a worm-infested cocktail.

**Casting Call:** Troy Garity received a Best Actor Golden Globe nomination for his role in *Soldier's Girl* (2003).

**Title Tale:** House is trying to reunite the team, fusing the old team with the new one. The patient and his wife seem to make a good team, despite their unconventional career choice. One of the diagnostic team's original members moves on.


## 6.09 "Ignorance is Bliss"

**Writer:** David Hoselton **Director:** Greg Yaitanes
**Patient of the Week:** Jimmy (Esteban Powell)

A genius physicist, who's left his research for a career as a deliveryman, collapses on the job. The team diagnoses thrombotic thrombocytopenic purpura (TTP), but the indicated splenectomy has no effect on Jimmy's symptoms.

While tracking down other diagnostic leads, House realizes that Jimmy has been "Robitripping": using dextromethorphan (like the cough suppressant Robitussin, which is also known as DXM). It's not until House discovers that

Jimmy tried to commit suicide years earlier that he puts together the last piece of the diagnostic puzzle.

But House has not yet figured out the puzzle of Cuddy's new relationship with Lucas. Unwilling to let them be, House must interfere with their Thanksgiving plans, leading him into an elaborate cat and mouse game with Cuddy. In the end, however, after sending House on a wild goose (or shall I say turkey) chase, Cuddy tires of the games and tells House, "It's not fun anymore." She means it.

Chase attempts to deal with Cameron's abrupt departure by withdrawing. But he is frustrated when everyone insists on giving him advice — from seeing a shrink to going out for a Thanksgiving drink.

**Zebra of the Week:** It's TTP after all, a rare and poorly understood blood disorder that can cause spleen problems. A splenectomy should help Jimmy. But an injury years earlier has shattered his spleen into 16 accessory spleens, so the treatment doesn't cure him. (This is the second time TTP has been the culprit — see "Kids," 1.20).

**Epiphany!:** Jimmy tells House about a previous suicide attempt, mentioning that he broke his ribs jumping from a building. House realizes the fractured ribs may have created accessory spleens, which is why a standard (single) splenectomy doesn't cure him.

**Iconic Moment in *House* History:** Tired of everyone fussing over him, Chase has had enough. One last cutting remark from House about his marriage, and he slugs his boss in the face, sending him reeling to the floor. Interestingly, House lets Chase get away with it, refusing to rat him out to Cuddy or punish him for the deed. In the end, Chase confesses to House that he hit him just to get the rest of the team off his back. House accepts Chase's explanation without comment.

**Clinic Duty:** House is nice to clinic patients, but he has an agenda, wanting to impress Cuddy.

**A Fine Bromance:** Wilson is bemused by House's rather pathetic game to intrude on Cuddy and Lucas' Thanksgiving.

**House Is a Jerk:** House is more of a manipulative ass than usual, trying to score a Thanksgiving invitation from Cuddy. For the second episode in a row, House is a pretty irredeemable jerk through most of this episode. He is only redeemed by . . .

**House *Isn't* a Jerk:** Realizing that the Robitripping provides Jimmy's only chance for happiness, House returns his dextromethorphan, giving his not-so-tacit blessing to DXM misuse. Throughout the series, House has always understood those patients who, like him, find happiness a daunting goal. House has often bent rules to help others have a chance to attain it.

**Patients Know Best:** Jimmy picks up on House's isolation, commiserating with him about the loneliness of being an intellectual outlier.

**Housian Ethics:** After empathizing with Jimmy's isolation when he's off the DXM, House provides him with a bottle of cough medicine. Taub can't believe that House would condone DXM abuse. Although the drug is an over-the-counter medication, some states now require signatures to obtain it.

**Shipper Alert!:** House vows to break up Cuddy and Lucas with a cunning plan that completely backfires when Cuddy one-ups his game. Supposedly anguished about losing her, House is waiting for Lucas when he returns from Thanksgiving dinner. Appearing to be a drunken wreck, House discloses that he's always been in love with Cuddy, but doesn't deserve her. You can't help but feel a frisson of sympathy for House's torment — until he tells Wilson shortly thereafter that the drunken admission is just part of the plan.

**Casting Call:** Esteban Powell played Arnie Swenton in the CBS drama series *The Cleaner* (2008–2009).

**Title Tale:** Using DXM to tone down the volume on his overactive brain, Jimmy knows it will render him blissed out enough to find an escape from his loneliness. He is happy in a relationship with a pretty — yet not genius-level — woman, and for him the sacrifice of genius for happiness is a fair trade. House is ignorant of Cuddy's scheme to have a peaceful Thanksgiving dinner with Lucas, while Cuddy is ignorant of the depth of House's real feelings for her. In the end, when House knows where he stands with Cuddy, he decides to leave them in peace. Everyone is ignorant about Chase's desire to be left alone — except House.

## 6.10 "Wilson"

**Writer:** David Foster **Director:** Lesli Linka Glatter

**Patient of the Week:** Tucker (Josh Malina)

*House* is nearly always experienced from House's point of view: his universe, his actions. In this episode we experience life from Wilson's perspective as he diagnoses a friend for a possible cancer recurrence. We see and experience House and his team through a different lens — and see House in a different light. We also observe Wilson as the head of the Oncology Department. He has his own fellows (a lot of them), a snarky assistant, and even the occasional ability to think like House.

Tucker is Wilson's longtime, but currently cancer-free, leukemia patient. They are also friends. When Tucker collapses during an early morning turkey shoot, Wilson insists it's not a recurrence of his friend's cancer. But House knows that Wilson isn't being objective.

House has an intense dislike of Tucker, believing that he uses Wilson like a doormat (pot, meet kettle). Although Wilson brushes it off, it becomes clear that House is right: Tucker is a jerk. He makes House look like Mother Teresa by comparison. When it becomes clear that Tucker needs a liver transplant, he calls upon Wilson's generosity, guilt, and friendship to donate part of his liver — something with which House and Cuddy vehemently disagree.

**Zebra of the Week:** Tucker suffers from acute lymphoblastic leukemia.

**Iconic Moment in *House* History:** After Wilson agrees to donate part of his liver for the needed transplant, he asks House to be at the surgery with him. House declines, admitting that he's scared of losing Wilson: "If you die, I'm alone." The disclosure isn't easy for the usually guarded House.

**A Fine Bromance:** As Wilson recovers from the transplant surgery, House stays nearby, whether laughing with him or quietly reading at his bedside. Wilson buys a larger condo — the one Cuddy has also been bidding on for herself and Lucas. Wilson is trying to change — be less of a "nice guy," and get back at Cuddy for hurting House.

**House Is a Jerk:** Although not quite in Tucker's league, House does his best to annoy Wilson by being a complete slob around their shared condo. But House is trying to make a point (in the most obnoxious way possible) that perhaps it's time to move on — to a bigger place, and more important, away from memories of Amber.

**House *Isn't* a Jerk:** House goes to great effort trying to procure a donor liver for Tucker so Wilson does not feel compelled to donate his own. And later, as Wilson undergoes the liver surgery, House appears in the operating room gallery, overcoming his fears to be there for his friend.

**Housian Ethics:** In the emergency room, House discovers a matching donor liver for Tucker. Religious beliefs prevent the donor's sister from agreeing to the donation. House and Wilson visit her at home, where House pressures her in his own inimitable fashion. Although he is eventually successful in gaining her consent, they are too late; the liver has exceeded its shelf life.

**Shipper Alert!:** Concerned that House is not reacting at all to Cuddy and Lucas' growing relationship, Wilson wonders how well he's coping. Of course, House's default position is "I'm fine," but he eventually admits that he's not. He's just trying to be an adult about it.

**Metaphorically Speaking:** House and Wilson have two discussions about the possibility of change. For once, House believes that change is possible. (Could this be the result of his therapy with Nolan?) Using the metaphor of a table, Wilson argues that a table will always be a table, to which House counters that all a table needs is a coat of paint to change — to be transformed.

**Casting Call:** Josh Malina plays a recurring character on the TNT drama *In Plain Sight* (2009–present). He is probably best known for his portrayals of Jeremy Goodwin on ABC's *Sports Night* from 1998 to 1999, and Will Bailey during several seasons of the acclaimed NBC series *The West Wing* (1999–2006).

**Title Tale:** The episode is primarily about Wilson. But "Wilson" is also the tale of his two friends. Both are jerks — externally, at least. But which one is the better friend — and better person? The contrast provides us insight into House's current state of mind — and his evolving position on change.

## 6.11 "The Down Low"

**Writers:** Sara Hess, Liz Friedman **Director:** Nick Gomez
**Patient of the Week:** Mickey (Ethan Embry)

Mickey arrives in the clinic after falling down during a drug deal. House notices minute details, including the likelihood that guns were involved in whatever led to his fall. Realizing that Mickey's relatively minor injuries may be the least of his concerns, House proves his point by loudly banging his cane. Mickey goes down again; it's loud-noise-induced vertigo. Is it an auditory issue or a problem in Mickey's brain?

Insisting that they deal "in textiles" and nothing illegal, Mickey and his close associate Eddie don't make it easy on House, who needs to rule out illicit drugs and the toxins with which they are often cut. But the team soon finds itself in the middle of a 16-month drug sting operation; the patient is an undercover cop.

Mickey continues to worsen, but he refuses disclosing anything that might short-circuit the sting operation. With the major drug bust imminent, Mickey is willing to risk his life rather than give away the game.

As House and Wilson settle into their new condo, they meet their beautiful neighbor Nora. Learning that Wilson wants to pursue her, House suddenly takes an interest, but there's a hitch. Nora believes that House and Wilson — two middle-aged guys living together — must be gay. As each tries to outdo the other in pursuit of Nora, their game escalates to operatic proportions.

Meanwhile, "13" orchestrates a plan to screw with the chronically serious Foreman over their respective salaries. She claims it's because the arrogant senior fellow needs to be taken down a peg; Chase wonders if it's revenge for Foreman firing her earlier in the year. But Foreman turns the tables, proving he can give as well he gets (and that he has a sense of humor).

**Zebra of the Week:** It's Hughes-Stovin syndrome, a rare autoimmune disorder. The disease has progressed too far in Mickey's case; there is nothing they can do for him.

**Epiphany!:** House discloses to Nora that Wilson isn't the good guy he appears to be. Suddenly, House realizes that Mickey's symptoms may not be caused by the fungal infection they appear to be. He makes the long associative leap to the correct diagnosis.

**Iconic Moment in *House* History:** Escalating their game, Wilson crashes House's dinner date with Nora — to propose to House! How could House resist such an offer?

**A Fine Bromance:** As part of his pretense, House buys an oversized *Chorus Line* poster for the condo, practically swooning over it in front of Nora. Once the game is over, House is ready to rid himself of it. But Wilson wants to keep it to annoy him, making his point when he serenades House with a song from the Broadway hit.

**House Is a Jerk:** House tries to exploit Nora's perception of his sexuality to win her affection and confidence. Using overly effeminate charm (turned up to a very cheesy "11"), he's more than obvious, but not to the clueless Nora.

**Housian Ethics:** House understands that no matter how many guys are busted in the sting, it's a futile exercise. Their places will be quickly taken by others, ready and waiting.

**Shipper Alert!:** The question on the mind of every House-Wilson shipper is whether there's an element of truth to the game with Nora. The series' creative team has teased at House and Wilson's relationship for years; those who believe it is more than platonic (or should be) have waited since season one to see it outed.

**Metaphorically Speaking:** Mickey and Eddie insist they're in the frock business, not the drug business. But House needs to know more about the exact nature of their wares. Trying to find a mutually agreeable language, House tries his hand at textile-speak: Cocaine becomes "culottes"; heroin is "hosiery."

**Pop Culture References:** House screams, Jack Bauer of *24* style, "I need the drugs!"

**Casting Call:** Ethan Embry (Mickey) starred with *House* alumni John Cho and Kal Penn in *Harold & Kumar Go to White Castle* (2004). Character actor Nick Chinlund (Eddie) was memorable playing death fetishist Donny Pfaster in two episodes of *The X-Files* (1995, 2000).

**Title Tale:** Nothing and no one is what they appear to be; everything is on the "down low" in this episode about secrecy and perception: Mickey isn't a drug dealer; he's an undercover cop. Eddie, who turns out to be a good friend in

Mickey's time of need, isn't quite as evil as Mickey believes. Nora's perceptions of House and Wilson's relationship are wrong — or are they? Chase and "13" scam Foreman, making him believe that he's the lowest-paid member of House's staff. But Foreman can be just as sneaky, and playing on his colleagues' perceptions of him, turns the tables and gets even. Not even Mickey's disease is as it seems. "Down low" is also urban slang for two people who define themselves as straight, but have same-sex relationships. Clearly the title is a nod to those who believe this term applies to House and Wilson.

### 6.12 "Remorse"

**Writer:** Peter Blake **Director:** Andrew Bernstein
**Patient of the Week:** Valerie (Beau Garrett)

The team treats Valerie, a high-powered businesswoman with sudden, severe pounding in her ears, taking the case because, as Foreman notes, "she's hot" — and because House is intrigued by a patient who is hot while her husband is not. "Thirteen" has a bad feeling about her, however.

Sensing Valerie's coldness and mannerisms around her homely husband (who has a multimillion dollar trust fund), "13" nails her as a psychopath. House briefly wonders if the patient's unique underlying psychology is a symptom, but discards the idea when other symptoms don't fit. Valerie continues to worsen, as her heart, kidneys, and liver become involved. Her bones are so brittle that "13" accidentally breaks her arm just moving it. It's not until Valerie's sister appears that the team is able to correctly diagnose and treat her.

We learn that part of House's therapy with Nolan involves apologizing to someone he has wronged. House chooses Wibberly, a medical school classmate with whom he swapped final papers in a genetics class. Wilson criticizes House for choosing a virtual stranger — taking the easy way out — rather someone he actually cares about (like him or Cuddy). But now, after House apologizes in a letter, Wibberly wants to renew contact and have lunch, which House futilely tries to avoid.

House is distressed when Wibberly reveals that the swapped paper caused him to flunk out of medical school, and he now works as a grocery store bag boy. Feeling responsible, House tries to help him financially. But everybody lies, including Wibberly. Not only did he score an A-plus with House's paper, but he became an orthopedic surgeon. He tanked his own career and only seeks to punish House for being an ass when they were in school.

**Zebra of the Week:** Valerie's body is unable to process copper. She has Wilson's disease, which made its first appearance on *House* back in season one ("The Socratic Method," 1.06).

**Epiphany!:** Noting that Valerie hasn't always been a cold bitch, her sister reveals that she changed around puberty, putting psychopathy back on the table as a symptom. The psych symptoms lead House to Wilson's disease.

**Iconic Moment in *House* History:** House tries to take Wilson's advice and goes to Cuddy's office to apologize for defacing her photograph. Observing her in intimate conversation with Lucas, House can't cross her office threshold, simply standing and staring through the glass.

**A Fine Bromance:** Wilson plays his familiar role as House's Jiminy Cricket, haranguing him about choosing to apologize to Wibberly.

**House Is a Jerk:** Not realizing a photograph in Cuddy's office has special significance for her, House defaces it, trying to make a rude statement about Lucas. The snapshot is the last memento she has of her father, who shot the photo.

**House *Isn't* a Jerk:** Realizing that it doesn't matter whether his act had actual consequences for Wibberly in the end, House still feels compelled to help him.

**Judgmental Fellow Alert:** "Thirteen" suggests that House has a few psychopathic tendencies of his own.

**Patients Know Best:** Usually it's the patients with wounded spirits who detect a kindred soul in House. But the psychopathic Valerie perceives a different sort of kinship, believing that like her, House is disengaged from conscience. House denies it, but seems unnerved, wondering whether there is an element of truth in her observation.

**Housian Ethics:** "Thirteen" comes very close to violating Valerie's privacy several times, trying to unveil the calculating amoral interior beneath her sweet, demure wife's mask.

**Shipper Alert!:** Wilson tells House that Cuddy has loved him for years. **Shipper Alert #2:** Foreman and "13," at each other's throats since "Epic Fail" (6.03), finally begin to make peace with their relationship.

**Lost in Translation:** House visits Wilson in the clinic as he treats a Hispanic man. House and the patient engage in animated, rapid-fire Spanish. The entire conversation goes completely (and amusingly) over Wilson's linguistically challenged head.

**Casting Call:** Beau Garrett is a spokesmodel for Revlon cosmetics, and appears as Siren Jem in *Tron Legacy* (2010), which also stars *House* regular Olivia Wilde.

**Title Tale:** Valerie's psychopathy means that she has no conscience; she can feel no remorse. She suggests to House that conscience is an animal instinct that can be ignored if self-interest demands, which House often claims as his prime motivator. Is "13" right, then, when she notes that Valerie reminds her of

House? Does House, like Valerie, act with freedom from conscience? Is he incapable of remorse and regret? Clearly not — although he often acts like he wishes he had no conscience. But the encounter with Valerie weighs heavily, leaving House to wonder about the validity of "13's" and Valerie's observations. Perhaps that's what drives him to force money on Wibberly, even after he learns Wibberly has been lying. Is House trying to prove to himself that he's not like Valerie? That he has the humanity and the conscience she lacks?

### 6.13 "Moving the Chains"

**Writers:** Garrett Lerner, Russel Friend **Director:** David Straiton
**Patient of the Week:** Daryl (Da'Vone McDonald)

When a college football player suddenly goes into a rage during a practice scrimmage, House initially thinks steroid abuse. But as Daryl becomes sicker and his heart, liver, and kidneys become involved, the team believes his symptoms may reflect paraneoplastic syndrome. But none of the tests for cancer come back positive, baffling the team.

We meet finally meet Marcus, Foreman's gang-member older brother, newly paroled for the umpteenth time. Foreman is distressed at the news, and even less happy to learn it from House, who has taken an uncommonly keen interest in the elder Foreman brother.

Going ballistic when House hires Marcus as his new assistant, Foreman justly questions his motives. Is it, as Foreman believes, pure and evil manipulation — or might it be the sort of diabolical yet somehow benevolent puppet mastery that House has honed so well over the years? Is House just trying to screw with his humorless senior fellow — or heal Foreman's family? Of course, House denies any altruism when Wilson asks about it, insisting that he is simply gathering information to use against Foreman when the time is right. Wilson isn't buying it.

Speaking of screwing with people, Lucas declares war on House (and Wilson). Trying to mark his territory, Cuddy's current boy toy cuts a wide swath: he unleashes an opossum in Wilson's bathtub, tampers with its grab-bar (injuring the disabled House), sabotages the condo sprinkler system, and trips House in the hospital cafeteria.

**Zebra of the Week:** Melanoma (skin cancer) hiding in an obscure location — between Daryl's toes.
**Epiphany!:** The team tells House that they've looked everywhere inside Daryl's body for evidence of cancer. "But what if it's not inside?" asks House, won-

dering if his patient has skin cancer, something rare in African-Americans, but impossible to find when it's located on Daryl's football-punished feet.

**Iconic Moment in *House* History:** House and Wilson lie in wait for their unknown condo saboteur late at night in the kitchen. Their vigil proves futile when the sprinkler system suddenly triggers, destroying everything in its path, including their new beloved flat-screen TV.

**Clinic Duty:** House treats an Iraq War soldier about to deploy for a third tour after a stop-loss order. About to become a father, the young man is willing to do *anything* to remain stateside. House has no sympathy for the young man . . . or does he?

**A Fine Bromance:** Wilson is upset with House for using his bathtub instead of the shower stall in his own bathroom. House, who has installed a grab bar in the tub, insists that soaking his leg helps with the pain.

**House Is a Jerk:** House mercilessly baits the overly serious Foreman using Marcus' treasure trove of personal information. The provocations go too far when House violates Marcus' confidence and reveals the recent death of their mother — something Foreman had kept secret from everyone.

**House *Isn't* a Jerk:** Wilson suggests that House's actions are really intended to unite the brothers against him, providing them a common enemy and allowing them to begin to heal their broken family. House only mildly denies the accusation.

**Judgmental Fellow Alert:** Foreman is unwilling to give his brother another chance after too many disappointments. Wilson unfairly blames House for the opossum hissing in his bathtub.

**Housian Ethics:** After a weary, stop-lossed soldier shoots himself in the foot, House warns him that it's not enough to avoid another tour of duty. Just what is House advising the soldier to do when he explains that unless he takes the prescribed antibiotics, he will likely lose the entire foot — something that will keep him from another Iraqi tour?

**Shipper Alert!:** Lucas remains concerned that Cuddy still cares too much for House.

**Props Department:** As House and Wilson lie in wait for their unknown saboteur, House's weapon of choice is a cricket bat, a self-referential nod to actor Hugh Laurie. Laurie plays, and is a fan of, the game, which is a national sport in his native Britain.

**Casting Call:** Orlando Jones, who plays Marcus Foreman, was an original cast member of *MADtv*, Fox network's offbeat sketch comedy series.

**House Canon:** In "Pilot" we learn that Foreman was arrested at 16 for breaking into a house. Now we learn he was 14, and it was a car. The Powers That Be changed it to a car by the second season, leading many to believe it may have been Foreman's second offense, but given what's revealed in "Moving the Chains," that would have been impossible, since Foreman turned his life around after the incident.

**Title Tale:** Every time a football team gets a first down, they "move the chains" towards the goal line. Ten yards at a time, the ball is moved down the 100-yard field, subject to blocks, fumbles, interceptions, and sacks behind the line of scrimmage. "Moving the chains" is also urban slang that signifies small but meaningful steps down a relationship's path towards a "score." Each of the plots and subplots mark forward motion towards another start, suggesting the pain and sacrifice sometimes involved in moving even slightly down the field. A college student tries to better his and his mother's life by making the pros; Marcus and Foreman begin anew; Lucas establishes his territory with Cuddy; a young soldier begins life without a foot — but with his wife and newborn child. All season, House has tried to "move the chains" down the field of his own life.


### 6.14 "5 to 9"
**Writer:** Thomas L. Moran **Director:** Andrew Bernstein
**Patient of the Week:** None

Like "Wilson," "5 to 9" is an off-formula look a day in the life of another resident of the House universe — Cuddy. Her day is off and running at the crack of dawn, when she tries to sneak in a some yoga before baby Rachel demands Mommy's attention. Nearly out the door, Lucas arrives wanting a little morning delight. From there the day goes quickly downhill.

Playing a game of brinkmanship with a mega insurance provider, Cuddy argues that the payment rates being offered to Princeton-Plainsboro are an insult to the hospital's integrity. But the corporate negotiator is a pompous and more than slightly sexist ass who doesn't think Cuddy knows how to play hardball. He is mistaken.

Throughout her day, Cuddy defends her difficult diagnostician, treats a clinic patient who wants to try breast milk to cure his cancer, and argues with the intransigent head of surgery, who accuses Cuddy of favoritism towards House. Learning that drugs are missing from the pharmacy, she plays the pushover with her prime suspect, a pharmacy tech, while luring her into a trap that will bring an end to her drug dealing days.

**Iconic Moment in *House* History:** When Cuddy is at the end of her emotional rope, feeling as if she's lost the power game with giant insurance company, she flees to the solace of her car, certain the game is over. House finds her there, and she seems to derive resolve and gain confidence from his honest, wise counsel. It's the first moment since "Known Unknowns" (6.07) that we perceive an ember of the warmth and trust that has defined their relationship since the series' start.

**Housian Ethics:** After Cuddy and other doctors have refused to prescribe mothers' milk for a cancer patient, House agrees to write a prescription for the unconventional treatment. Understanding that the man is terminal, House explains to Cuddy that the mothers' milk can't harm him — and cites some alternative medicine evidence that it can help, so why not?

**Title Tale:** A play on the 1980 movie *9 to 5*, which chronicled working life in the secretarial pool, we now know that Cuddy's workday begins at the crack of dawn and goes on late into the night.


## 6.15 "Private Lives"

**Writer:** Doris Egan **Director:** Sanford Bookstaver
**Patient of the Week:** Frankie (Laura Prepon)

This week's patient, Frankie, blogs the intimate details of her (and her significant other's) private lives. After an argument with him she begins to bleed under the skin and through her gums. Initially leaning towards rat poison, the team is perplexed after Frankie's urine turns muddy, which indicates kidney involvement — and not poison. Lymphoma is next, but the vaccine for it triggers a deadly response and she spikes a fever, suggesting a rampant infection. Eventually reaching a dead end, the team believes that Frankie is going to die — and soon.

After House outs Wilson's accidental (but brief) career as a porn star, Wilson seeks ammunition to likewise embarrass House. Chase informs him that although House *appears* to be reading *The Golden Bowl*, the book is far too skinny to be Henry James' lengthy novel. Whatever House is reading, he must be enough embarrassed about it to hide the real title. When Wilson discovers that House is really reading a book of inspirational sermons by a Unitarian minister, he is alarmed, wondering if House is having so much difficulty that he's grasping at straws, seeking answers in an antithetical worldview. But Wilson grows intrigued, noting the book jacket photo of the author — it's House's biological father, recognized from John House's funeral ("Birthmarks," 5.04).

**Zebra of the Week:** Frankie has Whipple's disease, a rare and sometimes fatal infection of the gastrointestinal tract.

**Epiphany!:** Wilson harangues House about why he would be so interested in reading religious "crap" — even if it is his father's writing. The word "crap," triggers the synapses, leading House to wonder if Frankie's problem is in her colon.

**Iconic Moment in *House* History:** Believing that House is beginning to isolate himself again, Wilson drags him to a speed dating event. Chase tags along, though House thinks he has an unfair advantage with his good looks and sexy accent. **Iconic Moment #2:** Wilson confronts House about why he's reading his father's words rather than taking the emotional risk of actually trying to connect with him. He determines that House must be seeking to understand something about himself through his father's writing. House's sad truth, notes Wilson, is that he is "way out there on the fringe somewhere," always alone. "Half the time, I don't understand you," he says. Wilson theorizes that House is trying "to look across the gulf and know there's someone else like you."

**A Fine Bromance:** What's more bromantic than tandem speed dating?

**House Is a Jerk:** "Be not afraid! The forest nymphs have taught me how to please a woman." House outs Wilson's starring role (or non-role) in a porn movie made when he was in college.

**Judgmental Fellow Alert:** Chase calls House a hypocrite for insisting he's an atheist while at the same time intensely studying a book of religious sermons. Wilson discovers that House is reading this book, which seems to make no sense given House's worldview. Wilson immediately jumps to the conclusion that House is back on Vicodin and desperate — the only thing that would drive the atheist House to a religious book.

**Shipper Alert!:** After his speed dating success, Chase begins to wonder if the only reason women find him attractive (including the estranged Cameron) is his looks. He begins doubting that Cameron had ever really loved him.

**Casting Call:** Laura Prepon played Donna in the long-running Fox hit *That '70s Show*.

**Title Tale:** Frankie explains that sometimes it's easier to open yourself up to strangers. But it can become destructive when sharing secrets with your readers surpasses the importance of maintaining your spouse's privacy. House has always found it easier to unburden his secrets to strangers. Outwardly his life is an open book: he's an unabashed jerk who (as Chase points out) brings hookers to the hospital and openly gambles with bookies. But House has another, more introspective side, one that he keeps essentially private (even from Wilson and Cuddy). Of course, no one's life is private with the hyper-observant House around, especially if he finds it amusing — like Wilson's porno past. But as House says, "We all need secrets. As long as they don't kill anybody, they keep us safe and warm."

## 6.16 "Black Hole"

**Writer:** Lawrence Kaplow **Director:** Greg Yaitanes

**Patient of the Week:** Abby (Cali Fredrichs)

Abby stops breathing while watching a planetarium sky show on a high school field trip, and something unpleasant oozes from her mouth. The case, of course, finds its way to House, where the team first thinks infection. But after Abby's aorta "dissects" and they have to perform emergency open-heart surgery, "13" thinks Abby has had a severe allergic reaction to her boyfriend's semen.

When Abby begins suffering hallucinations along with her other symptoms, House believes that like nighttime dreams of waterfalls and running brooks tell the dreamer that he or she has to go to the bathroom, Abby's subconscious is trying to tickle her conscious mind and tell her something. Her hallucinations have meaning.

Foreman vehemently disagrees, thinking House is insane for wanting to pursue this unproven diagnostic path, but House believes that cognitive pattern recognition is really their only hope to save Abby, no matter how crazy it seems.

In the meantime, House harasses Wilson for still not having furnished their new condo (they don't even have a dining table). Suggesting he is so devoid of personality, that he is incapable of even choosing furniture for himself, House challenges Wilson to purchase a single item for the condo.

**Zebra of the Week:** It's cerebellar schistosomiasis delayed hypersensitivity reaction: a severe allergic reaction caused by the remains of a parasite that Abby's immune system killed.

**Epiphany!:** House harasses Taub about having affairs with women half his age, suggesting that he's now old enough to be their "daddies." Making a leap that the man of Abby's visions is her boyfriend's father, House consider that the father might actually be the source of her disease.

**Iconic Moment in *House* History:** Wilson visits a furniture store and tries to "find himself." It's a great dialogue-free moment for Wilson as he bounces, sits, and examines — but doesn't buy. **Iconic Moment #2:** We've had too few of these the last couple of years, but we get a classic scene of House, alone, contemplating Abby's symptoms, staring at scans, thinking, sitting, and processing when his diagnostic trail reaches a dead end.

**A Fine Bromance:** Wilson finally purchases something for the condo on his own after hiring a decorator for the rest. True to Wilson's personality, it's not for him — it's for House. The organ is a lovely gesture, given that House's piano is still back at his apartment — and very Wilson. House is delighted and can barely wait to put his fingers on the keys.

**House Is a Jerk:** House outs the fact that Abby had sex with her boyfriend's father. It's important information for the case, but still!

**House *Isn't* a Jerk:** House plays anonymous cupid to Rachel and Taub, instigating romance in his own Housian way.

**Judgmental Fellow Alert:** Foreman wins hands down for being unremittingly dismissive of House's ideas. He's an intransigent jerk, especially in light of House's open-mindedness to Foreman's suggestions during the case.

**Shipper Alert!:** Taub and Rachel are having marital problems — trust issues, perhaps? He tries to make amends by romantically proposing to renew their marriage vows. House compliments him for rededicating himself to his efforts, but he is disappointed when he observes Taub chatting with a physiotherapist.

**Musical Notes:** Add the organ to House's list of musical instruments. House seems equally at home with Bach and the blues as he plays the Bach-infused opening organ line in Procol Harum's "A Whiter Shade of Pale" — a metaphorical ballad on the complexities of relationships.

**Casting Call:** Cali Fredrichs appeared in the intriguingly titled video, *OC Babes and the Slasher of Zombietown* (2008) and the short film *Psycho Hillbilly Cabin Massacre* (2007).

**Title Tale:** "Black Hole," is all about opacity and trying to find the truth within a densely constructed façade. The episode explores the opacities and closely guarded interiors of not only the patient, but of Wilson and Taub as well.


### * 6.17 "Lockdown"

**Writers:** Eli Attie, Peter Blake, Garrett Lerner, Russel Friend, David Foster
**Director:** Hugh Laurie
**Patient of the Week:** Nash (David Strathairn)

After a newborn goes missing from the hospital's Obstetrics Unit, Cuddy places the entire building on lockdown — no one enters or leaves, and everyone stays exactly where they are.

Wilson and "13" are stuck together in the cafeteria where they engage in a game of "Truth or Dare." Taub and Foreman are trapped in an old records room where they think they've found the gold mine — House's personnel file. Chase is confronted by Cameron as she comes to personally hand him the divorce papers. House ducks into a patient's room, only to find a dying man — a patient named Nash whose case he had once refused, and who will likely die within hours.

House observes Nash, a classics professor: his room lacks flowers, photos, and any other evidence of human contact. When House offers to put him into a morphine haze to end his hours in "blissful sleep" rather than in intractable pain, Nash wonders if it's for his comfort — or House's. But Nash also believes that fate has brought the two of them together at this particular moment in time.

**Zebra of the Week:** This week, the mystery isn't really medical. The missing baby is found under towels in a linen bin, put there by a woman on the housekeeping staff with a seizure disorder.

**Epiphany!:** Cuddy notices the woman's odd behavior and realizes she's been having seizures. She might well have put the baby in the linen bin without even realizing it.

**Iconic Moment in *House* History:** Chase and Cameron finally get closure on their now seemingly ended marriage. It's a wonderfully raw scene, with all of Chase's and Cameron's insecurities finally coming to the surface, but too late. In the end, they come to some peace and part amicably. **Iconic Moment #2:** Foreman and Taub get stoned on Vicodin trying to walk in House's shoes. Unlike House, however, they are barely able to stand in them, much less practice medicine.

**Clinic Duty:** The only action in the clinic is between Cameron and Chase — and it's considerable.

**A Fine Bromance:** In House's absence, "13" stands in, bringing out the bad boy in Wilson, daring him to "steal a dollar" from the cafeteria cash register.

**House Is a Jerk:** When Nash recognizes House as the doctor he had approached earlier with his symptoms, House condescendingly snipes that Nash's illness "is beneath my pay grade."

**House *Isn't* a Jerk:** House persuades Nash to place a call to his estranged daughter so he can tell her he loves her before dying. After the lockdown ends and House is free to leave, he continues caring for Nash, before putting him out with morphine.

**Patients Know Best:** Seeing that House is limping heavily, Nash notes that he must be having a "bad pain day." After House acknowledges that he's had a month of those, Nash suggests that House's pain might originate not in his physical injury, but the emotional pain of "long lost love." Deflecting, House turns Nash's keen insight on its head wondering who *he's* lost. Persisting, the dying Nash promises, "Your secrets couldn't be safer — unless you're keeping them from yourself." House confesses that Lydia ("Broken," 6.01/6.02) has changed him from someone who believes he's better off alone to someone who craves human connection.

**Housian Ethics:** What are the ethics of House's medical practice? On one hand, he selects the cases he wants to pursue; on the other, those he ignores probably die waiting for a diagnosis that never comes. It leads us to wonder how many other "Nashes" House has dismissed as "boring." On the other hand, as House (rather arrogantly) says, "It's really a good argument for there being more than one me."

**Shipper Alert!:** Chase and Cameron finally get a chance to discuss their relationship and its death. They talk about what went wrong — and the good times.

**Shipper Alert #2:** Wilson tells "13" that he's thinking of dating his first ex-wife, Sam Carr.

**Casting Call:** David Strathairn received Oscar, BAFTA, Screen Actors Guild, and Golden Globe nominations for his unforgettable portrayal of Edward R. Murrow in *Good Night, and Good Luck* (2005).

**House Canon:** Wilson's condo is at 519 Morehall Street, and Wilson is listed as House's physician and emergency contact. (Although the record is proven to be a huge setup by House, there's no reason to believe that this "factual" information is incorrect.)

**Title Tale:** The obvious: Princeton-Plainsboro in lockdown. Less obviously, as everyone is stuck in place during the lockdown, boredom and the unusual situation cause them to let down their carefully constructed and padlocked guards and open up to each other.

**Why It's a Classic:** Hugh Laurie's debut as a *House* director allows us deep within House's emotional landscape as he comes face to face with a patient he refused to treat.

## 6.18 "Knight Fall"

**Writer:** John C. Kelly **Director:** Juan J. Campanella
**Patient of the Week:** William (Noah Segan)

A jealous king, a brave knight wannabe (with a couple of secrets that could get him burned at the stake back in those good old days), and a soon-to-be wedded queen: there's intrigue at court. Is this the latest installment of *The Tudors*? No, my liege, it's "*House* goes to the Renaissance fair."

Young knight William (Noah Segan) feels himself unworthy of the Renaissance acting troupe's queen, who is about to marry the king. But it's clear from the teaser that the queen has feelings for the young man, whom she chooses as her champion in a swordfight. The much smaller (and geekier looking) William prevails against the king's hulking captain of the guard, stunning the king, the queen — and his opponent — in battle. But William falls suddenly, his eyes demon red.

House and the team are perplexed even after investigating the young man's home (where they find he's into witchcraft and potions) and the Renaissance fair campgrounds, at which he spends most of his time. There's plenty of evidence and sources for environmental and organism-borne illness in both places as the team considers everything from sanitary conditions and crowding at the fairgrounds to the possibility he's been poisoned with hemlock by the king.

In the meantime, House probably wishes he had some hemlock as Wilson and his ex-wife Sam begin dating. He does his hemlock-free best, however, to break up the new couple; he says it's to protect Wilson's from another failed (re)marriage, but House has a history of self-interested interference. Is he being noble — or a jerk?

**Zebra of the Week:** Anabolic steroid use enhanced by hemlock ingestion.

**Epiphany!:** When Sam pleads with House to stop trying to sabotage her relationship with Wilson and allow nature to take its course, House realizes that the hemlock has accelerated William's anabolic steroid use. Neither William in his quest to be a knight, nor the king, who is jealous, is willing to let nature take its course. It's an odd and obscure connection, but House is pleased enough with it to kiss his sword.

**Iconic Moment in *House* History:** House and "13" attend the Renaissance fair in full costume. House looks spiffy in leathers, brocades, and feathers.

**A Fine Bromance:** House perceives Wilson slipping away from him, just as Cuddy has. Will he be left alone as they move on with life?

**House Is a Jerk:** House does all he can to subvert Wilson and Sam's new relationship.

**House *Isn't* a Jerk:** House enlists Lucas to help him get rid of Sam by doing his private-eye best to get the goods on her. And he has acquired a sealed envelope full of revealing intel. Instead of using it to further disrupt her relationship with Wilson, House's better angels prevail and he throws it away, allowing Wilson this chance at happiness.

**Judgmental Fellow Alert:** "Thirteen" tells William that he's wimping out by not telling the queen how he feels.

**Shipper Alert!:** Cuddy advises House not to push Wilson to make a choice about Sam, reminding him that he might not be happy with the result.

**Casting Call:** Cynthia Watros (Wilson's first ex-wife, Sam Carr) played Libby Smith on ABC's hit series *Lost* (2005–2010).

**Title Tale:** This is a tale of a knight who has to watch his lady fair be with another man day after day with little hope of winning her. Who does that sound like? It applies to this week's patient, certainly. But there are resonances here for House as well. As William believes himself unworthy of the queen, House may feel the same way towards Cuddy. But Sir Gregory, the knight-errant of

Princeton-Plainsboro, possesses his own unique nobility, integrity, and fealty to his friends.

## 6.19 "Open and Shut"

**Writers:** Liz Friedman, Sara Hess **Director:** Greg Yaitanes

**Patient of the Week:** Julia (Sarah Wayne Callies)

Julia falls ill in a hotel room grabbing her abdomen in agony. She asks her young lover Tom to get her husband, who has just left the room. It's a case of open marriage, and no matter the medical crisis, it's bound to interest House, who is ever curious about unique relationships.

In addition to the abdominal pain, Julia is also running a fever. When she develops an arrhythmia, the team thinks she must have a parasitic infection from sexual contact. But without evidence, Chase and "13" break into the patient's home. They think they find the answer in Julia's loofah sponge, which may be contaminated with parasites. But that isn't the answer either — and by now Julia has developed a clotting disorder, followed by abdominal inflammation.

Intrigued by Julia's relationship, Taub is skeptical, believing that a "functional open marriage is a unicorn." As pretty a notion as they seem, they simply do not exist. At first, House isn't sure, wondering if Julia and her husband indeed have something special — until that is, they discover that the husband isn't participating, but is lying to his wife about money. The unicorn is simply a "donkey with a plunger stuck to its face."

Taub asks Rachel to consent to the same sort of relationship, which would free him to philander guilt-free. Eventually agreeing, she ultimately she backs out; Taub does not.

Vowing to stop interfering in Wilson's new relationship, House argues that Wilson needs to say what's on his mind rather than passive-aggressively letting annoyance simmer and boil over into a toxic mess. So House gives Wilson a little push, which provokes a heated argument between the formerly married couple. The airing of grievances proves House right, and strengthens the renewed relationship, but Sam and Wilson agree not to credit House.

**Zebra of the Week:** Henoch-Schönlein purpura, a systemic inflammation of the blood vessels that can wreak havoc throughout the body's systems.

**Epiphany!:** House notices that Julia's husband brought lilacs from their garden. House recalls that his mother grew lilacs, but his father made her stop because there were too many bees. House suggests Henöch-Schonlein because it can be sometimes triggered by a bee sting. They had ruled it out because Julia has no apparent rash, but on closer examination the purpura are there, but hiding in her throat.

**Iconic Moment in *House* History:** House returns to the condo to find Sam and Wilson intimately engaged in a card game. With Wilson barely acknowledging his presence, House has probably never felt so trapped and alone as the third wheel to this new tight twosome — something he, himself, has inadvertently helped to engineer. He walks away, barely noticed and without a word, thus beginning an inevitable fall towards despair.

**A Fine Bromance:** House helps Wilson in the only way he can — by provocation.

**House Is a Jerk:** After Wilson tells House that Sam has ended their relationship, House cavalierly asks if he wants to "grab some dinner."

**House *Isn't* a Jerk:** House argues that his motivation in interfering is altruistic — to get Wilson to air his feelings rather than let them boil over.

**Shipper Alert!:** "Thirteen" uncovers a truth about House: that he believes in monogamy. She perceives what many viewers already know: that House is at heart a romantic — cynical, certainly, but always hoping to be proved wrong about his cynicism. **Shipper Alert #2:** Chase admits his jealously of Cameron and House, "although she never touched him." But the perceptive "13" suggests that Chase isn't counting the "emotional fondling." **Shipper Alert #3:** House buys Cuddy an espresso machine after "doing something nice" for Wilson leads to Sam breaking it off (albeit temporarily). House feels the karma in doing something "nice" for Cuddy, because doing nice things leads to nice things happening in return. Perhaps Lucas will die, suggests House sarcastically, in explanation of his gift, or perhaps he'll receive oral sex (presumably from Cuddy). "*Namaste*," says House, without another word. Used in India and Nepal, the expression means, more or less, "I bow to you." Cuddy tries hard not to be, but she is amused.

**Props Department:** The whiteboard makes its first real appearance of the season, but Chase, not House, controls the markers. House's universe is not yet set back in order.

**Casting Call:** Sarah Wayne Callies starred as prison doc Sara Tancredi in the Fox series *Prison Break* (2005–2009).

**Title Tale:** Nothing is ever "open and shut" — as simple as it seems on the surface. An open marriage — created to prevent the deceptions that come with too many longtime relationships — blows up over a betrayal, but is saved by the underlying love between the partners. House believes he's tanked Wilson's relationship with Sam, only to find that he's instead made it stronger, yet he himself is cut off and alone. Taub believes that an open marriage is the panacea he's been seeking to cure his philandering ways, only to learn it ain't so easy. Even the beautiful spring lilacs can't be simple when they attract bees that trigger fatal illnesses. And on *House*, that most complex of medical dramas, nothing is *ever* open and shut.

### 6.20 "The Choice"

**Writer:** David Hoselton **Director:** Juan J. Campanella
**Patient of the Week:** Ted (Adam Garcia)

The team treats Ted, a young man who faints at the altar just before the exchange of wedding vows in a big church ceremony. Presenting in the emergency room with aphasia, House doesn't quite believe him, and sticking him with a needle, Ted can suddenly express himself. But when he passes out again, unable to breathe after being discharged, this time with a pleural effusion (fluid around the heart), House and the team are stumped.

Breaking into Ted's old apartment to look for toxins or anything else that may be causing the symptoms, "13" and Taub are interrupted by Ted's old roommate Kotter, who claims to be not just a roommate, but Ted's former boyfriend. Ted insists he's not gay; however, the bisexual "13" wonders if he's being honest, and it's not until she discovers that Ted has undergone conversion therapy to "become" straight that the team heads down the right diagnostic path.

Taub continues to be unfaithful to his wife, Rachel. And under the guise of trying to destroy his marriage by outing him, House manipulates him into breaking off the affair.

Wilson worries about House's emotional state when he wakes up in the neighbor's bed, having let himself into the wrong apartment, too drunk to notice. House admits it to Cuddy, and she also becomes concerned, fearing that House is beginning to withdraw and may be headed for trouble. Wilson's solution is to pay House's fellows to keep him company.

**Zebra of the Week:** Ted was born with a Chiari malformation, a structural defect in the cerebellum. It causes the brain stem to be pushed downward, affecting the flow of cerebrospinal fluid (CSF), and causing all of Ted's symptoms. The condition kicks into high gear after receiving electroshock therapy as part of his "conversion" therapy.

**Epiphany!:** Arguing with Wilson about the possibility of change, House asserts that wisdom is knowing the "difference between what you can change and what you've been born with." Stopping mid-sentence, it suddenly dawns on House that Ted has a genetic malformation — his symptoms are caused by something with which he was born.

**Iconic Moment in *House* History:** House goes to a karaoke bar with Chase and Foreman, performing the 1973 Gladys Knight and the Pips' classic "Midnight Train to Georgia." Chase sings lead while Foreman and House play the "Pips," complete with harmonies and choreography. **Iconic Moment #2:** House is like a kid in a candy store accompanying "13" to a lesbian bar. House "window shops" and he and "13" talk about each other's self-pity. But when House sees her hand shake, a symptom of her evidently worsening Huntington's symptoms, a flash of real concern crosses his eyes.

**A Fine Bromance:** When House realizes that Wilson is behind a sudden rash of dinner invitations, he calls him on the manipulation. Initially, House refuses to go along; however Wilson admits that he's engineered it in his own self-interest. He wants to be able to spend time with Sam guilt free. House agrees to do it — just for Wilson. After House admits he's had a good time out with his fellows, of course Wilson must turn it into a life lesson about the possibility to change.

**House Is a Jerk:** House continues to goad Taub about his infidelity, but with a purpose: to force him to make a choice.

**House *Isn't* a Jerk:** House agrees to go out with his fellows to please Wilson; he also saves Taub's marriage — but in the most Housian way possible.

**Judgmental Fellow Alert:** "Thirteen" accuses Ted of being untrue to himself and unfair to his bride-to-be.

**Shipper Alert!:** Concerned about House, Cuddy stops by his office to make small talk and invite him to dinner, which House declines, refusing her pity. She wants assurance that despite her ongoing relationship with Lucas their friendship is intact. "I just want us to be friends," she says. In relationship terms, "just friends" is a stake in the heart to anyone who wants more. "Friends," he replies, "is that last thing I want us to be." **Shipper Alert #2:** Taub ultimately ends his affair, largely due to House's manipulations — and Taub thanks him for saving his marriage.

**Gross-out Moment:** House grosses out his fellows by feigning to ingest milk secreted from the patient's bizarrely lactating nipples — for no particular reason.

**Casting Call:** Ted is played by Adam Garcia, an Australian stage and screen actor, whose best known roles include Doody in a 1998–1999 London production of *Grease*. Susan Sarandon's daughter, Eva Amurri, plays Ted's girlfriend, Nicole. The resemblance between mother and daughter is striking.

**Title Tale:** Do we get to choose how we live our lives? Ted believes it's true — or is he just trying to prove it to himself because the idea of being gay frightens him? There are paths we can choose, and destinies with which we are born — difficult, if not impossible, to change. Can House change his story? Is his misery something with which he's cursed, or is a night out with his fellows proof that he's making a conscious choice when he withdraws again afterwards? We make choices in our relationships all the time, and in the end, House makes a choice not to settle for being "just friends" with Cuddy. With the pain increasing in his leg, hopelessness begins to take hold in House's heart. Here, he makes a choice as well, pouring from a flask of single malt whiskey, knowing that over-the-counter ibuprofen tablets will not be adequate to dull the pain.

## * 6.21 "Baggage"

**Writer:** Doris Egan, David Foster **Director:** David Straiton
**Patient of the Week:** Sidney (Zoe McLellan)

House treats Sidney, a young woman with amnesia. As House relates the case during a psychotherapy session to his psychiatrist, Dr. Darryl Nolan (who we first meet in "Broken," 6.01), Nolan wonders why House is so focused on this particular case. Through flashback and non-linear storytelling, we are taken through House's week.

House first encounters Sidney in the emergency room. Unaware of her past, she doesn't even recognize her husband, Jay, once they locate him. All she's certain of is that the shared life he describes to her rings false.

Jay explains that after a family tragedy, Sidney wanted to find more "meaning" in her life. Changing course, she went from a surfer girl to high-powered attorney. But with no memory of this life-altering tragedy, she has reverted to the surfer girl she had always intrinsically been. Now, a stranger to who she has become, she is also a stranger to her husband of several years.

With an initial diagnosis of a prion disease, a progressive and potentially deadly neurological condition, Sidney and Jay must face with a choice: a needed surgery will likely eradicate her memories permanently; without it, she will die. Sidney consents, but Jay argues that she is incapable of consenting in her condition. Refusing to allow the surgery, he is afraid of losing a cherished relationship with the woman he loves.

Fortunately, Sidney doesn't have a prion disease — and doesn't need the surgery. Her symptoms are caused by a vestige of her past life, barely visible, even in bright light. House's week is complicated when Wilson decides it's time for House to move out — and by the reappearance of Mayfield roommate Alvie.

**Zebra of the Week:** Allergic reaction to the vestiges of a not-quite-removed tattoo.
**Epiphany!:** As Sidney passes beneath an ultraviolet light, House notices a faded tattoo on her ankle, barely visible even under lights. House speculates that the

ink from the tattoo got into Sidney's bloodstream when she recently became a very serious long-distance runner.

**Iconic Moment in *House* History:** Nolan asks House, "What did you screw up?" after he notices that House may have intentionally gotten himself beat up in a bar fight. He is really asking House why he feels he deserves to be punished. House has no ready answer.

**A Fine Bromance:** House defends Wilson's actions to Nolan.

**House Is a Jerk:** Finding Alvie living in his apartment — and in the middle of redecorating it — House orders him to leave, but not until he puts the place back in order.

**House Isn't a Jerk:** House finds a unique way to help Alvie when he has problems with Immigration and fears being deported.

**Shipper Alert!:** We learn that House has acquired a valuable medical text written by Cuddy's great grandfather — something he's been saving to give to her for a "special occasion."

**Casting Call:** Zoe McLellan is probably best known for her role as Navy Petty Officer Jennifer Coates in the CBS drama series *JAG* from 2001 to 2005.

**Title Tale:** Everyone has baggage — some more than others. Sometimes coping with that baggage, dealing with it, discarding it, is the only way to really move on and grow. Has nearly a year of psychotherapy enabled House to begin addressing his?

**Why It's a Classic:** With its almost play-like structure, "Baggage" is a riveting episode featuring two powerhouse performances. It's one of the series' best episodes.

---

### On the Couch with Dr. House:
### A Closer Look at "Baggage"

Since his release from Mayfield last autumn, House has continued his therapy with Dr. Nolan between the lines and behind the scenes. But in "Baggage" (6.21) we are flies on the wall as he takes Nolan through his week. Running the gamut from belligerent and sarcastic to vulnerable and fearful, House walks Nolan through his most recent case, which has emotional significance for him.

Nolan immediately notices that things seem "off." Among other things, House is late to his regular appointment, a rare enough occurrence for Nolan to wonder if something is wrong. House insists that his week has been uneventful, but when Nolan challenges him, House can only glare.

411

Backed into a corner, House reveals the events of his week as Nolan questions every action and reaction for meaning and subtext. Revisiting House's latest case we learn that House's week has been far from ordinary.

Treating Sidney, a woman with amnesia, House grows upset when her husband, Jay, seems willing to risk her life rather than risk the possibility that she may never remember him. It's a horrible choice to make, knowing that by saving his wife's life, he risks losing her forever. Frustrated that Jay seems to value the relationship over Sidney's life, House explains to Nolan that people get stupid when they're about to lose someone they love.

Sidney remembers nothing about her current life, including her marriage. Jay forges ahead, as if can somehow convince her to remember their life together. But Sidney is put off by his aggressiveness; his approach is too familiar — too intimate. To Sidney, he is a stranger. When Jay suddenly alters his approach, courting his wife as if wooing her for the first time, interestingly, Nolan senses House's touch. What does Nolan understand about House to draw this conclusion — something House only lightly brushes off?

Does House perceive Jay making the same mistakes he has made, blowing up relationship after relationship? And is House coming to an understanding about himself? Like Jay, House knows he is losing someone he loves (two, if you count Wilson). Trying to connect through familiar language and shared memory is impossible for Jay, since these are no longer part of Sidney's experience.

For House, familiar territory includes elaborate game playing and lusty innuendo, but Cuddy is no longer interested. She's grown up and away, leaving House alone and lost. Can he alter his tactics? Is it too late for him to court Cuddy as he has advised Sidney's husband? Is this what's on House's mind as he talks through the case with Nolan — and why it seems so important to him?

But Sidney's story is not the only thing troubling House. Wilson has now decided that it's time for House to move out as Sam prepares to move into the condo. And it's not Sam who wants to be rid of House — it's Wilson.

Nolan is surprised that House doesn't feel betrayed, but House shrugs it off as inevitable given Wilson's new reality. But when House returns to his old apartment, he finds it in disarray, with Alvie, his Mayfield roommate, having made himself at home in House's absence. He finds that Alive has pawned several of his books, one of which is an antiquarian medical text by one Dr. Earnest Cuddy.

Wilson soon reverses his decision and invites House to return to the condo, but House smells collusion with Cuddy. Through House's point of view, we observe Wilson and Cuddy argue like divorced parents about whose turn it is to be House's caretaker, ever-vigilant to ensure he's not crushed beneath the weight of his own emotional fragility. Nolan challenges House's pessimistic assumptions with an alternate scenario. Nolan asks: what if the eviction suggests only that Wilson believes House is ready to move on? Whoever is correct, the fact remains that House sees Wilson distancing himself just as Cuddy has done.

Noticing a bruise on House's arm, Nolan questions how he got it. Not wanting to discuss, but feeling impelled to do so, House replies simply, "I fell." Going on, House reveals that was too drunk to remember what happened, but assumes that he provoked a brawl — getting himself beat up.

Suggesting that "on some level" House is trying to punish himself, Nolan has an epiphany. Wondering suddenly why House feels he "deserves" to be punished, he asks pointedly, "What did you screw up?"

The answer eludes House, and the reveal upsets House so much, that he drops his defenses just long enough for Nolan (and us) to see it. It's not about the case: House hasn't screwed that up. It has to be more significant than that anyway. So Nolan assumes it's about a relationship, which is why House seems so keen about discussing Sidney. Jay fears that he is losing his wife; House fears he has lost Cuddy — and is about to lose Wilson. Has House pushed his relationship with Wilson too far? House angrily (almost violently) denies it.

Nolan makes the connection between the pawned medical text and Cuddy. Recognizing the title and — after a Google search — the author, Nolan realizes that the pawned book isn't just any book. A rare tome, worth thousands of dollars, House acquired it a long time ago, and when it's been pawned is desperate to recover it. Written by Cuddy's great grandfather, House purchased the book to give to her "for a special occasion" — a special occasion that has never come, and now may never come.

House is in full-on denial that it's the relationship with Cuddy upsetting him so much — to the point of self-destructiveness. Playing it cool, House dismisses Nolan's suggestion, protesting that he's not even involved with her at this point. And just as Nolan may have hit on something, touching a raw nerve, House decides he's had enough of Nolan — and of therapy.

He's done everything Nolan has asked. Psychotherapy, medication, and getting off narcotics were all supposed to have helped him claw his way out of misery, but House finds himself no better off than where he started. "You're a faith healer," House angrily accuses Nolan, deciding in the end, that he's had enough. There is nothing in Nolan's bag of tricks to help House. He feels betrayed and preyed upon, his efforts unrewarded, and for all he's tried changing, he is still miserable. As he has over the seasons, House has wanted to believe in the possibility of transformation — and once again he believes he's walking away empty-handed.

So House backs away, allowing both Cuddy and Wilson room to breathe in their new relationships. Withdrawing into a bottle of single malt, House is more alone than ever. But the answer to Nolan's pointed "What did you screw up?" may have only been partially answered — the remainder left to the season finale. . . .

### * 6.22 "Help Me"

**Writers:** Russel Friend, Garrett Lerner, Peter Blake **Director:** Greg Yaitanes
**Patient of the Week:** Hanna (China Shavers)

House and Cuddy are called to the scene of a crane collapse to help with a massive seach and rescue attempt. At first reluctant to participate, House is drawn in when he discovers a young woman trapped beneath the rubble. With her leg caught beneath tons of debris and the rescue team talking amputation, House connects with Hanna as he revisits a fateful decision made about his own leg years ealier, confessing that had he agreed to amputation all those years ago, he might not be the miserable, bitter person he has become. Against this intense backdrop, Cuddy informs House that she and Lucas are now engaged.

**Zebra of the Week:** The medical mystery is in discovering what made the crane operator drop his payload. Was he unconscious or asleep at the wheel? It turns out to be a cyst on the spinal cord that caused the disaster.
**Epiphany!:** The epiphany this week has less to do with either Hanna or the crane operator than with House himself. After Cuddy verbally slaps him with a visceral reality check, House sees the root of his misery in a new and harsh light.
**Iconic Moment in *House* History:** There are several in this powerful episode. House's regretful disclosure to Hanna about his leg; an intense and gripping scene in which House amputates Hanna's leg; the moment House knows that she's doomed, and of course, the final image of season six: House and Cuddy's

clasped hands with the promise of their future before them.

**House *Isn't* a Jerk:** House demonstrates what lies beneath his misanthrope's façade: a man of great integrity and depth, nobility, and compassion — and a doctor of tremendous skill with a devastating bedside manner.

**Shipper Alert!:** Cuddy declares to House that she cannot help but be in love with him after breaking off her engagement to Lucas. They kiss (for real this time) and end the season with their hands clasped.

**Casting Call:** China Shavers has appeared in numerous television and film projects, including *ER* and *Boston Public*, and the film *The Glass House* (2001).

**Title Tale:** At a press conference a couple of years ago, *House, M.D* star Hugh Laurie referred to a scene in a classic *Star Trek* episode in which Captain Kirk looks out over the cosmos, saying, "Somewhere out there someone is saying the three most beautiful words in any language." But, says Laurie, those three words are not what you would expect. They're not "I love you." They are, Laurie recalled (though not completely accurately), "Please help me." Laurie went on to suggest that "House is a character in need of human contact and some kind of redemption. That 'please help me' aspect I think is an important element in the show." In "Broken," at the beginning of season six, his defenses finally shattered, House asks Nolan to "help him" — to heal him. And now at the end of season six, House hears those other words, words he probably heard too seldom growing up, and, with the possible exception of his time with Stacy, not often since. But our battered and bruised antihero ends season six knowing that he is loved by someone he loves in return. It is certainly a new path for him — and the series. Where will it take him? Where will it take us? Only season seven will tell.

**Why It's a Classic:** House's revelation about his leg and what it's cost him is matched by the final scene, with House and Cuddy finally together. Laurie's quietly brilliant acting and a tightly written script make this episode a perfect lead-in to the next chapter of House's story.

> "We earned this happy ending by really putting House through the ringer this season. Through the psychiatric hospital, this emotional angst with Cuddy, and finally — literally — having a building fall on top of him. And then he has to crawl out from underneath this thing. It felt like he really deserved it."
>
> **— Executive producer/writer Russel Friend, May 2010 interview**

"[The] cliffhanger is in what this relationship is going to look like. Can it work? Has House changed enough? Will Cuddy be able to tolerate him? After all, House will still be House. Hopefully all those questions are cliffhanger enough that people want to see those questions answered."

— **Executive producer/writer Garrett Lerner on season seven, May 2010 interview**

## Redemption: A Closer Look at "Help Me"

The broken man sits on his bathroom floor: a mirror image of a year ago. In pain, adrenaline rush gone after a grueling day in battlefield hospital conditions, he is tormented by a happiness always beyond his grasp. And in his hand are two pills: his ruin — or his salvation?

A year clear of Vicodin, House could take just two, and the pain in his leg and the pain in his heart would fade into a light narcotic haze. Just how long has House been pondering those pills when we first see him sitting there?

We are transported eight hours into the past, where this hellish day begins with a simple gesture. Resigned to Cuddy and Lucas now living together, House presents Cuddy with the antique medical book written by her great grandfather. A conciliatory move, he gives it to both Lucas and a skeptical Cuddy, wishing them well. But when Cuddy reacts oddly, House perceives a glimmer of hope, wondering if there's "trouble in paradise."

But there's no time to reflect as Cuddy insists they get to the site of a crane accident. The operator has presumably fallen asleep causing the giant machine to topple an adjacent building. Of the 100 people inside, fewer than 70 have been rescued.

But with no desire to play the heroic rescuer at the scene, House quickly finds a medical mystery and a ticket back to the comfort of his office (so he thinks), examining the crane operator. Insisting that a neurological problem caused him to pass out, House wants to bring him back to Princeton-Plainsboro to diagnose him, but Cuddy has other ideas. Sending Foreman back to Princeton-Plainsboro, she orders House to stay and do his job.

House is more interested in analyzing Cuddy's reaction to the gift than in treating the wounded, but just as he's found a safe spot away from the action to discuss the Cuddy situation with Wilson, he hears banging on a pipe. Although the rescue team hears nothing, House's curiosity gets the better of him and he follows an exposed pipe into a small space beneath the collapsed parking structure. Though he sees and hears nothing, something suddenly grabs his cane. It's a young woman. "Help me," she says simply, a direct link back to the season premiere when House screamed, "Help! Someone help me!" while in the midst of narcotics withdrawal. The young woman's voice is barely a whisper — but it's a direct appeal to House.

In the meantime, House learns the reason for Cuddy's discomfort about his gift. She and Lucas are not "moving in together." They're getting married. The force of this disclosure hits House like a blow to the stomach. It's a truth for which he's not ready: Cuddy is truly lost to him.

And for the remainder of the episode, we are transfixed by this very personal tale of loss and redemption as House gives up the last vestiges of hope, only to be brought back from the brink of despair.

"Help Me," says the episode's title. But help who — and how? Does the title refer to the young Hanna — or to House? Or are the fates of Hanna and House inextricably bound? House is only slowly sucked into this tenuous relationship despite his best efforts to remain disinterested. But then the chief of the rescue unit suggests they amputate Hanna's leg. Suddenly, House is personally invested, insisting they have time before amputation becomes necessary. Irrationally protective of Hanna's leg, House has come full circle — returning at last to the real source of his misery, and perhaps the rest of the answer to Nolan's question to House in "Baggage" — "What did you screw up?"

"I'm the only one here who knows the value of a leg," House argues, double-teamed by Cuddy and the rescue chief. Hanna trusts only House to do the right thing by her. But will he? Or will his still-bitter memories of his own leg injury cloud his objectivity?

House seems correct as the battle to rescue Hanna begins. They can save the leg if they can get her out in time; amputation in these conditions risks almost as much as waiting.

As time goes on, a secondary structural collapse makes rescue more unlikely without amputation. But House refuses to budge — Hanna's leg shall not be cut off! Cuddy assumes his intransigence is a reaction to her engagement to Lucas, but House's attitude has little to do with Lucas and much to do with history — his and Cuddy's — and *the leg*. They are right back at that life-altering point so many years past: House's choice to die rather than lose his leg, Stacy's betrayal, and Cuddy's suggestion of a compromise. A conspiracy of poor decisions destroyed a loving relationship and ruined a physician's life.

The cutting cruelty of Cuddy's words reminds House of all that he's lost — what keeping his leg has done for him. "You're alone," she snaps. "You have nothing." A decision made long ago, keeping his leg has caused him nothing but pain and suffering.

Cuddy's words are a slap across House's face, and in the glare of cold, hard truth proclaimed aloud and unvarnished, they are a wake-up call to which he has no choice but to listen. Stalking off, Cuddy demands that if he has any humanity remaining, House will simply stay away while she attempts to convince their frightened patient to consent to amputation.

House marshals his resolve and confronts himself. Hanna is his patient, and House is fundamentally a healer — it's all he really has left. He cannot fail her, no matter the emotional cost to himself. In a way, this moment is his dark night of the soul.

Returning to Hanna's side, and in Cuddy's presence, House tells Hanna about his leg. "You asked me what happened to my leg," he begins. Haltingly and with great emotion, he explains the devastation wrought by refusing to allow the amputation of his own leg. "It changed me," he tells Hanna. "Made me a harder person — a worse person." For Cuddy, hearing these words is transformative; we want to believe that House saying them is cathartic: a pivot point in his life, but it is not to be. And echoing Stacy's words to him in "Three Stories," House tells Hanna, "It's just a leg."

Is House's admission the answer to the question, "What did you screw up?" He is certainly punishing himself for something. The answer is not about a patient, not about Cuddy, not about Wilson. With Cuddy's cruel words ringing in his ears, it all comes clear. That screwup happened long ago and lying in a hospital bed ("Three Stories," 1.21). It changed House profoundly, eating away at him for years, corrosive and more poisonous than anything else might have been.

How difficult must it have been for House to perform the emergency surgery himself after all he's been through? Sitting outside, listening to Hanna scream as House slices through her leg, Cuddy knows it, too. This moment is transformative for her as well.

As the EMTs lift Hanna into the waiting ambulance, Cuddy is speechless, looking into House's hurt eyes — there is nothing left to say. Then, in the ambulance, Hanna dies of a fat embolus. Always a risk during amputation, there is nothing they can do for her. House peers helplessly into Hanna's eyes, silently begging her for forgiveness — powerless to stop her from slipping away.

There is nothing left for him but to go home to be alone with his pain, his misery, his failure. Cuddy's words still likely ringing his ears, he understands their truth even more keenly now in the aftermath of Hanna's death. Cuddy is right. Even his medical mojo has fled — and he has nothing else. Everyone that matters has moved on and away from him.

A million what-ifs must be churning in his head as he makes his way through the darkness of his apartment and looks into his own face in the bathroom mirror. It's not his face he sees staring back at him, but Hanna's. No longer able to look himself in the face, he smashes the mirror and sees there, hidden away, a sort of salvation. Two bottles of Vicodin have been hidden for God knows how long, waiting and ready to make it all go away.

House has come far in a year; this from the man who insists that people don't change. A year earlier, House would have anesthetized himself with more and more Vicodin. Now he thinks twice, five, ten times — for hours. Sitting on the floor of his bathroom, an eerie mirror image of his "Under My Skin" delusion, he has a choice.

And then, *she's* there. A vision in pink scrubs. Full circle — back to "Under My Skin" (5.23). Then, as now, Cuddy appears to save him from himself. Then, she was the cruel joke played by House's battered psyche. Is his mind again playing tricks? It's certainly possible: he's lost a lot of blood, he's beyond exhausted, in terrible pain, and has been through a physical and emotional minefield. And it's Cuddy to the rescue?

It's improbable as hell; yet it's not. She's not there to rescue him. This is not an intervention. This is no hallucination. She is there because sitting inside a horrific disaster scene, Cuddy remembers with absolute clarity why she loves him.

# Appendix A:

## And When It's Very, Very Good: Awards for *House, M.D.*

*House* has been nominated for numerous awards over its six year run. It's won a few as well, including awards for writing, directing, and acting. For his starring role as Dr. Gregory House, Hugh Laurie has won two Golden Globes, two Screen Actors Guild Awards, two Satellite Awards, and two Television Critics Association Awards.

The show has been recognized for the way in which it approaches some of the themes and serious issues addressed on show, including a Humanitas Prize (which honors work that helps to "break down the walls of ignorance which separate us") and several Prism Award nominations and commendations (which honor shows and performances that are "not only powerfully entertaining, but realistically show substance abuse and addiction, as well as mental health issues"). *House* has also been honored with a prestigious Peabody Award for being "the most distinctive new doctor drama in a decade."

The series has also scored nominations and wins as favorite series, and for Hugh Laurie as a favorite actor in more populist awards like the People's Choice Awards and the Teen Choice Awards. While not a comprehensive list, here are the major awards for which *House* and its stars have been nominated. Wins are starred (*).

### Emmy Awards

Outstanding Drama Series: 2006, 2007, 2008, 2009
Lead Actor in a Drama Series: Hugh Laurie — 2005, 2007, 2008, 2009
Guest Actor Drama Series: 2007 (David Morse for season three)
Outstanding Writing for a Drama Series: *2005 (David Shore for "Three Stories")
Outstanding Directing for a Drama Series: *2008 (Greg Yaitanes for "House's Head")

## Golden Globes

Best Television Series Drama: 2008, 2009, 2010

Best Performance by an Actor in a Television Series: Hugh Laurie — *2006, *2007, 2008, 2009, 2010

## Television Critics Association Awards

Outstanding Individual Achievement in Drama: Hugh Laurie — *2005, *2006, 2007, 2008, 2009

Outstanding Achievement in Drama: *House, M.D.* — 2005, 2006

## Screen Actors Guild Awards

Outstanding Performance by a Male Actor in a Drama Series: Hugh Laurie — 2006, *2007, 2008, *2009, 2010

Outstanding Ensemble in a Drama Series: 2008

## Writers Guild Awards

Episodic Drama: *2006 (Lawrence Kaplow for "Autopsy"), 2008 (Doris Egan, Leonard Dick for "Don't Ever Change"), and 2009 (Russel Friend, Garrett Lerner, David Foster, David Shore for "Broken")

## Directors Guild Award

Outstanding Directorial Achievement in Dramatic Series — Night: 2006 (Paris Barclay for "Three Stories")

## Producers Guild Award

Producer of the Year Award in Episodic Drama: David Shore, Katie Jacobs — 2007, 2008

# Appendix B

## "Time Is Not a Fixed Construct":

## Continuity and the Series Timeline

House once noted, "It is well established that time is not a fixed construct" ("Three Stories," 1.21). And that's probably a good thing in House's universe. The series timeline is nearly impossible to completely untangle. Despite the longevity of most of the series' writers, and their intimate familiarity with the characters and story lines, scripts still contradict known "facts" (canon) about House and the other characters that have been established in earlier episodes.

Every time a missing bit of information about a character or story line emerges in an episode, fans rejoice as another piece of the jigsaw puzzle clicks into place. Unless, that is, it contradicts another established fact. Then it becomes the subject for intense Internet debate for weeks.

The events in House's world unfold in "real time." When it's autumn in the "real world," it's also autumn in House's world. When a new season begins, the story picks weeks later, skipping over whatever may have happened after last year's final scene.

Of course that frustrates the fans, who wonder what happened after House was shot at the end of season two ("No Reason," 2.24), and how he coped when season four left him seriously injured and in the hospital ("Wilson's Heart," 4.16).

Fans feared the same thing would happen after season five, when House suffered an emotional breakdown. If the typical pattern had been followed, the new season would have picked up with House back in his office, and only refer to whatever may have happened to him over the summer. Much to the credit of the House producers, that didn't happen, and viewers were not cheated. Instead, season six began with "Broken" (6.01, 6.02), a transitional episode that focused on House's two-month stay at Mayfield Psychiatric Hospital.

### A Hypothetical Series Timeline

Measuring everything from the start of the series and based on a few fixed time points established by the ongoing narrative, it's possible to extrapolate most of the timeline. We know, for example, that House has been practicing medicine about 20 years when the series begins ("Occam's Razor," 1.03). That's confirmed when House's old medical school nemesis Phillip Weber comes to the hospital to give a lecture ("Distractions," 2.13).

House, like the actor who plays him, was born in 1959 ("No Reason" 2.24), which would make him about 26 when he began practicing, which makes sense, given that medical school is four years. So far so good, right?

However, the season one episode "Socratic Method" (1.06) takes place in autumn, and Cameron acknowledges that House's birthday is imminent. At the end of the next season, when House is hospitalized in "No Reason," his hospital bracelet identifies his birthday as June 11, 1959 (Hugh Laurie's actual birthday). Is this a true timeline goof, or can it be somehow explained? (Or is it, as some fans call this sort of rationalizing, "fanwanking?")

We know that except the first and last few minutes, "No Reason" takes place entirely in House's mind. So House is likely an unreliable narrator. Or was the show's creative team sharing an inside joke? Who knows? But it is just the sort of detail likely to be noticed within the fan community, launching a thousand debates and "fanwanks."

So, here are "the facts" as we know them:

House is 45 years old at the start of the series (give or take a few months). He lived with Stacy for five years, and she left five years before the season one finale, "Honeymoon" (1.22). That would mean House met Stacy when he was 35 in 1994, a young doctor, probably not long after he finished his second sub-specialty fellowship. (House has dual sub-specialties in nephrology and infectious diseases.)

Stacy left five years later, in 1999, sometime after an infarction (arterial blood clot) in House's right thigh left him disabled. House had been working for Princeton-Plainsboro Teaching Hospital for eight years ("Mob Rules," 1.15), but owed Cuddy six years in clinic duty time ("Pilot," 1.01).

So it appears that House must have worked for two years at the hospital before the infarction, perhaps as a staff doctor, or in private practice with privileges. Cuddy was House's doctor in "Three Stories." And it's possible that after the infarction, House resigned and tried working elsewhere before coming back. So, here it is folks:

A Highly Speculative *House* Timeline. (Entries with an asterisk have been extrapolated from the narrative and are pure speculation.)

*1984 — House finishes medical school; he's about 25 or 26 years old. He then completes a residency in internal medicine, with subspecialty training in infectious diseases and nephrology. We know from "Known Unknowns" (6.07) that House first attended the University of Michigan Medical School, and from "Distractions" (2.12) that he attended Johns Hopkins Medical School. He was expelled from both schools, but as of the end of season six, we do not yet know where he completed his medical training.

1991 — Wilson and his first wife Samantha break up ("Lockdown," 6.17) after being married since 1990.

1991 — House and Wilson meet in New Orleans at a medical convention ("Birthmarks," 5.04; "Lockdown," 6.17). Wilson is probably 25 or 26 years old, making him about four years younger than House.

*Circa 1991 — Wilson marries Bonnie, wife number two, possibly on the rebound. However, this date is contradicted by "House Training" (3.20) in which Bonnie mentions that the dog she and Wilson bought 17 years earlier as a puppy was named after House. The episode takes place in 2007, and Hector would have been born in 1990, while Wilson was married to Sam. It's possible that Bonnie and Wilson married in 1991 and Hector could still have been considered a puppy then. That's my story and I'm sticking to it!

1995 — Stacy and House meet at a paintball tournament — doctors versus lawyers ("Honeymoon," 1.22; "Son of Coma Guy," 3.07).

Circa 1996 — Wilson sees his long lost (and presumed homeless) brother, Danny, for the last time until he turns up in season five ("Histories," 1.10; "Social Contract," 5.17).

*1996 — House begins to work at Princeton-Plainsboro (eight years before we meet him in "Pilot").

*Circa 1998 — House suffers the infarction to his leg, leaving him disabled and in chronic pain.

*1998 — Post infarction, House resigns from Princeton-Plainsboro, and works for four other hospitals, before Cuddy rehires him ("Humpty Dumpty," 2.03).

2000 — Stacy leaves House ("Honeymoon," 1.22).

2002 — Stacy and Mark Warner marry ("Honeymoon," 1.22).

2003 — Chase begins working for House ("Pilot," "All In," 2.18).

2004 — Cameron starts working for House.

2004 — Foreman starts working for House.

2005 — Stacy returns to House's life ("Three Stories," 1.21).

2005 — Chase and Cameron have sex for the first time ("Hunting," 2.07).

2005 — House adopts Steve McQueen the rat ("Hunting").

2006 — House tells Stacy to go back to her husband ("Need to Know," 2.11).

Spring 2006 — Wilson's third marriage ends ("Sex Kills," 2.14).

Spring 2006 — Foreman nearly dies from a Naegleria infection ("Euphoria, Part 2," 2.21).

2006 — House is shot by a former patient or the husband of a former patient. We do not know if he was ever caught ("No Reason," 2.24).

2006 — House undergoes an experimental pain treatment using the anesthetic ketamine ("No Reason," 2.24; "Meaning," 3.01).

Autumn 2006 — House returns to Princeton-Plainsboro Teaching Hospital after a three-month recovery, including two months of physical rehab ("Meaning," 3.01). The ketamine treatment fails within a week ("Cane and Able," 3.02).

Fall 2006 — House arrested for drug fraud ("Fools for Love," 3.04).

Early 2007 — House enters rehab ("Words and Deeds," 3.11); the drug charges are thrown out at the preliminary hearing after Cuddy lies to protect him.

February 2007 — Chase and Cameron begin a "friends with benefits" relationship — no intimacy, just sex ("Insensitive," 3.14).

Spring 2007 — Chase decides he "wants more" from their relationship; Cameron disagrees.

Spring 2007 — Foreman resigns ("Family," 3.21), Chase is fired, and Cameron resigns ("Human Error," 3.24).

Fall 2007 — House hires a new team of fellows.

Spring 2008 — Wilson becomes involved with fellow candidate Amber Volakis ("Frozen," 4.12).

Late Spring 2008 — Amber dies, and House is badly injured in a bus crash ("Wilson's Heart," 4.16).

Fall 2008 — Wilson resigns from the hospital — and from his relationship with House ("Dying Changes Everything," 5.01).

Fall 2008 — House's father dies. House confirms John House is not his biological father. Wilson returns both to Princeton-Plainsboro Teaching Hospital and House ("Birthmarks," 5.04).

Winter 2008 — Cuddy adopts a baby girl ("Joy to the World," 5.11).

Spring 2009 — Wilson finds his long lost brother ("Social Contract," 5.17); Kutner commits suicide ("Simple Explanation," 5.20); Chase and Cameron become engaged ("Saviors," 5.21).

May 2009 — House commits himself to Mayfield Psychiatric Hospital suffering delusions; Cameron and Chase marry ("Both Sides Now," 5.24).

Summer 2009 — House has a brief affair with Lydia, the sister of a patient at Mayfield ("Broken," 6.01, 6.02).

Fall 2009 — House is released from Mayfield and continues therapy with Dr.

Darryl Nolan; Chase assassinates African dictator Dibala by falsifying lab records ("The Tyrant," 6.04).

Fall 2009 — Cuddy begins dating Private Investigator Lucas Douglas ("Known Unkowns," 6.07).

Fall 2009 — Cameron leaves Chase in the aftermath of the Dibala Affair, heading to Chicago ("Teamwork," 6.09).

Spring 2010 — Cameron serves divorce papers to Chase ("Lockdown," 6.17); Wilson and first wife, Sam, get back together ("Knight Fall," 6.18).

May 2010 — Remy Hadley requests a leave of absence from the hospital; after years, House and Cuddy are finally on the same romantic page ("Help Me," 6.22).

## Acknowledgments

This book has been a labor of love (my husband would call it obsession), and there are many to thank for helping me bring it to fruition — people without whose help, I could not have written it. First, I would be remiss in not thanking David Shore and the incredibly creative minds that make every episode of *House* food for thought, discussion, and debate for millions of viewers. Thank you also to Hugh Laurie for his brilliant and insightful portrayal of the complex Dr. Gregory House.

I would like also to acknowledge the kind folks who run maintain the numerous *House*-related websites, blogs, and forums that provide a valuable resource to fans, and whose content helped me immeasurably in recalling the details of six seasons. Particular thanks to the Clinic Duty Live Journal, Polite Dissent, Hang Dog, the House Episode Wikipedia Pages, the Fox Official House Fan Site, and Television Without Pity.

Thank you to my loyal readers, whose thoughtful weekly commentary and debate have made my *Blogcritics* feature, "Welcome to the End of the Thought Process: An Introspective Look at *House, M.D.*" one of the best places on the Internet to discuss the series. I am grateful to *Blogcritics* publisher Eric Olsen and executive editor Lisa McKay for giving me a cozy corner at *BC*, for encouragement, and for making me feel welcome as an editor and member of the writing community there.

Thank you to Arachne Jericho for his insights on the Holmes-House connection, and to Dr. Robert Spector for his professional take on House's psychological issues. I would also like to thank the many people who have offered their advice and support in crafting this work. Their constructive criticism, editorial suggestions, and encouragement have been extremely valuable. My friends at the Too Handsome for Paperwork forum have encouraged me from the start in this endeavor. Particular thanks are due to Harriet Schabes, Patricia Eliot Tobias, Sandy DeMartini, Laurie Koen, Edna Schrank, and especially Mary Dagmar Davies, who first encouraged me to put my passion for writing into writing about *House*.

I am grateful to my agent (and fellow über-*House* fan), Katharine Sands of Sarah Jane Freymann Literary Agency, for her support, friendship, and guidance — and for finding the perfect home for this book. Very special thanks also to Ted Weinstein of Ted Weinstein Literary Management for introducing Katharine and me, and for his sage advice early in this project.

I am grateful to everyone at ECW Press for believing in this book and me, especially publisher Jack David, editor Sarah Dunn, and copyeditor Emily Schultz.

My mother passed while *Chasing Zebras* was being edited. All her life, she had wanted to be a published author, and when she realized that was never to be, she took delight in the idea that her daughter would provide her with vicarious fulfillment of that dream. Mom, in a way, this book is the fruit of your lifelong appreciation for writing and reading — and the direct result of making me a television addict at an early age.

But, I am most grateful to my soul mate, Phillip. His undying encouragement and support have gone way beyond the call of duty. Although not a *House* fan, he knows the show almost as well as I do, and has sat these several years through countless re-watchings of DVDs, listening to me read long narrative chapters aloud to him (while rubbing his feet), and offering me constructive criticism all the way through, particularly while writing the episode guide.

The most intense months of writing began while we were planning a wedding for our daughter, Shoshanna, and getting our son, Adam, ready for his first year in college. Even during those chaotic months, Phillip made sure I had the space and time to chase this dream while living on pita and pizza for months in a messy house. This book is dedicated to him.